HEBREW HISTORY

FROM

THE DEATH OF MOSES TO THE CLOSE OF THE SCRIPTURE NARRATIVE.

By REV. HENRY COWLES, D.D.

"Hast thou marked the old way which wicked men have trodden who were cut down out of time?"—Job xxii: 15, 16.

"Light is sown for the righteous."—Ps. xcvii: 11.

WIPF & STOCK · Eugene, Oregon

Wipf and Stock Publishers
199 W 8th Ave, Suite 3
Eugene, OR 97401

Hebrew History
From the Death of Moses to the Close of the Scripture Narrative
By Cowles, Henry
ISBN 13: 978-1-5326-8070-0
Publication date 1/30/2019
Previously published by D. Appleton & Co., 1878

PREFACE.

THIS volume aims to present the entire Sacred History of the Hebrew people from the death of Moses to the close of the Old Testament. Its special objects are—to trace the hand of God in this history, and to suggest the advancing revelations made of his character and moral government; to develop the leading human characters, and the significance of the great historic events; to explain difficult passages; to bring out the connections between sacred and profane history, in order both to illustrate and to confirm the records of Scripture; to place the History of the Old Testament by the side of its Psalmody and its Prophecy, in order to infuse into the History somewhat of its own living soul, and to give to the poetry more of its bodily form and earthly relationships, and to Prophecy its due illustration and impression. The author's aim and hope have been, not to supersede the reading of these historical books entire, but rather to stimulate and aid such reading by setting forth incidentally the exquisite beauty of its narratives, the interest of its historic events, and its great wealth of most precious truth—every way worthy of an Author truly divine All history is useful in so far as it makes truthful revelations of man's doings and of God's agencies in and above them; how, then, does it behoove us to honor and to study this one unparalleled history in which the relations of God to men and of men to God are traced with God's own unerring finger! How rich are we in having one model history of which we know that God himself is the Author!

HENRY COWLES.

OBERLIN, OHIO, *October*, 1874.

CONTENTS.

THE HEBREWS IN CANAAN.

CHAPTER I.
PAGE
Introduction to the book of Joshua, ... 1

CHAPTER II.
Conquest of Canaan, ... 10
Crossing the Jordan, ... 13
Memorial stones, ... 15
Fall of Jericho, ... 18
Achan and Ai, ... 20
Ebal and Gerizim, ... 26
The two great decisive battles, ... 29
The sun and moon stand still, ... 30
The victory over the kings of the North, ... 35

CHAPTER III.
Allotment of Canaan, ... 37
Caleb and his inheritance, ... 37
Cities of refuge, ... 40
The altar of witness, ... 41
Joshua's last words, ... 42

CHAPTER IV.
The book of Judges, ... 48
Eglon of Moab and Ehud, ... 50
Deborah and Barak, ... 51
Scenes in the life of Gideon, ... 65
Jephthah and his vow, ... 70
The story of Samson, ... 76
Micah, the religious idolater, ... 80
The nameless Levite; Gibeah of Benjamin, ... 85
The period of the Judges; Great declension, ... 88
Chronology of the book of Judges, ... 91
The story of Ruth, ... 92

(v)

CHAPTER V.

	PAGE
Introduction to the books of Samuel,	95
Samuel and his mother,	97
Samuel a prophet; Eli and his sons,	102
The ark in captivity,	107
Samuel as judge,	109
The order of prophets,	111
The schools of the prophets,	114

CHAPTER VI.

Saul, and the rise of the monarchy,	123
The kingdom renewed to Saul,	126
Samuel's last words to the people,	128
Saul and Jonathan,	130
Saul and Amalek,	133

CHAPTER VII.

THE HISTORY OF DAVID,	136
The evil spirit in Saul,	138
David and Goliath,	141
David and Saul,	146
Saul and the witch at Endor,	160
David and Ziklag,	163
Death of Saul,	165
David's elegy upon Saul and Jonathan,	166
Saul's character,	168

CHAPTER VIII.

Introduction to Chronicles,	171
David as king,	175
His steps to the throne,	175
The ark located in Jerusalem,	179
Public worship reorganized with sacred song,	182
The great Messianic promise,	187
David's wars,	193
David's great sins,	196
David's domestic calamities,	199
The sin of numbering the people,	205
David's work for the temple,	209
Arrangements for the succession,	214
David's last words and character,	216
Relations of the Hebrews to other nations,	220

CHAPTER IX.

Introduction to the books of Kings,	223
Solomon,	227
Solomon's dream and choice,	228

CONTENTS. vii

	PAGE
Solomon's wisdom and writings,	231
His building and consecration of the temple,	235
His foreign relations,	239
His apostasy from God,	241
His repentance; The evidence in the case,	242
Religious influence of Solomon's reign,	244
Contact of sacred history with profane,	249

CHAPTER X.

THE REVOLT,	252
Jeroboam,	255
The agency of prophets in Israel,	257
Jeroboam; Abijam; Baasha,	261
Ahab and Elijah the Tishbite,	264
Elijah, Ahab, and the rain,	266
Elijah in Horeb,	273
Review of Elijah in Carmel and Horeb,	275
History of Ahab,	279
Ahab, Jezebel, and Naboth,	283
Ahab, Jehoshaphat, and Ramoth-Gilead,	285
King Ahaziah and Elijah,	290
Elijah's translation,	291
King Jehoram, second son of Ahab,	293
Mesha; The Moabite stone,	296
The Prophet Elisha,	297
Naaman, the Syrian,	300
Elisha; Samaria besieged and delivered,	303
Jehu; His work and dynasty,	308
Jeroboam II. and the prophets,	312
Menahem; Pekah; Pul of Assyria,	313
End of the Kingdom of Israel.	314
Connections of sacred history with profane,	316
Review of the Northern Kingdom,	320

CHAPTER XI.

History of the Kingdom of Judah,	322
Rehoboam; Shishak,	322
Asa; Zerah the Ethiopian,	325
His reformation,	327
Jehoshaphat; His deliverance and reformation,	328
Jehoram; Ahaziah; Athaliah,	333
Jehoiada and Joash,	336
Amaziah; Uzziah; Jotham,	339
Ahaz,	342
Hezekiah; His reformation,	346
Manasseh; Amon,	355
Josiah; His reformation,	358
The sons of Josiah,	362
The Captivity,	364
Sacred history confirmed by profane,	369

CHAPTER XII.

	PAGE
THE AGE OF THE RESTORATION,	371
Its antecedents,	372
History of the restored people; Book of Ezra,	374
Decree of Cyrus; Genealogical record,	375
Foundations of the temple laid,	376
Samaritan opposition,	377
Temple finished,	378
Ezra arrives; His commission,	379
Intermarriages with idolaters,	380
Scenes of prayer,	381
Steps toward reform,	382
Character of Ezra,	383
Book of Nehemiah,	384
Nehemiah's story,	385
Arrives at Jerusalem,	386
Rebuilding of the city walls; Opposition,	387
A chapter on the poor and the rich,	389
Opposition to the wall-building,	391
Great meeting for Scripture reading,	393
Great feast of tabernacles,	394
National concert of prayer,	395
The Psalms of this period,	397
Events of Nehemiah's second sojourn in Judah,	398
Review of Ezra and Nehemiah,	399
Origin of the Samaritan community,	401
Esther—book of, etc.; Author and date,	403
The story of Esther,	404
The feast of Purim,	410

CHAPTER XIII.

Revelation progressive throughout Hebrew history—in what particulars,	410
APPENDIX—Chronological Tables,	419

HEBREW HISTORY.

THE HEBREWS IN CANAAN.

It is proposed in this volume, *First;* to treat of the canonical authority and authorship of these historical books;——*Secondly;* to consider the events and characters here presented, *as matters of history*, designed to throw light upon the character and ways of God, and upon the heart and life of man.——*Thirdly;* to explain difficult passages, giving due attention to those facts and events against which objections have been raised.

CHAPTER I.

INTRODUCTION TO THE BOOK OF JOSHUA.

On what grounds is this book included in the Canon of Scripture?

These grounds may be arranged under four heads as follows:

I. *The concurrent testimony of all Hebrew history;*
II. *The intrinsic demand for such a book as this in the Canon;*
III. *The provision made nationally for a continuous Hebrew history;*
IV. *The indorsement of Christ and his apostles.*

I. In speaking of the concurrent testimony of Hebrew history, I call attention,

1. To the *fact;*——2. To the *value* of the fact as testimony to the point in hand.

1. The fact is sustained

(1.) By repeated references to this book in subsequent

books of the Canon, both of the Old Testament and of the New.——The book of Judges links itself to this book of Joshua in its first verse: "Now after the death of Joshua, it came to pass," etc. Also by the fact that two passages are quoted with little variation from Joshua and incorporated into the history of the Judges, viz., Josh. 15: 13–19 into Judges 1: 10–15; and Josh. 24: 28–30 into Judges 2: 6–9.——Again we have a striking reference to Josh. 6: 26 (the malediction pronounced by Joshua on the man who should attempt to rebuild Jericho), in 1 Kings 16: 34. The shape of this reference is: "According to the word of the Lord which he spake by Joshua, the son of Nun." This not only indorses the book of Joshua as part of the well-known collection of Hebrew historical records, but these words of Joshua as inspired of God.——In the Psalms of Israel we find repeated references to the great historic facts of the conquest and settlement of Canaan, as may be seen in Ps. 44: 1–3, and 78: 54, 55, and 105: 42–45, and 135: 10–12, and 136: 17–22.——The specially historic prayer of Nehemiah (9: 22–25) groups the great events of the book of Joshua with those of the books of Moses preceding and with the later books that follow. The sublime strains of Habakkuk (3: 3–15) are but the echo of the historic events of this book of Joshua, presupposing, therefore, the existence of this book.——In the New Testament we find references to this book in the historic speech of Stephen (Acts 7: 45), and in that of Paul (Acts 13: 19). Two other references appear in the Epistle to the Hebrews (4: 8, and 11: 30, 31). It is unfortunate that twice in the New Testament the name of Joshua is given "Jesus," viz., in Acts 7: 45 and Heb. 4: 8.

(2.) The book of Joshua stands in its place in all the ancient translations made of the Old Testament Canon, *e. g.*, The Septuagint and the Chaldee Targums. This is the strongest sort of historic testimony.

(3.) Its claim is supported by the unvarying testimony of all known Jewish writers, especially of Josephus and of the great lights of Jewish learning in the ages since the Christian era.

Here let it be carefully noted:—It is historically certain, apart from scripture testimony, that the Hebrew people in the infancy of their nation were in Egypt.

It is historically certain that Canaan was their home and country for many centuries anterior to the Christian era. How came they there? What history of the conquest of Canaan and of the location of Israel there has the world ever had except what is here in this book of Joshua? The fact that somehow they came into possession of this country—that at some time they did locate themselves there—is beyond question. Hence there is the strongest presumption that this book is a true history, and has always been a part of the sacred historic records of Israel.*

2. We next consider the *value* of this historic testimony.

It must be admitted that the early traditions of some of the oldest nations are fabulous. Why may not this book of Joshua be fabulous also?

I answer: It lies on the face of every page of this book

---

*It is in place to adduce collateral testimonies from profane history and monuments to corroborate the historic verity of this book of Joshua.

It is well known that the ancient Canaanites and Phenicians were a maritime people, traversing the great Mediterranean with their ships and commerce, and at a very early period planting colonies in North-western Africa. It is also clear from the narrative in this book of Joshua, and is probable from the nature of the case that the invasion of Canaan by Joshua smote those nations with panic, and, consequently, that some at least would naturally flee the country by water, following the well-known track of their commerce to the shores of Africa. In accordance with these probabilities, there comes down to us through three apparently independent witnesses the statement that in Numidia there stood one or more pillars with substantially this inscription: "We are they who fled from the face of Joshua the Robber, the son of Nun."——The three witnesses are Moses of Chorone, the Armenian historian; Procopius, the Secretary of Belisarius, who went to Africa with that distinguished general; and Suidas, the lexicographer, of the tenth Christian century. The inscriptions are given with slight variations by these three witnesses, the words of Moses being these: "When he (Joshua) was destroying the Canaanites, some fled to Agra and sought Tharsis in ships. This appears from an inscription carved on pillars in Africa which is extant even in our own time, and is of this purport: "We, the chiefs of the Canaanites, fleeing from Joshua the Robber, have come hither to dwell."——The words as first quoted above are from Procopius.—— Suidas, on the word *Canaan*, remarks: "And there are up to the present time such slabs in Numidia, containing the following inscription:—"We are Canaanites, whom Joshua the Robber drove out."——The account in full is given by George Rawlinson in his Bampton Lectures of 1859, pages 86, 87, 300, 301.

that it *was written in the interests of the true God*. Its aim was to make revelations of God's character and ways. It was written by one who feared God and was consecrated to his service. That he wrote under a deep sense of being near to God—near to the God of infinite truthfulness, purity, sincerity—is every-where apparent.

Here my argument is that the highest guaranty for the truthfulness of an historical book is the truthful spirit of its author. If there is truth anywhere among men, we must look for it where the influence of the God of truth is felt most strongly on the soul. If it be said that the Hebrew nation sometimes apostatized from the true God to idols, the answer is, Yes;—but *the books of the Old Testament never apostatized from God;* never drifted into the current of the national apostacy; never failed to protest most solemnly and at every peril against such apostacy. If the facts were otherwise; if the writers of these books had gone into apostacy from God, this argument, I admit, would lose its force. The devil is notoriously the father of lies. It would not be safe to assume that any book or any part of a book written in his interest is true.

II. *There was an intrinsic demand for such a book as this in the sacred Canon.* It was an indispensable link of connection between the Pentateuch and all subsequent Hebrew history. Whole pages of *promise* had been given to the patriarchs, pledging to their posterity the land of Canaan for their country and inheritance. Was there not, therefore, a demand for some record of the fulfillment? Was it not vital that all the future generations of Israel should know how this fulfillment was brought about? Did not all those future generations need the moral power of these great facts of their nation's history? Did not the Lord know they would need it? If it be true that the Lord opened the Jordan waters at high flood for their passage on dry ground; if it be true that the walls of the first city they came to fell before the blast of ram's horns and the presence of the ark of the covenant; if it be true that God discomfited host after host of Canaan's best armed thousands with storm and hail; is it not to be presumed that God would secure an authentic, reliable account of these great facts for the moral instruction of the future thousands of Israel, and indeed of the whole world?—But there is no other record competing with this. It is, therefore, this, or none.

Yet further; let it be said with emphasis: this argument will not appear in its full force until we consider the intrinsic demand for a history of these great events, not only truthful historically, but inspired of God—inspired in the sense of being brought out under divine direction, comprising what the Lord deemed it important to place on these historic records for the moral instruction of all coming generations. If the Lord planted Israel in Canaan by his own special providence, in fulfillment of his own long-standing promise, it admits of no rational question that he took care to have a reliable record of the fact under his own indorsement. If God was *in Israel;* if they were his chosen people; if he was using them for the purpose of revealing himself to our world—then it is simply impossible that those great deeds done by him for the very purpose of revealing himself, should be left to sink into oblivion unrecorded—impossible that they should fail of such a record as would answer the ends of God in a written revelation. That is to say; if the book of Joshua is historically true, it can not be less than inspired of God. If his hand was in those events, his hand was also in the record which has brought them down through all the ages to our hand.

It may aid toward a better conception of the force of these arguments if we put it as a supposition—That the entire books of Joshua, Judges, and 1 Samuel were never written—that this section of Hebrew history were left a dead blank, and we were launched from the death of Moses flush into the reign of David. At the point when Moses disappears from the history, the people were manifestly on the borders of the promised land; every thing seemed ripe for crossing the Jordan and taking possession. But the next record we have gives us the nation apparently long time planted in Canaan; a monarchical government in running order, and a young man of very marked qualities, admirable training, and high promise, ready to ascend the throne. What sort of Rip Van Winkle sleep has been upon the Hebrew people, or at least upon their historians, during all this period? What account can be given for this mysterious silence of Hebrew history? How has it happened (we ask it reverently) that the Lord permitted such a blank in the historic records of his own glorious achievements? Counted numerically or estimated in military science by the weight of their battalions, Israel was weak and Canaan mighty. How was this immense disparity overcome? Why did not the Lord tell all the world *how* he fulfilled his word to the old patriarchs and *how* he made his chosen people mighty through God to the casting down of the strongly walled cities of old Canaan?

III. With forethoughtful wisdom, God made provision in the Hebrew constitution for a continuous Hebrew history and for its preservation. The tribe of Levi and the family of Aaron were the learned class of the nation. Exempted largely from engrossing, exhaustive toil, it was one of their official duties to care for the religious instruction of the people. It was made both their interest and their duty to guard the archives of the nation; to keep the books of Moses and the later historical books as they were prepared. That the original plan assigned to them also the function of national historian is perhaps possible, but it is not definitely indicated. If such were the plan it was soon modified. Whether because of negligence on their part, or because their Levitical duties were all they could perform well, or because some special qualifications were naturally requisite for this service, it came to pass that very early after Moses the Lord raised up a series of *prophets* to write the history each of his own times. The sacred books show plainly that Samuel, Nathan, Gad, and other men of this class, became national historians. Their succession and their services were by far the more reliable from the fact that God himself filled their ranks; that they did not hold office by hereditary right or by any public appointment from men, but directly and immediately from God himself. What better guaranty than this can be rationally demanded?

The historic testimony, to show that a series of prophets became the historians of their nation, is of this sort:

1. Throughout the two books of the Kings, the writer closes his narrative of each king by referring the reader for any further information to the books of the chronicles of the kings of Israel or of Judah. With scarcely

the slightest variation in his method, if it be a king of Judah, he refers you to the chronicles of the kings of Judah; if of Israel, to the chronicles of their kings. The case of Solomon being very prominent, he writes thus (1 Kings 11: 41): "The rest of the acts of Solomon, and all that he did, and his wisdom, are they not written in the book of the acts of Solomon?"—showing apparently that his history was to be found in a special volume bearing his name.

In the two books of Chronicles the references to historic authorities for "the rest of the acts" of its several kings are less uniform, but for this reason more valuable. Of David we read thus (1 Chron. 29: 29, 30): "Now the acts of David the king, first and last, behold, they are written in the book of Samuel the seer, and in the book of Nathan the prophet, and in the book of Gad the seer; With all his reign and his might, and the times that went over him and over Israel, and over all the kingdoms of the countries"—which certainly indicates a very full history, not of Israel only and of David, but of outside powers. Here are three historians of David and his times—Samuel, Nathan, Gad.——Solomon also had the honor of three distinct historians (2 Chron. 9: 29)—Nathan, Abijah the Shilonite, and Iddo the seer. For further particulars of Rehoboam, the writer refers to "Shemaiah the prophet and to Iddo the seer *concerning genealogies*"—this important function falling within their province (2 Chron. 12: 15)——Closing his sketch of Jehoshaphat, he says (2 Chron. 20: 34)—"The rest of his acts are written in the book of Jehu, son of Hanani, who is mentioned in the book of the Kings of Israel"—a fact which is verified in 1 Kings 16: 1, 7.——Again, we have several references to "the book of the kings of Judah and Israel."—Moreover, "the rest of the acts of Uzziah," (the writer says) "Isaiah the prophet did write" (2 Chron. 26: 12); also, "the rest of the acts of Hezekiah and his goodness, behold, they are written in the vision [prophecy] of Isaiah the prophet"—as we may see in Isa. 36–39.—— This twofold reference to Isaiah suggests two points worthy of notice, viz., that these prophet-historians wrote largely as eye-witnesses of matters falling under their personal knowledge, and that in this one case we have in our hand the very authorities to which he refers us for further information. In the other cases (excepting what Samuel wrote of David), the historic authorities are no longer extant.

Comprehensively the facts on the subject of historic references to other authorities in writing are:——(1.) They include every case in which the writers of either the books of Kings or of Chronicles record the death of a Hebrew king, whether of Israel or of Judah.——(2.) They give us the names of at least eight such prophet-historians, and manifestly refer to works written by many others.——(3.) So far as appears, these prophet-historians of the acts of those kings wrote out and placed in the public archives the events of their own times, from which the writers of the books of Kings and Chronicles drew if they had occasion, and to which they referred their early readers for further information. The authorities referred to were extant when our canonical histories were written.——(4.) Comparing the historic sketches which have come down to us in the canonical books with those to which they referred but which are now lost, it is surely legitimate to infer that if the latter were written by men known as inspired prophets, yet more surely were the former, viz. the books preserved through all the future generations of Israel in their sacred canon.

IV. The proof that "Joshua" belongs in the canon of the Old Testament is properly completed by the indorsement of Christ and his apostles. They furnish this indorsement in two ways:

(a.) They indorse the entire Old Testament canon under its well-known names; "the Scriptures," "the Holy Scriptures," "the Law, the Prophets, and the Psalms," etc. See Luke 24: 44, and 16: 20, and John 5: 39, 46, 47, and Acts 28: 23, and 1 Tim. 3: 16, and 2 Pet. 1: 21.

(b.) They indorse the several books by quotations from them or by allusions to them as a portion of the sacred canon. The historic events of Joshua are definitely referred to by Stephen (Acts 7: 4, 5); by Paul (Acts 13: 19); and by the writer to the Hebrews (4: 8, and 11: 30, 31.)

I see no call for further argument beyond what will be found in these two closing suggestions: viz., (1.) That the points above made are the best evidence that is in the nature of the case possible—the very sort of evidence which might be expected for books really inspired, and *all* that ought to be expected;——and (2) that these proofs stand unimpeached. From reliable sources of testimony no counter voice has ever been heard.

There remains the less important question of *the original author of this book.*

Here I make two main points.

1. There is strong internal evidence that the original writer was contemporary with the events. In a few passages he writes in the first person, definitely including himself among the actors. "Until *we* were passed over" (5:1). "The land which the Lord swore that he would give *us*" (5:6). Note also what he writes of Rahab: "She dwelleth in Israel even unto this day" (6:25), showing that the record was written while Rahab yet lived.——Many passages give us the definite words of conversation had or directions given, as might be expected in a narrative made at the time and on the spot. The geographical allotments of Canaan among the tribes were matters of contemporary record—wisely, if not even necessarily. The narrative itself notes the fact: "The men went and passed through the land and described it by cities into seven parts *in a book*" (18:9). These are points of strong internal proof of a record made very near the time of the events.

2. That Joshua was himself the writer, or at least that it was done under his eye and at his instance, is eminently probable, on these grounds:——(a.) Trained under Moses—his first and most prominent servant, associate, assistant, and after the death of Moses, his successor, it is almost certain that he was competent to write this history—and that he did.——(b.) It is explicitly said that he wrote out one transaction (24:26): "And Joshua wrote these words in the book of the law," etc.——Against these points of strong probable evidence, there is so far as I know no counter evidence whatever.

CHAPTER II.

CONQUEST OF CANAAN.

We have reached another of the great crisis periods of Hebrew history, at once critical and momentous, eventful and inspiring. How critical it was, we shall better appreciate if we recall to mind the failure to reach Canaan when they came out of Egypt though they came forth " with a high hand;" or the yet more disastrous failure when they moved upon Canaan from Kadesh-Barnea; or if we remember how long they had been marching and countermarching and camping through the great Arabian desert in wanderings that seemed so fruitless and disheartening, in which there had been so much of hope deferred and of wearisome waiting for an end long sought in vain. It was *critical*, moreover, in view of the great military power of the old nations of Canaan, or the very unmilitary antecedents of Israel.——Naturally, the issues were to be momentous and eventful; for they were destined to make or unmake a great nation. They must issue in the rising and triumph of God's earthly kingdom, or in its dishonor, and in at least the long postponement of its success. Promises and covenants pledging Canaan to this people which God had been waiting through long generations to fulfill were either on the eve of their fulfillment or of another postponement of unknown duration. It is in human nature to feel a keen sensibility over the pending of issues so momentous and eventful.——Yet the hour was *inspiring* in just so far as there was evidence that God's hand was there and that he was about to inaugurate a great era of victory for Israel.

Fitly the history opens (Josh. 1.) by revealing God's agency in the movement—his great command from his lofty throne, bidding the people "go forward." Coupled with this, the history discloses the moral state of the people—the tone and temper of both the leader and the led in this eventful hour.——First of all the Lord spake to Joshua, transferring to him the leadership of Israel which Moses laid down at his death, and bidding him arise and go over Jordan—"thou and all this people." As if to inspire complete assurance of success, he said to him—"Not a man shall be able to stand before thee all the days of thy life; as I was with Moses, so will I be with thee; I will not fail thee nor forsake thee; be strong and of a good courage, for unto this people thou shalt divide Canaan for their inheritance." It was every thing toward success that the soul of their leader should be mighty in God and sure of victory; hence these words.——Forthwith orders go forth through his subordinate officers to all the people to be in readiness within three days to pass over Jordan. Was not that an hour of most thrilling interest to the thousands of Israel? Is their wilderness life at last to end? Are they so soon to plant their weary feet on the goodly soil of Canaan? Joshua has a special word for the warriors of the two-and-a-half tribes already located in their national home on the east of Jordan. It was in the bond that their men of war, leaving their families in their eastern homes, should go over before their brethren, unincumbered, harnessed for battle. The record sets forth their prompt response to this call. *We are ready!* We wait for marching orders. "Only the Lord thy God be with thee as he was with Moses. Be strong and of a good courage."——In these words we have the temper, the morale, of this army of conquest. The faith of God strong in their souls; their hearts on obedience to God; their eye on victory!

Here we may fitly arrest the historic narrative for the moment to *revise this group of facts and gather up their moral lessons*, as thus:

1. God is never afraid of *exigencies* for his people, however severe the strain they may occasion. Indeed exigencies are a part of his ordained scheme for their earthly discipline.

2. God never fails to be equal to any emergency into which he may bring his people.

3. It comes of his wisdom, kindness, and love that he prepares his people before hand to bear the great labor he proposes to put upon them. During full forty years of wilderness life under Moses he had been preparing this generation for the conquest of Canaan. Noticeably he began with them in their childhood.

4. It is every thing to his people, that their own God

should exhort them to "be strong and of good courage" (vs. 6, 7, 9). How ought such words to inspire their souls and tone up their faith to perfect assurance!

5. With God on their side, what have his people ever to fear? What can they not achieve against any foe, in the face of any obstacles, however weak they may be in themselves apart from God's strength given them in their need?

6. Though the scenes before them were in the highest degree exciting, yet God expected them to be cool, considerate, studiously careful to keep the book of his law in their mouth and in their heart, meditating thereon day and night (v. 8); for when God comes so very near to his people for their help, it behooves them to walk softly and solemnly before him, holding their mind to most implicit obedience to his revealed will, ever wakeful to learn what this will of God as to their duty may be.

Next, we have (Josh. 2) *the mission of the two spies* sent by Joshua "to view the land, even Jericho." Apparently this was a military movement, wise and forethoughtful; for a strongly walled city of the enemy, eight miles from the point of crossing the Jordan, might sharply contest the passage. If the men of Canaan had the heart to defend their country against this invasion, would they not muster at the fords of Jordan with their best forces? Yet this mission of the spies was not merely a thing of military policy, it was yet more a movement of God. His hand was in it. It served to show that this time— far otherwise than on the former mission of spies—the panic is all on the other side. Who guided these two spies to the harlot Rahab's house, the history saith not; but plainly God's hand was in this also. From her they learned that the men of Jericho had heard of the fall of Sihon and Og of Bashan; had heard also of God's great judgments on Egypt and of his marvelous presence with Israel through all her wilderness wanderings, and that their hearts melted with fear and dread till there remained no more spirit or courage in any man of them as against Israel, for they saw that the mighty God was with them.

Of the former history of this woman of Jericho we know nothing beyond what is told in that one sadly significant word "the *harlot* Rahab." But on this record she appears a woman of thoughtful, vigorous, independent mind, who understood well the public feeling in her city and throughout Canaan; who had formed her own conclusions as to the great question of the times, and was more than ready in the face of some present peril to cast in her lot with Israel on the side of Israel's God. So she took the Hebrew spies to her house; skillfully protected them through their then present perils, and sent them to their people in safety. We notice that in stipulating for the rescue of herself and household when the city should fall, she enumerated "father and mother, brethren and sisters, and all that they have," but made no allusion to husband, and none to children. We are thankful that she had so many family ties, and a nobler nature than is wont to appear amid such surroundings—the best we could expect in a penitent "harlot." Plans for her rescue ere the city should fall were wisely laid. From her house on the town-wall a pendent scarlet thread guided the spies to their protector, where by agreement her household were convened in readiness; and they were put in safety before the city fell. This history leaves her with the statement (6: 25), "Joshua saved Rahab the harlot alive and her father's house and all that she had, and she dwelleth in Israel unto this day, because she hid the messengers whom Joshua sent to spy out Jericho." To the genealogical table of Matthew (chap. 1) we are indebted for the further fact that she became the wife of Salmon, the mother of Boaz, the grandmother of Jesse, and in the fourth generation the maternal ancestor of David. There was grand material in her, which, sanctified by her faith, made her truly a mother in Israel.

The Crossing of the Jordan.

The time in the year for crossing the Jordan was fixed forethoughtfully in the early spring. True, Jordan was then at high flood; the melting of the snows of Lebanon caused Jordan to flow all his banks;* but this made

---

* The usual width of the Jordan at this point may be one hundred feet; its depth eight or ten. When the Israelites passed it, its width is supposed to have been twelve hundred feet. The waters set back to Zaretan and Adam, near Beth-shean, thirty-five or forty miles distant." (See Coleman's Historical Text Book and Atlas of Biblical Geography, p. 83.)

the miracle the more signal, and the prestige of God's present hand became the greater and to the Canaanites the more appalling. The tenth day of the first month was the eventful one—four days before their feast of the Passover, and among the first days of the barley harvest.

The preceding night they encamped on the river bank. The grand scene of crossing the Jordan bed puts the ark of the covenant in the foreground. The priests bearing the ark came into the water's edge, dipping their feet in the Jordan; then the waters stood as if a dam were suddenly dropped across the entire river-bed; the waters from above set back, piling themselves higher and higher through all that momentous day; while the waters below that crossing line flowed on and away, leaving the river-bed dry. The priests held their position supporting the ark of God till the hosts of Israel had gone over, and then brought up the rear. When nightfall came over Israel they were in the long-promised land. They had crossed the Jordan. They had seen its waters mounting up higher and higher on their right all the day; but the glorious ark of God stood like a breast-work of the Almighty, and not a rill, not a drop, could force itself down upon their crossing host till the last man had passed over and till the feet of the priests who bore the ark were high on the Canaan side. Then the hosts of Israel were not only in Canaan, but were there with one more fresh testimony that their God was with them. Eventful days were before them; scenes of war and blood were in prospect; but the men of faith throughout all the camp of Israel sang their evening song with glad heart and rested on their arms feeling that it was enough for them that their God was there; had brought them into his own land of promise, and would carry the work of its conquest through in his own time and way.

We are in no danger of overestimating either the intrinsic interest or the moral significance of this grand event. Let us remember how many slow moving generations of the children of Abraham had held Canaan in distant prospect and in more or less confident hope. Now they are there—and there, by what stupendous agencies—through what astounding scenes! How they must have looked up to that solid wall of waters piling itself high and more high during all that memorable day in which full three millions of men, women, and children were crossing over into Canaan! What child even of that crossing host could ever forget the scene? How must the people have been impressed with a sense of the *power* of their own God—that God who had given them a symbol of his presence in the ark of his covenant!

Observe that this crossing was "right over against Jericho"—as if intentionally located almost under the very eye of that first strongly walled city of Canaan. But they had not the least reason to fear the armed men or the strong walls of Jericho. The fear was now on the other side. When his people have faith and walk humbly before him, God has reserved power enough to bring out in their behalf, so that they often need only stand still and see the salvation of God. This was the beginning of God's glorious deeds for his people toward the possession of Canaan—the first, but not the last.

Memorial Stones.

Such an event was worthy of commemoration. It ought never to be forgotten. Stones have often served the dying generations of men for a memorial. A pile of them, even though they hold no written letters, may hold a tradition of their significance age after age. The number twelve was suggestive of the number of their tribes; therefore, twelve stones were placed together for a memorial.——It should be noticed that this memorial was duplicated. There were two such memorial piles; one on the east of Jordan, and one on the west; the former on the spot where the feet of the priests first touched the waters—that is, at high water mark on the east side of the river, and at the point of their crossing. As these stones were at hand and needed no transportation, it is said (4: 9) that Joshua set them up. Obviously they would serve a threefold purpose; to indicate high water mark; also the place of crossing; and to provide a memorial which the tribes on the east of Jordan might consider as theirs.——The second memorial pile cost more labor. Twelve men, one from each tribe, were selected and ordered to pass over before the ark, and take each a stone from the midst of the river channel, and bear it to the place of their first encampment, viz., Gilgal, about five miles from the Jordan, on the rising bluff which overlooks the Jordan vale and river. This memorial pile was readily accessible to the tribes on the west of Jordan, and from the manner of its construction would hold within itself traditionary memories likely to endure from age to age among the Hebrews of Canaan. Gilgal continued for several years to be the head-quarters and fortified camp of Joshua and his host. This memorial pile stood for ages to suggest to the youth of Canaan the inquiry, What mean these stones? and to afford to Hebrew fathers the opportunity of repeating and so perpetuating the ancient story.——So let all the great works of God be held forever in the hearts of his people. It is wholesome to fathers to repeat the story, wholesome to children to hear it and place it deep in their memories, till they in their turn become fathers and tell it to their children.

The historian (chap. 5) records two facts, manifestly correlated to each other. First, that the tidings of this wonderful passage over the dry bed of the Jordan flashed over the hills and valleys of Canaan, bearing terror and dismay to all hearts. Alas, said they, who can stand before this mighty God of Israel! "Their hearts melted, neither was there spirit in them any more, because of the children of Israel" (5:1).——The second fact is that Joshua proceeded to the most unmilitary *act of circumcising* all his men of war—indeed all the children of Israel.* With apparently not the least fear lest the Canaanites should muster their

---

* The sense of the passage (5: 9) has been earnestly debated. "The Lord said to Joshua, this day have I rolled away the reproach of Egypt from off you: Wherefore the name of the place was called Gilgal (the *rolling* place) unto this day."——The best view assumes that Egypt had reproached Israel with their failure to reach Canaan during the long wanderings of forty years in the wilderness, and that God was then to roll off this reproach by visibly taking the people again into covenant relation with himself, indicated by this circumcision, and so would give them Canaan. That circumcision had been omitted in the wilderness, especially after the unbelief in the matter of the spies, implied that God's covenant with his people was temporarily inoperative because of that unbelief. At Gilgal the Lord was returning to them in his great mercy.

forces and fall suddenly upon them—with a deep feeling obviously that his first concern was to be right before God, and to have all his soldiers and people right in heart and true to every precept of their God, he suspended all military movements; gave his enemies time to recover from their panic; halted his army not only for some days of circumcision but for the *feast of the Passover* seven days—all as if religion was indefinitely more than military strategy—as it truly was!

Let us note that this Passover, far beyond any other yet, was suggestive of the scenes of the original institution of it forty years before — on that most eventful night of doom to Egypt, but of joyful redemption to Israel. The redemption begun there in Egypt was consummated, in a measure, here in Canaan. This crossing of the Jordan must have suggested the crossing of the Red Sea by their fathers, three days after the first Passover night. That earlier crossing put the Red Sea between them and Egyptian bondage: this latter crossing put the Jordan between them and their wilderness life. The most precious thought of all would be that God was equally in both—his uplifted right arm was made glorious for their redemption, both there and here. It must have been inspiring to all devout souls to celebrate the majesty and loving-kindness of their fathers' God.

Among the new experiences of their Canaan life was a supply of bread from the corn (not as in our English "the *old* corn," but the corn) of the land. The manna ceased as suddenly as it began. Forty years (less one and a half months) it had been the nation's bread, fresh each morning (save the Sabbath) from God's lower heavens. The period of its fall measured their wilderness life. This being past the manna ceased.

Another event of striking significance stands in the history at this point. While Joshua was near by Jericho, apparently alone, taking a military survey of the city and its approaches, suddenly raising his eye, he saw a man over against him with a drawn sword in his hand. True to the instincts of his military spirit, and with apparently no sensation of fear, Joshua advances near him and puts the main question—demanding the countersign—*for us?* or *against us?* Friend art thou; or foe?——As promptly the answer comes:

"Nay, but as Captain of the Lord's host am I now come." Instantly Joshua recognized in this Personage his divine commander-in-chief; and prostrating himself in worship, asks—"What saith my Lord unto his servant?" The Captain of the Lord's host made this his first reply: "Loose thy shoe from off thy foot, for the place whereon thou standest is holy; and Joshua did so." His further reply appears in chap. 6: 2–5. ——This suggests to our minds the scene with Moses at the burning bush; much more surely must it have made the same suggestion to Joshua.——It would seem to have been the main purpose of this manifestation to give Joshua a sensible and vivid impression of his superior officer. To the day of his death let him never be tempted to think of himself as at the head of the armies of Israel. Let him never forget the presence, the look, the voice, the words of his supreme commanding officer, the real "Captain of the Lord's host." Critics have raised the question, Who was this Personage? Was he human, angelic, or divine?——But one answer it seems to me can be given: *Divine;* the same who spake to Moses at the bush; the same whose record and description appears in Ex. 23: 20–23; "Behold, I send an angel before thee; beware of him and obey his voice; provoke him not, for he will not pardon your transgressions; for *my name is in him.*"

Jericho Falls.

According to the principles of military tactics this strongly walled city ought to have commanded the passage of the Jordan. It failed to make the least demonstration in that direction. Yet Joshua found the city standing in its strength, too near his encampment at Gilgal (which lay between Jericho and the Jordan), and too important in every respect to be passed. What shall be done with it?

The problem must come to issue, What of these strongly walled cities of Canaan? Is this undisciplined and half-armed host of Israel equal to their subjugation? With none of the powerful enginery produced by military science for the assault of strongly walled cities; with no battering rams, no catapults, and far indeed from having field artillery and Rodman guns—

FALL OF JERICHO. 19

what can they do before the walled cities of Canaan? We shall see.

Here also, as in the crossing of the Jordan, the ark of the covenant appears in the foreground. Seven priests surround it with rams' horns. Its place is assigned between the battalions that precede and those that follow and bring up the rear. The whole armed host of Israel is put in motion—one half to precede and the other to follow the sacred ark and its attendant priests. The first day they march around the city once, the priests blowing their rams' horns, but every human tongue silent; and return to their camp for the night. Five more days they encompass the city daily in the same marching order—all silent save the horn-blowing.——What did the men of Jericho think of this new and strange type of tactics? Had they ever seen a walled city invested after this sort? Even if they felt somewhat uneasy the first day and the second, did not their fears begin to subside and the whole movement begin to appear farcical and ridiculous before the eventful seventh day opened upon them? Be this as it may, the seventh day came. Up betimes in the morning under fresh orders, moving at double-quick, they encompass the city seven times—every rams' horn blowing, but all human voices silent till the word of command resounds through their marching hosts, *shout!* Then the welkin rang with the shouts of victors in battle!

All suddenly the entire wall of the city is flat upon the ground. Wheeling toward the city from every point, armed men rush over the fallen walls; with sword and fire they lay the city utterly desolate. All its silver and gold, all its vessels of brass and of iron, are consecrated to the Lord and come into his treasury; all else was doomed to destruction. Jericho is no more! Its fall gave new impulse to the panic which shook the stoutest hearts among the men of Canaan. They could not but see that a new power was among them and that their city-walls were of no particular account before this strange people. We may imagine how anxiously they are saying—Who can stand before this unknown enemy and their more wonderful and wonder-working God?— It may be noted that throughout the subsequent history of the conquest of Canaan, the siege of walled towns is scarcely noticed. This first master-stroke of divine policy seems to have made city-walls, gates, and bars practically useless.

Some may raise the question (more curious than wise)—What could be the use of all that marching and horn-blowing? Why was not one day's investing as good as seven? And why a seven-fold encompassing on the seventh day?

To these questions it might suffice to answer in general, that the Lord has his own thoughts in regard to the preliminary service or doing which shall precede a miracle. Very possibly we should fail to fathom all those thoughts if we should attempt it. The requiring of some human activity in connection with God's miracles has been the rule—"Go, Naaman, and wash thou in Jordan seven times and thou shalt be clean "—of thy leprosy (2 Kings 5: 10). To spit on the ground—to make clay of the spittle, and rub it upon the eyes of the man born blind and then to bid him "Go, wash in the pool of Siloam "—preceded his restoration to sight;—but not at all as natural remedial agencies. Those antecedents stood to the miracle in moral relations only. We may suppose, not unreasonably, that God proposes in these preliminaries a certain trial of human faith. In this case the Lord was doubtless quite willing that the men of Jericho should have their attention thoroughly aroused to these transactions before the fatal hour. In general, it is a thing of wise economy not to perform a miracle until every thing has been done to give it a telling moral power. Let there be no waste of force even though the power that works miracles be (as to the arm of the Almighty) so infinitely abundant that we might suppose it cheap. The laws of the human mind being what they are, divine wisdom will suggest a close economy in the putting forth of miraculous powers lest they lose their due impression.

Achan.

The seventh chapter discloses a scene of trouble. Suddenly the progress of Israel's victorious arms is blocked; their prestige of victory is dimmed; their bright prospects are clouded over. The feeling in the most sagacious minds is scarcely less than consternation.——What has happened? The warriors of Israel are smitten and flying before the men of Ai.* Joshua falls on his face in agony. This is so unlike his anticipations! He had felt sure that God was with him and with his army; but this appears quite otherwise. He cries to the Lord for help. Nay more; he thinks this a matter of most serious moment. We read: "Joshua rent his clothes and fell to the earth upon his face before the ark of the Lord until the eventide, he and all the elders of Israel, and put dust upon their heads. And Joshua said, Alas! O Lord God! wherefore hast thou at all brought this people over Jordan to deliver us into the hands of the Amorites to destroy us? O Lord, what shall we say when Israel turneth their backs before their enemies?" To which he adds, quite in the spirit of those great prayers of Moses for Israel; "For the Canaanites will hear of it, and will environ us round, and cut off our name from the earth, and *what wilt thou do for thy great name?*" Instantly the Lord replies: "Get thee up; wherefore liest thou thus upon thy face? *Israel hath sinned;* they have transgressed my covenant; they have taken of the accursed thing; have stolen and dissembled, and have put it even among their own stuff. Therefore it is that Israel could not stand before their enemies; neither will I be with you any more except ye destroy the accursed thing from among you." (vs. 6–12.) To make the strongest possible impression upon all minds, both of the enormity of this sin, of the purity of their own holy Lord God, and of his all-searching eye before which no sin however concealed from men can be hidden, the whole people are brought up standing before him, and by the sacred lot first, from all the tribes Judah is taken; then onward by families, by households, and lastly man by man, until at length the guilty offender stood out before the assembled hosts of Israel—Achan, by name; *the sinner* who had brought this great trouble upon Israel. To him Joshua said: "My son, give glory to the Lord God of Israel, and make confession unto him; and tell me now what thou hast done; hide it not from me." Achan

---

* The site of Ai has been identified by Dr. Robinson, twelve miles north-west from Jericho; ten miles north-east from Jerusalem; three miles south-east from Bethel. The valley of Achor was a short distance south of ancient Jericho. (Coleman, p. 84.)

confesses: "Indeed, I have sinned against the Lord God of Israel, and thus have I done: When I saw among the spoils a goodly Babylonish garment, and two hundred shekels of silver, and a wedge of gold of fifty shekels weight, then I coveted them, and took them, and behold, they are hid in the earth in the midst of my tent, and the silver under it."——The stolen goods are soon found and brought out before all the people; Achan and all his were brought down into the valley of Achor [trouble] and there stoned with stones and burned with fire after being stoned. A great heap of stones was raised over him—a memorial of his awful doom. "So the Lord turned from the fierceness of his anger." (7:26).

The reader will notice some striking points of analogy between this case of Achan at the opening of the Canaan dispensation, and the case of Ananias and Sapphira at the opening of the Christian age. Covetousness, the love of money, was the root-sin in each case. The demand for fearful judgment and vigorous retribution in the outset to head off a great temptation and to protect the people of God in scenes of fearful peril, constitute yet other points of obvious analogy. There are times and seasons when justice of the sterner type toward individual offenders is the only real mercy to the masses.

It may seem to some readers that this punishment was excessively severe, and that the occasion scarcely justified such manifestations of God's displeasure. In reply to such views I suggest that it behooves us to approach such a question with reverent reserve, and to beware of any rash thought or word derogatory to the Most High, not because it is intrinsically improper to exercise the sense of justice and right which God himself has given us, but because we are very liable to take limited, imperfect, very inadequate, or even distorted views of the case. Let us never assume that God's views are short-sighted or his judgments morally perverse! In both these directions, men may err, and do; but God, never!

In regard to the case of Achan, it is within our limited vision to see if we will that the Hebrew people were in most critical circumstances. They were just entering upon a scene of great and searching temptation. The people and cities of Canaan were rich; the Israelites were poor. Canaan had the resources of a somewhat high civilization; gold, silver, vessels of brass and of iron; goodly Babylonish garments—all dazzling before the eyes of a people forty years in a barren wilderness, and antecedently four hundred years afflicted in Egypt. Now, suppose the Lord had given them free license to plunder, to steal and hide, and appropriate all they could lay hands on! This movement for the conquest of Canaan would have become a savage, plundering, marauding expedition, not a whit above the demoralizing wars of all barbarous tribes upon nations largely in advance of themselves in wealth and luxury. Could the God of Israel become a party to such a war of plunder? Would it be to his honor to fulfill his promise of Canaan to the godly patriarchs in such sort as this? Would such avarice, and theft, and selfishness have improved the morals and the piety of the children of Israel? Would such license to his people have inured to the honor of Israel's God?——And yet further; these fascinating spoils—these glittering prizes of gold and silver and these ornaments of the cultured Canaanites—were linked in on every hand with idolatry. Art and wealth, in Canaan as in every other heathen nation, lent their power to augment the attractions toward idol-worship. If God would shut this flood-gate of idolatrous influence sharply down, he could not have done less than he did in the case of Achan—make the first offender a fearful example of severe and terrible, but just and righteous, punishment.

But these considerations, though in point and of great force to show the aggravation of Achan's sin, yet fall far short of the whole truth. The strongest points of the case appear in the special features as given in the history. God lent his miraculous power for the destruction of Jericho on the special stipulation ("covenant" he calls it in 7: 11) that the city should be *devoted*—it and all therein to the Lord; the sense of this devotement being that whatever was appropriate should go into the treasury of the Lord, and all else be given up to absolute destruction. The Hebrew word (*cherem* or *hherem*), translated either "devoted" or "accursed," is used continually in this record (6: 17, 18, and 7: 1, 11). Moreover it was most explicitly stipulated that all the silver and gold and vessels of brass and iron were consecrated wholly unto the Lord (6: 19); "they shall come into the treasury of the Lord." Joshua and the people so understood it, and acted accordingly, for the history is definite: "They burnt the city with fire, and all that was therein; only the silver and the gold and the vessels of brass and of iron they put into the treasury of the house of the Lord" (6: 24).—— Yet further; the utmost pains were taken to have this matter well understood beforehand. The preliminary precautions ran—"And ye in any wise keep yourselves from the accursed thing *lest ye make yourselves accursed* when ye take of the accursed thing, and make the camp of Israel a curse, and trouble it" (6: 18).——The sin of Achan had, therefore, these points of highest criminality.——(a.) It was a "presumptuous sin," against known and most explicit prohibition, and in contemptuous defiance of God's authority:——(b.) It was sacrilege—*stealing* from God; taking property that was devoted to God by special stipulation. By all right-thinking men in every age, this sin has been accounted as of the highest enormity. To this it may be added that all the wealth of Jericho and the city itself fell into the hand of Israel by special miracle, wrought of God under these express stipulations.——(c.) God being their Supreme King, the sin of Achan had the crowning element of being *high treason.*

Contemplating the moral applications of this case, the question may arise: What bearing has it upon the responsibilities of associated bodies of men for the sins of individual members of the association?——Some bearing, all must admit—at least a bearing in some cases and under some circumstances. The principle which underlies this case certainly *may* apply in other cases. But obviously much will depend upon the power of the associated body (suppose it to be a local church) to detect and prove the offense. In the case of Achan the Lord interposed to detect the crime and single out the criminal; and in ways which we can not expect him to repeat. Yet his providences are various and not infrequently put their finger upon the Achan in no doubtful way. Or the offense may be in its nature so public as to remove all doubt.

Next arises the question of power to deal effectively

with the offense. When offenses and scandals occur in a local church, light as to duty is sometimes sought by laying the case alongside of this case of Achan. In this comparison there may be danger in assuming that the same sort of treatment is appropriate in these church cases as in that case in ancient Israel. It is not well to forget that the first and chief responsibility of a church to its erring members is to bring them to repentance—to proceed in the spirit of love and not of sternness (much less of vindictiveness), and with tenderness, and tears, and prayers, labor for their return to Christ and righteousness. The highest glory of church discipline is to save, not to root out; to purify the body, not by amputation of its members, but by restoration to soundness and life. Resort to expulsion should be regarded as a somewhat humiliating (certainly a sad) confession by the church of the impotence of her spiritual forces.——The case of Achan stood in such relations to Israel, to her national work and to her national exposure to idolatry, that nothing short of extreme severity could be rationally thought of. It can not be well to draw inferences from such a case to church discipline in our times without carefully considering the wide difference between that case and these. ——And yet we have lessons to learn from the case of Achan. As every individual Christian is taught in God's Word to say—" If I regard iniquity in my heart the Lord will not hear my prayer," so every church must learn to say—If we tolerate flagrant scandalous sins in our communion, how can we hope that God will hear our church prayers and bless our associated labors? If we place ourselves in such relations to God that he can not bless us without publicly indorsing the scandalous lives that (in a supposed case) go unrebuked among us, what ought we to expect from him other than his frown?——The two great moral lessons taught for all time by this case of Achan are——(a.) That God is holy, of purer eye than to behold iniquity save with abhorrence;——and (b.) That men, associated, may become responsible to a certain extent for the sins of their individual members, so that the innocent must needs suffer with and for the guilty, until they meet their social responsibilities and use their social power in solemn fidelity against scandalous sin in their body.

The Fall of Ai before Israel.

After the repulse before Ai and the trouble that came of Achan, Joshua and his army needed some word of encouragement. God gave it. Their confident assurance of victory had received a painful shock. It was vital to their work that it be toned up again. The Canaanites had now for the time the prestige of victory, and would therefore be formidable in battle. No great commander ever appreciated better than Joshua how greatly success in war depends on the spirit—the courage, the real expectation—of both the officers and the fighting men. Consequently he advanced upon Ai with the greatest caution. He said to himself—I must have victory here at any cost. Chap. 8 informs us of his well-laid stratagem and of its complete success—till Ai lay in ashes—an heap of desolation forever.

Ebal and Gerizim.

This done, we note another brief pause in his military operations to give due attention to certain religious duties, enjoined through Moses shortly before his death (see Deut. 11: 29, 30, and 27: 1-13), viz., the erection of an altar on Mt. Ebal; the setting up of great plastered stones, the writing of the law upon them, and the solemn public proclamation of the blessings and curses from these specified mountains, Ebal and Gerizim,* in the presence and with the response of all the people. (See Deut. 27 and 28.

This was now done, also a copy of the law of Moses (supposeably as repeated in abbreviated form Deut. 12-26) was written on plastered stones as Moses had prescribed. Much as the laws of war might demand that he follow up this last victory with telling blows, swift and fast falling, Joshua well knew that religious duties were every thing to his right standing with God, not to say also to the intelligent, well-grounded assurance of his army. It was not, therefore, lost time or lost opportunity for

---

* Geographically these summits were near Shechem, twenty to twenty-five miles north from Ai. They rise 800 feet above the valley between them, this valley being about one-third of a mile in width, and from two to three miles in length.

them to pause for a fresh renewal of their covenant before the Lord.*

Recurring to the transaction itself, we have a grand theme for the imagination to paint. Think of 600,000 adult men, besides women and children, marshaled in equal divisions on two opposing mountains, 800 feet high and one-third of a mile from one summit to the other; the ark surrounded by the priests

---

*It has been doubted by able critics whether the passage (8: 30–35) —of the scenes at Mt. Ebal and Gerizim—is in its chronological place immediately after Ai and before the deception of the Gibeonites. This question not being of very great importance, let it suffice to say briefly:—That the objections to this chronological location of the scene are mainly—that at this stage Joshua had not penetrated into Canaan so far; that in Chap. 9: 6, and 10: 6, 7, 15, 43, we find him still in camp at Gilgal; that the distance from Gilgal to Shechem (twenty-five to thirty miles) is too great to admit the probability that Joshua and all his people traversed it, going and so soon returning, for the mere purpose of performing this religious service at that designated place; not to say that, not having at that time subjugated either the powerful Southern Kings or the Northern, it would have been in a military point of view unsafe.——Moreover, in the version of the Seventy there is some diversity in the location of this passage, some of the manuscripts placing it between vs. 2 and 3 of chap. 9.

In favor of retaining the order of our text and of locating the scene at Ebal and Gerizim chronologically as here, may be urged— (1.) That the compilation of the materials of this book should be presumed to be correct, unless very important reasons appear to the contrary.——(2.) That the divine command through Moses (Deut. 11: 29, and 27: 2, 4, 12) required this service on Mts. Ebal and Gerizim very soon (not to say immediately) after their arrival in Canaan. "When the Lord hath brought thee into the land," etc., thou shalt put the blessing upon Mt. Gerizim, etc. "And it shall be on the day when ye shall pass over Jordan, thou shalt set up great stones, plaster them with plaster, and write upon them all the words of this law." "It shall be when ye be gone over Jordan, ye shall set up these stones in Mt. Ebal," etc. Doubtless Joshua and the people were in the mood of prompt obedience to this word of the Lord through Moses, and therefore could not (as some critics suppose) have delayed to perform it until after the great battles recorded in Chaps. 10 and 11. The command was definite to do this *after* going over Jordan, not after they had subdued the Canaanities. In the order of reason and religion it came *before* the subjugation of Canaan, not *after*.——(3.) The objection on the score of safety in a military point of view is of no account, because the fall of Ai had given fresh force to the panic of the armies of Canaan, and because God never failed to shield his people from sudden assault while they were engaged in special and required religious solemnities. For these reasons, although this view as well as the other has its difficulties, I prefer to retain the chronological order as in our version.

and Levites in the intermediate valley; the solemn rehearsal of the blessings and the curses in tones loud and clear, in the hearing of the gathered thousands; and then the thundering "Amen," resounding from both mountain summits: — What could have been more impressive! How must this scene have fixed the attention, especially of the young, and solemnly deepened the conviction—This law is *our* law; these blessings are to be *our* reward, and these curses *our* doom, according as we obey or disobey this law of our own holy Lord God! Whatever power of impression upon the human mind is possible through the senses—the eye, the ear, and the personal utterance of awe-inspiring words—is all present here in its intensest form. Truly here are scenes for every eye to see; sounds for every ear to hear; scope for the fullest utterance of every human voice. Here is every thing to bring out a volume of common sympathy, rolling deep and strong, sustained throughout the entire transaction—the whole to be remembered through all future years as *the* great religious meeting of their lives.——Are there any lessons in the philosophy of religious impression for us to learn from this national assemblage of the ten thousands of Israel on these lofty mountain summits for the solemn announcement of the blessings and curses of their law?

The crafty policy of the Gibeonites * (chap. 9) affords strong proof that fear had fallen upon the inhabitants of Canaan. The crossing of the Jordan and the fall of Jericho and of Ai had brought a new power to their very doors. The men of Gibeon chose submission rather than resistance. By stratagem they obtained a treaty with Joshua and his princes, under which they served in the most laborious occupations for ages.——It is noticeable in this case that "the congregation" of Israel—the common people—dissented strongly from the action of their princes in sparing the Gibeonites. How much their views were influenced by their indignation against such duplicity, and how much by a close construction of the divine behest for extirpating the

---

* Gibeon, "a great city as one of the royal cities" (10: 2), was situated on a high eminence six miles north of Jerusalem. Three other cities, lying near, Chephirah, Beeroth, and Kirjath-jearim (9: 17), acted with Gibeon, in alliance or subjection.

devoted nations of Canaan, does not appear. The princes, however, recognized the obligation of their oath, and the Lord manifestly approved their action—which seems to show that the Canaanites might have been spared upon their submission, or (probably) if they had voluntarily surrendered the country to Israel and removed themselves beyond its bounds. Their destruction came, therefore, of their assault upon Israel —as the history proceeds to show.——It may be noted that the servile condition of the Gibeonites would go far to make their influence toward idolatry harmless. Only in the most menial status could it have been safe to spare them to live among the people of Israel—active idolaters.

The Two Great Decisive Battles.

Canaan was virtually subdued before the arms of Joshua in two great decisive battles; the first against five confederate kings of Southern Palestine (chap. 10); the second, against a similar but larger confederation of the petty kingdoms of Northern Palestine (chap. 11). The first was precipitated by the action of Gibeon which those southern kings regarded as treachery against the common interests of their country. At the instance, therefore, of the king of Jerusalem, four other kings, viz., of Hebron, of Jarmuth, of Lachish, and of Eglon, combined in an assault upon Gibeon. The Gibeonites sent at once to Joshua for help. The Lord said to Joshua: "Fear them not; for I have delivered them into thy hand; there shall not a man of them stand before thee." (10: 8). By a forced march of a whole night, Joshua was soon there, probably surprising his enemies and thus completely discomfiting them with great slaughter. The statement is:

"And the Lord discomfited them before Israel, and slew them with a great slaughter at Gibeon, and chased them along the way that goeth up to Beth-horon, and smote them to Azekah, and unto Makkedah. And it came to pass, as they fled from before Israel, and were in the going down to Beth-horon, that the Lord cast down great stones from heaven upon them unto Azekah, and they died: they were more which died with hailstones than they whom the children of Israel slew with the sword. Then spake Joshua to the Lord in the day when the Lord delivered up the Amorites before the children of Israel, and he said in the sight of Israel, Sun, stand thou still upon

Gibeon; and thou Moon, in the valley of Ajalon. And the sun stood still, and the moon stayed, until the people had avenged themselves upon their enemies. Is not this written in the book of Jasher? So the sun stood still in the midst of heaven, and hasted not to go down about a whole day. And there was no day like that before it or after it, that the Lord hearkened unto the voice of a man: for the Lord fought for Israel." (10: 10–14.)

Joshua's military character being studied on its human side, his forte as a general would lie in creating a panic and then making the utmost possible use of it. In this case his rapid march of a whole moonlit night brought him upon his enemy yet (we may suppose) in their morning slumbers, all unprepared for battle. Then the panic becoming a route, he chased them up the ascent to the upper Beth-horon; then down the descent to the lower Beth-horon, along which descent the Lord met them with a most terrific hail-storm, crashing among their broken ranks with that awful enginery of heaven, slaying more with his hail-stones than all whom Joshua slew with the sword. When just out from Gibeon, Joshua saw that the tide of victory had turned against his enemy, already routed and fleeing. With the instinct of a great commander he felt that his time had come to annihilate that host. Now, thought he, let this victory be made complete; O for a day long enough to finish them utterly! Then and there, moved by a divine impulse, he cried aloud "in the sight of all Israel—Sun, stand thou still over Gibeon, and thou Moon, in the valley of Ajalon! And the sun stood still, and the moon stayed until the people had avenged themselves upon their enemies."

The geographical localities named concur with the facts stated to show that it was during the morning hours of the day, and not toward the evening hours, that the sun and moon were arrested in their course by this miracle. The direction of this flight and pursuit was *westward*. Joshua had passed the highlands on which Gibeon stood, so that Gibeon lay eastward from his point; while the valley of Ajalon was still some distance in the west. The sun had risen above Gibeon, perhaps nearly half way to his meridian, so that it stood still "in the *midst of heaven, i. e.* coming near the middle of its diurnal circuit in the heavens; while the moon, somewhat past the full, hung over the valley of Ajalon.

THE SUN AND MOON STAND STILL. 31

The narrative represents that the sun and moon "hasted not to go down *about a whole day*."

No miracle recorded in the Scriptures has been assailed more violently or discredited more generally than this. The forms of assault are chiefly these two:——(1) To attribute the appearance of miracle in the statement to the embellishments of poetry:——and (2.) To reject the whole as scientifically impossible, and therefore incredible.

The former class of critics make large account of the incidental allusion to the "book of Jasher," and also of the poetic parallelism which appears in the words— "Sun, stand thou still upon Gibeon; and thou Moon, in the valley of Ajalon." The "book of Jasher" is claimed to be a poetic legend in which this overwhelming defeat and route of the five kings of Canaan—work and glory enough for *two* days—is represented as filling out two days of time—*as if* the sun and moon waited in midheaven for this stupendous work to be well and thoroughly done!

The proper answer to this construction of the passage is that, *as an interpretation of language*, it utterly fails in the vital point—that of *giving the sense*. The words of our record declare that, in the sight of all Israel, Joshua cried aloud, commanding the sun and moon to stand still; that thereupon the sun and moon *did* stand still for about one whole day; that this day was unlike any other before or since, in this vital respect—that the Lord hearkened to the voice of a man and granted his prayer—to the result of this great miracle. This is what the words standing here must mean. That these words of command assume somewhat the form of the usual poetic parallelism does not modify their legitimate meaning one particle. The loftiness of the thought, the grandeur of the conception, demanded from any Hebrew mind this style of expression. A prosaic style would be so unnatural as to raise legitimate doubt of its genuineness.——That this great event should be recorded in the book of the upright ["Jasher"] is not the least disparagement to its veracity. Such an event *ought* to be recorded in any and every *book of Jasher*. All the records of those times made by upright men, or made for the reading of upright men in all future ages, should include this great transaction.

Some very able and excellent critics—men who accept the true doctrine of miracles and find them elsewhere in the Bible, yet hold that in this case the day was not really prolonged as to time. In their view Joshua's prayer was answered in its spirit, not in its letter; *i. e.* only by making his victory complete before the usual darkness of night came on. In support of this view they urge that this case is not referred to elsewhere in scripture as a miracle; that all Joshua could desire in his prayer was the complete discomfiture of his enemy—in spirit, this: O let not the day close till my enemies are perfectly routed! and that this prayer was granted by smiting them with hail-stones from heaven, and by giving Joshua's men almost superhuman endurance and energy in battle. Especially they maintain that the entire passage (vs. 12–14, and perhaps also v. 15) is quoted from the book of Jasher, of which we learn from 2 Sam. 1: 18, that it was written in the boldest style of ancient Hebrew poetry. Regarding it thus as a quotation, these critics make large allowance for bold poetic diction, as Deborah sung—"The stars in their courses fought against Sisera" (Judg. 5: 20); while some raise the question whether this book of Jasher was inspired and its representations altogether truthful, and also whether the compiler of the book of Joshua must be held to indorse them.

Replying briefly to these points in order; it must be conceded that this miracle is not clearly referred to elsewhere in scripture.* This argument *from silence* can have, however, but very limited force. It may be quite impossible to explain the reason of this silence, yet there may have been reasons other than the absence of all miracle here.

As to the form of Joshua's prayer, the record is entirely definite. It states that Joshua prayed—not thus: O give me a perfect victory! Let my soldiers do the work of two days in this one!—but precisely this: "Joshua spake to the Lord in the sight of all Israel (and of course in the *hearing* of many): "Sun, stand

* It is plainly referred to in the Apocryphal book Ecclesiasticus (46: 4); "Did not the sun go back by his means, and was not one day as long as two?" This shows the current opinion of the Jews at that date.

thou still upon Gibeon, and thou Moon, in the valley of Ajalon!" Then the narrative proceeds to say—not merely that the Lord answered his prayer in its spirit. yet not in its letter; not merely that the Lord gave him a finished victory, routing and almost annihilating his enemies; but this: "And the sun stood still, and the moon stayed until the people had avenged themselves upon their enemies." Then follows a reference to the "book of Jasher" as corroborating this wonderful fact, after which we have the statement, not in poetic parallelism or diction, but in the plainest sort of prose: "So the sun stood still in the midst of heaven and hasted not to go down about a whole day." Nor does the passage end with this, but again reaffirms the vital fact: "And there was no day like that before it or after it, that the Lord hearkened unto the voice of a man"—a statement which can not mean that God never before or after this day answered the prayer of man, but which must mean that never, before or after, had God heard man's prayer *in this way*—to the result of *such a miracle.*

——Hence I am compelled to dissent from even such critics as Hengstenberg, and quite decline to resolve this miracle into poetic embellishment, or pass it over to the doubtful or denied inspiration of the "book of Jasher."

To those who reject this miracle as scientifically impossible, and therefore incredible, the proper answer is, that *the author of nature is the Lord of nature*, and has never perpetrated the folly, not to say the impossibility, of tying his own hands by any system which vacates his absolute control of the universe he has made. If it be said that the disturbance in the planetary system by such an arrest of the earth's revolution on its axis is too great to be thought of as admissible, the answer is: He who is able to arrest the earth's revolution twelve hours, is also able to prevent any disastrous disturbance from such arrest. It is not incumbent on us to show *how* this supposed disturbance was prevented; nor even to show *how* the Lord applied his divine power to stop the sun in the heavens; *i. e.* to stay the revolution of the earth on its axis. The question *how* is simply an impertinence. We might as well discredit the creation of light because we can not answer the question *how* God could "speak and it was done."

Fundamentally, this objection to miracle must assume one or the other of these two alternative positions.

(1.) That *there is no God*—no being who has power to stop the sun in the heavens for twelve hours; or,

(2.) That God, having created the universe, put it under the control of laws, which laws he either lacks the power to deviate from, or having this power, has bound himself never to use it.——The last alternative is more generally adopted than either of the others. The proper answer to it is: *Where is the proof?* Who knows that God has bound himself never to interpose and suspend for the occasion the normal laws of nature? Let it be granted that he will never do this without good reason; yet who knows that there never has been and never will be a good reason? Who is able rationally to deny that for this once the Lord might listen to the voice of a man, and prolong the fighting day twelve hours for the purpose of breaking down the military power of Canaan, and giving the land of his promise to his believing people? Who knows that during the progress of those great events which make up the wonderful record of inspiration—which go to *make the Bible*—which were intended for great witnessing facts, giving to the ages of human history the proofs of God's present wonder-working hand—there would not arise occasions for real miracle—for a manifestation of God's hand of such sort and sustained by such proofs as no then living witness could gainsay or resist?——If the objector says, with Hume: At all events the proof of miracle must always be unsatisfactory and (rationally considered) insufficient, because it is more probable that history should lie than that God should work a miracle, the answer is a flat denial. It is *not* more probable that all history—the strongest and best historical testimony—should lie than that God should under any circumstances work a miracle. For, under some supposable circumstances miracles are not only credible but are even probable—to be expected. A written revelation from God being a moral necessity for man, and God being a kind Father to his moral offspring, it is far more than probable that God would make one; and in order to make it available, authoritative, to intelligent beings, would give a miracle to indorse it. Therefore it would

THE BATTLE OF HAZOR. 35

be marvelously strange if God did not resort to miracle to substantiate his written revelation and to manifest himself to a moral world like this.

We return to our history. Night-fall came at last and closed the pursuit. The men of Joshua's host who had marched all night from Gilgal to Gibeon, and then fought, not twelve hours only, but perhaps twenty, must have had almost miraculous powers of endurance—attributable, doubtless, to that inspiration of soul which makes small account of the weakness of human flesh and blood.——One little incident of this day reveals the spirit of their commander. The five confederate kings fled and hid themselves in a cave at Makkedah. The fact is reported to Joshua. Instantly he gives orders:— Wall them in and set a guard to keep them; and stay ye not, but pursue after your enemies and smite the hindmost of them; let none escape to enter into their fenced cities. We can look after the five kings when our other work is done.——So they did, and when that double-day's work was done, the army returned and made their first camp at this Makkedah. In due time those kings were brought out and laid prostrate before Joshua and his men. Perhaps to heighten the courage of his captains or to counteract their fear of kings in arms—stalwart, gigantic men they may have been—he said to them, "Come near and put your feet on the necks of these kings." Done; and then Joshua said; "Fear not, nor be dismayed, be strong and of a good courage; for thus shall the Lord do to all your enemies against whom ye fight." (vs. 24, 25).——These kings having been disposed of, Joshua followed up this great victory by passing rapidly in his victorious march from one royal city to another, capturing in their order Makkedah, Libnah, Lachish, Gezer, Eglon, Hebron, and Debir—thus subjugating all Southern Palestine. "All these kings and their land did Joshua take at one time; because the Lord God of Israel fought for Israel." Thus tersely the historian ascribes these victories to God.

The Victory over the Kings of Northern Palestine (Josh. 11).

This history is given with very little detail. Hazor, quite near the northern limit of Palestine, and on the southern extremity of the Anti-Libanus range, being

THE BATTLE OF HAZOR.

the strongest of those cities and kingdoms, took the lead, its king inviting into this confederation all the kingdoms of Northern Palestine as far south as the latitude of Jerusalem; also those adjacent on the north-west and the north-east. Mustered for war, they were a great host—" much people, even as the sand that is upon the sea shore in multitude, with horses and chariots very many (11: 4).* They encamped near the waters of Merom (the modern El Huleh), a basin of water near the sources of the river Jordan, and really an expansion of that river. Joshua, in his camp at Gilgal, is waiting for marching orders from the "Captain of the Lord's host." In due time they came: " Be not afraid of them; for to-morrow about this time will I deliver them up all slain before Israel." So short a time signified another forced march, doubtless by night, up the line of the Jordan valley. The record has it: "So Joshua came and all Israel with him against them by the waters of Merom *suddenly, and they fell upon them:* "—Another of those rapid movements according to the military policy of Joshua—dashing upon his enemy after a forced march, smiting and slaughtering before they are aware that he has even broken camp at Gilgal. Thus he demoralized that vast host with panic, and then chased and cut them down with fearful slaughter. In this battle his enemy fled in various directions—some to the north-west, whom he chased even unto great Zidon; others up the "valley of Mizpeh" eastward along the lake and marsh of Huleh beyond which some might pass up the valley lying between Lebanon and Anti-Lebanon, while others might bear away "eastward by Baneas toward Damascus" (Coleman p. 87).——To hough and so to disable their horses and to burn their chariots in the fire was at once the command of the Lord and the dictate of the soundest policy.——This great battle having broken his enemy into fragments, it only remained to follow it with the capture of his cities and the slaughter of all his resisting forces. This was a work of time, since we read; " Joshua made war a long time with all those kings" (11: 18). Not a city made peace

---

*Josephus reckons their number at 300,000 foot, 10,000 horse, and 20,000 chariots. It is safe to assume that these figures are too great, yet that the host was immense, relatively to the number under Joshua.

ALLOTMENT OF CANAAN;—CALEB.

with Israel save Gibeon. It was of the Lord that the rest were persistently hardened in their opposition, fighting to the bitter end and to their own terrible destruction. Thus Joshua took the whole land as the Lord had promised to Moses and to the earlier patriarchs, and then gave it to the tribes of Israel for their inheritance.

CHAPTER III.

Allotment of Canaan.

THE ensuing chapters give further particulars of the conquest, and then of the distribution of the conquered country. In chap. 12 the historian gives a list of the cities and kings subdued, both those on the east of Jordan and those on the west. In chap. 13 is a brief sketch of the sections ("very much") yet remaining to be possessed (vs. 2-6); and next we find the distribution of territory east of Jordan to the two and a half tribes previously located there.

Caleb and his inheritance.

In chap. 14: 6-15 the writer gives a special account of Caleb, the associate of Joshua in the minority report when twelve spies were sent up into Canaan from Kadesh-barnea. (See Num. 13 and 14.) At this time, eighty-five years old, still hale as at forty, still strong in the faith of Israel's God, he asks for the special inheritance which Moses had promised him—which promise Joshua with good heart gratefully fulfills.*

The reader will notice that Caleb makes a strong point of his hale and vigorous old age. To see this in its full force we need to ask—Where were the ten spies

* The dates given in this brief personal history of Caleb avail to show that this transaction was seven years after the crossing of the Jordan. Caleb being forty years of age at the mission of the spies from Kadesh-barnea and eighty-five now, the difference (forty-five) allows thirty-eight years for the remaining wilderness sojourning, and seven for residence in Canaan. These seven years measure the duration thus far of the wars of the conquest.

who, forty-five years before, brought in the majority report, so full of unbelief, so faithless as to the God of the patriarchal promises? Where were the thousands of that unbelieving generation? Alas! not a man of them lived to see the goodly land of Canaan; not one survived through the remaining thirty-eight years of wandering in the wilderness. But here is Caleb, not only living, but as vigorous as ever—as hardy and robust for war, as fresh for enduring the rougher tasks of human strength as when in his full maturity at forty. His testimony stands here, therefore, to prove that piety is wholesome, not to the soul only, but to the body; not for the culture of noble character only, but for the less yet not insignificant good of health, vigor, and years. ——If the fearful mortality among the unbelieving multitude at and after Kadesh-barnea gave occasion to the plaintive strains of Moses in Ps. 90, the total contrast between their case and that of Caleb and Joshua might no less naturally have suggested the contrasted strains of Ps. 91. Look into the case of those two men; hear the inspiring words of personal testimony which Caleb gives here, and learn to sing—"He that dwelleth in the secret place of the Most High shall abide under the shadow of the Almighty. . . . He shall deliver thee from the noisome pestilence: he shall cover thee with his feathers, and under his wings shalt thou trust." "Thou shalt not be afraid of the terror by night, nor for the arrow that flieth by day: A thousand shall fall at thy side, but it shall not come nigh thee." . . . "With long life will I satisfy him and show him my salvation."——It need not be maintained that all good men and good women will be healthful and strong down to the advanced age of Caleb the son of Jephunneh; and yet there is no lack of testimony that godliness has the better "promise of the life that now is." Virtue is always more wholesome for health and long life than vice; temperance than excess; a loving, trustful spirit, than a soul made bitter by hate and unrestful by its hostile attitude toward him who controls all things in both this world and the next.——It is pleasant to think of the cheery tone and trustful spirit in these words of the venerable Caleb. There were few to enjoy better than he the entrance into Canaan and the victories that gave them possession of that goodly land. He had occasion to remember the noble testimony he bore for God at Kadesh-barnea; he could not fail to see that God remembered it too. The earthly rewards of his faith and obedience were magnificent, yet not really greater than God is wont to give for like faith and obedience in all ages; albeit there may have been in his case an unusual measure of those rewards given in "the life that now is."

Chap. 15 locates the tribe of Judah, enumerating the cities given them, 112 in number, with their villages, showing that this portion of Canaan was densely peopled.——Chaps. 16 and 17 similarly give the location of Joseph, *i. e.* of Ephraim and of the half tribe of Manasseh—this territory, like that of Judah, stretching quite across Palestine from the Jordan to the Mediterranean.

The next important event is the fixing of the religious center at Shiloh in the territory of Ephraim* (chap. 18)—a much more central location than Gilgal. Thenceforward for many generations this was the home of the tabernacle, and practically the capital city of Israel.

The Location of the Tribes Completed.

Seven tribes were yet without location.† Arrangements were therefore made for the survey of all the yet unappropriated territory. Three men from each tribe constituted the surveying party. Instead of mapping out the country by its natural boundaries (rivers or mountain ranges) or by lines of latitude and longitude, they described it by cities and their adjacent villages. The whole was thus divided into seven parts, and these

---

* The precise location of ancient Shiloh has been ascertained beyond reasonable question by Dr. Robinson, after having been long unknown. See his Researches, vol. 3, pp. 85–89. It lies a little off and eastward of the great road from Jerusalem to Shechem, about twenty-four miles north from the former, and twelve miles south of the latter city, quite central to Palestine, west of the Jordan.

† Levi not being counted in the allotment of territory—to this tribe being assigned only cities and their suburbs, and these scattered among all the tribes, Joseph counted two, viz., Ephraim and Manasseh. Two and a half tribes were already provided on the east of Jordan, and two and a half on the west, viz., Judah, Ephraim, and the other half of Manasseh. Hence only seven remained; viz., Benjamin, Simeon, Zebulon, Issachar, Asher, Naphtali, and Dan

parts assigned to the seven tribes by lot. As Judah
and Ephraim were found to have a disproportionate
share, Benjamin's allotment was taken from theirs, and
also the allotment for Simeon was cut from the S. W.
portion of Judah.——The allotment of the remaining
tribes is given in chap. 19. A good map of the Palestine of that age will give the reader the best view of
their location. That of Coleman (Historical Text Book
and Atlas), frequently referred to in these pages, may
be safely recommended as made with care and on the
best and latest authorities.

The ultimate location of all the tribes in their own
cities and territory was an event of profound significance, worthy to be long remembered. A great people,
four hundred years oppressed in Egypt, forty years
wandering homeless in the deserts of Arabia, full seven
years up to this date in the conquest of Canaan, and
therefore unsettled—in a state of war, living in camp:
but now they fold up their tents and make their permanent homes in cities already built; in houses constructed, not to say, furnished ready to their hand.
Around them are lands under tillage, fruit trees in
bearing condition, every thing prepared for living with
all the comforts of oriental life. Indeed so great are
their resources for comfort and abundance that now
their dangers lie morally in this very line—the temptation to self-indulgence, to sensuality, and to most guilty
forgetfulness of their great Benefactor.——But God has
fulfilled his great promises made long ages ago to Abraham and renewed to his godly descendants. He has now
given them a land flowing with milk and honey—the
glory of all lands. Will they live worthily of their
mercies—worthily of their covenant relations as servants of their own Jehovah? Will they remember his
mercies and honor him with grateful hearts and consecrated lives?

Cities of Refuge.

Chap. 20 recites the Mosaic law in respect to cities of
refuge, and names them as assigned by Joshua, viz.,
those on the west of Jordan: Kedesh in Naphtali,
Shechem in Mt. Ephraim, and Hebron in Judah:—with
three on the east of Jordan, viz., Bezer from the tribe
of Reuben, Ramoth in Gilead from the tribe of Gad,

THE ALTAR OF WITNESS.   41

and Golan in Bashan from Manasseh. All these were from cities given to the Levites.*

Chap. 21 names the cities assigned to the Levites, forty-eight with their suburbs. The priests had all their cities in the territory given originally to Judah, and consequently were located conveniently for their ultimate service at Jerusalem.

Let it be noted that this chap., 21, closes pertinently with the statement that by this conquest and division of Canaan, God had thoroughly fulfilled all that he had promised to Abraham and the patriarchs in regard to the gift of Canaan to him and to his posterity. "The Lord gave unto Israel all the land which he had sworn to give unto their fathers, and they possessed it and dwelt therein." The Lord gave them rest round about and victory over all their enemies. "There failed not aught of any good thing which the Lord had spoken to the house of Israel; all came to pass." (21 : 43–45). The main purpose of the whole book of Joshua is to record this fulfillment of a long series of promises. It was quite in place, therefore, that at the close of these numerous details this comprehensive statement should have a place.

The Altar of Witness.

Chap. 22 recites the public services connected with the dismission of the men of war from the two and a half tribes after the conquest of Canaan was mainly finished; and coupled with this, the slight, or rather the transient, misunderstanding between the western and the eastern brethren, growing out of the erection by the latter of an altar of witness near the Jordan crossing which their western brethren assumed to be designed for sacrifice. The eastern wing, it at length appeared, had none but the best intentions. The jealousy of their western brethren moreover sprang from none but a good heart. Of course there was great wisdom in their sending an embassy of inquiry and investigation, and great joy when they learned the real purpose and meaning of this altar. The facts are of value historically as evincing a most excellent spirit in both the eastern

---

* The Mosaic law in regard to these cities of refuge, its occasion, spirit, and purposed operation are fully presented in my Pentateuch, pp. 282, 283, and therefore need not be repeated here.

brethren and the western; and are also useful suggestively as indicating how a bad and painful misunderstanding may be amicably disposed of, to the joy of both parties.

This case may, at first view, seem to indicate a secondary class of altars already in established usage, viz., for purposes of memorial witness. But if such had been the case, there would be far less justification for the jealousy and alarm of the western brethren when they heard of this altar. The presumption is strong that they knew of no such usage, and therefore could see no explanation of this act of their eastern brethren.—— Observe also that the record here states that this altar of witness was built "after the pattern (v. 28) of the altar of the Lord which our fathers made." It does not, therefore, indicate any secondary usage of altars, other than for sacrifice. It was an extraordinary, not an ordinary or customary institution, and was gotten up purely for memorial purposes, to testify along the course of future generations that they, equally with their brethren on the west of Jordan, had rights in the great altar of burnt-offering at the holy tabernacle. It was the result of a fear in their minds lest at some future period their rights in the holy place on the west of Jordan might be ignored and their children repelled.

Joshua's last words.

Chapters 23 and 24 transmit two discourses of Joshua to the assembled people of Israel, both of which meetings and addresses must have been near the close of his life. It is not perhaps certain, though probable, that there were two different meetings rather than two addresses at the same meeting, since that of chapter 23 is made specific by its *note of time*, viz.: "A long time after that the Lord had given rest to Israel and Joshua had waxed old." (23: 1); while that of chapter 24 is made definite by a *note of its place:* " Joshua gathered all the tribes of Israel to Shechem " (24: 1). In both cases the call embraced "all Israel," with their " elders, heads, judges, and officers." The general purpose of each meeting was the same; yet the things said by Joshua in each were quite different. In the second meeting, the national covenant was solemnly renewed at Shechem

(24: 25).——In the first meeting Joshua reminded the people of all the Lord had wrought for them *in Canaan*, subduing their enemies and giving them the land so long before promised to their fathers. Upon the basis of these great facts he exhorted the people to courage and faith in whatever conflicts of arms might be yet before them; but especially implored them to stand invincibly against idolatry and cleave to the Lord their God alone, assuring them that as God had faithfully fulfilled all his promises of good to the nation while obedient, so would he as faithfully fulfill his threatenings of evil if they apostatized to idols.——In the second meeting and address Joshua takes a larger range of historic review, sketching the history of Abraham even from his native home on the other side of the great Euphrates ("the flood," as our translators render the Hebrew word "*the river*"); then continuing his sketch through Isaac, Jacob, Esau, Moses, the Exodus, Balak, the wars of Canaan, and finally the possession of lands put under cultivation by other laborers and cities built by other hands. All this history is presented for the purpose of enforcing his final appeal; "Now, therefore, fear the Lord and serve him in sincerity and in truth, and put away the gods which your fathers served on the other side of the Euphrates." The strong point of this historic allusion seems to be of this sort; the Lord called Abraham out from Ur to remove him and his posterity from the social temptations existing there to idolatry. Now, do not frustrate his main purpose by plunging yourselves again into forms of idolatry no less vile than those.——Then, giving a new and sharp turn to his appeal, he says: "If it seem evil unto you to serve the Lord;" if it be a hardship and ye on the whole prefer to be like the heathen around you, "then choose ye this day whom ye will serve;" be whole-hearted one way or the other; "As for me and my house, we will serve the Lord."——The people answer with apparent earnestness and decision, certainly with excellent logic: "God forbid that we should forsake the Lord to serve other gods." It is this very Jehovah who has brought us out from Egypt; borne us through the wilderness; shielded and blessed us by miracle, and given us Canaan: "therefore we will serve the Lord, for he is our God."—— To put the case yet more strongly, Joshua takes still a new turn and in very remarkable words says: "Ye can not serve the Lord, for he is a holy God; he is a jealous God; he will not forgive your transgressions nor your sins. If ye forsake the Lord and serve strange gods, then he will turn and do you hurt and consume you after that he hath done you good."

It is important to us to use our plain common sense in construing these words of Joshua. It can not reasonably be supposed that he meant to say: "It is entirely impossible for you to serve a God so holy and so jealous, to his satisfaction, and you may as well desist from the attempt in despair at the outset. If this had been his meaning, why did he not live up to his own doctrine? With what reason could he say—"As for me and my house, we will serve the Lord?" No, his meaning is rather this: God will have your *whole heart*, or nothing. It is not pleasant to him to be insulted by having other gods thrust up before his face in preference to himself. It can be of no use for you to profess to serve him or even to make a small and faint beginning, and then turn back to serve idols. Interpreting Joshua's words in view of his own drift of thought, *i. e.* comparing v. 19, "Ye can not serve God," with v. 20; "If ye forsake the Lord, he will consume you," we get his meaning: ye must serve God if at all *with persistent and persevering steadfastness;* for if ye turn back to serve idols, all your former service of God goes for nothing and can not save you from his consuming judgments. Ye can not serve God *so!* Such service can never avail you at all! Ye might serve idol gods to their satisfaction in this way—but never the Great Jehovah! He takes no such offerings!——With apparent sincerity the people respond: "Nay, but we will serve the Lord."——"Ye are witnesses in this matter," replies Joshua. "Now put away the strange gods that are among you"—which suggests but too plainly the reason why Joshua is so thorough and searching in this exhortation against idolatry. Even then idol gods were secretly held and worshiped by some of the people. A special and most solemn covenant is therefore ratified in Shechem—all the people pledging themselves to cast away their idol gods, and give their hearts entirely to the God of their national covenant.

Next we read: "Joshua wrote these words in the

book of the law of God." What "*book*" is this? What and how much did it contain? Something more than the decalogue; more even than the decalogue with the addition of "the statutes and judgments." To be the appropriate place for this record, it must have been *historical* as well as *preceptive*—the book which contained whatever God had said and done of which a permanent record was kept; which brings us to this result; that this phrase, "The book of the law of God," included the Pentateuch and whatever subsequent matter, like the account of this proceeding, it was important to put on permanent record for the use of future generations.

——Again, studying the usage of this phrase, "The book of the law of God," we first meet the fact that the phrases, "The book of the law," and "The book of the law of Moses" are in very frequent use to indicate the Pentateuch (*e. g.* Deut. 28: 61, and 29: 21, and 30: 10, and 31: 26; and Josh. 1: 8, and 8: 31; and 2 Kings 14: 6). The phrase as here (Josh. 24: 26), "The book of the law of God," occurs rarely, yet manifestly stands related to those cited above, only substituting "law of God" for "law of Moses"—a substitution which indicates, (a) that it is inspired;—(b) that it is a continuation of the Pentateuch, being a "law" in the same sense, yet not the law of *Moses*, but only a continuation of it.

Joshua made another memorial of this transaction—a great stone set up under an oak near the sanctuary of the Lord. This usage—a memorial stone—appears as far back as Jacob in Bethel; and also in Joshua's history at the crossing of the Jordan. With remarkable vividness of imagination, Joshua says; "This stone shall be a witness, for *it hath heard* all the words of the Lord which he spake unto us; it shall be, therefore, a witness unto you, lest ye deny your God" (v. 27).

The book of Joshua then closes with the statement of his age and death—of course annexed by some later hand.——V. 31 states that Israel served the Lord, not only during the life of Joshua, but of all the elders that survived him, and had seen those great works of the Lord that he had done for Israel. This is gratifying proof that a rich and wholesome moral influence came in from those great manifestations of power and of faithful loving-kindness in the fulfillment of long standing promise. The best generation, morally, in the entire history of Israel is this which served under Joshua, amid miracles, wars, and the grand fulfillments of God's ancient promises.

Of Joshua it is pleasant to note that his character as presented in sacred history is faultless. Morally he appears under all circumstances true-hearted and inflexibly firm in steadfast obedience to his God.——Like the other great men whom God has raised up for some special work, Joshua was made for his. Undeniably he was one of the world's greatest generals. Against an enemy long skilled in war, and abounding in the best appliances of the military science of the age, he developed out of the most crude material an army really invincible—an army that may be said never to have lost a battle. Joshua seems under God to have inspired them with his own dauntless heroism and lofty faith. Make whatever discount we may for the occasional presence of miraculous manifestations, it is quite plain from the history that Joshua's men performed prodigies of valor, and evinced a celerity of movement, a terrific fury of onset, and an amount of physical endurance which are almost incredible. The presence of miracle did not supersede the demand for the very highest qualities of the true soldier and of the great commander. Everywhere in his military life, Joshua evinces the finest qualities of the general.*

* Before we lay aside the conquest of Canaan under Joshua, let us note the masterly movement, in a military point of view, by which this conquest was achieved.——Comparing the two supposable points of invasion; that from the south, say in a direct line from Egypt, or coming up from Kadesh-barnea (Num. 14: 40-45), with the approach from the east across the Jordan near Jericho, the latter had an immense advantage in several most vital points.——(1.) It flanked the enemy and struck them in their most vulnerable point;——(2.) It cut their forces in two, placing Joshua's army between the old Amorites and Canaanites on the south and the great Hittite nations on the north;——(3.) It gave Joshua the facility of making his forced marches immediately preceding his two great battles, along natural thoroughfares of travel, viz., that from Jericho westward to Joppa, and that northward up the valley of the Jordan, instead of crossing the great mountain ranges of Judah, as he must have done had he entered the country from Kadesh, and instead of encountering a cordon of immensely strong cities, as he must have done advancing from Egypt. It should be borne in mind that Southern and South-western Canaan was full of the strongest walled cities (Lachish, Gaza, etc.), all constructed to withstand an enemy approaching *from the Egyptian side*. The early history of Egypt shows that their military expedi-

In his last address to his people the reader will notice the same striking decision of character and thorough independence of thought and will which we have seen in all his military life. To the people he said, "If ye see fit to serve other gods, make your choice, *As for me and my house, we will serve the Lord.*" My house will go where I lead. My decision is made, and can never be reversed; *we serve the Lord!*

It is sad to think that the last days of so good a man were shaded by the painful apprehension that the people whom he had led to victory and conquest, and had planted in this glorious land of promise, already gave but too plain indications of relapsing into idolatry. Was it that "fullness of bread" and rest from toil were begetting effeminacy; or was it due to the social attractions of idol-worship from a somewhat cultured people, suffered to dwell among them? Be the cause what it may, the fact is apparent. Joshua, it would seem, both *saw* and *foresaw* that idol-worship was and was to be the giant sin of Israel. How then could he die in peace without bearing his most emphatic testimony against this sin? No wonder he accumulated the utmost force of appeal, of historic testimony, of earnest presentation, of solemn covenant, and of impressive memorial, to stem this anticipated and already apparent tendency to idols. Venerable man! How closely did he follow in the footsteps of Moses! How grandly did he fill the sphere God had assigned him! Now so near heaven, about to close a life so eventful, it is sad that his anticipations of the future of his people should be so shaded—but blessed to think that amid these painful apprehensions, he yet did his duty so fearlessly, so wisely, so well.

tions were almost universally toward the north-east, against or through Canaan.——If we add to all these natural advantages of his point of approach, the fact that crossing the Jordan miraculously at high flood and taking Jericho by miracle, must have astounded his enemies and smitten their souls into the weakness of panic and terror, we can not fail to see that God's hand was present to make this conquest easy. For war, as seen on its merely human side, and as military force is measured of men, Israel was weak; Canaan was powerful. Yet with God on their side, Israel was mighty, and Canaan, against them, virtually powerless. Israel's hosts had been trained in their wilderness life only to foot marches; scarcely at all to the shock of arms in battle; none to the subjugation of walled cities or the construction of fortifications. Curiously they made the best possible use of their celerity and endurance in forced marches and carried both of their great battles largely by means of this power.

CHAPTER IV.

The Book of Judges.

As to the author of this book, it can scarcely be necessary to add to what has been said already in the introduction to Joshua. A history of Israel was provided for—to be made up either by learned priests, or by a succession of prophets. Some contemporary record of the leading events of this book may very probably have been put in writing before the age of Samuel, and he may have put it in its present form. The demands of faith in this book as a part of the inspired oracles are satisfactorily met by the existing evidence,——(1.) That a history of the great events in Israel was secured under God's special arrangements (as above);——(2.) That this growing book of the law of God, when complete, was fully indorsed by Christ and his inspired apostles as the oracles of God.

The *General Scope* of this book is obvious, and, moreover, is brought out very fully in chap. 2, especially in vs. 11–23. Relapses into idolatry incurred the displeasure of God; this was manifested in strengthening their enemies against them and bringing Israel under severe oppressions. Then the people cried to God for help, and he raised up Judges who delivered them from their oppressors. In most cases these men judged Israel in peace and prosperity during their remaining life. Over and over we have these alternations: sin; punishment; repentance, and prayer for help; help coming through special instruments raised up of God.

The careful reader will notice that chap. 1 resumes and continues the history from the death of Joshua. "Now after the death of Joshua it came to pass" etc. (1: 1).——What the tribes did, and what they did not accomplish in the way of driving out the Canaanites in their respective localities is mainly the theme of the first chapter.——It has been already noticed above (p. 2) that the passage (Judg. 1: 11–15) appears substantially in Josh. 14: 15–19. Also the passage (Judg. 2: 6–10) appears with some variations in Josh. 24: 28–

CONDITION OF THE OLD CANAANITES.

31. These references in the latter book to the earlier are entirely natural in an author whose purpose is to resume and continue the history onward.

The history of the book of Judges can not be thoroughly understood unless the reader take into account the condition of the old Canaanite population, and also the religious state of the Israelites. Let it then be borne in mind;——(1.) That Canaan, though conquered, was only partially subdued. Their armies had been defeated in battle, pursued, scattered, broken, and most of their strong cities captured and more or less thoroughly destroyed; yet still they remained in very considerable force in the country, holding some of their strong points of defense. Especially along the western border of Canaan, "the lords of the Philistines, the Canaanites, the Zidonians, the Hivites of Mt. Lebanon" (3: 3) remained in great strength. It is one thing to gain a great battle, and quite another to exterminate an entire population.——(2.) It was of the Lord to leave some of their old enemies on the soil of Canaan in strength. This point is distinctly made in the history. "These are the nations which the Lord left" (3: 1). "I will not henceforth drive out any from before them of the nations which Joshua left when he died" (2: 21).——(3.) The reason for this policy on the part of God is given plainly; viz., the people transgressed their covenant; relapsed into idolatry; needed to be scourged and chastened to bring them back; and, therefore, God suffered these tribes of Philistia and Canaan to remain in sufficient strength to prove Israel, and try them, and scourge them back from their apostacies. This is the reason which the Lord himself assigns (2: 19–23, and 3: 1–4).

Hence this "book of Judges" is little else than an alternation from prosperity to adversity, corresponding to the moral alternations of the people from obedience and penitence for their sin to transgression and apostacy. Forgetting their own God; falling under the social influences of their idolatrous neighbors; drawn by intermarriages into dangerously intimate relations, and so into idol-worship, they incurred the wrath of God, and he brought them into political bondage to some adjacent hostile power.

Chap. 3 records two distinct scenes of apostacy,

EGLON OF MOAB AND EHUD.

oppression, and deliverance.——(a.) "God sold them into the hands of Chushan-rishathaim, king of Mesopotamia—Syria of the rivers (Euphrates and Tigris). Eight years under his yoke brought the nation to penitence and prayer. Then the Lord raised up Othniel, a nephew or younger brother of Caleb, for their deliverer. Expressively it is said that "the Spirit of the Lord came upon him, and he judged Israel and went out to war, and the Lord delivered this Syrian king into his hands." No special incidents of this deliverance are on record, save that after his victory the land had rest under his administration forty years—to his death.

(b.) The people, having relapsed again into idol-worship, the Lord strengthened Eglon, king of Moab against Israel. He drew to his alliance Ammon and Amalek, and smote Israel, and "possessed the city of palm-trees."* This servitude to Moab continued eighteen years. Then the people cried to God for help; and he raised up Ehud of the tribe of Benjamin. Of his deliverance of his country from Moab's king and oppressions, some striking incidents are told; *e. g.*, that he prepared a double-edged dagger of a cubit's length; concealed it under his loose oriental tunic upon his right thigh—an unusual and therefore unnoticed position; that he was sent with others to bear the national present to king Eglon, then residing in Israel at or near Jericho as in his own conquered country; that having delivered the present and set out upon his return, he suddenly dismissed his attendants, and went back to the king, saying—"I have a secret errand unto thee, O king." Eglon—his thought being apparently on some royal gift and not upon daggers—ordered his attendants out and received Ehud to his private summer chamber. Ehud came near, saying, "I have a message from God unto thee." The king arose from his seat: Ehud buried his dagger in the king's bowels —blade and haft—and fled that chamber, locking the door behind him, and made good his escape. Before the king's death was known he had distanced his pursuers; and then lost no time in rallying an army from

---

* This "city of palm trees," mentioned under this name Judg. 1: 16, is definitely said (Deut. 34: 3, and 2 Chron. 28: 15) to be Jericho.

DEBORAH AND BARAK. 51

Israel and seizing the fords of Jordan. In the issue he cut to pieces the army of Moab—ten thousand men— thoroughly broke their yoke, and gave his country rest eighty years.

In this narrative the Hebrew reader would notice that the word translated "errand" ["a secret errand"], and "message" ["a message from God," etc.] is the same, being the usual Hebrew term for *word*, but having in some cases the sense of thing, a matter. A private word for thee; a word from God to thee—would well express his meaning.——The word translated "quarries" (vs. 19, 26) is probably the name of a place—Pesalim, and was near Gilgal, and of course not far from Jericho, the city of palm-trees, where Eglon fell.

In Judg. 3: 7, we read: "They served Baalim and the *groves*"—as if the groves were an object of their worship as well as Baal. The Hebrew word is Asherah, probably equivalent to Ashtoreth or Astarte—a well-known Phenician goddess, often associated with Baal as the corresponding female and male gods of the Phenician system of idols. As Baal bore some relation to the sun, so did Asherah [Ashtoreth] to the moon, or, as some suppose, to Venus. Her usual image was an upright wooden pillar, or often the upright trunk of a tree—its head and branches removed. This circumstance may have led to the translation "groves," which, however, lacks authority. This worship was horribly obscene and debasing.

Deborah and Barak.

The next apostacy began probably some years after the death of Ehud, since we can scarcely suppose he lived to judge Israel full eighty years after the deliverance from Moab. The next great oppressor, permitted of God to scourge the nation, was Jabin, king of Canaan, reigning in Hazor, that strong northern city which led the combination of Northern Palestine against Joshua (Josh. 11). The city was again strong, its king having at command nine hundred chariots of iron. Twenty years he mightily oppressed Israel.

This time deliverance came through a woman, Deborah the prophetess, who was judging Israel, dwelling under a palm-tree which bore her name, between Ramah, the home at a later day of Samuel, and Bethel, the spot made sacred by Jacob's early visions of God. Moved by the Spirit of the Lord to heroic daring, she sent for Barak of Kedesh in Naphtali, and said, "Hath not the Lord God of Israel commanded, saying, Go and draw toward Mt. Tabor, and take with thee ten thousand men out of Naphtali and Zebulun? Then I will draw out to the river Kishon Jabin's chief captain Sisera, and all his host, and I will deliver him into thy hand."——Barak promptly answered, "If thou wilt go with me, I go; otherwise, I go not." Deborah replied, "I go; but it shall not be so much to thine honor; for the Lord will sell Sisera into the hand of a woman"—a prediction which seems to have had a double fulfillment, for a woman (Deborah) was virtually the head of the armies of Israel, and another woman (Jael the wife of Heber the Kenite) took the life of Sisera and no small share of the glory of this deliverance.——Barak gathered his ten thousand men on Mt. Tabor. Sisera came to join battle with him in the great plain of Esdraelon [Jezreel], lying at the foot of Tabor, through which flows the Kishon.*

Adjacent to the locality of this battle lived Heber the Kenite, a descendant of Hobab, who was brother-in-law to Moses—his family, holding a somewhat neutral position between the great contending powers, Israel and Canaan. The battle was joined in the great valley of Jezreel; the host of Sisera broke; he leaped from his chariot and fled on foot through some by-way doubtless, and turned in, weary, to the tent of Jael. She met him with inviting words; laid him to rest in her tent, and covered him with a mantle. Thirsty and hungry, he asked and obtained water and milk; drank and then slept. Whether it came of Jael's faith in Israel's

* This remarkable plain, in form, roughly put, a triangle; the base, its east line about fifteen miles long; its north side, formed by the hills of Galilee, about twelve miles long, and its south side, skirted by the Samaria range, about eighteen miles. Through its apex on the west flows out the Kishon draining its waters into the Mediterranean.——This plain has proved to be one of the most celebrated battle-fields of all history. Here, after Barak, fought Gideon and the Midianites; here Saul fell before the Philistines; Josiah before the Egyptians under Necho; here, in later times, fought Vespasian, the Crusaders, and Buonaparte.

God, or of her historic memories of Moses and of Israel, or of her recent sympathy with a long and sorely oppressed people—which, or all combined—we may not be able to say; but some heaven-born impulse moved her soul to the heroic deed. Armed with a workman's hammer and a tent-spike, she stole up softly and smote this tent-pin deep into his temples, and fastened it through his head into the ground—to his death.
——Barak, in hot pursuit, came up ere long, and Jael called him in to show him the man he was seeking—Sisera dead; the nail through his head to tell the story of his fall! So God subdued Jabin that day before Israel.

Deborah embalmed this story in sacred song. Her emotions of joy, gratitude, and praise were too strong to be suppressed—too rich to find fit utterance otherwise than through poetry and music. Why should not such a woman's heart indite poetry and pour itself forth in holy song? So we have in this fifth chapter of the book of Judges—one of the oldest songs known to the literature of the world—a beautiful specimen of Hebrew poetry, and of its felicitous adaptation to music, praise, and thanksgiving.

This song opens (v. 2) with the briefest reference to the great theme of praise; calls triumphantly (v. 3) on all kings and princes to give ear to her song; sets forth in lofty poetic conceptions the coming of Jehovah from the south, in earthquake, tempest, and storm for their help (vs. 4, 5); then falls back to give historically the state of the country prior to this great victory (vs. 6, 7); refers to the giant sins which brought on these foreign wars (v. 8); calls on men of every grade, rulers and people, to join in her song (vs. 9–11); then summons herself and Barak to their tribute of praise (v. 12). Again she resumes the history of this great event—how she called the people to battle (v. 13); how one tribe after another responded or did not respond to this call (vs. 15–18); how the kings of Canaan came and fought, but took no spoil (v. 19), because God and his stars in the heavens and all the forces of nature fought for Israel (vs. 20–22). God's angel bids them curse Meroz who would not come to the help of the Lord (v. 23); but blesses Jael the Kenite—whose exploits the song spreads out in ample detail (vs. 25–27), not omitting a home picture of the scenes in Sisera's houshold and the kindling expectations there which were never realized! (vs. 28–30); closing with the prayer that all God's enemies may perish in like manner; and his loving friends be as the sun going forth in his might (v. 31).

1. Then sang Deborah and Barak the son of Abinoam on that day, saying,
2. Praise ye the LORD for the avenging of Israel, when the people willingly offered themselves.

In the phrase translated here, "for the avenging of Israel," critics have held diverse views, mostly adverse to our English version. The best lexicographers (Gesenius, Fuerst, and Robinson) give it—"for the leading on of the leaders in Israel," corresponding to the next clause— "And for the hearty volunteer service of the people." The first theme of her song is that both rulers and people led off so freely and so nobly in this uprising for freedom. The test word—the noun rendered "avenging"—occurs elsewhere only in Deut. 32: 42, and there in the sense of ruler.

3. Hear, O ye kings; give ear, O ye princes; I, *even* I, will sing unto the LORD; I will sing *praise* to the LORD God of Israel.

Are these kings and princes those of Israel or of Canaan? Doubtless of Canaan. This summons to them comes of her full heart, of her dauntless spirit, and of her piety. She would show them the might of Israel's God, and invite them to solemn consideration.

4. LORD, when thou wentest out of Seir, when thou marchedst out of the field of Edom, the earth trembled, and the heavens dropped, the clouds also dropped water.
5. The mountains melted from before the LORD, *even* that Sinai from before the LORD God of Israel.

So God came in glorious majesty. This poetic conception of the coming of God for the help of his people (technically called a "theophany") is by no means uncommon in the lofty strains of Hebrew poetry. Examples may be seen in Deut. 33: 2, and Ps. 18: 7–14, and 68: 7–9, and Hab. 3.——In point of interpretation the only question is whether it describes historically God coming on Sinai at the giving of the law, or conceives poetically of God as having his abode in that wilderness where his personal manifestations were so striking, but as coming up from that quarter in tempest and storm for the help of his people against the Canaanites as he came forth of old on Sinai. The latter construction is preferable. The song (vs. 20, 21) indicates a terrific storm—the stars of heaven (perhaps thought of as ruling the elements) fighting against Sisera, and the old river Kishon, suddenly swollen by the torrents of rain, sweeping away their foes, the living and the dead, in masses piled.——" The heavens dropped"—rather let their waters *drop;* poured them forth—oceans of water.——In the phrase "the mountains melted," modern critics universally favor another root for the Hebrew verb, with the sense, *tremble, shake* with mighty convulsions.

6. In the days of Shamgar the son of Anath, in the days of Jael, the highways were unoccupied, and the travelers walked through by-ways.
7. *The inhabitants of* the villages ceased, they ceased in Israel, until that I Deborah arose, that I arose a mother in Israel.

Shamgar (Judges 3 : 31) and Jael seem to have judged Israel next before Deborah. The phrase "in the days of" implies that they were public and prominent men, and forbids us to suppose that this Jael was the heroine of our song.——The public highways were unoccupied, no one daring to travel there. Life was so insecure, men feared to go from place to place except through unknown tortuous by-ways.——In v. 7, the word "*inhabitants*" has no Hebrew equivalent, and the word translated "villages" should be rulers. The rulers—the magistrates of the country who should have protected life and enforced law, were inactive—practically powerless. The protecting power of law was suspended, virtually dead, until Deborah arose, a true "mother in Israel," to shield property and life—to restore law and order.

8. They chose new gods; then *was* war in the gates: was there a shield or spear seen among forty thousand in Israel?

The sense of the first clause is controverted, the better opinions being *with* our version, referring the phrase to idolatry, as the sin which brought foreign wars upon them even to their gates. These wars found them almost utterly unarmed—a fact which made this great victory the more striking and the more glorious to God. The resistless enthusiasm of Israel's warriors supplied the place of shield and spear

9. My heart *is* toward the governors of Israel, that offered themselves willingly among the people. Bless ye the LORD.

"My heart is toward"—might without violence be taken to express her gratitude. Yet since this verse closes with the words, "Bless ye the Lord," and the next two verses are in the same strain, it seems better to give the words this turn: My heart goes out to the governors of Israel, exhorting them to unite with me in blessing and praising our great Jehovah.

10. Speak, ye that ride on white asses, ye that sit in judgment, and walk by the way.
11. *They that are delivered* from the noise of archers in the places of drawing water, there shall they rehearse the righteous acts of the LORD, *even* the righteous acts *toward the inhabitants* of his villages in Israel: then shall the people of the LORD go down to the gates.

"Speak," *i. e.*, in praise to God; give utterance aloud to your joyful thanksgivings.——"Ye that ride on white asses;" men holding office and honored with this distinction.——"Ye that sit in judgment," should rather be, ye that recline on splendid carpets, luxurious tapestries. The Hebrew words demand this sense.—— "Walk by the way." These are the people in the humbler walks of life who travel on foot, having no means of riding.——In v. 11, the poet has in mind the joyful scenes of dividing the spoil at the great watering places where the returning victors halted to rest. She calls on them to suspend that division of spoil for a song of praise to rehearse the glorious things God had wrought, and then go in peace to their homes. Our English version fails in several points to give the sense of the original. Better thus (following Dr. E. Robinson): "At the voice of those who divide the spoil by the watering troughs. There shall they celebrate the victories of Jehovah, the victories of his princes in Israel. Then shall the people of the Lord descend to their gates." Or the more precise sense of the Hebrew translated "at the voice" may be, *more than—high above*—the shouts of joy over the dividing of the spoil, let their songs of praise to God ascend, etc.; or possibly—*Because of* those shouts of joy, etc. We meet with a historic scene of revelry over spoils in 1 Sam. 30: 16, and poetic illustrations from such scenes in Isa. 9: 3.

12. Awake, awake, Deborah: awake, awake, utter a song: arise, Barak, and lead thy captivity captive, thou son of Abinoam.

Deborah will not fall behind in this outpouring of grateful song. In lofty self-excitation she calls upon herself and Barak to lead off in this celebration.——"Lead thy captivity captive"—means, Lead thy captives away into captivity.

13. Then he made him that remaineth have dominion over the nobles among the people: the LORD made me have dominion over the mighty.

The English translation of v. 13 is very defective; (a) In (apparently) following some other than the received and best supported text: (b) In omitting the verb, "I said, which" manifestly should be supplied, as it often needs to be in Hebrew poetry at the commencement (as here) of a new strain. The verbs of the verse (in our English) "made him have dominion;" "made me have dominion," most obviously signify—*go down* (imperative), *i. e.*, into the battle. The poetess throws herself back to the point where she summoned the men of Israel from all the adjacent hills of Palestine to come down into this great valley of Esdraelon to the battle, and invokes the Lord Jehovah to come with them. I would translate (with Robbins, Bib. Sacra, July, 1855, p. 608).—"Then I said, Descend ye residue, to the aid of the nobles of the people, descend for me, Jehovah, against the mighty.——" Ye residue," means all ye surviving people who have escaped death during the desolating wars and oppressions then recent. The nobles of the people are ready, in advance of the rank and file of the army. The latter are, therefore, specially exhorted to come on! Nothing could be more appropriate than this call upon Jehovah also to come down in her behalf among these heroes for their help.

14. Out of Ephraim *was there* a root of them against Amalek; after thee, Benjamin, among thy people; out of Machir came down governors, and out of Zebulun they that handle the pen of the writer.

15. And the princes of Issachar *were* with Deborah; even Issachar, and also Barak: he was sent on foot into the valley. For the divisions of Reuben *there were* great thoughts of heart.

16. Why abodest thou among the sheepfolds, to hear the bleatings of the flocks? For the divisions of Reuben *there were* great searchings of heart.

Here with a few rapid touches she indicates the various responses given to her call by these several

tribes. "Out of Ephraim" [came those] "whose root"
—home, dwelling-place—was on Mt. Amalek. (See
Judg. 12: 15 for this locality.) "After thee was Benjamin among thy people." "From Machir" (representing Manasseh) "came down leaders; out of Zebulun,
those who bear the ruler's scepter. The princes of
Issachar were with Deborah; Issachar was the support
of Barak; they rushed down into the valley at his
feet." The song is with the history (4: 10, 14) in the
fact that the main force, especially the rank and file,
were from Issachar and Zebulun.——What is said of
Reuben is, to say the least, doubtful praise. The latter
part of v. 15 opens this subject: the verse should have
begun at that point. The English translation is by
no means felicitous. Reuben on the east of Jordan was
a well watered country, of the finest pasturage, and
covered with its flocks and herds.——Instead of reading, "For the divisions of Reuben," read—" Alongside
or at the streams of Reuben " (where they were leading
and feeding their flocks) " there were great resolves of
heart"—[nothing more!] Hear the expostulations of
the poetess: "Why didst thou sit down" [at thine
ease] "to listen to the bleatings of thy flocks?" Was
that the right thing for men—loyal-hearted men—to
do when summoned to arms for their country and for
their country's God?——Then with a touch of sarcasm
she repeats with only slight variation, and that a play
upon the former word; "At the streams of Reuben
there were great searchings in thought." They pondered over this matter full long, and talked great resolutions—but all came to nothing! Their country in
her peril gat no help from Reuben!

17. Gilead abode beyond Jordan: and why did Dan remain in
ships? Asher continued on the seashore, and abode in his breaches.

Gilead, the mountainous region east of Jordan, held
by the two and a half tribes, seems here to represent
Gad, and perhaps the half of Manasseh—Reuben having already received special consideration. Gilead
abode [at his ease], all quiet as if with no care for his
imperiled brethren on the west and north. Dan and
Asher, lying upon the shore of the great sea—why did
they sit down at their ease by their ships and around
their harbors? Just far enough removed from the

scenes of this great battle to be (probably) safe themselves, why should they be so selfish as to sit stolidly down, and leave their brethren to imperil their lives to the death on the field of blood?

18. Zebulun and Naphtali *were* a people *that* jeoparded their lives unto the death in the high places of the field.

Zebulun and Naphtali were the people who made no account of their lives on the heights of the battle-field. Literally, they "scorned their lives;" accounted life a matter of no special consequence, compared with the salvation of their country.

19. The kings came *and* fought; then fought the kings of Canaan in Taanach by the waters of Megiddo; they took no gain of money.

In this one verse with briefest words the song puts before us the mighty conflict of arms. "*Kings came and fought.*"——The precise battle-ground—designated here as "Taanach"—has been identified in modern times, near the "waters of Megiddo," *i. e.*, the river Kishon, which drains the great plain of Esdraelon into the Mediterranean.——What was the result of the battle? This: *they took no spoil.* We see below (vs. 29, 30) that this was the chief end thought of and sought —at least by the women of these warriors. But they got none. This sufficiently signifies that they lost the battle.

20. They fought from heaven; the stars in their courses fought against Sisera.
21. The river of Kishon swept them away, that ancient river, the river Kishon. O my soul, thou hast trodden down strength.
22. Then were the horse-hoofs broken by the means of the prancings, the prancings of their mighty ones.

Why this vast army and their hundreds of war chariots made no better fight is told here. *God was against them.* Great powers "fought from heaven." The Hebrew verb being impersonal—"There was fighting from heaven"—we are left to supply the person—which could be none other than the mighty God.——"The stars in their courses fought"—should probably be taken to mean that all the agencies of the lower heavens— tempest, storm, lightning—were in this battle, God's angels of death, to whelm in ruin those hosts of Canaan.*

* Describing this battle Josephus (Book V. chap. v.) says—"When they were come to a close fight, there came down from heaven a

As the men of Canaan worshiped the heavenly bodies, it was an astounding, terrible retribution that those stars and the elements of the lower heaven should join Israel in this battle against them.——It seems that Barak and these powers of heaven drove the men of Canaan with fearful rout into the deep ravine through which the Kishon drains this great plain. The river, swollen to flood by the mighty rain storm, drowned many of the living and swept off the dead.—— "That *ancient* river," called "ancient," not because it was older than other rivers, but either because it (poetically) "covered itself with glory," and embalmed its name in history to be ever remembered; or, in a different sense of the original word—river of battles, or of combatants—those who meet you *in front* as opponents. The primary sense of the root is to be in front or before; and is applied to *time* in the sense of ancient, or to an opponent.

The poetess thinks now of the fall of her mighty foes, and accosts herself: "O my soul, thou hast trodden down the mighty"—*i. e.*, the *strength* of mighty men.——The rapid flight of the mounted warriors is prominent in her poetic conception of this battle. Thus v. 22: "Then did the horses' hoofs smite the ground through the haste—the haste of their valiant riders." The original word suggests horses leaping, prancing, sweeping round in circles as when under training.——To speak of flying horsemen as brave, valiant ("mighty ones"), may be slightly sarcastic. Brave men they were, were they? But how they fled! ——These touches complete her sketch of the battle scene.

23. Curse ye Meroz, said the angel of the LORD, curse ye bitterly the inhabitants thereof; because they came not to the help of the LORD, to the help of the LORD against the mighty.

great storm, with a vast quantity of rain and hail, and the wind blew the rain in the face of the Canaanites, and so darkened their eyes that their arrows and slings were of no advantage to them; nor would the coldness of the air permit the soldiers to use their swords; while this storm did not so much incommode the Israelites, because it came in their backs. They also took such courage, upon the apprehension that God was assisting them, that they fell upon the very midst of their enemies and slew a great number of them, so that some of them fell by the Israelites, some fell by their own horses which were put into disorder, and not a few were killed by their own chariots."

Meroz, a village or city unknown to fame or history save through this dishonorable mention, seems to have lain near the scene of this battle, or, perhaps, of this retreat, where her warriors might have done ready and effective service if they had come forth to the help of the Lord, *i. e* ., of the Lord's army. *With* their own warriors, is the sense required by the Hebrew, rather than *against* the mighty hosts of Canaan.

This command to curse Meroz, she is inspired to declare, comes from "the angel of the Lord." How made known to her, we are left with no means of certain knowledge. It is supposable that she had an impressive consciousness that God moved her in this entire uprising against Jabin and his allies; and thus God's angel was present to her soul as the captain of the Lord's host (Josh. 5: 13-15), inspiring both her call to Israel's warriors, her rebuke of the tribes that made no response, and her malediction upon those who like Meroz had the finest of opportunities for most effective help, but would not come.

24. Blessed above women shall Jael the wife of Heber the Kenite be; blessed shall she be above women in the tent.

25. He asked water, *and* she gave *him* milk; she brought forth butter in a lordly dish.

26. She put her hand to the nail, and her right hand to the workmen's hammer; and with the hammer she smote Sisera, she smote off his head, when she had pierced and stricken through his temples.

27. At her feet he bowed, he fell, he lay down: at her feet. he bowed, he fell: where he bowed, there he fell down dead.

The transition of thought from Meroz to Jael—from those who would not come to the Lord's help, to her who would, and who so nobly did, is both natural and full of force. Let her be honored among women, yea above all women who dwell in tents.——The reader will note how the poetess dwells on each prominent fact with impressive reiteration, as if she could not hold these points before her mind's eye too long. You see all the transaction; how she puts forth one hand to the tent-pin; another, her right hand, to the workmen's hammer; how then she smote with her might and sent it crashing quite through his head; it passed through his temples. Our translators slightly missed the sense in supposing that she beheaded her victim. Neither the words of the song as here, nor those of the history (4 : 21) mean that. Rather she drove the nail quite through his head and fastened him to the ground. Four Hebrew verbs in succession depict this scene, the last three nearly synonymous in this sense of piercing through, crashing along, transfixing. Then we have the struggle of the dying man till all is over! How true to the genius of graphic poetry!

28. The mother of Sisera looked out at a window, and cried through the lattice, Why is his chariot *so* long in coming? why tarry the wheels of his chariot?

29. Her wise ladies answered her, yea, she returned answer to herself,

30. Have they not sped? have they *not* divided the prey; to every man a damsel *or* two; to Sisera a prey of divers colors, a prey of divers colors of needlework, of divers colors of needlework on both sides, *meet* for the necks of *them that take* the spoil?

Why the *mother* of Sisera, rather than his wife or sister? Is this historic fact, or poetic imagination? Probably fact, because fiction would be very unlikely to say mother. If fact, it indicates a contemporary writer, intimately familiar with the minutest circumstances of the case.——Why does his chariot *shame* us [Hebrew] as to its coming? *i. e.*, delay so long as to shame our expectation?——Her lady attendants are represented as shrewdly ["wise"] forecasting the cause of this delay and relieving her anxiety. The army of Sisera are of course victorious, and are delayed only to divide the great spoil. Noticeably in this enumeration of spoil, female captives stand first in order and highest in value; then ornament, dress, decoration, and nothing else! A woman's conception of woman's estimate!— true enough, if not to nature, at least to fact!——This is only one among many points in this song which indicate a woman's pen and conception. A military historian (say Cæsar) would have shown us the position of the contending hosts and given the science of the battle; but in this song of thirty verses, not more than three (19–21) are given to the battle proper. On the other hand, Deborah's part in this whole movement—a part entirely appropriate to a "mother in Israel"—stands in the foreground throughout. Her Christian soul indites the thanksgiving, and never loses sight long of the mighty hand of God in their deliverance. She tells us of her efforts to call out the brave men of every tribe; in what cases she succeeded and in what she failed; how her womanly, noble heart honored the former and upbraided the latter; and, not least, how she sympathized with the spirit, so kindred to her own, which was in Jael the wife of Heber the Kenite. If the genius of any song were ever true to its author, bearing internal evidence of being the production of its author and not of another, this song may claim such evidence of being genuine.

31. So let all thine enemies perish, O LORD: but *let* them that love him *be* as the sun when he goeth forth in his might. And the land had rest forty years.

She does not take time to tell us how Sisera's mother and her wise ladies met their disappointment and saw their pretty fancies vanish in one short moment; but she suggests that it reminds her of the way in which all God's enemies perish and all their thoughts and plans against him come to abortion. Nay more, her *heart* is in the result of this; her sympathies are intensely deep and strong, and withal are thoroughly *for* God and *against* his enemies. With what terseness and force does she put it! So let all thine enemies perish, O Lord; whenever, anywhere in the lapse of the ages, they take up arms against Thee, or how strong soever they may be in chariots and in horsemen—let them go down quick to such a doom as this! But let all who love God and put themselves with heart and hand upon his side, be as the rising sun sweeping up the eastern heavens in his might and glory!——Could any thing be more beautiful, nay, rather, more sublimely grand in poetic conception than this?

But some one may say (more than one has said), that such joy over scenes of human carnage is at least unwomanly if not inhuman and unchristian, and will ask—as if the very question carried their argument—Is this loving one's enemies? Is this blessing those who curse us, and doing good to those who persecute us, and praying for our murderers?

A full answer must include several points, mainly reducible to these three:

1. The utterance of her heart said to God, "*thine* enemies," not *mine*. Not mine merely; not mine (as in her thought) mainly; in fact not mine with sufficient prominence to come into notice at all. She never even alluded to them as her own personal enemies. More-

over, by contrast and implication they are those who do *not* love God. Her prayer is that all who love God may be as the rising sun in his glory.

2. Nothing said here forbids that she may have felt sincere compassion for those dying Canaanites considered as sentient and suffering, although she prayed and labored for their overthrow as God's enemies. This discrimination is certainly not unknown to Christian experience, however remote it may be from the conception of those who criticise and condemn this prayer of Deborah.

3. It is sufficient to reply comprehensively, once for all, that the sympathies of this prayer and of this woman Deborah were *with God*—with God most thoroughly, most intensely, and (so far as appears) were nothing other or else. She loved God's honor, God's people, God's cause on earth; she gave to it her best wisdom, her great social power, her noble heroism, her highest womanly powers of piety, poetry, song, and praise. What more or other than this can be reasonably demanded of a great and noble woman? She adjusted herself precisely to the circumstances in which God placed her. She lived, not in our age, but in her own— when God's people stood against their enemies by dint, not of patient suffering, but of heroic fighting, imperilling their lives on the high places of the bloody fields of real war. It is quite idle for us to hint that it would have been more Christian for Deborah and her people to have suffered even to martyrdom rather than take the life of their enemies. It is somewhat out of place for us to review the policy of the God of Israel and suggest that it would have been a better example and a better spirit if he had forbidden his people to take the life of their and his enemies. No; it rather becomes us to withhold our criticism upon the ways of God, and admit that he may have had the best of reasons for the policy under which he disciplined and ruled Israel in those ages.

As to Deborah, it must suffice for her vindication that she put herself in full sympathy with God, and met the circumstances and conditions of her time with the truest Christian heroism. If she had lived in Judea with Christ and his disciples, or in Rome with Peter and Paul, she would (with the same spirit) have suffered, like Jesus and like the martyred apostles, even to death, praying withal for her very murderers. The former—the life she actually lived—was neither more nor less than adjusting herself to the demands of full sympathy with God under her actual circumstances. The latter—the life of apostles and martyrs —was nothing more or higher than this. Under any and all conceivable circumstances, there can be no higher, no nobler, virtue for mortals than to be in perfect sympathy with God. Falling sweetly, bravely, wholly into his will; doing or suffering all that obedience to that will demands, is man's highest virtue and truest glory. To do this is not piety and virtue in the age of Paul, but malignity and sin in the age of Deborah. To assume that it is would imply a radical change in the moral character of God, taking place between the times respectively of Deborah and of Paul.

Scenes in the Life of Gideon.

The recorded history of Gideon fills three chapters (6–8), and illustrates one great central lesson. It also presents certain subordinate points, deserving brief notice.——The central lesson is that the Lord saves according to his wisdom, by many or by few; it being all the same with him, inasmuch as "the excellency of the power" is altogether of God and never of man.

This lesson stands in somewhat special adaptation to the character of Gideon. When the Lord first proposed to Gideon to send him against the Midianites, he replied, "Wherewith shall *I* save Israel? Behold, my family is poor in Manasseh, and I am the least in my father's house" (6: 15). Here it was pertinent for the Lord to answer, "I will be with thee," and that is always enough. The God of Israel is mighty to save, whether by few or by many. He can save by the smallest man in the small half-tribe of Manasseh. And the Lord shaped the circumstances of this case to bear toward the illustration of this great lesson.

Some of the antecedents deserve notice. Israel had fallen again into idolatry after Deborah had passed away, and the Lord brought them under subjection to Midian seven years. The men of Midian and Amalek came up from the populous east, like "grasshoppers for multitude," and like the locusts also in their ravages, devouring the harvests of the land and leaving the people to famish with hunger. Want brought them to reflection and to prayer. They cried to God for help. First he sent to them "a prophet" (6: 7–10), to remind them of his past mercies and of their recent sins. The reader will notice that this is the first recorded instance, since Moses, of a prophet raised up and sent of God. His name is not given.——God introduced himself specially to Gideon by means of an angel; yet this angel is repeatedly called "the Lord" (6: 14, 15, 16, 23 24). Gideon seems to have understood that this call meant business, and was to him a summons to action. Consequently he felt that he must become well assured that the call came truly from God. We may note with pleasure that this was the *only* doubtful point in his mind; for he seems never to question God's power if only it be truly God. "If now I have found grace in thy sight, then show me a sign that *thou* talkest with me" (6: 17). Perhaps it was not quite settled in his mind whether this personage were angelic or divine. Wishing to do him all honor whichever he might be— moved, it may be, by the impulses of oriental hospitality, he besought the stranger to remain in that place till he could prepare his offering, which consisting of a kid ready for the table and unleavened cakes, was of a sort to be eaten as food, or consumed otherwise, at the option of his visitor. The angel directed him to place his provisions (or offering) "upon this rock." Gideon did so; and the angel, having touched the flesh and cakes with his staff, fire came forth from the rock and consumed them. Then Gideon knew him to be an angel of the Lord, and cried out: "Alas for me! for I have seen an angel of the Lord face to face." The Lord gave him an answer of peace, and Gideon built an altar of the memorial sort, giving it a name significant of this great fact: *Jehovah—peace*. Thus Gideon is becoming acquainted with God and prepared for more intimate personal relations.

In the next stage of these events the Lord directed him to tear down the altar of Baal and cut down the tall wooden pillar (not "grove") in Heb. Asherah, otherwise called Astarte—both of which seem to have been the property of his father. The men of the city (probably Canaanites) appear to have worshiped here, for they were offended and indignant. Further, the Lord commanded Gideon to take his father's young bullock* and offer him as a sacrifice on this altar with the wood of this idol image. This bold act evinced the spirit of Gideon and put him right on the record before the people as being in sympathy with the true God, and against all idolatry. It legitimately prepared the way for Israel's deliverance from Midian by his hand.

Then the Spirit of the Lord came mightily upon Gideon; he blew the war-trumpet, calling forth the people to battle against Midian. The men of Abiezer, his own tribal family, first gathered after him. He sent messengers to other tribes, and soon had an army of 32,000 men. Yet still Gideon's mind is not at rest toward God as to his promised help, but craves some unmistakable sign. He proposes to put a fleece of wool on the open, unsheltered threshing-floor over night, and suggests that the sign be—dew on the fleece only; none on the earth about it. Done; yet still Gideon begs the Lord to make it more decisive by one other test—dew on all the ground about it, and none on the fleece. This also the Lord granted; and Gideon seems to have been quite satisfied. Perhaps it was for the sake of his followers as well as for his own that he sought these manifold and manifest proofs of God's present hand. We must admire the patience and forbearance of God in consenting to put himself thus on trial and in meeting so kindly what had at least somewhat the aspect of unbelief.

The small army of Gideon (32,000 men) were now in camp quite near the almost countless hosts of Midian. The Lord came to Gideon to say—Your men are too many, "lest Israel vaunt themselves against me" as having gained their victory by their own numbers and valor, and without God. Send home all who are fearful and faint-hearted.† 22,000 went home; 10,000 remained. Again the Lord came to say—There are still too many. They must be sifted again. By the Lord's direction Gideon marched his men down to a stream of water. The test turned on the manner in which the men drank.

* It is not quite clear, from the original, whether the command included two bullocks or only one.
† This was in accord with the Hebrew war-law; Deut. 20: 9.

One class dropped upon their knees and drank from the stream; another class dipped up water in the palm of the hand and then lapped it. Whether this latter mode of drinking from a stream indicated more power of endurance or less—more martial zeal or less—we are left to form our own opinion. The number of this latter class was 300. The Lord said, These are the men for the victory over Midian; send home the other class—9,700 strong.——To assure Gideon's faith yet the more, the Lord sends him down to the border of the camp of Midian to listen. There he hears a man of Midian report his dream to his fellow, who interprets it of the sword of Gideon into whose hand God had delivered Midian and all their host (7: 13, 14). This is to Gideon an *inspiration*. He accepts it as the voice of God, and strikes for victory. Arming his 300 men with trumpets and dark lanterns (a lamp concealed in a pitcher), he puts his men in a circle investing the whole camp, with orders to follow his example. When all had reached their position, Gideon blew his trumpet and shouted: "The sword of the Lord and of Gideon;" then broke his pitcher and let his lamp blaze out. Instantly three hundred trumpets and three hundred voices are in chorus, and three hundred lamps are gleaming on every side of the camp of Midian. It was the beginning of the middle watch, *i. e.*, toward midnight. The panic was complete. "All the host ran and cried and fled." The Lord set every man's sword against his fellow, with no discrimination of friend or foe. Doubtless the darkness in dead of night conduced to this mutual slaughter. Of course the men of Israel rallied for the pursuit, and seized the fords of the Jordan. "There fell on that day 120,000 men that drew sword" (8: 10). Midian was subdued, and Israel was again free.

Incidentally the historian records the extreme and petty jealousy of the Ephraimites because they were not called out among the first. Gideon (of the tribe of Manasseh) answered them adroitly by magnifying their exploits—an offering to their vanity. "What have I done now in comparison of you?" Perhaps this was the wisdom of the serpent. It proved perfectly successful, acting like a charm on the human nature of the Ephraimites. (See 8: 1-3).

The closing incident of this history brings out another sad proof of the amazing, not to say unaccountable, propensity of the Israelites to idol-worship. The pillage of the fallen or routed Midianites brought great quantities of gold into their possession. For reasons (if there were any) not apparent, Gideon while nobly refusing to take the scepter offered him by the people, did request each of them to "give him the golden ear-rings of his prey "—*i. e.*, the share falling to each in the division of the spoil. Gideon (it is said) made of this gold " an ephod, and set it up in his city, and all Israel went thither a whoring after it; which thing became a snare unto Gideon and to his house" (8: 27). This word "ephod" usually indicates the outer robe of the priests. Some have supposed that here it must mean a golden image regarded as an idol. Others, that it rather implied the accompaniments of a system of idolatry. The former view is favored by the great quantity of the gold; by the fact stated of its being "*set up*," and by the idolatry which ensued. It certainly became the occasion of a sad relapse after this great deliverance, and involves Gideon's character in both weakness and sin.——The phrase—" go a whoring "—conceives of Israel as under covenant with God, analogous to the marriage covenant, so that idolatry in them was the sin of adultery and whoredom toward God. This figure of speech, as it was intensely expressive, became very common, almost the standard illustration of this giant national sin.

Judg. 9 is a digression from the general current of Hebrew history to give a series of local incidents in which Abimelech, son of Gideon by his concubine, is the central actor and Shechem the principal locality. The historic incidents are numerous and need not be given in detail here. I refer to it as developing the true idea of history—viz., to *illustrate great principles in God's government of men, moral and providential*. The principle in this case is definitely stated in the conclusion of the story, in the words—" Thus God rendered the wickedness of Abimelech, which he did unto his father, in slaying his seventy brethren: And all the evil of the men of Shechem did God render upon their heads: and upon them came the curse of Jotham the son of Jerubbaal." (Judg. 9: 56, 57).

This rendering of men's wickedness upon their own

head, which is simply a righteous retribution, is one of the great laws of God's administration over men, whether as communities, nations, or individuals. For the illustration of this great law, the chapter before us is on record. We find the same law written everywhere in the events of human life. How wonderfully does it make up the warp and woof of human history! Oh, would men but open their eyes to see and read it, and their hearts to receive its admonitory lessons!

Resuming the thread of events, the historian (chap. 10) alludes in passing to the judgeship of Tola and of Jair, and then proceeds to describe more at length the great defection of Israel into idolatry, in which, it would seem (10: 6) that they introduced the idol-gods of all the contiguous heathen nations—the gods of Syria, Zidon, Moab, Ammon, and Philistia. Their scourging in this case came from the Philistines and Ammonites, the tribes east of Jordan suffering first and most severely, and Gilead under Jephthah taking the lead in the resistance. The history sets forth God's expostulation with his recreant people. "Did not my uplifted arm save you from Egyptian bondage and deliver you of old from the very same enemies under whom ye are now groaning—the Ammonites and the Philistines? Yet ye have forsaken me, and served other gods; wherefore I will deliver you no more. Go and cry unto the gods whom ye have chosen; let them deliver you in the time of your tribulation."——We can not say less than that this rebuke was terribly truthful and just; but alas for Israel if the Lord had given them only simple and stern justice!——The reply of the people as given here was the best possible for guilty sinners to make: "We have sinned; do thou unto us whatsoever seemeth good unto thee; only deliver us, we pray thee, this day."

Moreover, they not only offered this very suitable prayer with the humblest submission to whatever chastisements the Lord might inflict, but they put away their strange gods and served the Lord. Then (as we read) "his soul was grieved for the misery of Israel." His pity and compassion were moved. Resentment, revenge—there was none in his heart. The way was fast being prepared for their deliverance.——
Jephthah became God's instrument for this result. An illegitimate son, cast out from the family by his half-

JEPHTHAH AND HIS VOW. 71

brothers, he fled to Tob where "vain men" (so-called) gathered themselves under him as their head, following a life of plunder and adventure—a kind of life not unknown to the Arab freebooters of the same country to this day. The fact is mainly important in this history as having given him the training of a fearless, hardy, capable military leader, with, however, only very meager advantages for religious knowledge and culture. When the men of Gilead looked round for a man equal to this service of leadership in war, their eye rested on this Jephthah.——We may note that Jephthah, remembering how his brethren of Gilead rudely and cruelly cast him out of the family, stipulated in this case that if the Lord delivered Israel from the oppressions of Ammon by his hand, they should make him their head—manifesting in this a spirit that does not compare favorably with that of Gideon (8: 22, 23).——Remarkably, in this uprising against the oppressions of Ammon, negotiations preceded war. The history recites the arguments as put by Jephthah, and answered by the men of Ammon (11: 12-28). This effort having utterly failed, the Spirit of the Lord came upon Jephthah (v. 29), and he passed round among his people, rallying them to arms, and then marched down upon Ammon. At this point Jephthah vowed a vow unto the Lord and said— "If thou shalt without fail deliver the children of Ammon into mine hand, then it shall be that whatsoever cometh forth from the doors of my house to meet me when I return in peace from the children of Ammon shall surely be the Lord's, and [perhaps *or*] I will offer it up for a burnt-offering."——Jephthah gained a great victory, subdued Ammon, and redeemed his people from their oppressions. The sequel of his remarkable vow is fully given in vs. 34-40—in substance thus: Returning in peace to his house, he was met first by his only child—a daughter, rushing forth to greet him with timbrels and dances as at once a father and a conqueror—the savior of his country. The father's heart is dead to this joy, overwhelmed with anguish because of his vow. "Alas, my daughter" (he cried), "thou hast brought me very low; thou art of them that trouble me;" no trouble has ever befallen me like this, for I have opened my mouth to the

Lord, and I can not go back."——It is probable though not, perhaps, entirely certain that at this stage the daughter fully understood the vow. The agony of the father was fearfully significant, yet she bears herself nobly. "Father," said she, "if thou hast vowed to the Lord, go on and perform it, since the Lord has given thee such victory over thine enemies." She asks but one favor—two months' delay, that she may go out to the retirement of her native mountains, and there with her companions "bewail her virginity." This was granted. Then she returned; and the record has it— her father "did to her according to his vow, and she knew no man." It is not said definitely *what* he did with her. This remains somewhat an open question— with, however, a strong preponderance of critical opinion and also of evidence favoring the view that he made her a burnt-offering, taking her life and burning her dead body entire upon the altar.——Finally, it became a custom for the daughters of Israel to gather four days each year "to lament the daughter of Jephthah." The margin reads, not "lament," but *talk with*, on the supposition that her doom was not death, but perpetual virginity. The Hebrew word, little used, signifies to celebrate with praises, to give forth the voice; but apparently not as in conversation, but rather as in song and praise.

Turning our thought now to the main question, *What was done to Jephthah's daughter?* we must answer in the first place, she was in some way *devoted to God*. This is obvious, and indeed unquestionable. The only possible point of doubt lies in the *way and manner* of this devotement. The alternatives here are these three:——(1.) Death as a burnt-offering;——(2.) Absolute consecration to God—the term, "burnt-offering" being on this supposition used figuratively, and so not implying consumption upon the literal altar, but complete and unreserved devotement to God's service. So Paul (Rom. 12: 1) exhorts that "ye present your bodies a living sacrifice:"——or (3.) Perpetual virginity.

In making our choice between these three alternatives, we should be governed ——(a.) By the current usage of the language, especially the words of the vow. ——(b.) By the force of the facts given in the narrative. ——(c.) By the usages of Jephthah's time and by the notions and ideas, superstitious or religious, which he may be reasonably supposed to have held.

The usage of the language comes legitimately first. Men must be assumed to say what they mean—to speak in order to be understood, and, therefore, to use their words in the customary sense of those words among the people at the time.——Now, interpreting Jephthah's vow by the use of words in the Mosaic law, we are compelled to think of an animal laid whole upon the altar and there consumed.——The force of the attendant facts narrated here bears in the same direction. The agony of the father when his daugther rushed out to meet him; the heroism of the daughter; and the annual commemoration of this event four days in each year—all look strongly toward this excessively sad, agonizing result.——But over against these considerations there are others, worthy of notice, which favor a different conclusion. Perhaps we can not assume that Jephthah knew much about the Mosaic ritual law. If he had, he would have seen that a rash vow like this should have been repented of, and not performed in its letter. If he had he could not have thought it pleasing or due to God to murder his daughter.—Then further, we may ask—What could he have been thinking of as likely to come forth first from his house to meet him on his return? He knew there was but one child there—his only daughter—more likely, therefore, to be this *"whatsoever"* than any other living being. There was only the smallest probability that this animal would be a lamb, a bullock, or a kid—*i. e.*, of the class permitted for burnt-offerings. As to domestic animals, dogs, pets of nameless kind—we know quite too little to make even a conjecture.——Jephthah used the masculine gender; literally thus: "It shall be that the outcomer (masculine) which shall come forth from the door of my house .... shall be for the Lord, and I will offer *him* (masculine) as a burnt-offering."—— I infer from this that he certainly did not think of his daughter as likely to be this forthcoming person or animal. His surprise and agony when he saw her coming bear to the same point.——I am aware it may be replied to this that rash vows do not imply much forethought; that the great mistake, not to say sin, of Jephthah lay in the fact that he *did not think;* that he opened his mouth under the pressure of intense emotion, pressed by the momentous crisis, and feeling that something must be done to propitiate the favor and gain the blessing of God; and that under these emotions he spake most unadvisably and with no proper consideration.

In interpreting this transaction, it is our weakness that we know so little of Jephthah—of his early education, of his religious or superstitious ideas, and of the current notions and usages of the people on the east of Jordan. What were their notions about vows? What about human sacrifices? What about devotement to God in ways other than by burning entire on the altar? If we had light on all these points; especially if we had proofs of a usage in which young men or young women either, were devoted to God by a life of seclusion from society, celibacy, perpetual virginity —we should have some foothold for the opinion that this vow issued in such a result. But in the absence of proof or indication as to this we can not rest in this opinion. It is much more probable that Jephthah sympathized with notions respecting human sacrifices which are known to have been prevalent in Syria and in Moab. For the latter, see 2 Kings 3: 26, 27. As to the former, Porphyry (cited by Eusebius, Prep. Evan. IV : 16) says—"In all great emergencies of war, of famine, or drought, the Phenicians used to designate by vote one of their nearest and dearest as a sacrifice to Saturn, and their descendants, the Carthaginians, sacrificed their finest children to the same god." This usage of the Syrians is the more probably the origin or suggestive occasion of Jephthah's vow, from the fact that according to this record (Judg. 10: 6) "Israel served the gods of Syria, and of Zidon, and of Moab."

The prominence given to her "virginity" as the paramount evil in her case somewhat favors the opinion that her doom was not death. It was this that she and her female companions bewailed upon the mountains; this that appears in the record as the consequence of her father's performing his vow (vs. 37, 38, 39); "She knew no man."

The construction placed second (above) in the list of possible alternatives, which would make Jephthah's words figurative, and his meaning only that he would

JEPHTHAH AND HIS VOW. 75

fully consecrate to the Lord in the spiritual sense whatever should first come forth from his house, lies open to these two objections:—(a) It is too early to look for a figurative use of the burnt-offering. Usages like this take time to work themselves so perfectly into the public mind that they naturally become figures of speech for corresponding ideas in the spiritual world.—— (b) There is the greatest reason to fear that spiritual ideas were not sufficiently developed in the mind of Jephthah to justify such a construction of his words as we may reasonably give to the words of Paul. Jephthah and Paul were not on the same plane of religious thought and culture. We may wish they were, and may feel that it would be an immense relief to us to think of Jephthah as only consecrating his beloved and noble daughter to most sacred service for the living God. But with this sense to his word, why should he be so stricken with grief in the thought of performing his vow?

That Jephthah was in the main a good man—so good that the Lord could use him for the deliverance of his people, is obvious. Was his record as to this vow given here to show that God can use very imperfect and erring men, provided they are honest? or to show how crude and semi-heathenish were the current notions of that age and country, and how little the true spirit of the Mosaic code had leavened society? On these and similar questions we seem to lack the data we so much need for decisive opinions.

The little fragment of history with which Jephthah's record closes (chap. 12) shows him rather rash than prudent and conciliating, putting him in sharp contrast with Gideon under similar circumstances. Those jealous Ephraimites come to light again, complaining indignantly that they were not summoned first to the war and to the glory of this victory. They must have crossed the Jordan in great force to demand reparation or to take vengeance for this assumed tribal insult. In the issue they attacked the men of Gilead, who smote and drove them back; took the fords of the Jordan; tested the Ephraimite by his provincial pronunciation of "Shibboleth;" and put to the sword 42,000 men—a terrible punishment upon a very ridiculous jealousy and a very rash, unjustifiable assault. We get here a dark view of social and national life in Israel.

Jephthah's judgeship was of six years only, and was apparently limited to the region east of the Jordan. At least there is no indication of its extending to the western tribes.

This chapter (12) closes with the briefest notice of Ibzan as Judge, from Bethlehem in Judah; of Elon, Judge from Zebulun; and of Abdon of Ephraim.

The Story of Samson.

Of the four chapters (13–16) which tell the story of Samson, the first records the antecedents of his birth. His mother, long childless, had a vision of an angel, of whom, reporting the case to her husband, she said: "A man of God came unto me, and his countenance was like the countenance of an angel of God, very terrible." It was one of those manifestations of the Holy One in which the personage is called interchangeably "the Lord" or "God;" and "the angel of the Lord"—such as appears in the history of Abraham (Gen. 22: 11–14); of Jacob (Gen. 32: 24–30); of Moses (Ex. 23; 20–23); and of Gideon (Judg. 6: 11–24). This personage, being questioned as to his name (13: 17, 18) declined to give it, "seeing it is Pele" (Heb.), meaning *wonderful* (not as in the English text "secret")—the very name which appears in the list of names given to the glorious Messiah by Isaiah (9: 6): "For unto us a child is born; unto us a son is given; and the government shall be upon his shoulders, and his name shall be called *Wonderful*, Counsellor, the Mighty God, the Everlasting Father, the Prince of Peace."——Following the example of Gideon in a similar case, Manoah begged the privilege of entertaining his guest with a kid and a meat-offering, but received from him the suggestion that his guest was divine, not human; and the appropriate hospitality would be a sacrifice suitable for God, and not food for the eating of man.

When he had placed his offering to the Lord upon a rock, the angel "wrought wonderfully" (according to the import of his name); for when the flame arose from the burning flesh on the altar, the angel ascended in that flame—and the vision was no more!——He had previously made his communication, first to the mother, last to the father of the child Samson, whose birth he came to herald, and whose training he came to prescribe. He would have this child a Nazarite to God from the womb to his grave under the solemn vow to drink neither wine nor strong drink, and that no razor should ever pass over his head. The mother also was to maintain a like abstinence from strong drink and from all unclean food. The case of the Nazarite was provided for in the Institutes of Moses, the record of it standing in Num. 6: 1–21. This vow might run for a limited time or for life—the case of Samson and also of Samuel being of the latter class. Paul (as in Acts 18: 18) was a case of the former sort.——By this vow the subject was brought into peculiar relations to God. In the present case the supernatural strength of Samson and his special fitness for his mission as a scourge upon the Philistines and a Redeemer and Judge for Israel turned upon his faithful observance of his vow. We may notice the connection between being filled with the Spirit and *not* filled with wine, as in Eph. 5: 18.

——An interesting point of this brief history is the very appropriate solicitude of the father of Manoah to see the angel for himself and learn from his own lips what they should do to the child that should be born. "Now let thy words come to pass" (said he). "How shall we order the child, and what shall we do unto him?"—better; what shall be *his doing*, *i. e.*, what shall *he do?* (13: 8, 12, 13.) And the angel repeated the points previously given to the mother (vs. 4, 5, 7). So all legitimate consecration of offspring to God under his proposed covenant carries with it the obligation to train them from birth for the service and work which God has for them to do. Let parental solicitude concentrate itself upon this point with never-ceasing interest and care! Is it not a solemn, momentous, and royal thing to train sons and daughters for the use of the Great King of heaven?

In several points the case of Samson resembles that of Samuel; *e. g.*, the long barren, prayerful mother; her abstinence from wine and strong drink; the Nazarite vow for her son involving his consecration to God all the days of his life (1 Sam. 1: 28). Some have thought that Samson and Samuel were contemporary; but this view seems to lack authority.

Passing the antecedents of Samson's birth, we come to his *life, exploits, and personal character.*——It can scarcely be necessary on these pages to report or even condense the very full account of his adventures.*

The story is told plainly; every child reads and loves to read it. I propose only to call my readers' attention to a few points which seem worthy of remark.

1. Samson only *began* to deliver Israel from the Philistines, as the angel promised (13: 5): "He shall *begin* to deliver Israel," etc. He never entirely broke their yoke, but left much of this work unfinished. No complete deliverance was effected short of the age of David.

2. Remarkably he achieved all he did by the power of his single arm. It was done by courage and muscular force. "With the jaw-bone of an ass heaps upon heaps"—so a thousand men lie dead before his unwearied arm; or when waylaid in the house, he is up at midnight and walks off with the doors of the city gates and the two posts; and for a final exploit he put his hands severally upon the two great central pillars on which Dagon's temple rested, and while three thousand men and women were on the roof, exulting and shouting over their blind prisoner, he lifted his soul in one prayer for help; then bowed himself with his returned strength and fell with thousands of his enemies, slaying more at his death than through all his previous life. Unlike the Judges before him, he planned no stratagem; created no panic among his foes; never set them upon mutual slaughter; never rallied the warriors of Israel's tribes to his standard, and apparently never had their help at all. Indeed it was with some difficulty that he persuaded his brethren of Judah to keep their own hands off from himself. They seem to have utterly succumbed to the Philistines and demanded of him the same submission.

On the point of the divine purpose in this peculiar type of manifested power, we may, perhaps, in the absence of revealed suggestion, indulge ourselves in

* The only point of special difficulty in this narrative is in the translation "foxes" (15: 4) where the animal is without doubt the *Jackal*—a gregarious animal caught and harnessed for such a service without difficulty. The fox as we know him is both too cunning and too alert for such harnessing and service.

some conjecture. The Lord manifestly sought *variety* in his methods of revealing his power to save. In the case of Gideon he "chose the weak things of the world to confound the mighty"—a few men, only a very few, to rout and destroy an almost countless host. Over against that case he puts this, of one man's physical might. This was equivalent to saying before all Israel and all Philistia—What if the Lord should raise up an army of ten thousand Samsons?——Yet further, may we not conjecture that this power given to Samson was specially adapted to Philistia, where the giant race of champion warriors was not yet extinct, and whose pride in her Goliath comes to view presently in David's history? The case of Samson witnessed before those lords of the Philistines that the Great God of Israel could raise up champions against whom no Goliath from their ranks could hope to stand.

3. It is a striking fact that Samson came into contact with the Philistines in the line of social life, through amatory relations to their women. It is intimated that while his father and mother protested strongly against his choice of such women—as we might expect faithful Hebrew parents would—yet " they knew not that it was of the Lord that he sought an occasion against the Philistines " (14: 3, 4). Probably we shall be obliged to leave this divine purpose among his inscrutable ways, for these connections seem to have tempted Samson above what he was able to bear, and in the result brought dishonor, not to say disaster, upon Israel through his manifold infirmities.——In Samson we note a strange blending of courage and physical strength with a weakness toward women. Was it partly for the sake of the moral lessons enforced by such an example that these painful facts were permitted to occur and the record of them to appear in the sacred history? We read it with a painfully quickened sense of the weakness of some of the strongest men.——Moreover, it does undoubtedly throw light upon the dangers continually incident to the close social contact of Israel with the Canaanites remaining in the land. Those families of ancient Canaan had art, culture, beauty; and when these qualities were found by the men and women of Israel, associated with an attractive sensuous idol-worship, we can readily see how subtle and perilous

the temptation became. There is no definite proof that Samson was weak toward idolatry; but being so weak toward idol-worshiping women, he might have been fearfully tempted in that direction.

4. Yet, on the whole, I see not how we can deny to Samson a place among the heroes of faith. The writer to the Hebrews (chap. 11 : 32) finds a niche for his name in that glorious temple. The record here reveals him a man of prayer and of power with God.——While, therefore, we are sad and humiliated for our human nature in the view of such moral weakness, it may, perhaps, be a legitimate consolation that God can forgive such human weakness, and put away even such great sin, and still employ to his praise men who are very imperfect, provided, always, that they are sincere and true hearted.

Micah, the religious idolater.

In the order of the chapters in "Judges" we come next to a very remarkable story (chapters 17 and 18) of a man named Micah, of Mt. Ephraim. It is a story rather of domestic, private life, than of national affairs, but is exceeding interesting and valuable for the light it throws upon the inner religious history of the people (or at least *some* of the people) of Israel at this age, showing how they mixed together religious and heathen ideas of God, and sought to improve upon the great law of Jehovah—no idols or images of God of any sort—by introducing both graven and molten images. This man Micah had " An house of gods," a temple on his own private account, with the accompaniments of the "ephod"—the insignia of the priest; the teraphim—household images of worship; and, moreover, he set apart one of his sons for his priest.* In process of time a wandering Levite, out of employment, passing that way, he hired him into his service as priest for the very humble compensation of ten shekels of silver and one suit of clothes per annum, and his board. This change quite improved his religious establishment and raised his hopes of God's favor to an assured confidence : " Now (said he) I know that the Lord will do me good, seeing I have a Levite for my priest " (17 : 13).

---

* It is worth noticing that the Hebrew phrase for "consecrate" (17: 5) is *filled the hand*, in the sense of giving one full occupation and making this his special business.

This arrangement, so very satisfactory to Micah, was quite broken up by a series of accidents, narrated chap. 18. Five men of the tribe of Dan deputed to go north and search out a new home for a portion of their tribe, turned into the house of Micah on Mt. Ephriam to enjoy his hospitality, and chanced to recognize his Levite priest as an old acquaintance. They drew from him the terms of his contract with Micah and improved their opportunity to ask counsel of God through him as to the success of their mission. With his very favorable answer they went on their way, inwardly purposing, we must suppose, to call again. ——Having found a fertile region in the extreme north of Palestine, held by a people quite unprepared to defend themselves, and withal consciously secure and off their guard, they reported to their people their success. Forthwith an armed force of six hundred men are on their march to this new home of the Danites. They make it in their way to pass the house of Micah. The five spies suggest to them how fine a lot of plunder lay here at their mercy—all this household of gods and the Levite priest besides. The latter was readily persuaded to break his contract with Micah for the sake of becoming the high priest of this tribe of Dan; and seems to have had no particular scruples against taking his images, ephod, and teraphim—the implements necessary for his service—with no thought of asking Micah's consent or offering compensation. It was the old doctrine of "Might against Right," and suggests that the religion of these men was not embarrassed with ideas about rights of property, claims of justice, or bonds of social compact. Micah is stripped of both his priest and his gods; expostulates to no purpose, and is compelled to succumb before superior brute force. His expostulation is in pitiful tone, revealing a broken-hearted man: "Ye have taken away my gods which I made, and the priest, and ye are gone away; and *what have I more?* And now what mean ye to say unto me, What aileth thee?" But no heart was moved to pity by this sad wail.——It is plain that his religious hopes have perished. He no longer "knows that the Lord will do him good." "Alas," he cries, "what have I more?"——He must have been a very *sincere* idolater.

If sincerity insures salvation, he should have had nothing to fear.

These are the outlines of the story. There are several points which should have more particular attention.

The mother of Micah had by some means accumulated quite an amount of silver—eleven hundred shekels.* Suddenly it is missing. She seems to have lacked the grace necessary to accept this dispensation submissively, the remark of her son being this—"About which thou *cursedst*.† Whether this cursing awakened the son's superstitious fear or aroused what little conscience he may have had, the result was that he said to her: "Behold, the silver is with me; I took it." The overjoyed mother gives him her devout benediction; "Blessed be thou of the Lord, my son." Very religious is she now—in her words! May we suppose that her case was in the mind of the Apostle James when he said (3:10): "Out of the same mouth proceedeth blessing and cursing. My brethren, these things ought not so to be."——Perhaps it was a relief to them both to give two hundred of these silver shekels toward a set of silver gods. It may have helped the son to atone for his theft, and the mother for her cursing. It is quite in harmony with human nature, under the darkness of sin, to comfort itself in this sort of atonement for conscious misdeeds. It was presently arranged between them to make this disposition of so much of this silver; and the family became thereupon very religious!

Now, we very naturally ask whether this was a sample or an exceptional family in Israel. May we take it to represent the morality and the religion of the masses, or was this case rather special and unique?——If it represented Israel somewhat justly, their case readily accounts for those frequent and fearful relapses into idolatry which give character to this whole book of

---

* On the authority of Webster, the shekel is equal to a half ounce avoirdupois, 62½c. The weight would thus be 38⅜ pounds, and the value $687.50.

† It is supposable that this "cursing" should be taken in the sense of adjuring, and not of passionate imprecation. The former would be according to the law of Moses—a rule, however, for the magistrate—perhaps not for the private citizen. It is to be feared that the spirit of the mother favors the sense assumed in my exposition.

MICAH, THE RELIGIOUS IDOLATER. 83

Judges. Yet we may certainly hope that this was rather the darker side of the national character. We may note that both this case of Micah, and that of the nameless Levite who went for his concubine to Bethlehem-judah (recorded chap. 19), originated on Mt. Ephraim. Now, although Joshua was of that tribe, and although his bones lay on that very Mt. Ephraim (Josh. 24: 30), yet the men of Ephraim have not by any means a worthy record in this book of Judges. The reader will remember how they appear in the history of both Gideon and Jephthah—very proud, very jealous, and far less ready to be foremost in toil and peril for their country than to be first in the glory of victories achieved by others' valor. In estimating their tribal character it may be considered that they were populous, numerically strong, and very proud of it; were centrally located in Western Palestine, with the first religious capital (Shiloh) in the bosom of their tribe (since Josh. 18: 1); but they never distinguished themselves for either patriotism or piety. No Judge arose from that tribe to redeem Israel in her seasons of political servitude, unless Abdon may possibly be an exception. He was buried in the land of Ephraim (12: 15).——In the hill country of Judah were fairer religious homes, and nobler men, if we may judge by the records of Boaz, Jesse, and David. On the whole, we may hope that the average religious life of Israel was above the examples furnished from Mt. Ephraim in these closing chapters of the Judges.

Let us not fail to notice very definitely that this picture of domestic life on Mt. Ephraim witnesses to a radical apostasy from the fundamental principles of the divine law in these several respects:

(1.) First and most vital of all—in the making of images with which to worship God. It is, perhaps, not quite certain that Micah purposely ignored the true God, and intentionally offered his worship to these images as being themselves gods; for he may have thought to worship the God of Israel *with the help* of these images. But we must note that he cried out: "Ye have taken away my gods, and *what have I more?*" —as if there was no God left to him after these silver images were taken away. This case shows, at least, that the distinction between worshiping God by means of images, and worshiping images as themselves gods, was but dimly defined in his mind, if at all—a distinction of only the smallest practical account. The divine law attempted no distinction between these supposably different forms of idolatry; and this case sufficiently indorses the wisdom of God's law in this particular.

(2.) The divine law explicitly forbade the offering of sacrificial worship, with the ceremonials of their religion, elsewhere than *at the one place* which God might choose. In the case before us, this precept was utterly disregarded.

(3.) The law also debarred from the priesthood all men save the descendants of Aaron. But this Micah first put into his family priesthood one of his own sons, and then a Levite, not of the family of Aaron. Thus recklessly, if not even defiantly, was the divine law in these very vital points overruled and set aside.

This picture of the inner life of Israel is darkly shaded by the facts recorded respecting the men of Dan. An armed banditti, six hundred strong, marching through the land of Israel, amenable to no authority; subject to no law save that of *might;* stealing whatever they chose to steal; threatening the owner's life to silence his complaint:—verily, such a case gives significance to the historian's frequent remark: "In those days there was no king in Israel."

One further remark is suggested by this fragment of history:—It is scarcely supposable that the three great national festivals and the Great Day of Atonement were fully observed by the nation and practically accounted by the masses as their own religious system—the media of their own personal approach to God and communion with him. At best the Mosaic system could have had only a feeble influence and a very limited observance. With the developments of the book of Judges fully in our mind we can understand why David, of spirit so devout and with views of the national character and national want so broad and discriminating, should, on coming to the throne, feel the necessity of making a religious capital powerful and imposing as a home for the ark of the covenant, and of investing the entire Mosaic worship with the richest attractions of ceremonial and song. There was, doubtless, a most

THE NAMELESS LEVITE: GIBEAH OF BENJAMIN.

imperative need for that re-enforcement to the power of the religious institutions of Moses.

The name of this Levite who became priest to the tribe of Dan is given (18: 30)–"Jonathan the son of Gershom, the son of Manasseh." Some have supposed that he was a grandson of Moses—their ground for this supposition being that the eldest son of Moses bore the name of Gershom (Ex. 2: 22, and 18: 3); and that in our Hebrew text, this word "Manasseh" is written with the letter (n) suspended above the line, indicating a doubt of its authority. Without this (n), the consonants of the word will be those of the name Moses.—— Evidence of this sort seems to me quite unreliable. Gershom was a family name in the tribe of Levi. (See 1 Chron. 6: 1, 16, and also Ezra 8; 2.)

This suspended (n) in "Manasseh" very naturally classes itself with Rabbinic conceits. This theory of a grandson of Moses may possibly be true, but not probably. We may be allowed to hope that no grandson of Moses had fallen so low as this.

The incidents recorded Judges 19–21, disclose a gloomy state of morals in *Gibeah of Benjamin*. The case implicated the whole tribe inasmuch as they defended the guilty perpetrators of this horrible crime with their entire military force and to the bitter end.

A Levite sojourning on Mt. Ephraim had taken a concubine from Bethlehem in Judah. She had proved false to him and had returned to her father. He visited her there to bring her home; was welcomed warmly and detained long in the customary convivialities. On his journey home night found them at Gibeah of Benjamin, hospitably entertained by a temporary resident who came from his own Mt. Ephraim. Some of the men of Gibeah, "sons of Belial," cognizant of the presence of traveling strangers in the old man's house, gathered about it to renew the shameful, horrible crime of the men of Sodom. The expostulations of the host were of no avail. The traveler's concubine was abused by them till the morning, and then found dead with her hands upon the threshold. Her lord bore the dead body sadly to his home; and then, to place this terrible outrage in its true light before the tribes of Israel, he cut her body and bones into twelve parts, and sent them forth among all the tribes. The public indignation was irrepressible.

The people came together *en masse;* heard the Levite's story of this outrage; sought counsel of the Lord; first demanded in vain the surrender of the guilty; and then, they by divine counsel attacked Gibeah with arms. It is not altogether clear why the issues of battle on the first two days were adverse to the warriors of Israel, resulting, according to the figures here, in the slaughter of 40,000 men. But on the third day the men of Benjamin were cut to pieces. 25,000 men fell, and only 600 escaped. The cities of Benjamin were also fearfully devastated, and the population of the tribe cut down to these 600 surviving men.

The narrative records the grief of the whole nation over this fearful scene of destruction—sad that one tribe in Israel should be brought so near to utter extinction. A national feeling that the integrity of the twelve tribes must be maintained, coupled with compassion for these surviving 600, led to conciliation and to special arrangements to provide them wives;* and thus this sad scene of horrors—shameless lust, persistence in defending the guilty, bloody war, and almost the extinction of one tribe from Israel, came to its close. On the one side of this picture we have a fearfully low and debased condition of social life; but on the other, the uprising of virtuous indignation, resulting in fearful retribution upon the guilty city and tribe, and a moral lesson, not soon or easily forgotten.

There remain two subordinate questions pertaining to these two cases—that of Micah and that of the Levite and his concubine—viz., the date of the events, and the date of this record made of them. The casual reader is liable to the mistake of assuming that their place in the book of Judges indicates their relative date as being subsequent to all its other events. In fact the place assigned them in this book gives no clew whatever to their date. They are a sort of appendix to the book, disconnected from the thread of its national history. All the other historic incidents were national in their character—successive chapters of national history. But

---

* The history of Saul (1 Sam. 11, and 31: 11–13) will bring to light a specially kind feeling between Gibeah of Benjamin and Jabesh-Gilead—a feeling naturally strengthened by the circumstance that 400 of the 600 mothers of the resuscitated tribe were of the spared daughters of Jabesh-Gilead.

DATE OF THE EVENTS IN JUDGES 17-21.

these five concluding chapters are not primarily national, but rather are fragments of family history.——
It is generally held that their chronological place is quite early in the book of Judges, perhaps even before the Judgeship of Othniel (3: 9–11). It is every way probable that this migration of a part of the tribe of Dan to the extreme north of Palestine occurred soon after the allotment of the tribes, their original territory being found too limited. One of the encampments of the 600 near Kirjath-jearim (18: 12) gave the place the name, Mahaneh-Dan (the camp of Dan)—a name which appears subsequently in the history of Samson (13: 25). Samson was, therefore, certainly later than this march and encampment of the 600.

Again, in the second of these narratives (20: 28) we are told that Phineas, the son of Eleazer, the son of Aaron, stood before the ark as high priest in those days. But this Phineas was in the vigor of his manhood (apparently) in the scenes recorded Num. 25, *i. e.*, before the death of Moses. His father's death is noticed in close connection with the death of Joshua (Josh. 24: 33), showing that he came into the high priesthood at least as early as Joshua's death. The transactions of these last three chapters of Judges must, therefore, be located in time very early among the events of this book.

As bearing upon the *date of the record*, the remark four times made in these five chapters, "In those days there was no king in Israel" (17: 6, and 18: 1, and 19: 1, and 22: 25), implies that the historian contrasts those days of no king with his own in which there was a king.——The statements made (18: 30, 31) to the effect that Jonathan and his descendants held the priesthood for the tribe of Dan "till the day of the captivity of the land," and that Micah's graven image stood among them all the time that the house of God was in Shiloh, imply that the writer's knowledge comes down to the dates of those respective events—the transfer of the tabernacle from Shiloh to Jerusalem in the reign of David, and "the captivity of the land." What "captivity" is here referred to may be somewhat uncertain, though probably it is that of the ten tribes (B. C. 722).——
Moreover it is quite possible that these two verses are an appendix to this story by some later hand—a sort of foot note by some compiler, long after the body of the

story was written.——Finally, it may be considered probable that the book of Judges was written by Samuel, excepting these two verses (18: 30, 31) which may have been added by some subsequent compiler.

The facts stated in these two verses are of more importance to us than the date of their writing. The facts are sadly significant of the feeble influence of the Mosaic system out on the northern confines of the land —that this special priesthood for the tribe of Dan, entirely distinct from that of Aaron, should have been sustained there through so many ages, and that this idol-image should have maintained its place down at least to the reign of David.——Let us note, however, that this fact, though sad, is abundantly corroborated by subsequent historic allusions. Isaiah (9: 1, 2) speaks of the outlying regions of Zebulun and Naphtali as having long lain in dishonor, oppression, and spiritual darkness, until Jesus came among them, revealing a truly blessed light. (See my notes on the passage). The received English version translates it very imperfectly.——The current feeling in the time of Christ runs in the same strain: "Can any good thing come out of Galilee?" "Out of Galilee ariseth no prophet." The Galilee of the gospel age included the territory of this northern Dan, and also of Zebulun and Naphtali. The Jews of Jerusalem had for ages looked upon that as a heathen country, early and long apostate from the religion of their fathers.

Reviewing briefly the great religious declension of Israel during the period covered by the book of Judges, we may profitably turn our thought,

I. To the *evidences* of such declension :

II. To the *causes* which contributed to produce it:

III. To the *agencies* introduced by the Lord in his providence to counteract it.

I. The fact of great declension is entirely obvious throughout this book. We have seen proofs of it in the sketches of family history in chaps. 17–21. We saw them through all the previous chapters in the perpetually recurring relapses into idolatry after the death of each prominent Judge, and after the deliverance wrought under his hand. The fact is fully implied in the statement (Josh. 24: 31) that "Israel served the Lord all the days of Joshua, and all the days of the elders that outlived Joshua, and who had known all the works of the Lord that he had done for Israel "—but (so it is implied) no longer with like steadfastness. Then followed a series of sore declensions.——This great relapse was foretold by Moses in his song (Deut. 32). And finally, it was manifestly anticipated, and with earnest endeavor resisted and forefended by Joshua in his last words to the assembled people. He seems even then to have seen the causes working, and the indications of weakening moral stamina to withstand pernicious influences already apparent.

II. Among its causes we may name,

1. The example and social influence of the cultured, wealthy, and powerful Canaanites left in the land, or residing close upon its confines. Something may, perhaps, be due to the inexperience of the people in regard to the prodigious evils of idolatry. We marvel that they should not have accepted God's law as the expression of his wisdom and love, without the aid of bitter experience. But such is frail, sinning man.

2. "Fullness of bread;" the growth and development of self-indulgence—perhaps we may say, comparative luxury. The change from being poorly fed throughout their servitude in Egypt; from manna and water forty years in the wilderness, with only an occasional taste of animal flesh, to this copious supply amid the wealth of Canaan, would press upon their frail human nature in one of its weakest points. We place this among the causes of their declension with the more confidence because it was foreseen and declared by Moses in his prophetic song (Deut. 32: 13–18); in the words, "Jeshurun waxed fat and kicked; thou art waxed fat; thou art grown thick; thou art covered with fatness. *Then he forsook God who made him*, and lightly esteemed the Rock of his salvation," etc.

3. Ephraim, the central tribe territorially, the head tribe numerically, and the location of the religious capital during the entire period of the Judges, indeed down to David, had, as we have seen, *a bad record*, and, therefore, constituted an uncongenial locality for the great religious center. It is inevitable that such influences should contribute largely toward national declension and make a change of place for the religious capital a real necessity.

THE GREAT DECLENSION.

4. It is quite apparent that both politically and religiously the mutual relation of the tribes to each other was far too loose for the best results. While the tribal feeling was strong—we may even say, clannish—the national feeling was feeble, and greatly needed more concentration. All through the period of the Judges, it was only under some powerful impulses that the whole national force could be brought to bear against any foreign enemy. The histories of Deborah and Barak, of Gideon, and of Jephthah, are full of facts bearing to this point. It is scarcely supposable that during the long period of the Judges, the tribes went up *en masse* three times a year to any great religious center to strengthen at once their national piety and their national patriotism at the shrine of the same national God.

III. Of the agencies brought forward in God's providence to counteract this declension and fortify the nation against it, we may note,

1. The stern discipline of suffering. This book is mainly a record of the successive visitations by which "the Lord sold them into the hand of cruel enemies," who mightily oppressed them and put them to great hardship and suffering. Then, when they were brought to repentance and to earnest cries to God for help, he raised up for them some deliverer. The next relapse made necessary the same process of discipline, repentance, prayer, and help, designed to impress the same great moral lessons.——At the extreme point of their calamity, the ark of God was taken away into captivity [Heb.] seven months among the Philistines (1 Sam. 6: 1) and twenty years in Kirjath-jearim (1 Sam. 7: 2). The two sons of the aged and pious but weak High Priest, Eli, were slain in one day, and with the loss of the ark "the glory was indeed departed from Israel." ——To rally the nation from this extreme point of depression, the Lord brought out Samuel, and through him developed into fullness and strength the prophetic order—an event which will demand more particular attention in the sequel.

Finally, the Lord suffered the form of government to be so far modified as to become monarchial. He granted the request of the people for a king, securing thus a much greater degree of consolidation and making provision for a more vigorous nationality, both political and religious. At length the Lord raised up David, a king "after his own heart," and through him withstood more successfully the temptations to idolatry under which Israel suffered so fearfully during the period of the Judges. These agencies for the better development of the nation, religiously, as well as politically, will be the special theme throughout the two books of Samuel.

Chronology of the Book of Judges.

The vexed questions of sacred chronology have been somewhat fully discussed in my volume on the Pentateuch—the chronology of the period of the Judges on page 60. This question is resumed here chiefly to refer to the extreme diversity of views held by critics, of which a conspicuous example appears in the Speaker's Commentary, pp. 118–121. Here the entire period of the Judges between the death of Joshua and the judgeship of Samuel is brought within 140 to 160 years. This is done by ruling out the authority of the historian in 1 Kings 6: 1, which makes this period 339 years; and of Paul (Acts 13: 20), who declares it to be about 450 years; of Jephthah (Judges 12: 26), which assigns 300 years between the death of Moses and that day; and, substantially, of the oft-repeated statements within this book of the periods of "rest" from oppression, viz., of 40 years thrice said (Judg. 3: 11, and 5: 31, and 8: 28), and of 80 years (3: 30), which alone amount to 200. These figures having been set aside, the author accepts as the only reliable authority, the various genealogies which appear in the Scriptures stretching over this period, e. g., of David, of Zadok, of Abiathar, etc. In making these only his data, the author seems to overlook two important facts, viz., (1.) That the period of one generation. i. e., the age of the father at the birth of his son in the given line, is by no means a fixed quantity; and (2.) That in the Hebrew genealogical lists it is undeniable that some names are occasionally omitted, as in the tables of Matt. 1: 2, and of Luke 3, and as I think must be admitted, between Levi and Moses. (See my Pentateuch, pp. 63, 64.) It is, therefore, by no means obvious that we reach the best results by rejecting those general comprehensive statements which appear in the historian of 1 Kings, in Paul, in Jephthah, and in the Book of Judges generally, and by relying exclusively upon the authority of genealogical lists which make no allusion whatever to chronology.

Doubtless we must all accept the conclusion that no absolutely certain data exist for a complete chronology of the Book of Judges.

The Story of Ruth.

This story, in four chapters, is legitimately a sequel to the book of Judges, since it belongs to the same period—"in the days when the Judges ruled" (Ruth 1: 1), and, like the story of Micah and that of the nameless Levite on Mt. Ephraim, gives us, not so much national as private life. Unlike the two last named, it opens to view neither idol-worship, nor horrible vices, nor desolating wars; but presents the quiet scenes of home, savored with sincere and humble piety. Such Hebrew life it is grateful to the heart to contemplate. Let us lend to it a few moments' quiet consideration.

A family of Bethlehem, consisting of the father Elimelech, his wife Naomi, and two sons, Mahlon and Chilion, were driven by stress of famine to seek bread in the country of Moab. For some reason not given, their stay there was protracted through ten years. During this time the two sons married each a daughter of Moab—Orpah and Ruth. But these ten years brought to this family, not marriages only, but funerals. The father died, and his two sons were laid in early graves. Three human hearts were widowed and desolate. Sore was the burden of grief and responsibility upon the heart of Naomi. The narrative appreciates this: "The woman was left of her two sons and of her husband" (1: 5). No wonder her thoughts turn toward the land of her fathers' sepulchers and the people who worshiped the God of her trust.——But what shall she say to her widowed daughters-in-law? They have been kind to her and to her dead; but what more can she do for them? They are childless; and for this sore trial she has no relief to offer. She therefore proposes to them to return each to her own father's house, and start again in Moab life as the ways of Providence may open it before them.——In their first reply they are at one in protesting that they can not leave their mother-in-law, but must go with her to her Bethlehem home. When she responded, putting the case yet more strongly, Orpah gave her mother the parting kiss, but Ruth clave unto her. Naomi probed the depth of her love yet once more: "Behold, thy sister-in-law is gone back unto her people and *unto her gods:* return thou after thy sister-in-law" (1:15). These last words serve to bring out the noble and truly religious heart of Ruth: "Entreat me not to leave thee." Her words are very strong: Do not assail—do not *strike* me [Hebrew] with such painful words. "Do not ask me to return from following after thee, for where thou goest, I will go; and where thou lodgest, I will lodge: thy people shall be my people, and thy God my God. Where thou diest will I die, and there will I be buried. The Lord do so to me and more also if aught but death part thee and me." She meant this for a final, decisive answer. It was. No words could have made it stronger. The solemn oath, "God do so to me and more also," left nothing stronger to be said. Her heart is with her mother; and what is yet more, is with her mother's people and with her mother's God. Her sister may go back to her people, and if she chooses to her people's gods; but for herself she can do no such thing. Her heart is with the God of Israel, and she hails the day that shall transfer her home and her church relations (so to speak) to the country and the people who had given her that godly mother. The religion and the God of Israel had met the great wants of her soul—daughter of Moab though she was—and she rejoices to make them in every sense her own. Godly souls, Jewish and Christian, through all the ages, have welcomed this Moabite daughter to the fellowship of the saints and to the household of God, grateful to accept her case as a precious harbinger of the day when "they shall come from the East and from the West, from the North and from the South, and sit down in the kingdom of God."

In the sequel, we have a lovely picture of home-scenes and of common life in Bethlehem among the laboring classes. It was the beginning of barley-harvest when the welcome news ran to and fro among the friends of her youth—Naomi, the widow of our Elim-

elech, is again among us from the land of Moab, and with her one of the daughters of Moab, cleaving to her in her widowhood with true and daughterly fidelity. Forthwith this young woman is out with the maidens of Bethlehem, gleaning after the reapers, the ordering of a forethoughtful providence assigning to her a place in the field of a certain man Boaz, here introduced to us in the story as a young man of their kindred. Though not the nearest blood-relative to the deceased Elimelech, yet he seems to have been the second—only one standing in nearer relationship. Elimelech left some real estate which, by Hebrew law, it was the right of Naomi and her daughter to redeem by the aid of any relative or friend. With this redeemed estate was associated, by usage, the hand of Ruth in sacred marriage, that no family might become extinct in Israel. We need not be surprised that, in the simplicity of those early ages of the race, the hearts of mothers and daughters, of fathers and of sons, all alike beat strongly with the love of offspring, nor that they honored the family relation and the sacred institution of marriage, and felt an interest, of which none were ashamed, in perpetuating the family line, that no household might fail of posterity. The strength of this feeling, the joy felt in happy and virtuous marriages of the young, and especially the gratification when a widowed, desolate household, on the verge of extinction, became re-established in the divine order, stand forth with great, and let us say, very interesting prominence throughout the sequel of this story. —— Yet we can not pass this case without suggesting that the method, proposed by Naomi and carried out by Ruth, of introducing herself to Boaz, and, in a sort, claiming her rights under the Mosaic law, is not to be recommended for any other age or people. —— We shall note, perhaps with some surprise, that an excellent and virtuous mother made this proposal, and that Boaz seems to have nothing less than the fullest confidence in the virtuous purity of Ruth. While it behooves us to exercise a free and large charity toward the recognized usages of an age so early in the progress of civilization, we may hope that the intrinsic impropriety of this usage made it very short-lived. No trace of it appears in subsequent Hebrew history. ——
With this single exception every feature in this picture

of home life in Israel is full of sweet and charming simplicity and fragrant with the aroma of moral purity. —— In the result Boaz became the husband of Ruth, and through this union the father of Obed, from whom next in the line of descent were Jesse and David. Thus Ruth, of the daughters of Moab, and Rahab, of the doomed nations of Canaan, came by virtue of their faith in Israel's God into the nationality of Israel, and also into the particular family line of the ancestry of the nation's Messiah.

Of the *author and date* of this book, nothing can be known with certainty. It is probable, yet not certain, that the genealogical table at the close (4: 17–22) is part of the original book. If so, it must have been written after David came into some prominence. On the concurrent testimony of all the ancient authorities it is part of the Jewish Canon of books written and compiled by their prophets. We must rest it on their authority, indorsed subsequently by Christ and his apostles.

CHAPTER V.

Introduction to the two Books of Samuel.

On the concurrent testimony of all the legitimate authorities, the two books of Samuel were originally one. Every reader will notice that what is now called the second book continues the history of Saul's death and of David in the same strain, with not the least indication of another author, or of a different purpose in the construction of the history. There is no appearance of transition at this point from one author to another. It need not be assumed that the entire two books of Samuel were written by one man; but only that there is no indication of change of author between the last chapter of the first book and the first of the second book.

On the whole question of *authorship* of the Hebrew historical books (Samuel; Kings; Chronicles), the following points are important:

1. With Samuel commenced a regular succession of prophets—the order being sustained by continued accessions to their number so that their functions were kept up from generation to generation down to the age of Malachi. This point will be discussed more at length below.

2. One among several functions of the prophetic order was that of committing to writing the important events of their national history. They were the annalists of the Hebrew people. (See more of this under the head of the "Order of Hebrew prophets.")

3. That Samuel wrote the first part of the first book of Samuel—probably so much as could have been written by him before his death—is rendered highly probable, almost certain, by the following considerations:

(a.) That the author of Chronicles (1 Chron. 29: 29) tell us that "the acts of David, first and last, were written in the book of Samuel the seer, in the book of Nathan the prophet, and in the book of Gad the seer," etc.

(b.) That, inaugurating a system of historic annalism, and making it one of the functions of the prophetic order, it is altogether reasonable to suppose that he would give it the force of his own example, and, indeed, would introduce and inaugurate it specially by means of his personal example.

(c.) To this we may add the concurrent testimony of all Hebrew tradition.

It is, therefore, more than probable that Samuel wrote, not only the first chapters of 1 Samuel, but also the books of Judges and of Ruth.

4. The three following considerations render it more than probable that Gad and Nathan continued the history known as the books of Samuel from the point where Samuel closed; viz.:

(a.) The testimony of the author of Chronicles (as above) that Samuel, Gad, and Nathan wrote the acts of David.——(b.) The fact that they stood in specially intimate relations to David; Samuel having anointed him and received him as his guest and friend at his prophet-college and home in Ramah (1 Sam. 19: 18); Gad being more than once called "David's seer;" and Nathan having been sent of God to reprove him for his great sin, and being specially prominent in the efforts necessary to secure the succession to Solomon. Such intimacy coincides with the other evidence to indicate these prophets as the successive authors of the history in the books of Samuel—the two latter completing what the first began.——(c.) It is every way probable that both Gad and Nathan commenced their prophetic training under Samuel, and thus became first acquainted with David through this aged prophet-father. Not improbably Gad was sent from Samuel to David while in Moab (as in 1 Sam. 22: 5).

5. The books of Samuel differ decidedly from the books of Kings and Chronicles in this one point, viz., that they contain no references to other documents in the national archives for more full information; while such references occur constantly throughout the books of Kings and Chronicles. Consequently the work of the author in the case of Kings and Chronicles was largely that of *compiler* from other documents previously written. On the other hand the books of Samuel have no such references, but seem to have been written by men personally cognizant of the facts they record. The business of historic annalism was then in the forming stage of its development. This is as we ought to expect on the assumption that Samuel himself set the example and inaugurated the practice—having however, such illustrious examples as Moses and probably Joshua before him. The special work of Samuel was to inaugurate the system and provide the requisite agencies for its permanence.

In striking confirmation of these views is the internal evidence in the early chapters of 1 Samuel that its author was an eye-witness—personally cognizant of the important facts he narrates. Who but Samuel could give the story of his first call to the prophetic work as we have it 1 Sam. 3? So also of his reported addresses to the people, chaps. 7, and 8, and 12.

The First Book of Samuel.

The prominent individual characters in this book are Samuel and his mother; Eli, the high priest, and his sons; Saul, the first king of Israel, and David the second. The important historical facts are those which pertain to the national worship at the tabernacle in Shiloh; the conflicts with their Philistine enemies; the captivity and fortunes of the ark of the covenant; the rise and development of the prophetic order in and by means of Samuel; the establishment of the kingdom under Saul; his reign and death; and the scenes of David's early peril, discipline, and growth toward the greatness and goodness of Israel's best king.

Noticeably we have here an unquestionable allusion to an annual festival to the Lord at the religious capital, Shiloh—the first well defined allusion since Joshua kept the Passover in Gilgal (Josh. 5: 10, 11). "A feast of the Lord in Shiloh yearly" is referred to (Judges 21: 19–21) as a scene of virgin dances. It may, perhaps, have been the feast of tabernacles—how true to its original purpose it is difficult to say. But here we have the record of a man of Ramathaim-zophim,* Elkanah by name, who "went up out of his city yearly" (it is not said three times a year) "to worship and to sacrifice to the Lord of Hosts in Shiloh." There were, therefore, some pious families who remembered the requirements of the law of God through Moses. The frequent and fearful relapses of the tribes into idolatry had not utterly extinguished the national worship yearly at the tabernacle.

In the scenes of this chapter and the next, Hannah, one of the two wives of Elkanah, is the central personage. For years the living grief of her heart had been barrenness. She had the love of her husband, but the proud scorn of this second wife of her husband who had children. This woman, Peninnah, is spoken of (1: 6) as "her adversary," provoking her with sore temptations to fretfulness. These griefs of Hannah's heart are

---

* The locality of Elkanah's home and of Samuel's is assigned variously. Were they the same? Was Elkanah "*of Mt. Ephraim*" in the sense of living there then, or merely of having previously lived there? Is this "Ephrath" (as in other passages) the same as Bethlehem in Judah? There is a well known Ramah six miles north of Jerusalem. Was this the locality of their "house" (1: 19)? Or, as Dr. Robinson concludes, was their home at Sobah, four or five miles west of Jerusalem?——These questions have scarcely sufficient importance to justify more extended discussion here. See Biblical Researches in Palestine, vol. II: 40, 141, 331, and 334; and Bib. Sacra. 1843, p. 506; and Smith's Bible Dictionary, Ramah (2) and Ramathaim-zophim; and Coleman, 105.

brought before us to show why she cast her burden so earnestly upon the Lord, and how it came to pass that Samuel was a child of many and mighty prayers before he was born. Indeed, he was specially consecrated to God, a Nazarite from the womb, before his birth, and the fact embalmed in his very name *Samuel*, one asked of God—a gift sought in prayer, and therefore fitly lent back to the Lord for his whole life's service.——If in her grief, and vows, and prayers for a son whom she might consecrate to God, Hannah fails to gain the sympathy of her sex in our age by reason of current notions as to maternity, let it bear, not to her dishonor, but to theirs. Her heart was too noble to think it a disgrace to be a mother. She was too true to her divine mission to repel the responsibilities, the care, or even the pains of maternity. The highest ambition of her soul was to be the mother of a son whom she might give to the Lord and train for any service the Lord might please to assign. No ambition in the heart of woman can be purer or nobler.——To such a woman God gave the child Samuel. Her record as a praying mother is priceless for our common humanity. It can not be said too emphatically that hers was the true idea of woman's mission. The names of only a few women stand embalmed for all time on the pages of God's ancient word. Almost without exception, those few names are there, exalted to that high honor because they were true mothers.

The Lord remembered Hannah with the gift of a son; and she gratefully remembered her vow. In pursuance of it, she retained him at her bosom so long as his infancy required, and then brought him to the altar of God at Shiloh with the customary sacrifice, and there consecrated him to the Lord, to be taken back no more. Her words to Eli on this occasion were few but expressive: "O my Lord, as thy soul liveth, I am the woman that stood by thee here, praying unto the Lord. For this child I prayed, and the Lord hath given me my petition which I asked of him: therefore also have I lent him to the Lord; as long as he liveth he shall be lent to the Lord."——If we ask how this praying mother felt at this hour; if we are curious to hear how she herself expresses the gratitude and exultation of her soul when the Lord so signally heard her prayer and accepted her offering, we may be gratified. Her prayerful song is here before us in ten full verses (1 Sam. 2: 1–10). The first words strike the key-note: "My heart rejoiceth in the Lord; mine horn is exalted in the Lord; my mouth is enlarged over mine enemies, because I rejoice in thy salvation. There is none holy as Jehovah: for there is none beside thee: neither is there any rock like our God." With frequent reiteration she tells us that God shapes and reverses human destiny, lifting up the lowly, casting down the proud—for she can not forget how the Lord had remembered her low estate; had heard her prayer, and put this grateful song into her mouth. Ere she closes, her song rises to the grandest generalizations. "The pillars of the earth are the Lord's, and he hath set the world upon them. He will keep the feet of his saints, and the wicked shall be silent in darkness. The adversaries of the Lord shall be broken to pieces; out of heaven shall he thunder upon them; the Lord shall judge the ends of the earth; and he shall give strength to his king and exalt the horn of his anointed."—— This anticipation of a "king" over God's chosen people, and this first use of the term Messiah ["his Anointed"], are distinctly prophetic of the changes in the national form of government then near at hand, and of these human kings of David's line as foreshadowing the Lord's Great Anointed.

Samuel is left at the sacred tabernacle to be under the care of the priests during his early childhood, employed in such ministries about the house of God as his maturing powers were adapted to perform. We are told that year by year his mother made and brought up for him "a little coat"—an outer tunic, worn by those who ministered before the Lord. Thus she refreshed her spirit with the evidences, growing year by year, that the Lord had accepted her gift, and was training her Samuel—rather, *his own* Samuel—for yet higher services.

"The Lord had need of him." Samuel represents, not himself alone, but the prophetic order. This new and vastly important religious agency had its rise as an institution, *in him*. There had been individual prophets before Samuel, but no established order, no sustained succession, no definite, constant service; and no

SAMUEL AND HIS MOTHER. 101

organized agencies to train men for it. With Samuel, this new order took its rise.

It is pertinent here to note that the history interweaves the youth and developments of Samuel with startling proofs of the astounding degeneracy of the priesthood—as if to indicate the moral necessity for introducing new and more reliable spiritual agencies.——Eli seems to have been in some points true to his responsibilities—a man of some right impulses, but alas, sadly, pitifully weak in the training and control of his two sons. Hophni and Phinehas, then in active service in the priesthood, are said and shown to be "sons of Belial" (2: 12), guilty of outrageous sacrilege in appropriating to themselves the offerings brought by pious Israelites according to Mosaic law, taking what they chose in defiance of the laws of sacrifice. The Mosaic law specified the parts of the several offerings (sin, trespass, and peace-offerings) which belonged to the priests. (See Lev. 6: 26, 29, and 7: 6–10, 28–34, and Num. 18: 8–14, 18). But the law gave no permission to thrust a three-tined fork into the seething flesh, to take out the choice pieces for the priest, nor did it permit him to make his first grab into the unsodden flesh before the cooking process commenced. By this double gouge, skillfully manipulated, the priest secured for himself the choicest and probably the greatest part of all the animal offerings. His threat to take what he would *by force* indicates a spirit reckless at once of God and of man, of piety and of common decency.——The Lord through his prophet expresses his sense of this insult in the words translated: "Wherefore *kick* ye at my sacrifices and at my offerings which I have commanded?"—the true sense of the Hebrew being rather—Wherefore do ye *trample under foot*—tread upon, as if with supreme contempt?

To this horrible sacrilege—so flagrant and scandalous that men abhorred the offering of the Lord and were repelled from his sanctuary—they added shameless adultery with the women who assembled at the door of the tabernacle—making God's own house their brothel!
——No wonder that the Lord rebuked Eli—not so much his sons who were hopelessly doomed to a swift and fearful death, as the aged father for his unpardonable dereliction in both parental and official duty toward those

sons. This rebuke was duplicated—the first sent by a man of God, not named in the record (2: 27–36); the second, by the child Samuel (3: 11–14). In the first rebuke the salient points are—Did I not give to thy tribe and family the high honors and emoluments of the priesthood? Wherefore, then, hast thou honored thy sons above me in allowing them to commit sacrilege at my altar? Why in the person of thy sons hast thou trampled under foot the sacrifices designed for God's honor in his earthly dwelling? I have said that thy house should stand before me in the priesthood forever; but now "the Lord saith—Be it far from me;" I can endure these insults no longer. "Them that honor me I will honor; and they that despise me shall be lightly esteemed."——The judgments threatened were, that his posterity should be cut off in youth, none ever attaining to old age; that their life should be only a consuming grief; that when joy should come to Israel, it should bring no joy to his posterity;* and that the sign and pledge of these crushing calamities should be that his two sons, Hophni and Phinehas, should both die in one day. God would raise up a faithful priest and make for him a sure house, while the posterity of Eli, doomed to abject poverty, should beg the humblest pittance and most menial service for a bare subsistence.——The reader may notice that, according to the very common law of divine judgments, this followed closely in the line of the sin punished, so as to be a perpetual reminder of that sin. The sin was (in part) sacrilegiously clutching from God's sacrifices at his very altar all they could get their hand on. The judgment was that they should beg around the same altar for the most menial service and for the merest pittance of bread.

Samuel Becomes a Prophet.

The second prediction of judgment on Eli and his

---

* "Thou shalt see an enemy in my habitation in all the wealth which God shall give Israel"—has been construed variously, *e. g.* ——(1.) Thou shalt see a *home-enemy*, an adversary of the house or home—in all that may be well for Israel, *i. e.*, in all her prosperity. ——(2.) Thou shalt see straitness of habitation—straitness, narrowness of place, in all Israel's prosperity (Gesenius);——(3.) Thou shalt look with a distressed look upon all the prosperity of Israel (Fuerst).——All these constructions concur substantially in the general sense given above.

SAMUEL BECOMES A PROPHET.

sons was sent through the lips of "the child Samuel." The inspired record gives a simple and beautiful account of the way in which the Lord first made himself known to young Samuel. "The word of the Lord was rare (Eng. version 'precious') in those days; there was no open vision"—the word for "open" having usually the sense of *spread abroad* before the public. Possibly the idea may be—no vision which clearly made known God's thoughts and words.——Samuel was sleeping in an apartment near to that of the aged Eli, and was suddenly awaked by a voice calling his name. He ran to Eli to answer this call. Eli said—"I did not call thee; lie down again." The third time Eli saw that this call was the voice of God to the child, and, therefore, instructed Samuel to answer, "Speak, Lord, for thy servant heareth." The Lord *did* speak:—"Behold, I will do a thing at which both the ears of every one that heareth it shall tingle." I am about to fulfill against Eli all I have said concerning his house, "beginning and finishing." I have told him that I will judge his house forever for the iniquity of which he was cognizant—that when his sons were bringing a curse upon themselves, he restrained them not. The translation "made themselves vile" (v. 13), comes short of the full sense of the Hebrew, which means, not merely that they were bringing dishonor upon themselves, but *curses*. They were drawing down upon their guilty heads the very thunderbolts of heaven. Their father should have known this; yet he "restrained them not." The fatal mistake of this too indulgent father was that his methods of discipline lacked adaptation—were far behind and below the point of depravity which the sons had reached; had a tone of very tender and gentle expostulation, "Why do ye so?" which might have been well for young sinners of quick and vigorous conscience, but never for old and hardened offenders. Their case demanded of him the most stern and vigorous punishment; such restraint as they could not but feel. Because the father's hand failed to restrain them, God took their case into his own hand, and not only launched those curses upon the sons, but doomed the posterity of Eli to virtual exclusion from the priesthood. "I have sworn to the house of Eli, that the iniquity of Eli's house shall not be purged with sacrifice nor offering forever."

The secret is now in the bosom of Samuel; shall he divulge it to Eli? It is one of the sore trials of the prophet's mission; "he feared to show Eli the vision." But Eli would know. Consciously guilty, his conscience was more than half a prophet of doom. He adjured Samuel most solemnly to tell him every word—and he did. Here a shade of light falls on this picture, otherwise all dark;—Eli's answer breathes submission to the terrible decision of Jehovah. "It is the Lord; let him do what seemeth to him good."

The word of the Lord has now gone forth; events hasten, therefore, to their fearful consummation. The Philistines came forth in strength for battle. Israel was smitten; four thousand men fell on the field. The elders of Israel ask, Wherefore is this? What shall we do? They remember how the presence of the ark of God rolled back the waters of Jordan and brought down the walls of Jericho; so they said, The ark shall go forth with us to the battle. God will surely appear to defend his own ark of the covenant, and to give us victory. So they sent to Shiloh and brought forth the ark. With it came the two sons of Eli. The feeling of the army was shown when the ark came into the camp: "All Israel shouted with a great shout so that the earth rang again." Now they were sure of victory.——The Philistines heard the shouting, and learned with no little solicitude that the ark of the Lord had been brought into the camp of Israel. Ah, they had heard of the wonders wrought by the God of Israel in Egypt and in the wilderness:—but the second thought was that of resolute courage and a more desperate conflict. "Quit you like men, and fight." They did fight; and Israel was terribly smitten; thirty thousand footmen fell; the ark of God was taken, and, as the Lord had said, Hophni and Phinehas were both slain in one day. A man of Benjamin ran the same day to Shiloh with the tidings. Eli, ninety-eight years of age, was sitting on a seat by the wayside watching, "for his heart trembled for the ark of God." At the tidings the men of the city sent up their wail of woe, which Eli heard, and anxiously inquired—"What meaneth the noise of this tumult?" The messenger rehearsed the sad tale, one

MORAL LESSONS IN THESE EVENTS.

calamity after another: Israel fled; a great slaughter of the people; thy two sons dead; *the ark of God taken!* The old man bore it all till the last words—the ark taken, and then fell backward from his seat, and heavy as he was, his neck brake and he died. The wife of Phinehas was near the point of child-birth; the tidings brought upon her the pains of travail; she lived to name her new-born child *Ichabod*—Where is the glory? and then gave up her life, for she said: "The glory is departed from Israel, because the ark of God was taken," and her father and her husband were with the dead.——Thus the judgments on Eli's house began on that fearful day and hastened toward their consummation.

The events of this fourth chapter have moral bearings in two directions, viz., (1) As illustrating the judgments of God in time on great sinners; and (2) As showing the utter worthlessness of the mere forms and externals of religion to shield sinners from God's retributions. 1. Here was a case of flagrant wickedness. The head and front of the offense was in the priesthood. But the people were largely implicated. Such sacrilege and such abominations of lust in the very house of God could not go on year after year without involving fearful guilt on the part of the people at large. Not the priesthood only, but the very nation had made itself loathsome before God; and, consequently, terrible judgments from the Lord must needs witness to his hatred of sin and to his justice in its punishment; and were moreover demanded as the last hopeful means for the moral reformation of so many as were not yet hopelessly hardened. Hence came this one day of accumulated horrors. A lost battle; Israel panic-smitten and fleeing; 30,000 of her dead strown on the field of battle; the two sons of Eli, acting priests, slain in one day; the ark of God in the hands of uncircumcised Philistines; the aged Eli and the wife of Phinehas dead—the dying mother giving the key-note to the sad wail of that day: "The glory is departed from Israel!" Thus it behooved the God of Israel to testify that he is of purer eye than to behold iniquity; that he can never wink at such flagrant abominations, and, least of all, in those who minister at his altar.

2. The last remark suggests the second great moral les-

son of these events; viz., the utter worthlessness of the mere forms and externals of religion to shield sinners from God's retributions. There can never be a finer opportunity than this to test the value of the mere forms and rituals of religion as means of saving a sinning people from the deserved judgments of God. If any ritualities, or sacraments, or religious symbols ever carried with them the divine presence, this ark of the covenant did so, for it was God's resting-place and visible abode. If the mere presence of any thing sacred to God can save men *in their sins* and despite of their sins, men might surely expect that the ark of God's covenant would carry victory with it, and that God would not allow his name to " go to protest " before idolaters. If there be any saving power in the mere ritualities and sacraments of our holy religion, here was a splendid opportunity to test and display it. Let it be supposed that God had made his ark the talisman of victory on this eventful day; that he had said—" I can not afford to dishonor my name before the uncircumcised hosts of Philistia when the very ark of my presence is borne to the fight by my priests in their holy garments. Bad as my people are, I must have respect to these symbols of my presence, and shield my professed worshipers." Had the Lord said this, the genius of ritualism would have been baptized in glory! No event since the world began has ever borne such a testimony to its value and its power as a victory given to the sacred ark on that day would have borne. All down through the ages men would have reverted to this palpable testimony of fact as proof that God does spare and bless even the wicked when they hide themselves beneath the wing of his cherubim, though it be done in the *outward* only; when they put the sacred ark between their guilty souls and the arrows of God's retributive justice. Oh, how would men, conscious of damning sin upon their souls, have hastened to the holy sacraments of the altar and sought to hide under sacred vestments and the hallowed emblems of God's presence! How would souls quivering on the verge of hell have cried out for the priests of God that they might but touch the hem of their garments, receive the holy water from their sacred hands, and take the symbols of Christ's death to their dying lips with the refreshing assurance that God will honor such symbols of his love as these, and *for their sake* blot out human guilt and save a dying sinner from perdition!——But alas! such a testimony to the power of the mere forms of religion has never yet been given from heaven! The events of this chapter stand solid against all such vain hopes.

The Ark in Captivity.

The thread of the history (1 Sam. 5 and 6) follows the ark to the land and the cities of the Philistines. First, they of Ashdod have it in charge. Whether as being the only appropriate place for it they could think of, or for insult to the conquered symbol of Israel's humbled God, "they brought it into the temple of their Dagon and set it by Dagon." This Dagon (it is well that we remind ourselves) was a fish-god, with human head, breast, and arms, and all the rest *fishy; i. e.*, the lower half of the trunk, and the lower limbs were supplied from the headless fish. Whether in their science of idols, this fish idea were in honor of their fisheries as a source of their wealth, or a symbol of fecundity, has been disputed, and we may afford to let it remain disputed, for all science of idolatry is only human folly. ——In the present case, the ark of God and this Dagon were brought face to face to spend the night together. When they of Ashdod arose early in the morning and hastened to their temple, lo, Dagon had fallen upon his face to the earth before the ark of Jehovah. Most significant!——"They took Dagon and set him in his place." Perhaps they were not quite sure of the significance of this fall; so they put up their god to another "round" (as the pugilists would say)—one more trial in combat. When they arose early the next morning, behold, Dagon was not only fallen on his face to the ground before the ark, but his head and both palms of his hands were cut off upon the threshold; only the fishy part remained to him. By one of the curious and unaccountable freaks of superstition, the priests and worshipers of Dagon commemorated this significant and to them disgraceful fall and dismemberment of their god by never stepping on the threshold of their temple. The writer remarks that this usage was in force to his day.

Not the god Dagon only, but the men of Ashdod were smitten sorely. The record is: "The hand of the Lord was heavy upon them of Ashdod, and he destroyed them and smote them with emerods." This scourge was so severe that they said, We can not have this ark of God among us. So they called a council of Philistine lords, and it was agreed to try it in Gath. "They carried the ark to Gath, and there the hand of the Lord was against the city with a very great destruction, and he smote the men of the city, both small and great, and they had emerods in their secret parts."——There seems to have been some form of pestilence fatal to life, expressed under the word "destruction;" and also another great affliction, under the name "emerods." This name is unfortunately blind to many English readers because the word is mostly obsolete, being a corruption of the medical term "hemorrhoids"—the painful disease currently known as "the *piles*."

The cities of the Philistines were by this time thoroughly alarmed. Not one would consent to have the ark in its keeping. Another council was summoned; the priests and diviners were called in, and it was concluded to send the ark back to Israel, not empty (said these diviners), but with a trespass-offering. Remarkably this trespass-offering is described as "five golden emerods and five golden mice"—the number of each corresponding to the five principalities of Philistia, for the one plague was common to them all. Moreover, it is clear that these golden emerods and mice were representations *in form* of the plagues under which they suffered so terribly, and that their purpose was to "give glory to the God of Israel"—a very explicit acknowledgment of his supremacy, and of their own defeat and suffering before him. By these tokens of their suffering they said, to their own shame—"We can not stand before these manifestations of Jehovah's presence and power." Urging the adoption of this method of joint confession and restitution, they said—"Wherefore, then, do ye harden your heart as the Egyptians and Pharaoh hardened their heart? When he had wrought wonderfully among them, did they not let the people go, and they departed?" Be not ye stiffnecked, after that ancient and fatal example of Egypt and her king; but yield promptly, humbly, gracefully;

and acknowledge that ye can in no wise stand before Jehovah and his fiery judgments!

As if to make it more sure whether these judgments were fortuitous, or came from the hand of Israel's God, they said — Make a new cart; harness to it two young heifers with young calves, never in yoke before; shut up the calves at home; then start them. If they take the way to Israel's cities, and go on despite of their instincts toward their young confined at home, then may ye know that God is with his ark, and that these sore afflictions are from his hand. —— The experiment was decisive. The young cows moved off by the route to Israel, lowing for their calves as they went, and halted not till they brought up at Bethshemesh, a city of Israel. Thus ended these scenes of seven months' captivity of the ark among the Philistines.

It will readily recur to every reader that the fortunes of the ark in its captivity among the Philistines suffice to solve the problem whether God were able to take care of his own ark of the covenant without the aid of his chosen people. For the ark went forth into that captivity alone. Not a man of all its appointed guardians stood by to protect it. No cordon of armed Levites, zealous for God, often firm of hand and brave of heart for battle, remained for its body-guard. The Lord alone stood by for its defense, and the history shows with what result. Plainly the Lord labored under no lack of resources to shield his ark from insult, to scourge its Philistine enemies, and make them but too glad to send it back. These showings of Jehovah's power might, we must suppose, have been wholesome and admonitory to the men of Philistia, had their minds been in any wise open to conviction of the truth as to the God of Israel.

Samuel as Judge.

The history of Samuel as Judge of Israel is brought chiefly within 1 Sam. 7. The ark, moving back from the Philistine land by stages, tarried twenty years in Kirjath-jearim.* It is not surprising that pious hearts

* This was one of the cities of the Gibeonites, on the S. W. border of the territory of Benjamin, six or seven miles N. W. from Jerusalem and eight or ten N. E. from Bethshemesh. Its ancient site is now recognized in the modern Kuriet El Enab, determined satisfactorily by Dr. Robinson.

in Israel mourned its absence, nor that those who valued it only as embodying the ritualities and forms of their worship should feel unrestful. It is said, "All the house of Israel lamented after the Lord" (7: 2). At this point Samuel comes to view. With the pertinence of blended good sense and piety, he said to all Israel, "If ye do return unto the Lord with all your hearts, then put away the strange gods and Ashtaroth from among you, and prepare your hearts unto the Lord, and serve him only; and he will deliver you out of the hand of the Philistines" (7: 3). "Then the children of Israel did put away Baal and Ashtaroth, and served the Lord only." It was the moment to strike for a national reformation, and Samuel was too wise to let it slip. So he issued his proclamation: "Gather all Israel to Mizpeh and I will pray for you unto the Lord." They came; "they drew water and poured it out before the Lord (perhaps in symbol of broken hearts and flowing tears); and they fasted on that day, and said there, We have sinned against Jehovah." After this penitential scene, it is said that "Samuel judged the children of Israel in Mizpeh."——The Philistines heard of this great convocation of Israel, and probably suspecting that it contemplated some general uprising against themselves, they came up for battle. The Israelites feared to face them, and therefore cried unto Samuel: "Cease not to pray to the Lord our God for us, that he will save us out of the hand of the Philistines." Samuel took a sucking lamb for a whole burnt-offering and cried to the Lord for Israel. The Lord heard. While the sacrifice was still in progress the Philistines drew near, and the Lord thundered with a great thunder that day upon the Philistines and discomfited them, and they were smitten before Israel. The men of Israel took heart, rallied, and smote their enemy until they came under Beth-car. Samuel set up a memorial stone and called it "Eben-ezer"—stone of help, saying—"Hitherto hath the Lord helped us." The precious associations of that memorial stone still abide with God's people. The experiences of this eventful day must have been exceedingly wholesome, religiously as well as politically. They brought before the nation a present and most precious testimony that God hears prayer, and that piety toward God was the salvation of their country. How plainly they must have seen that if penitent toward God, they might depend upon his being on their side as toward their enemies, and that the prayers of even one good man might bring the agencies of heaven to their help and paralyze the power of even Philistia's hosts. These were indeed momentous lessons.

The events of that day turned the tide of political prestige and power against Philistia for at least the remaining years of Samuel's administration. The cities which they had taken from Israel were recovered, and Israel had rest from their hostilities. Samuel then judged Israel peacefully, administering justice by a circuit court arrangement, in which his seats of justice were Bethel, Gilgal, Mizpeh, and Ramah—his family residence being at the last-named place. "There he built an altar unto the Lord."——Samuel had no successor in this one respect—filling at once the functions of prophet and of Judge.

A man of rare qualities, of heart ever true to God and to the work for which God raised him up, his name was a tower of strength to Israel, and his life an era in her history. By him the Lord interposed to stem the current of religious and political declension which seems to have been setting in with accumulating force, during at least the latter part of the period of the Judges. From the scanty records that have come down to us it seems manifest that Samuel rose quite above any of the Judges that intervened between himself and Joshua, in the steadfast earnestness of his piety; in his prominent influence upon the religious life of the nation, and especially in those functions which pertained to the prophetic office. His name is naturally identified with the rise of the prophetic order—a new power which the Lord inaugurated in his person for the religious instruction of his people.

The Order of Prophets.

It is in place here to consider an event of very grave importance in the religious history of God's people, viz., *the rise and development of the order of prophets.*

It is conceded that this order properly began with Samuel. Let us consider briefly the following points:

1. *The meaning of the term prophet, and the functions of the office.* Our English word denotes primarily one who foretells future events. The most common Hebrew term (nabi) has a broader signification, viz., one who speaks for God, who is in communication with God, and who receives from him and bears to men his messages. These messages might or might not bring revelations of future events. It was after God had called to Samuel in his sleep and revealed to him the doom of Eli and his house, and after the declaration— "The Lord was with him and did let none of his words fall to the ground," that we read: "All Israel from Dan to Beersheba knew that Samuel was established to be a prophet of the Lord" (1 Sam. 3: 19, 20).——Important to the sense of this term "prophet" are Ex. 7: 1, and 4: 16: "I have made thee (Moses) a god to Pharaoh; and Aaron thy brother shall be *thy prophet*"—elsewhere expressed—"thy mouth ('spokesman') unto the people." Thus the prophet spake in God's behalf to the people, or as the case might be, to their king.——Note also that during the age of Samuel, the customary designation was changed from "seer" to "prophet" (1 Sam. 9: 9). The precise shade of difference between these terms is not clearly indicated. Perhaps the name "seer" (which English word very correctly translates the Hebrew) might imply that his chief function was to *foresee;* and that during Samuel's age the broader sense above referred to became more prevalent.

A very common designation of the prophet is "man of God," as may be seen 1 Sam. 2: 27, and 9: 6, 7, 8, 10, and 1 Kings 12: 22, and 13: 1, 5, 6, 11.

Of the functions of their office—their professional work—we may say, comprehensively, it was *moral instruction*, especially as sent directly from God to men. Their peculiar work was quite distinct from that of the priest who had special charge of the rites of worship—indeed, of the entire system of religious service as prescribed through Moses. Over against this, the prophets dealt with simple truth. They were teachers raised up of God. They gave religious counsel and sympathy to God's people in their domestic life, as we may infer from Elisha's relations to the woman of Shunem (2 Kings 4: 8–37). They gave moral support and special counsel to good kings. Gad

THE ORDER OF PROPHETS.

is twice spoken of as "David's seer" (2 Sam. 24: 11), by whom the Lord spake in the matter of numbering the people and the ensuing pestilence; also in 2 Chron. 29: 25, on the subject of sacred psalmody. Nathan appears as his reprover for his one great sin (2 Sam. 12). Isaiah was a bosom friend of Hezekiah (Isa. 37: 21, and 38: 1–8); Jeremiah, of Josiah (2 Chron. 35: 25).——To wicked kings they bore God's messages of rebuke and warning, of which we have examples in Elijah and Ahab (1 Kings 17: 1, and 18: 17, 18); in Micaiah as toward Ahab and Jehoshaphat (1 Kings 22: 7–28); in Ahijah and Jeroboam (1 Kings 14). The desolation that came over the heart of King Saul when he found no answer from the Lord, either by dreams, by the Urim, or through God's prophets, avails to show that the prophets were a recognized medium of communication from God to man, and we may perhaps say, especially to the kings of Israel. In their theocratic relations to God they must have often felt the need of such a medium between themselves and the nation's Supreme King.

They were annalists of the nation, writing out more or less fully the history of the kings, both of Judah and of Israel. The names of not less than eight* appear as having performed this service. See cases in 1 Chron. 29: 29, 30, where as historians of David we have the names of Samuel the seer, Nathan the prophet, and Gad the seer: also 2 Chron. 9: 29, where the biographers of Solomon are named—Nathan, Ahijah, and Iddo, all prophets.

It scarcely need be said that in later times they not only proclaimed their messages more or less in public, but committed them to writing, and thus left to all future ages those sacred and priceless messages sent of God to men through their tongue and pen.

Nor let us omit to note their useful and prominent labors upon the psalmody of Israel. In this service David himself appears as a prophet. With him and after him arose an indefinite number who contributed religious songs for the service of worship in the great congregation. To this order of Hebrew prophets, therefore, is the world indebted for the *written word of*

* Viz., Samuel, Nathan, Gad, Ahijah, Iddo, Shemaiah, Jehu the son of Hanani, and Isaiah.

God as we have it in nearly the entire Old Testament. Moses, one of the most eminent of prophets, lived before the order of prophets took definite form; of Job and of the books of Solomon, it is not in place here to speak particularly. The other books come clearly under the statement as above made.

2. *The requisite training—Schools of the prophets.* Such services demanded special qualifications, both natural and acquired. Nothing can be more obvious than the necessity of a special training for the proper performance of their varied and exceedingly responsible duties. Therefore, we naturally look for some traces of this special culture and training; and we find them from Samuel and onward. The earliest appear in the life of Samuel; the most full and decisive, in the history of Elijah and Elisha. The important passages are 1 Sam. 10: 5-13, and 19: 20-24, and 1 Kings 18: 4, and 20: 35, and 2 Kings 2: 3-7, 15-18, and 4: 38-44, and 5: 22, and 6: 1-7, and 9: 1-16.

In these passages from 1 Samuel his history brings to view a considerable number of young prophet-pupils, called "a company" (1 Sam. 10: 10), but the sense of this Hebrew word is rather that of *band*, a body of men closely affiliated. In 1 Sam. 19: 20, another Hebrew word for company occurs, found here only, but by general consent of critics meaning a troop or affiliated body of man.——Noticeably it is said that "Samuel stood as appointed over them," their recognized head and leader, that is to say, their professor, their prophet-father.

Two other points come to view in this second passage from Samuel respecting this group of prophet-pupils and their religious father. One relates to the word "Naioth," taken by our English translators as the name of a place. But the current of recent opinion sets strongly toward the sense—the college buildings in Ramah—the group of dwellings in Ramah. (See Fuerst's Lexicon, and the Speaker's Commentary.) The reader may notice that four times in close succession we have in our English version, "Naioth in Ramah," while in v. 18, it is equally plain that Naioth and Ramah can not be different cities, but the one must somehow be included *in* the other. The Hebrew word "naioth" means habitations, dwellings—a noun in the

SCHOOLS OF THE PROPHETS.

feminine plural. No traces of a place bearing this geographical name have ever come to light. We have, therefore, a reasonable certainty that the word here means the buildings fitted up for Samuel's college of prophet-pupils. That these schools of the prophets had special buildings for their accommodation is not only inferrible from the necessities of the case, but is touchingly indicated (2 Kings 6: 1–7) where we read that "the sons of the prophets" came to Elisha to say that their accommodations for students' rooms were too strait, and proposing to go to Jordan and its timbered bottoms, and take thence every man his beam [pole], and fit up more such humble accommodations for their shelter. He said, "go;" but they quietly suggest that he go with them; and like a true and faithful father-prophet, he went. It was fortunate that he did; for so he was on hand to bring the iron ax-head to the surface when by accident it had sprung from its helve and fallen into the Jordan. The cry—"Alas, master, for it was begged"—brought Elisha's miracle-working power at once to their aid. They were too poor to buy their axes. This man had to beg his—ask it as the Hebrew signifies—yet never in the sense of borrow. It is the word used in the history (Ex. 3: 22, and 11: 2) of the Israelites *asking* jewels and goods of the Egyptians—which was by no means "borrowing." All in all, this is a very pleasant inside view of college life in those ancient schools of the prophets—antedating by a few thousand years the experiences of some prophet-schools of our age which have struggled upward from the humblest beginnings amid many privations, and not a little morally wholesome manual toil, and occasionally some cheering tokens of a helping power from above. ——We will, therefore, recognize in our English version—"Naioth in Ramah"—really the *college dwellings in Ramah*—as the earliest scriptural notice of the existence of a Theological College.

3. *Music and the spirit of prophesying.* While yet these two passages from 1 Samuel (that of chap. 10 and this from chap. 19) are before us, let another incident be noted. We first see a company of prophets coming down from the "high place" (10: 5, 6) where probably they had been engaged in worship. Moving to the music of psaltery, tabret, pipe and harp, the prophetic

afflatus falls upon them; they prophesy; and the scene becomes so inspiring, the sympathies of men so moved go forth with such power upon other souls, that even Saul catches the inspiration and he prophesies! More extraordinary still is the second narrative (chap. 19: 18–24), for here Saul, like his namesake in the gospel history, comes "breathing out threatening and slaughter" against the youthful and innocent David. First, his "messengers," his armed "posse"—the king's royal executioners—men doubtless of iron nerve and of fearless brute courage—come within the range of this prophetic afflatus. We read—"When they saw the company of prophets prophesying and Samuel standing as appointed over them, the Spirit of God was upon the messengers, and they also prophesied." This is reported to Saul, and, with mingled astonishment and mortification, he resolves to try again, and therefore sends other messengers the second and the third time—with only the same result. Then what can he do but go himself? He goes, and lo, even Saul also prophesies!——Now, were these results purely miraculous, and quite independent of known psychological law? Or was there blended with this prophetic afflatus a joint operation of the power of music and of the law of mutual sympathy by which mind acts powerfully upon mind? To admit some power of the latter sort by no means precludes the divine hand. God's Spirit (then as now and ever) may have worked in harmony with the laws of mind—since God constructed the human mind to be moved by his own manifested presence and revealed truth in connection with music and the law of sympathy. It is clear that a very close relation existed between music, especially instrumental music, and that mental and spiritual exaltation, coupled with earnest, impassioned utterances which are expressed by the word "prophesy." It would seem that the utterances made under this spirit of prophecy might or might not be predictions of future events. In some cases they were, and in other cases apparently were not. The remarkable relation of music to this prophetic state is strongly suggested in the passage from Samuel which we have been considering. It was while they were coming down from the high place with the music of instruments that the young prophets prophesied and that Saul caught the inspiration. The same connection appears in strong light in 1 Chron. 25: 1-3, 6, in which the sons of Asaph, Heman, and Jeduthun are said " to prophesy with harps, with psalteries, and with cymbals;" "who prophesied according to the order of the king;" "who prophesied with a harp, to give thanks and to praise the Lord:" "all these were under the hands of their father for song in the house of the Lord with cymbals, psalteries, and harps for the service of the house of God," etc. This stated service of song for thanksgiving and praise was expressed by the term " prophesy."——For yet another illustration of the presence of music in the loftiest songs of praise, see the exercises when David brought the ark into his royal city (1 Chron. 13: 8, and 2 Sam. 6: 5): "David and all Israel played before God with all their might, and with singing, and with harps, and with psalteries " etc.

4. The *localities* of these schools of the prophets.— In the history of Samuel we find them at Gibeah and at Ramah; Gibeah, the home of Saul, and Ramah, of Samuel. The mention of Gibeah in the English version is obscured by translating it as a common, not a proper noun—once (1 Sam. 10. 5) "the hill of God," instead of Gibeah of God—the name of God being attached probably on account of its being consecrated as a place of worship; and in another case (v. 10) simply "the hill" instead of Gibeah. That this place was Saul's city appears from v. 11.——To the school (college) in Ramah we have seen references in 1 Sam. 19: 18-24.

Under Elisha we find these schools at Gilgal (2 Kings 2: 1, and 4: 38-44); at Bethel (2 Kings 2: 3); at Jericho (2 Kings 2: 5, 15, 16); and perhaps on Mt. Ephraim, since Gehazi (2 Kings 5: 22) said (truly or otherwise) that two young men, sons of the prophets, had come to him from that place.

5. *Number of students.*—We read of one hundred at Gilgal (2 Kings 4: 43); of fifty at Jericho in the account of the ascension of Elijah (2 Kings 2: 16). During the reign of Ahab, Obadiah shielded from the vengeance of Jezebel one hundred prophets in two companies of fifty each, feeding them with bread and water in a cave. It is merely probable (not certain) that these men were taken in a body, and, therefore,

may have been residing together in their prophet-college. So many God providentially rescued from Jezebel for future service.

6. The question naturally arises, *How were these schools of the prophets supported?* Their prophet-fathers—how did they get their bread, and shelter, and clothing? And the young men; how were they fed (the first necessity), and how sheltered and clad?

In the outset we may dismiss all thought of palatial buildings, amply endowed professorships, and charity funds for the support of students. [I make this remark with not the least purpose of disparaging the more costly appliances of modern times for similar services.] There is no hint that the wealth which came into David's hands from the spoiling of his vanquished enemies, or the yet more abundant riches of Solomon, went into this channel of benevolence. The temple and the vastly expensive ritualities of the Mosaic worship drew from these sources largely; but we read of no buildings, endowments, or other charitable aid for the schools of the prophets, coming from the treasures of either David or Solomon. Less expended on the temple and its sacrifices, and more upon these ministries that bore more directly upon the truly religious life, would certainly seem to us a wiser distribution. But it pleased God, so far as we may judge from his direction, whether through his providences or through his prophets, to expend immensely upon the former, and very sparingly, if at all, upon the latter. It may fitly be considered, however, that the reigns of David and Solomon were the golden age of the Mosaic system; and, therefore, this system naturally attracted most of the religious thought and effort of the times. The schools of the prophets are not even noticed during those otherwise memorable reigns.

Returning to our theme, the few notices we find (*e. g.*) in the history of Elisha, touching the questions of finance, subsistence, and the comforts of life generally, betoken poverty of resources, an average straitness, with occasionally pinching want, sometimes relieved by miracle. It may be questionable how far we are authorized to draw general conclusions from special cases of distress in a country subject like theirs to dearth and consequent famine. These cases, however,

SCHOOLS OF THE PROPHETS.

(such as that in 2 Kings 4: 38-44) show that they had no invested funds to fall back upon—no fixed sources of supply, good for bridging over a season of dearth. The temporary relief brought by the man from Baal-shalisha—some "bread of the first-fruits; twenty loaves of barley," etc.—suggest how these schools were sometimes relieved from pinching want; albeit even this seemed very insignificant to set before one hundred very hungry men. But Elisha's miracle-working power had been drawn upon before to augment little into much; and it availed here.

We have already seen (in 2 Kings 6: 1-7) that the "rooms" at one of these colleges (probably the one at Jericho, that being near the Jordan) were very limited, and that the young men took axes—one of them had to *beg* his—and went to the Jordan valley for poles to put up what must have been at best a very rude structure to live in. We have also a very touching case of want brought to the knowledge of Elisha by the widow of one of these students. She cried out to him: "Thy servant, my husband, is dead; and thou knowest that thy servant did fear the Lord; and the creditor is come to take unto him my two sons to be bondmen" (2 Kings 4: 1-6).——Here was a prophet-student with a young family. It is not said that hardships hastened his death—but he died—died young, and leaving his estate in debt. The last resort for the collection of debts in those days—a terribly cruel and heartless one —was to take the debtor, or his wife, or his children, for slaves. The widowed mother's heart felt the bitterness of this affliction. Very properly she brought her case before Elisha. Her provision-stores were reduced to one pot of oil—manifestly a small one; but according to the promise of Elisha, and under the miraculous hand of God, the oil-can kept pouring out oil till all the vessels she had faith to borrow were full, and then stayed. So she paid her debts, kept her sons, and lived—gratefully, we must think—on the rest.——Let us note also that this was a *home* scene, adapted for the best home influences. "When thou art come in, thou shalt shut the door upon thyself and thy sons, and shalt pour out into all those vessels," etc.—none present save thyself, thy sons—*and God;* and the door shut. Eyes that are mainly curious, and tongues that are only chatty, might well be spared. God would have those dear boys remember that flowing oil to the end of their days. Let us hope that they did, and also the great and kind giver!——The life-history of Elisha is remarkably filled with supernatural incidents. Plainly a double portion of the spirit of Elijah did rest on him, as was promised (2 Kings 2: 9, 10).

7. The question naturally arises: From *what class* in the community were these prophet-students drawn? And by *what influences*, and by *whose agency*, were they brought into these training schools?

On the point first named we have no general statements—nothing beyond a few special cases. Elisha was called from the plow (1 Kings 19: 19–21), and from a field where twelve yokes of oxen were plowing—implying a farmer of some means. Amos (7: 14, 15) speaks of having been "a herdsman," "a gatherer of sycamore fruit," and also a "shepherd," up to the time when the Lord called him to go and prophesy unto his people Israel. Jeremiah was descended from the priests in Anathoth, and seems to have been (as the phrase is) "respectably connected" with some of the first and best families of Judah, and apparently on intimate terms with Josiah the king. [See introduction to my commentary on Jeremiah, pp. 9, 10.] Ezekiel, too, was in his family line a priest (Ezek. 1: 3). Isaiah, whatever his parentage, became a special friend and counselor of the good Hezekiah.——Beyond these few special cases I am not aware that any thing certain can be known.

On the question — How and by what agencies were these young men brought into these schools — the record is not by any means full; yet there are some facts bearing on the point. Samuel's case is given in ample detail. The voice of the Lord fell on his ear — the inner rather than the outer ear probably — for no one other than himself seems to have heard it. Elijah called Elisha (as we have seen), yet plainly God's voice also was felt to be in the call. Elijah's agency was quite like that of his Lord, long after, in calling the two sons of Zebedee and Matthew the publican. Several of the prophets who have left us their writings have left in them some allusion to their special call to the prophetic work, *e. g.*, Isaiah, Jeremiah, Amos, Jonah.——

The numerous cases in which God assigned to these prophets some special service by means of a special call, strongly support the opinion that we must allow a large place to the immediate call of God impressed upon their souls, to bring them into these schools of the prophets, and to prepare them thus for any future work the Lord might have for them to do. Yet this view of the case will not rule out the personal agency of Samuel and of Elisha in drawing young men under their instruction. They may have been guided of the Lord specially in their selection, or they may have made large use of their own judgment and knowledge of men. Any prophet-father (in that age or in this) who walks with God, and seeks divine guidance in a matter of such responsibility, need not fear that God will withhold it. This is one department of that wisdom which if a man consciously lacks, let him ask of God who "gives liberally, upbraiding not" (James 1:5).

8. If the further question be raised as to their college duties, their course of study, text-books, methods of study and training — it is easy to say that the Hebrew scriptures, so far as then extant, must have been chiefly their text-books. Fortunately for us, the writings of the prophets evince such familiarity with the previously written scriptures as can leave no doubt on this point. —— As has been already suggested, some place must be assigned for culture in music and for exercises in sacred song. Skill in music never comes without culture and somewhat extended practice, of which in their case we have some testimony on record (*e. g.*, 1 Chron. 25:7); "The number of them" [the families of Asaph, Heman, and Jeduthun] "with their brethren that were *instructed* in the songs of the Lord, even all that were cunning" [skilled], "was two hundred and eighty-eight." Out of these families arose several men whose culture and training, of the sort given in the schools of the prophets, were such that they became authors of a considerable number of the Psalms that have come down to us in the Psalter.

Moreover, the fathers who presided in these schools were men of large experience in the prophetic life. Samuel's history is full of instructive and thrilling events. So was that of Elisha. God was near to those holy men, often manifesting his special presence and his miraculous gifts. From time to time some special service would devolve by the call of God upon some of these sons of the prophets—a case in point appearing in 2 Kings 9, where Elisha sent one of them to anoint Jehu.

The fact that some of them became the annalists and historians of the nation involves the study of their nation's past history to some extent, and certainly a careful study of recent and present history. Those who became writers of prophetical books most obviously must have had some training and culture preparatory to this work of authorship, not only to gain the manual skill of writing (chirography), but practice in composition, and the power to express thought and to relate facts with clearness, beauty, and force. Such qualities they certainly had; and their possession, then as now, presupposes culture and training.

How long their course of study and training was we have no data whatever for deciding beyond what we know of the average time requisite in all ages to acquire such an education as those prophets manifestly had. ——It is not unreasonable to suppose that every man graduated when God called him away into some field of active service.

The circumstances in the age of Elijah and Elisha which manifestly called for and developed a very large increase in the number of these schools and of their pupils, we shall study to better advantage when the history of those times shall come fully before us. We now return to the age of Samuel to resume at that point the thread of Hebrew history.

CHAPTER VI.

Saul and the rise of the Monarchy.

Old age had come upon Samuel; his two sons, promoted to civil responsibilities, had not borne their honors nor their responsibilities well. It is said of them briefly that they "did not walk in the ways of their father," but "took bribes and perverted judgment." The people were dissatisfied, and not unnaturally thought that any change would be improvement. The elders, acting as usual for the whole people, came together and said to Samuel, "Now make us a king to judge us, that we may be like all the nations" (8 : 5). Subsequently they gave their reasons more in full (vs. 19, 20) ; "That our king may go out before us and fight our battles."—— Other nations on every side—the Philistines, the Hittites, Syria, Ammon, Moab, and Edom—seemed to them prosperous and strong under their kings. So, overlooking the fact that the Lord was their King, or, at least, making far too little account of it, they thought to rival their neighbors to better purpose if they too had a king. It is not altogether strange that the experience of several hundred years under the judges and without any judge should have made this political reasoning seem to them plausible. Their mistake had its roots in their leaving God out of the account and in overlooking their peculiar relations to him as their Sovereign, Redeemer, and Father.

Samuel was not pleased with their request, and therefore turned to the Lord in prayer. The Lord also was displeased with the *spirit* of the people. Their motives were by no means grateful to his mind; yet, apparently, he was not averse to this proposed change in the form of the national government. There were some good reasons for the change. The tribes of Israel, whether considered politically or religiously, needed more consolidation. Their national experience, from Joshua to Samuel, bore this testimony. In the midst of so many powerful enemies, the most effective union would give them none too much strength. And it had become manifest that the Mosaic religious system needed for its best results a great national capital which might become the religious as well as the political center of the whole people. As already suggested, the experience of several hundred years, since Joshua, had been impressing this lesson (we must presume) on the sagacious minds among the elders of Israel. Yet, according to the record, the more worldly consideration of being like the nations round about them lay in the foreground of their thought and of their petition.

It is well to notice the sagacity (whether in its origin human or divine) with which Samuel first met their request. Ye ask (he said to the people) for a king? But have ye well considered what a king would cost you? Royalty is an expensive luxury. Your king must have his court, his retinue of servants, a costly table, and the most sumptuous surroundings. Have ye duly considered that more government implies less personal liberty for the individual?—— So Samuel told them how the king would take for his use their noblest sons and fairest daughters; their best fields and most desirable possessions — until they would cry out under his extortions and find no response from the Lord to their cry. Yet still they persisted in their demand for a king; and the Lord yielded.

In chap. 9 : 17, the word chosen for the sense of *reign* over this people has normally the meaning *restrain*—a thought which the Lord takes pains to impress upon the people.

The manner in which Saul—the Lord's choice for their first king—was brought before Samuel appears in 1 Sam. 9; while in chap. 10 we see him brought into contact with the young prophets of Samuel's school, and ultimately before the whole people assembled at Mizpeh.

Saul—of the small tribe of Benjamin—a tribe made smaller by the fearful scenes narrated Judges 20 and 21 —was of tall, commanding person, and, as he first appears in the history, of rather prepossessing modesty. Sent from home with a single servant in pursuit of his father's lost asses, they traveled till their provisions were spent and till they came into the vicinity of Samuel's residence, "Zuph" (v. 5), which we must identify with Ramathaim-zophim, the place of Samuel's na tivity. Here, remarkably, it comes to light that Saul's servant knows more of Samuel than Saul himself—not the only case in which servants have known more of God and of godly men than their masters. The little Hebrew maid-servant in Naaman's slave-quarters helped him to a similar knowledge of Elisha, and consequently to a cure from his terrible leprosy. Saul's servant said: Just by us here in this city lives a man of God who can doubtless tell us about our asses. Saul replied: We have nothing for a present, and how can we call on him without? But the servant is equal to this emergency: a quarter shekel in his pocket will suffice. They found Samuel, and it came out that the Lord's hand had been shaping this whole movement. He had whispered it in Samuel's ear the day before that the king elect was coming, and that he must first entertain him at the religious festival then pending, and afterward in a private way anoint him king. Then in chap. 10 we read what signs Samuel gave him to assure him that this anointing was certainly from God; how well he kept his secret; how he returned to his own city Gibeah—a place mostly concealed from the English reader by the mistranslation which gives it "the hill" instead of Gibeah in both vs. 5 and 10, and only in v. 26 the true translation, "Gibeah."——Of his contact with the prophesying band of young prophets enough has been said in connection with the schools of the prophets.

Shortly the people are convened at Mizpeh, and by means of the sacred lot the tribe of Benjamin first, and ultimately Saul himself is brought out as the divinely chosen king for Israel. For himself he knew beforehand what the issue would be. Shrinking from the responsibility, or overcome by modest diffidence, he hid himself among the baggage (10: 22) brought together by the assembled thousands of Israel. It was only the all-seeing eye of God that disclosed his hiding-place. When his noble form appeared the people greeted him with the shout, then heard for the first time among the tribes—"God save the king."——Here again, and more fully than before (1 Sam. 8: 11–18), Samuel told the people "the *manner* of the kingdom," and "wrote it in a book and laid it up before the Lord" (v. 25). "The manner of the king" as explained to the people on the former occasion gave them one side of the case—the license he would take to make exactions upon them of all best things for his royal state; but here "*the manner of the kingdom*" seems rather to mean the royal charter or constitution according to which he was to administer the government under Jehovah their Supreme King. Inasmuch as the Lord had anticipated this very result— the demand and necessity for a king—and had provided for it in the civil code given through Moses (see Deut. 17 : 14–20), it can scarcely be doubted that this chapter of restrictions and regulations was precisely the royal charter which Samuel rehearsed on this occasion to the people and wrote it in *the* book (so the Hebrew), and placed it in the national archives. Among other things it provided that the king should have a copy of "this law" for his special use, that he might consult it daily in person and guide his administration by it through all his life.

After this ratification the people dispersed to their homes, a few only whose hearts the Lord had touched going with their new king to his home. The bad men (sons of Belial) stood aloof and withheld both their confidence and their gifts. The historian suggests that Saul took this very quietly—as said in our version, "he held his peace" (in Hebrew), acted as one deaf, who heard not their derisive words. It was wise in him to leave the issue with the Lord.

In form the people now have a king; yet there was need of other influences to place him high in public confidence and to give him the royal state of the monarch of Israel. Events soon occurred which hastened on these results, as we see in chap. 11.

The kingdom renewed and Saul put really at the head of the nation. (1 Sam. 11.)

Ammon on the east of the Jordan was a kingdom of considerable military power. Its king, Nahash, marched upon the two and a half tribes on his side of the Jordan and laid siege to Jabesh-Gilead—a city which, as appears in Judges 21, for some reason sustained intimate relations with Gibeah of Benjamin the home of Saul.* The forces of Nahash seemed to the men of

* How these intimate relations commenced does not appear. The men of Jabesh did not—probably *would* not—join in the war of the

Jabesh resistless. They, therefore, proposed a treaty under which they expected only some relation of servitude. The terms made by Nahash were that he should "thrust out [in Hebrew *bore* out] every man's right eye, and lay it for a reproach upon all Israel." This was not only mercilessly cruel but purposely disgraceful. Ammon retained for ages this pre-eminent character of barbarous cruelty—as we may see in Amos 1: 13–15, where God annihilated the nation at last because of their heartless violation of the dictates of common humanity.——The men of Jabesh were in deep trouble. They asked seven days, ostensibly for consideration—really for an effort to secure help from their brethren across the Jordan. Their messengers came naturally (providentially too) to Gibeah, not it would seem because king Saul was there, for "they told their tidings in the ears of all the people," and Saul seems to have heard the story casually (as any other man of Gibeah might) when he came in from after his herd in the field. But the tidings fired up his soul; "the spirit of the Lord came upon him;" he hewed his yoke of oxen into pieces and sent them by the hand of his own messengers over all Israel, summoning the men of war to his army headquarters in Bezek.

The method of this summons followed somewhat the one adopted in the scenes narrated Judges 19: 29, 30. The fear of the Lord fell on the people, and 330,000 men rushed to the rendezvous ready for war. In the result the army of Nahash was thoroughly routed—indeed so utterly that no two men were left together. Jabesh-Gilead was saved; and, not least, Saul was brought before the people as their hero, their king, owned of God, and competent to lead their armies on to glorious victory. It was the moment for renewing the kingdom to Saul; so Samuel leads the whole army to Gilgal where they performed the services of a solemn inauguration; sacrificed their peace-offerings before the Lord and rejoiced with great joy. Saul was now king of Israel indeed, with all the prestige for a successful reign that any monarch could desire.

tribes upon Benjamin. Consequently they suffered under a like fearful devastation of judgment (Judges 21: 10, 11), and in the result 400 of their virgin daughters became mothers of the future Benjamites—a fact which sufficiently accounts for the close relationship indicated here between Jabesh and Gibeah.

Let us note some additional particulars.——Jabesh Gilead was nearly twenty miles south of the Lake of Tiberias, and less than half that distance east of the Jordan. Bezek is supposed to have been near Beth-shean, and over against Jabesh-Gilead (the Jordan valley lying between), and distant probably fifteen or twenty miles. A rapid night march brought them near Jabesh-Gilead at the morning watch. There dividing his army into three companies, Saul seems to have surrounded and surprised his enemy.

The clemency with which Saul met the demand of the people for the slaughter of those sons of Belial who said, "Saul shall not reign," was every way admirable. We put it among the best features of Saul's character and reign.

Samuel's Last Words to the People.

In chap. 12 a moral exhortation by Samuel follows the political ratification or renewal of the kingdom to Saul—at once timely and pertinent.——In v. 2, the reason for alluding to his sons as being there with the people is not altogether apparent. Was it a hint that they had been passed by in the choice of Saul for king, or a suggestion that if the people had any more public service for them they were on hand; or if there was a demand for investigation into their official conduct, they were present?——V. 3 is a tacit allusion to the charge of bribery brought against his sons—as if he would say: Whoever else is guilty, I take you to record that I am not. I wash my hands before the nation. If my sons are guilty, it is not that they have followed my example or my counsel.——In v. 6, the Heb. word for "advanced" has commonly the sense *made*—meaning here, he *made* them what they became; gave them their high distinction as his servants.

In the brief and rapid sketch (vs. 9-11) of their nation's history from Joshua to that time, it can not be assumed that Samuel touched the great characters during the period of the Judges in their chronological order. The order in the Book of Judges differs from this, and is more likely to be correct.——In v. 11, Jerubbaal is another name for Gideon. With great probability "Bedan" is an orthographic error for *Barak*—the last two Hebrew letters being easily mistaken for each other. The invasion under Sisera was certainly before his mind (v. 9), so that the deliverance achieved by Barak could scarcely be omitted. Moreover, Barak's name follows Gideon's in Heb. 11: 32, which almost quotes these words of Samuel.——In v. 14, the Hebrew, closely translated, would read: "If ye will fear the Lord and serve him and hearken to his voice, and not rebel against the mouth [words] of the Lord, and if both you and your king who reigns over you will be after the Lord your God"—then all well!—these three last words being forcibly understood and implied.

The moral impression of this great thunder and rain in time of wheat harvest would be exceedingly heightened by the fact that in that climate neither is known during those weeks. Jerome, whose home was there, says: "I have never seen rain in Judea in the end of June or in July."——The people saw that God was displeased with their request for a king and became sensible of their sin in that request. With the greatest confidence in Samuel's prayers they beg his continued intercession on their behalf—a responsibility which Samuel could not throw off. Note that Samuel's hope in God rests, not on the merit or even the penitence of the people, but on the Lord's regard for his own great name; for he had committed himself to mercy toward his people. This moral lesson is too precious to be overlooked.

These are Samuel's last words spoken publicly before the people. His record as a thoroughly godly man—a true and representative prophet, raised up of God to sustain the religious life of the nation—deserves our careful attention. The point that most impresses us is that in his person mortal man stands so very near to God. We see him continually made the vehicle of communication from God to men. Over against this, he bears up words of prayer and of confession from men to God. The people recognize his wonderful power with God in prayer and put all confidence in his success before the throne. The time had then fully come in the history of the nation when there was need of such a medium of words from God to men, and also from men back to God. Such men are a great moral power in whatever age they appear. In some vital respects they may appear in any age—

known as living near to God, as taught of him, and as mighty in prayer. Samuel is a model man of this class, well worthy to be made a study and an example.

Saul's History.

The events of 1 *Sam.* 13 are involved in no small chronological perplexity. Saul seems to have been young when made king; but here is his son Jonathan in command of one third of his standing army, and evincing manly vigor, courage, and decision. Saul must have been reigning at this point more than three years. Yet the English version of v. 1 seems to affirm that the events of this chapter occurred during or immediately after the third year of Saul's reign.——V. 1 presents several other critical difficulties. The Septuagint omits it altogether, apparently in despair of making any thing out of it. The Hebrew for the first clause—"Saul reigned one year"—according to universal and therefore decisive Hebrew usage, must refer, not to the duration of his reign, but to *his age when he began to reign*. Saul was the son of——years in [at the point of beginning] his reigning. The numeral for either twenty or thirty has probably dropped out, the sense intended being—Saul was twenty and one years of age (or thirty and one) when he began to reign. A similar omission is probable in the second clause: "And when he had reigned [perhaps] twenty and two years over Israel," these events that follow took place.——That the Hebrew text has some errors, and more especially in *numerals*, ought to be frankly and fearlessly admitted. They affect no important doctrine or duty, and should not mar our confidence in the integrity of the Scriptures in all vital points as a revelation of God's character and of human duty.—— Another instance of numerical error must, I think, be assumed in v. 5, where the number of chariots is entirely out of proportion. 30,000 should probably be 300—300 chariots to 6,000 horsemen being nearly the usual ratio.

Saul's standing army stood at 3,000 men, two parts being under his immediate command; one part with Jonathan his son. The Philistines had a garrison in Geba (the modern Jeba), close upon the northern border of Benjamin and looking out northward upon the great ravine [the Wady Suweinit], on the opposite side of which stood Michmash, crowning the summit of the opposing mountain ridge. All suddenly Jonathan fell upon this garrison, smote and dislodged them. It startled the Philistines as would a clap of thunder from a clear sky, and the people of all Philistia seem to have rushed to arms to maintain their supremacy and to avenge themselves for this defeat. Vs. 19–22 show that the Philistines had managed to monopolize and control the skill of making and mending iron weapons, whether for agriculture or for war, so that Israel in this emergency had scarcely sword or spear in all their army.——In this crisis their men were spiritless (all save Jonathan), melting away in panic before the hosts of Philistia. Saul was in deep solicitude; it was his crisis of moral trial. Samuel had told him to tarry seven days till himself should come, when he would offer the requisite sacrifices, and seek help from their God. Saul waited till the morning of the seventh day; then, impatient of Samuel's delay, and lacking the repose of real trust in God, he ordered the sacrifice to proceed. Scarcely had he finished when Samuel came up; rebuked his disregard of the divine directions and his lack of faith in God; frankly told him he had done foolishly; had forfeited his position as the accepted king of God's people, and must be, sooner or later, superseded by one who would obey his divine Sovereign implicitly and trust him with all his heart. Thus Saul was weighed in the balances of this searching test and found wanting. Obedience less than implicit and absolute is no real obedience at all. Saul made shipwreck on the point of this vital distinction. From this time onward his career was downward and rapid. It was not possible that God could be manifestly on his side— evermore with him to make all his ways prosperous.

Jonathan.

1 Sam. 14: 1–46 records thrilling scenes. Jonathan and his armor-bearer, single-handed, under the inspiration of sublime faith in God, are seen moving upon the hosts of the Philistines, panic-smiting their vast multitude, turning the whole tide of war, and ultimately driving the Philistines back to their cities.——This

great victory was marred by the mistake, not to say the folly, of King Saul in imprecating a fatal curse upon any man who should touch a morsel of food during the entire day. Jonathan, who was off before this military order was issued, and who began his day's fighting with the morning light, became faint for want of food; helped himself to wild honey that lay in his path, and found "his eyes enlightened" (vs. 27–29)—the dimness of vision consequent upon faintness was relieved. But notwithstanding these lesser abatements from the benign results of the day, the victory was glorious—the honor being due, however, under God, not to Saul, but to Jonathan.——That the people interposed resolutely to resist Saul's purpose and save Jonathan from death under Saul's rash curse is proof that his power was not altogether absolute, also that the people were in heart enthusiastically with Jonathan.——The day taken in whole must have been not a little humiliating to the king. Jonathan's record shines with the splendor of sublime heroism, and of genuine faith in God—all the more so, because when the whole army, and even Saul, were trembling with fear, many deserting their nation's standard, and secreting themselves wherever they could, he rose high above every fear, and accounting that the Lord was mighty to save by many or by few, plunged in among the armed hosts of Philistia, and laid a full score of warriors low in the first assault, and thus sent panic through that host till they melted away before him, and turned their mad, wild hand upon each other. Thus began that day of glorious victory for Israel.

This spirit of heroism, resting upon his faith in God, is quite like what we see in David when he came first into the camp of Israel where Goliath was challenging them to send out some champion for single combat. No wonder two souls so kindred in spirit as David and Jonathan should love each other with love worthy of being embalmed in the sweetest strains of David's immortal song, as in 2 Sam. 1 : 17–27.

The closing verses (47–52) of this chap. 14, give a brief *résumé* of Saul's family history, with some notices of his wars.

Saul and Amalek.

Chap. 15 reveals yet more fully the fatal lack in the character of Saul, and is a natural sequel to the developments which appear in chap. 13. The test in this instance was a special commission to destroy Amalek—a commission perfectly explicit in its terms, and therefore one that could not be misunderstood. It called for an utter destruction—one that should spare nothing, man or beast, alive. Saul assumed the responsibility of making exceptions in the case of their King Agag, and of the best of the sheep, lambs, oxen, and fatlings. His reasons named were—not any want of military force, nor any considerations of compassion. Why he spared their king is not apparent, unless it were to grace his triumph. As to the cattle the record states that Saul *and the people* concurred in sparing them (v. 9); but Saul thrice over (viz., vs. 15, 21, 24), distinctly, yet probably not truthfully, laid the responsibility upon the people. The reason assigned was that they might offer them to the Lord in sacrifice—probably as being in their view a matter of economy—to save their own.

This new development of disobedience ("rebellion" the Lord calls it, v. 23) brought matters to issue between the Lord and Saul. The divine word came to Samuel; "It repenteth me that I have set up Saul to be king, for he is *turned* back from following me, and hath not performed my commandments" (v. 11.) This touched the pity and compassion of Samuel's heart. "It grieved Samuel" (we read), "and he cried unto the Lord all night." But the Lord's decision could not (honorably) be reversed. So Samuel himself, in reply to Saul's entreaties, was forced to declare; "The Strength of Israel will not lie nor repent; for he is not a man that he should repent" (v. 29). The Hebrew word for "strength" is not elsewhere applied to God, but according to its current usage should contemplate, not merely his power, but his ineffable glory, and especially the eternity of his being, and hence the permanence of every glorious quality of his character.

In this transaction the expostulations and reasonings of Samuel with Saul are pregnant with moral force for all ages. "Ye think" (he would say) "to please the Lord by sparing the flocks and herds of Amalek and then offering them to the Lord in sacrifice." No mistake could be greater or more fatal. "Hath the Lord as great delight in burnt-offerings and sacrifices as in obeying the voice of the Lord? Behold, to obey is better than sacrifice, and to hearken, than the fat of rams. For rebellion is as the sin of witchcraft, and stubbornness is as iniquity and idolatry." God asks the homage of the heart—the pure and perfect submission of the human will. No substitute for this can possibly be accepted.

Neither apology nor confession on the part of Saul could avail to change the divine purpose. Saul had shown himself untrue to his Supreme Sovereign and utterly unfit to be king over the Lord's people. It, therefore, only remained for Samuel to rebuke his sin sharply, to testify to him that the Lord had that day rent the kingdom of Israel (in purpose) from him and given it to a neighbor better than he ; and then to tear himself sadly yet firmly away from Saul and leave him to his wretched doom.——Yet as if to administer one last rebuke to Saul by giving him an example of what he should have done, he commands—" Bring ye hither to me Agag the king of Amalek." "Agag" (we read) "came to him *delicately*"—the sense of which Hebrew word may perhaps be *with joy*, assuming that his peril of death was past. Yet Fuerst gives the word the sense—*in chains*. The Septuagint has it "trembling." The first named sense, [*i. e.*, with joy] seems most probable, because in harmony with what follows.——Then the aged Samuel, rising to the stern demands of God's fearful retributions, proclaims—" As thy sword has made women childless, so shall thy mother be childless among women,"—and then "hewed the guilty king in pieces before the Lord "—the final clause "*before the Lord* " signifying that God was solemnly present to that scene, and that it was done in faithful though stern fulfillment of God's command. It was the moment for God's eternal justice to be vindicated. There was no element in Saul's character equal to such an emergency ; there was none in Samuel's that could shrink from fulfilling God's high behest. The contrast is a lesson in moral sublimity.

Does the divine mandate for the extermination of Amalek seem to any reader unreasonably severe and unworthy of God? Let it be borne in mind that Amalek

SAUL AND AMALEK.   135

stands before the world on the scripture record as foremost among the savage nations of those early times in her cruelty and in her ruthless violation of common humanity. Israel had scarcely crossed the Red Sea when Amalek fell savagely on the rear of his marching hosts, assaulting the infirm and weary, the aged, the mothers with babes. There, first, Israel was brought into conflict of arms with her causeless enemies. (See Ex. 17: 8–16). This is the scene which the Lord here speaks of remembering still. Let the reader note also the record (Deut. 25: 17–19) which recites the outrage perpetrated on Israel by Amalek (as above), and adds—" When the Lord hath given thee rest in Canaan, thou shalt blot out the remembrance of Amalek from under heaven; thou shalt not forget it."——Some fresh assault from Amalek seems to be referred to in this immediate connection (1 Sam. 14: 48) in the general reference to this onslaught upon Amalek: " And he (Saul) gathered an host and smote the Amalekites, and *delivered Israel out of the hands of them that spoiled them.*" It seems to be implied here that Amalek had quite recently fallen upon Israel for plunder and spoil, taking advantage probably of some period of special exposure in consequence of their wars with the Philistines. The reader will note also that Samuel prefaces the execution of Agag with words indicating precisely the idea of righteous retribution: " As thy sword hath made mothers childless, so shall thy mother be childless among women." It is one of the sublime prerogatives of the God of nations to hold men to righteousness and to deter them from outrageous inhumanity. There will be cases that must be made terrible examples of the punishment which such sinners deserve. It is simply inevitable that if nations as such are to be governed at all by the Great God of nations, they must have their punishment in the present world. It must be left to the option of divine wisdom to determine the *form* of this punishment—whether by a deluge of waters; by the volcano or earthquake; by pestilence or famine; or by the sword of war. The justice of such retribution is the same by whatever means it be executed. And if it please God to commission Israel to execute his retribution on Amalek, who shall question the wisdom of his pleasure? It may impress Israel with a fresh sense of God's righteous rule over the nations and of the wisdom of having the fear of God ever before them. The assumption—sometimes so hastily and thoughtlessly made—that real benevolence never can restrain sin by means of inflicted suffering, may sometimes seem plausible, but is sadly short-sighted, not to say puerile. It has never measured the mischiefs of unrestrained sin in the moral universe; has taken no account of the true interests of moral beings, or of the value of holiness; and does not even attempt to estimate the responsibilities of the Great Father of all to restrain and punish the free moral wickedness of his creatures.

CHAPTER VII.

The History of David.

From this point (1 Sam. 16) onward, the historic thread runs on the life of David, not of Saul. David is the primary character, Saul only the secondary. Whatever is said of Saul is here because of its relations to David; what is said of David is here for its own sake, to give us a full and connected view of his experiences during the interval between his being anointed and his being ultimately inaugurated as king of Israel.——After Saul has been publicly disowned of God the historian seems more than willing to let him drop out of his narrative, except as the history of David necessarily brings him to view. Around David the chief interest of the sacred story naturally gathers.

Opening this chapter 16, we are reminded again (v. 1) of the deep and honest grief felt by Samuel over the sad fall of Israel's first king. It was sad that the *first* king should make such a failure—that one of so much early promise should break down so utterly, and that, too, on the very first principle of true piety—implicit obedience to God.

In choosing the next king, the Lord looked for a man—not after the heart of Israel, but after *his own* heart. Consequently his choice was determined, not by the outer, but by the inner man; not by lofty stature and commanding presence, but by the far nobler qualities of a true, trustful, loving heart. He sends Samuel to a humble family of Bethlehem-Judah under instructions to take with him his horn of oil, and let his mind be guided by the word of the Lord given him on the spot. ——The reader will notice Samuel's solicitude lest Saul should hear of it, and under excited jealousy take the prophet's life. God's method of avoiding this danger throws light on a nice question of casuistry—viz., whether it is right to conceal a part of the truth from those whose known character and purpose make it certain that they would use this knowledge for evil. In this case Saul had no claim to know what God was doing in regard to the anointing of David. It was certain that the knowledge, if he had it, would fire up his selfish jealousy to mad fury and involve him in awful sin. It was, therefore, right and kind toward him to withhold from him this knowledge. The proposed method of concealing it involved no falsehood; it merely withheld part of the truth, and this from one who had no claim to know it, and who could not safely be trusted with this knowledge. The sacrifice was not a sham, but was an honest transaction, demanded by the solemnities of the occasion.——That the elders of Bethlehem "trembled" (v. 4) at Samuel's coming shows that the people were by no means at ease under the administration of Saul. Society was unrestful—as under some terrible despotism where no man can know that his head is safe upon his shoulders. A king who is consciously unfit to reign and painfully sensible that both God and man must know it too, is of all men most miserable. Such was the case of this degenerate king.

In v. 7 we see that, as hinted above, Israel's second king was to be chosen on the ground of qualities pleasing to God, and not of those that were popular with men. In the case of the first king the people had a man to their notion—of tall and commanding presence, who in these points might compare with the champion monarchs of the nations round about them. In the case of David the Lord sought and found a man whose chief qualities were that he knew and loved the Lord, and that his heart was true and trustful toward the God of Israel. Samuel very naturally assumed that the first-born would be the man, and the more so for his lofty stature and imposing mien. But the Lord soon set him right, coupling this correction with the statement of the grand principle: "The Lord seeth not as man seeth; for man looketh on the outward appearance, but the Lord looketh on the heart." Somewhat broader still was the doctrine taught by our Lord (Luke 16: 15): "God knoweth your hearts; for that which is highly esteemed among men is abomination in the sight of God."

Youngest of Jesse's eight sons came forth at last the youthful David, whom his father evidently thought quite ineligible, and therefore had not even called him in from his shepherd duties to be present on this occasion. The brief notice of his "personnel" makes no allusion to his stature. He was "ruddy" in complexion (red-haired like Esau, some of the critics think) but beautiful; of pleasing countenance. The aged prophet anointed him, and the Spirit of God indorsed this anointing by coming upon him from that day forward. This second and spiritual anointing gave him special qualifications for his new and coming responsibilities, in accordance with which the Apostle John wrote: "Ye have received an unction from the Holy One, and ye know all things;"..."The same anointing teacheth you of all things, and is truth" (1 John 2: 20, 27).

The Evil Spirit in Saul.

Here a striking fact appears in the case of Saul (v. 14), viz., that not only did the Spirit of the Lord depart from him, but an evil spirit from the Lord *troubled* him—"troubled" in the sense of the distortion of the normal activities of his mind—an abnormal state of his faculties—due to the terrible power of jealousy and to the mastery of evil influences over his soul. Psychologically considered, here are really three questions: (a.) What exactly was this mental state—this terrible condition of the soul?—— (b.) Was any spiritual agency from without himself concerned in its production, and if so, what?—— (c.) In what sense was this evil spirit "*from the Lord?*"

(a.) One vital fact in Saul's case is that he was apostate from God, and, therefore, inevitably wretched. He

THE EVIL SPIRIT IN SAUL. 139

had been too near to God, and knew too much of him to be at rest in a state of apostasy. Consciously unfit to reign; knowing but too well that God had forsaken him; cast off from all hope in God, and haunted with "a certain fearful looking-for of judgment," how could he be otherwise than melancholy, anxious, miserable? ——(b.) The next fact pertaining to the state of such a mind is that it presents a most congenial field for Satan's agency. He loves to torment such souls, and never misses his opportunity. His suggestions are naturally seconded and not even feebly resisted by the normal action of a human soul lost to God and surrendered to the power of evil.——(c.) It only remains to say that there is need of no other agency from God than the permissive.* Satan never needs to be *sent* on such a mission; it is only requisite that the Lord suffer him to go. Such permission is one feature in that awful retribution which God must send upon apostate souls. They having chosen sin and rebellion rather than obedience, and, consequently, evil rather than good, God leaves them to their own guilty choice, to "eat the fruit of their own way, and to be filled with their own devices." What can be said against his wisdom or his love in leaving sinners to their own chosen ways? What reason can be given why he should not thus leave them? How can sin be more effectually forestalled and resisted in a moral universe than by sometimes giving it scope to develop its full and fearful power to sink human souls under an unutterable desolation?

Next in this history (1 Sam. 16: 15–23) we meet the remarkable fact that music (especially that of the Hebrew harp) appears as the antidote to the agency of this "evil spirit." The record shows two things, viz., that in that age music was currently understood and believed to have this power; and that in Saul's case it proved effective.

---

*If permissive agency on the part of God be all the case requires, then it is unphilosophical to assume any thing more. The known character of God forbids us to go beyond this—unless the case demands it—as it does not. Moreover, Hebrew usage fully justifies this construction of the passage. Things done under God's permissive agency are usually said to be done by God. See the case of hardening Pharaoh's heart, and also God's agency in the sin of Joseph's brethren.

This fact is one of too much interest and value to be passed without a few moments' attention.——Let us inquire if there be any other known facts or laws of mind which may either illustrate or confirm this.

The ancient harp of the Hebrews we may not be able to reproduce with sufficient certainty to analyze its powers as compared with other instruments or with the human voice. But it is safe to assume that it was constructed for use in religious worship, and, therefore, doubtless, had adaptations to sacred song.——Next, let us note that its musical power was manifestly congenial to the presence and activities of the *Holy Spirit*—that Spirit under which prophets prophesied, and worshiped, and praised. This we have seen in our studies upon the music of the schools of the prophets.——From this fact we naturally pass to the conclusion that what was so sweetly in harmony with the Spirit of God must be out of all harmony with the spirit of the devil. The music and the songs that tune men's hearts to praise and to worship, and to love, must be intensely repellent to the spirit of hate, of discord, of cursing—of all evil.——Note also the well known fact that some forms of insanity yield (at least temporarily) to the power of soft, gentle music. It strangely charms such souls to rest, as if the spirit of their insanity could not resist its uncongenial influence. It is also well known that the violent (semi-satanic) passions of jealousy, anger, revenge, become at once conscious of the antagonistic force of music. He must be (one might almost say) more demoniac than the demons who can steel his sensibilities altogether against its power.

The case of Saul will be mostly relieved of mystery if studied in the light of his antecedents. Apostate from God; then forsaken by God; burdened with official responsibilities which he could neither bear nor throw off; consciously unfit to reign, and, worse yet, consciously guilty, as well as weak, why should not he be melancholy, troubled, wretched? If music can divert his thought from himself for even the moment, it will refresh him; if it can soothe the dreadful disquiet of his soul even transiently, he will breathe more freely. If we accept the supposition that Satan's hellish impulses were present in the case, then the music of the harp—so like heaven, so unlike hell—

may have made him but too glad to withdraw, and bide his time to return under more congenial surroundings.

It should be noted that this reference to the evil spirit upon Saul appears here to account for David's coming to court. He was brought there to relieve Saul in his paroxysms of melancholic insanity.

David (as appears here, v. 18) had other fine and promising qualities besides his skill in music—a mighty, valiant man, a man of war, of knowledge and skill *in words* (so the Hebrew); of agreeable person, and, as was well understood, a man who walked with God, and whose ways the Lord made to prosper. Hence, even Saul was favorably impressed, and, as the record puts it—"loved him greatly."

It has been thought by some critics that this paragraph (1 Sam. 16: 14–23) belongs in the order of time *after* the scenes between David and Goliath (chap. 17), and especially so because Saul seemed not to recognize David when he saw him go forth to meet that Philistine (17: 55). It is certain that David came to that battle-field, not from Saul's court, but from his father's house. Hence if his introduction at Saul's court preceded the slaying of Goliath, he returned home again. This may have been the case. As to Saul's failure to recognize David it should be noticed that the point of his inquiry was—not, Who *is* this young man, but, Who is his *father?* Amid the cares of a kingdom in time of war, he may have forgotten that this young man, for a time his musician and armor-bearer, was the son of Jesse of Bethlehem.——After the scenes with Goliath Saul would let him go home no more to his father's house (18: 2).

David and Goliath. (1 Sam. 17.)

Our study of this scene may fitly embrace two quite distinct inquiries:—(a.) Into its external history and circumstances;——(b.) Into its sublime significance as related to the character of David and the great conflict of arms beween Israel and her national enemies.

(a.) The geographical locality of this scene has been very satisfactorily identified by Dr. Robinson. (See his Researches, vol. ii, 349, 350). Shocho (or

Socoh) is found in the modern Shuweikeh, near the western border of Judah, nine Roman miles from Eleutheropolis, on the great road from Gaza to Jerusalem. The valley of Elah is here, the mountain ridges confronting each other and the valley between into which Goliath descended on forty successive days (v. 16) to challenge the army of Israel to send forth some champion to meet him and decide by single combat which nation should be master and which servant to the other. Goliath is spoken of as a "champion" —the Hebrew word signifying *a man between;* one who holds a middle position between two hostile armies. He and his opponent wield their respective destinies. Goliath's personnel and armor are fully described— his height about nine feet; the weight of his coat of mail five thousand shekels of brass (proximately, one hundred and sixty pounds avoirdupois). One of the survivors of the old Anakim race, clad with defensive armor so ponderous, complete, and strong that it might be expected to shield him perfectly from the missiles of ancient warfare; and with offensive weapons deemed sufficient to annihilate any ordinary antagonist—his confidence of victory in single combat was unbounded. All Philistia felt safe in committing their nation's destiny to his single arm as against any warrior whom the Israelites might bring out against him. His words of defiance coupled with his manifest power appalled the men of Israel: "They were dismayed and greatly afraid." The repetition of this challenge for forty days had not abated their fears, nor did they seem to approach any nearer to a final issue on the basis of this challenge.

At this critical juncture a new sort of hero appeared on the Hebrew side. The youthful shepherd of Bethlehem, sent by his father Jesse with army supplies for his three older brethren in Saul's army, happened there just at the moment when this Goliath strode down the hill for his morning challenge. His ear caught the taunting tones and words; his quick eye noted the panic which shook the Hebrew lines, and his soul was stirred within him. He soon learned the pending issues—the call for some hero to dare the single-handed fight in behalf of Israel; and he felt—what no one else had seemed to feel—the insult offered to Israel's God, and the inspirations of sublime confidence that their own Jehovah would surely avenge his own honor and wipe out this reproach, if only some one would go forth in his name to this conflict. He remembered how he had slain a lion and a bear, and he saw in that success a pledge that his God would give him an easy victory over this uncircumcised Philistine who had defied at once the God of Israel and the armed hosts of his people. He, therefore, modestly signified his readiness for this single combat; was brought before Saul and again declared himself ready. At Saul's suggestion he put on Saul's armor, but soon laid it aside as untried, lest it should trammel rather than protect or aid him. Really his views of the pending issue would not allow him to think of matching one coat of mail against another. His expectation of God's interposing arm did not lead that way. If we might allow ourselves to speculate upon his thought and plan for this fight, we should assume that his own good sense was at one with the impulses of God's inspiration within him to this point, that he must depend under God upon his tried weapons—the sling and stone—and that if these weapons seemed weak and insignificant, all the more would men see that "the excellency of the power was not of man but of God." David's sling had been with him in many a day of shepherd life; he knew how to put a smooth stone from the brook straight and swift to its mark. And however thoroughly shielded by his helmet and coat of mail Goliath might be, he could not fight without eyes nor see without exposing them somewhat to such a missile as a small smooth stone. How much space adjacent to the eye was exposed does not appear; not much was needful for David's mark. So the thing was done. The giant strode down into the valley, and looking about "saw the youthful David and disdained him," for he was but a youth, ruddy and fair— more fit, Goliath doubtless thought, to grace an assembly room than a field of battle. He manifestly felt himself insulted. Perhaps out of respect to his offended dignity, he may have raised the question whether he ought not to retire indignantly from the field. "Am I a dog," said he, "that thou comest to me with staves? And the Philistine cursed David by his gods." Proudly, champion-like, he tells what he can and will do.

"Come to me, and I will give thy flesh to the fowls of the air and to the beasts of the field."——David's reply reveals the source of his courage: "Thou comest to me with sword, and spear, and shield: I come to thee *in the name of the Lord of Hosts*, the God of the armies of Israel whom thou hast defied. This day will the Lord deliver thee into my hands; I will smite thee and take thy head from thee, and I will give, not *thy* carcass only, but the carcasses of the Philistine host to the fowls of the air and to the wild beasts of the earth, that all the earth may know that there is a God in Israel. And all this assembly (these gathered hosts crowning these mountain summits to witness) shall know that the Lord saveth not with sword and spear, for the battle is the Lord's, and he will give you into our hands."——Verily David had ideas and had words—grand ideas and fitting words—as well as courage of soul and a trusty sling. So when Goliath approached to meet David, David, too, hasted and ran toward the opposing army to meet his foe. One stone from his bag filled his sling; he hurled it and smote the Philistine in his forehead, where it sunk deep and he fell upon his face to the earth. The deed is done! It only remained to run to his fallen foe, draw the dying champion's sword and take off with it his head. The Philistine army, smitten with terror, betake themselves to flight. The men of Israel and Judah arose, gave one shout—the shout of a host—and then pursued the fleeing enemy even to their cities. Such in brief were the external points of that thrilling transaction.

(b.) Of its *significance*, what shall we say?——Here were new elements, a new spirit and new achievements, little known ere this in the wars of Saul; nowhere apparent indeed except in the somewhat analogous case of Jonathan and his armor-bearer, as we saw in 1 Sam. 14. If we study David to purpose we shall see that the secret of his courage, his coolness, his heroism, and his power, lay in the fact that *God was with him.* He had a sense of a present God, of a sort unknown to Saul—little known it would seem to the men of his army. In Christian phrase he had *faith*, and this faith took on in war-scenes the form of placid trust, cool courage, the inspiration of heroism. He knew that God had a care for his own glory, and he saw that the hour had come for its manifestations before Israel and before all the nations. Therefore, he could not doubt the issue of this conflict. He went out to it with no trepidation of doubt or fear. His eye was never more clear nor his right arm more true. Moreover these inspirations of faith were not new and heretofore unknown in his experience. Had this been the case, nothing less than miracle could have kept his nerves steady and his soul above perilous perturbation. We must, therefore, assume that this faith had become the quiet habit of his mind. Out on the hills of Bethlehem, caring for his flock by day or by night, he had walked with God. He had known the God of his fathers before he ever saw Samuel the prophet; but after that scene of the anointing, how often were his thoughts thrown forward upon that field of untried responsibilities, and soothed to rest only as he committed his unknown ways to the over-ruling care of the Great Father! Those days or months or years which intervened between his first meeting with Samuel and this meeting with Goliath were full of discipline and exercise to his faith in Israel's God. It is pleasant to think how often he had lifted his soul to God in humble prayer to order his unknown future and to give him the training requisite for his prospective responsibilities. Out of such communion with God in prayer, there is wont to come forth at length such easy achievements as these on this great day of Jehovah's triumphs through the hand of the youthful but prayerful David.

The scenes of this day had their significance also to the whole nation of Israel, and especially to the army of Saul, before whose eyes they transpired. Probably very few of them saw in David their future king; few were aware that their great prophet had poured the anointing oil on his head. Even Eliab who saw it done seems strangely far from having laid it in any sort to his heart. Yet there, before their eyes, was this astounding spectacle. In the very ears of some of them rang out those cheery, most inspiring words of faith in Israel's God—" That all the earth may know that there is a God in Israel; and all this assembly shall know that the Lord saveth not with sword and spear; for the battle is the Lord's." What a testimony was that fall of the Philistine giant before the sling of the youth ful David! How forcible the inference that, with God on their side, they were mighty against the mightiest of their foes! It is scarcely to be expected that Saul, hardened as he was, would take in these moral lessons; but we may hope that many a soldier in those ranks saw the moral teaching of this wonderful transaction and felt the force of its grand lessons respecting the God of his fathers. It is pleasant to think how many thousand times along the lapse of the ages since that day, the significance of its scenes has lifted up hearts ready to sink, and fired with sublime inspiration souls otherwise feeble and overborne with burdens and responsibilities. Reading this chapter of God's working through weak human instruments, "the feeble have become as David, and the house of David as God—as the angel of the Lord before them" (Zech. 12: 8).

We ought not to close this chapter without the passing remark that David came out from this brilliant victory (apparently) neither inflated with vanity, nor excited with unhallowed ambition, nor impaired in his simple-hearted modesty of unconscious greatness. He did not strike for the throne, nor drop the least hint that he thought his hour had come. It does not appear that *he even penned one Psalm to celebrate this great event.* There were other events along his life-path, some sad, some joyful, which brought inspiration to his poetic soul, and which he embalmed in song; but we find no special allusion in his Psalms to this conflict with Goliath. Was it that he intuitively felt the delicacy of his relations to Saul, and therefore could scarcely allow himself to whisper a word of those deeds which the Lord wrought by his hand? The fact of his silence is before us; we need ask no better proof that God was with him; no higher mark of true greatness.

The history of David continued: other results of his slaying Goliath. (1 Sam. 18.)

As one result, David became too valuable in the house of Saul to be spared any more for shepherd-life in Bethlehem (v. 2).——As might have been expected, a very warm friendship sprung up between Jonathan and David. Ah, with what eyes did Jonathan look upon the youthful David giving utterance to his lofty inspirations of faith and going forth to easy victory over proud Goliath! However those scenes may have impressed other minds in Saul's court and camp, there was one man who felt through all his soul the quickening of kindred sympathies and the mighty attractions of a kindred spirit. "When David had made an end of speaking unto Saul it came to pass that the soul of Jonathan was knit with the soul of David, and Jonathan loved him as his own soul" (v. 1). A covenant of mutual friendship was but a faint expression of their love. Jonathan, the heir-apparent to the throne, the man who next after Saul might be expected, under the impulses of depraved human nature, to be unrestful with jealousy—this Jonathan can not do too much for his new friend, David. He stripped himself of his outer robe and gave it to David, and of his military equipage, even to his sword, and bow, and girdle. We shall see yet more of this friendship in the sequel.

It was of the people, not of David, to celebrate this great victory. When Israel's warriors returned laden with spoils and aflame with the glory of victory, "the women came out of all the cities of Israel, singing and dancing to meet king Saul with tabrets, with joy, and with instruments of music!" Saul felt somewhat the impulses of this general joy, and all might have passed off well in his heart but for one word which came to his ear from their song. "Saul hath slain his thousands and David his ten thousands." Alas! this was a poisoned arrow to his heart. It touched him in a most sensitive point, and he seems never to have forgotten or forgiven it. Saul was very wroth, and the saying displeased him, and he said: "They have ascribed unto David ten thousands and to me only thousands; and what can he have more but the kingdom?"——Ah, what can be done for him who is consciously unworthy of the first praises and yet can not endure to miss them? Whence can help come to a spirit smitten with such grief?——The historian must needs give a place to these troubles in the heart of Saul, for they are the clew to his future policy toward David.

From that day forward Saul thought he saw in David a dangerous rival, if not immediately for his kingdom, yet at least for the love and confidence of his people.

"Saul *eyed* David from that day "—in the double sense of close watchfulness and of bitter jealousy. Brooding the livelong night over this higher praise given to David, in the morning the evil spirit was upon him again (v. 10), and, strange to say, "he prophesied in the midst of the house"—to which words it is hard in this case to give any other sense than that of pouring out the impulses of his excited, half-maddened soul —his utterances taking their character from the spirit which indited them, and evincing this character by the deeds they prompted him to do. David was called in to soothe Saul's mania with his harp; but with small success if we may judge from Saul's hurling his javelin to smite him. "David avoided out of his presence," *i. e.*, turned himself (Heb.) suddenly so that the shaft missed him, twice.——Saul's next policy was to put David into the thickest perils of war in hope that he might fall by the hand of the Philistines. Vain hope! for the Lord was with David to shield him from the deadly arrow. This policy served only to bring him the more fully and favorably before the people, and to inspire anew their love and confidence as to David. Thus every movement Saul made aggravated his trouble. "When he saw that David behaved himself very wisely he was afraid of him" (v. 15). The historian makes Saul's fear of David very prominent, naming it even the third time in this one chapter (vs. 12, 15, 29). "Fear" is altogether the right word, yet it was not fear that David would take or even plot against his life, but that he would inevitably have the hearts of the people; would eclipse the honor of himself as king, and ultimately become king by virtue of his greatly superior merit. The bitter self-consciousness of being forsaken of God and unworthy to reign, and a sense of David's superior worth to which he could not blind his eyes, conspired to make him the most wretched of men.

Saul plighted his eldest daughter to David to induce him to expose his life in forays upon the Philistines; then violated his pledge; then, hoping to succeed the second time, gave him Michal—but only to fail again in compassing David's death. All these events brought David the more fully before the people, and brought fresh trouble upon the jealous heart of Saul.——In **v.**

DAVID AND SAUL. 149

30 we read: "The princes of the Philistines went forth," *i. e.*, to war with Saul; and "it came to pass *when* they went forth," *i. e.*, whenever—as often as—they went forth, it served to set forth David's superior tact and wisdom, and to place him before the people as one worthy to be their king.

Chap. 19 presents Saul, not only plotting and personally attempting to take David's life, but commanding his servants and even his son Jonathan to kill him. Jonathan nobly expostulates with his father, and at first with apparent success. But Saul waxed worse and worse, so that Jonathan's subsequent expostulations proved unavailing (1 Sam. 20: 30–34). After this first success Saul seems to have been quiet, till a new occasion of jealousy arose; "war again" (v. 8); David went out and fought, and slew the Philistines with great slaughter, and they fled. Then the evil spirit of jealousy came again upon Saul; David played before him; Saul again hurled his javelin to kill him, with no better success than before. David not only evaded the shaft, but escaped from the house.——Next we learn that David was not safe from Saul even in his own house, for Saul sent men there to watch the house by night and slay him in the morning. By the artful policy of his wife Michal he eluded these men and made his escape to Samuel in Ramah.

Here we may begin to find definite points of coincidence between this history of David, written probably by Samuel or by Gad (David's seer), and his own Psalms. Ps. 59 is definitely located at this point in his history—"When Saul sent and they watched the house to kill him." Here, then, we may raise the question—What were the thoughts of his heart under these stern and sore afflictions? Did he look upward to God for help? Did he prove the priceless comfort of prayer in human emergencies?——He himself gives the answer. "Deliver me from mine enemies, O my God; defend me from them that rise up against me."—— Greatly to his comfort, he is conscious of innocence as toward Saul. "They lie in wait for my life, not for my transgression, nor for my sin, O Lord."——He thinks of them as going round the house by night and compares them to the oriental dog; but of himself he says, "I will sing of thy power; I will sing aloud of thy mercy in the morning." Sweetly, calmly, his soul abode in peaceful trust toward his Great Deliverer.——When we follow David from one scene of vengeful persecution to another, and our hearts are stirred to deepest sympathy for him, let it be a precious consolation to us, as it was to him, that he never sank under those burdens; that he was not left to bear them alone; that, looking upward, his eye always rested on One whose heart was quick to sympathize and whose uplifted arm was mighty to save.

Next he is with Samuel at the prophet-college in Ramah, and tells him all that Saul had done to him. It was here that messengers sent by Saul to take David's life—hard, bloody men—three companies in succession, were seized with the spirit of prophesying as they saw and heard the sons of the prophets prophesying, and quite forgot their bloody errand. At last Saul came himself, only to fall under the same mysterious (or perhaps we should say) sympathetic influence, and he too prophesied, and his purposes of murder were for the time quenched.

David's flight to Samuel at Ramah suggests how naturally he sought sympathy and help from the specially religious communities and men in Israel. It is not certain that they had met before, since the anointing at Bethlehem. David had a long story to rehearse, of fierce persecution from Saul; of constant plotting against his life; of hair-breadth escapes; of faith and trust in God; sorely tried, yet never altogether sinking. What Samuel said to him after hearing his story is not on record, yet is not hard to suppose. Some words of patriarchal sympathy; some fresh inspiration toward abiding faith in God; some new assurance of coming forth at last with God's peaceful blessing and the throne of Israel—such help from the aged Samuel must have made this meeting memorable through many otherwise desolate and weary days of David's perilous flight before Saul and his bloody "messengers."

Next we see David fleeing from Ramah and in deep consultation with Jonathan touching his own personal safety, and the designs of Saul upon his life. Jonathan's friendship for David was true and most self-sacrificing, as may be seen wherever he comes to view. The feast of the new moon would naturally bring Saul's family together—David included: will it be safe for David to come? Jonathan will sound his father and see, and then inform his friend. In the event he found Saul bitter and desperate, not to say infuriated with madness, so that he even attempted Jonathan's life as he had repeatedly the life of David.——There is no longer peace or safety for David in Saul's house. He fled next to Nob, then the location of the tabernacle and its services, and the residence of a large number of priests.* David reached the city with but few attendants; came before Ahimelech the priest alone and hungry, and asked for bread. There being none on hand save the show-bread which had been removed that its place might be supplied with fresh baked loaves, David asked and obtained this—a case to which our Lord alludes (Matt. 12: 3, 4), to illustrate the principle that exigencies sometimes justify the neglect of usages merely ceremonial and ritual.——This transient stay at Nob brought disaster upon the priests resident there, and fresh sorrow to David. Their friendly aid to him in the gift of bread and of Goliath's sword, being reported to Saul by Doeg, brought down on them his cruel vengeance through the bloody hand of this treacherous Edomite. Doeg also charged Ahimelech with asking counsel of the Lord for David, but this the priest denied (v. 15), and it must be put to the account of misapprehension or of slander. David's Psalm on this occasion (Ps. 52) charges Doeg with unmitigated deceit and falsehood (vs. 2–4).——Saul's vengeance was most unreasonable and cruel, showing what a mastery his madness of jealousy against David had gained over all the better elements of his character. The impressions made upon David by this transaction he has given, at least, in part, in Ps. 52, in which the bloody and lying spirit of Doeg stands in the foreground. It is quite remarkable that this Psalm refrains from the least apparent allusion to Saul. Was this silence due to his delicate relations to his sovereign? As he would not lift up his hand against the Lord's anointed, so also did he withhold tongue and pen from the least utterance that might be to Saul's detriment? The

* Nob was situated very near Jerusalem. No trace of its site has been found, but it must have been within sight of Jerusalem, on the northern slope of the Mt. of Olives. See Isa. 10: 32.

fact is at least a marvelous instance of self-control, and probably we should say of profound sagacity.

Next David fled his country and sought refuge with Achish king of Gath (1 Sam. 21: 10–15). To his astonishment and alarm he found that he was but too well known there as the greatest of Israel's warriors against the Philistines. Even the words of that song of triumph—"Saul hath slain his thousands, and David his ten thousands"—fell on his ear, and "he was sore afraid of Achish king of Gath." In this emergency he feigned insanity. As the Hebrew expressively puts it, "He changed his good sense"—seemed to have lost it—acted as one who had. He scribbled on the doors and let his slaver run down his beard, so that the king rebuked his servants for suffering such a man about the palace, and David escaped the pending danger.

Two precious Psalms have come down to us, disclosing the thoughts and experiences of David amid these trying scenes; viz., Ps. 34 and 56. (See my Notes on these Psalms). If the question be raised, What did David think of the policy of feigning insanity as a means of personal safety before Achish?—perhaps the utmost we can say is that he does not recommend it, nor is any word dropped which necessarily implies that he condemned it. Ps. 34 glows with thanksgiving and trust; exhorts to well-doing and against "speaking guile" (v. 13); and certainly does not distinctly assume that his own methods of self-protection were against his conscience, or inconsistent with entire trust in God.

Escaped from Achish, David sought refuge temporarily in the mountain fastnesses of Judah, making the cave of Adullam (a few miles south-east from Bethlehem), his retreat. Some of his heart-experiences during these days of exile and isolation appear in Ps. 57, the heading of which refers to his fleeing from Saul and finding his home in the cave. A lofty tone of exultation in God is the key-note of this Psalm—in striking contrast with the gloom and desolation of his external surroundings. "Be thou exalted, O God, above the heavens, and let thy glory be above all the earth." "My heart is fixed, O God, my heart is fixed; I will sing and give praise. Awake, all ye noblest powers; awake, psaltery and harp; I will awake early. I will praise thee, O Lord, among the nations," etc. Would it not have been at once strange and inspiring to hear this fugitive exile praising God with the sweet tones of psaltery and harp in those deep glens and among the dark, damp caverns of Judah's mountains? But there is no place on this earth where the presence and consolations of God can not waken joy in the souls that love and trust him. Verily this is the grandest moral sublimity—to rise above the depressing influence of the darkest surroundings and triumph in God only! It reminds us of Habakkuk, amid prospective scenes of famine and dire captivity, singing, "Though the fig-tree do not blossom . . . . . yet will I rejoice in the Lord;" and of Paul and Silas—their flesh still raw from the scourge—with probable death before them in the morning, yet singing praises to God from the depths of their dungeon. So the story of David in the cave of Adullam and among the fastnesses of Judah's mountains is only half told without the help of his Ps. 57. To see the whole of a man, we need to see both his external surroundings and the uprising of his heart to God above all their depression and gloom.

In this period of David's history we may locate also Psalms 55 and 58 — the former opening to view the great deep of his heart-trials, yet not less, his perpetual resort to God in prayer for help, and his placid trust, evinced in sweetly casting his burden on the Lord. In the latter, his soul is keenly sensitive to the sharp injustice under which he suffers from men in power, whom he warns solemnly of their responsibility to the righteous Judge of all. These Psalms give us yet more of that inside view of character which so finely supplements and interprets the external facts of David's history.

This chapter 22, shows us the classes of men who composed David's *band*—adventurers and personal friends; viz., every one that was in distress, or in debt, or discontented, literally, *bitter of soul;*—such gathered about him and followed him as their captain, making his fortunes their own. His father's family are now with him and other personal friends; others doubtless who had become alienated from Saul; some because they had faith in David as the "coming man" of the kingdom; and some who, being in bad case, assumed that any change must improve their condition: such were the classes who made up this somewhat motley band.——It must have been specially trying to David that there were not more among them who sympathized with his faith and patience under his call to the kingdom and his long waiting till God's hand should pave his way to the throne.

At this juncture David disappeared for a while from the eye of Saul, having made his way, perhaps, unobserved, into the land of Moab. The fact that his grandmother Ruth was of that land, coupled with the hostile attitude of Saul toward Moab (1 Sam. 14: 47) may have secured for him a favorable reception there. His special request to the king was that his aged father and mother might find a refuge there until the present crisis in his fortunes should be past. This seems to have been readily granted. David and his men also found a stronghold in that country where they made their camp, until called back to the land of Judah by a special message sent him through the prophet Gad (v. 5). It is supposable that Gad was sent by Samuel, direct from the school of the prophets at Ramah, and that, having fulfilled this mission, he returned to his college.——Gad appears in David's subsequent history as "David's Seer" in God's messages to David, because of his numbering the people (2 Sam. 24: 11-19); as his adviser (together with Nathan) in organizing the temple worship (2 Chron. 29: 25); and as his historian, coupled in this service with Samuel and with Nathan (1 Chron. 29: 29).

David's return to Judah brought him again within the knowledge of Saul whose cabinet meeting on the occasion is on record (vs. 6–11). His servants, members of his royal cabinet, seem to have been mostly Benjamites. Hence the style of his appeal: If David, of Judah's tribe, comes to the throne, will ye, Benjamites, stand any chance at all to keep the fat offices ye hold under me? Then, as if he were indeed a much abused man, he says—"That all of you have conspired against me, and there is none that showeth me that my son (Jonathan) hath made a league with the son of Jesse; and there is none of you that is sorry for me or showeth me that my son hath stirred up my servant against me to lie in wait as at this day (v. 8)? "Uneasy lies the head that wears a crown;" fear and jealousy had upset the balance of his mind, and put diseased, distorted fancies in the place of realities. Miserable man!——He is now in a mood for bloody vengeance upon somebody! Just here Doeg the Edomite is on hand to put fuel to the fire of Saul's rage, charging Ahimelech and the priests at Nob with conspiracy against Saul. Saul summons them all before him, and —too infuriated to listen with the least candor to their defense—commands and witnesses their causeless murder—eighty-five priests in one day; and only one— Abiathar—fortunately not with them at the hour of slaughter—escaped. From him David learned the sad tale. Thenceforward Abiathar the priest became David's companion in tribulation, and his fast friend, till the rebellion of Adonijah.

In 1 Sam. 23, we have new scenes in this great drama. Keilah, a walled town, its site no longer traceable, but associated (Josh. 15 : 44) with Achzib and Mareshah, and not many miles south and east from Gath; also the "wilderness of Ziph," in the vicinity of Hebron; were the geographical localities. The "wilderness of Ziph" suggests the contemporary Ps. 54, of which the heading is—"A Psalm of David when the Ziphims came and said to Saul, Doth not David hide himself with us?" The history shows that the men of Ziph came to Saul with this message twice. See 1 Sam. 23 : 19, and 26 : 1. Constant prayer for help and precious trust that God will help, are the theme of this sweet song. Outwardly every view before the eye of David was dark and frowning; but looking upward—lo, God was there—a very present help in every hour of need.

That the men of Keilah, suffering from plundering bands of Philistines, should have sought help from David rather than from Saul indicates his standing before the people and the service rendered to the country by his band of armed men. It astonishes us that Keilah, saved by David, is so ungrateful as to consent to surrender him to the power of Saul. The fact gives us a new sense of the trials incident to this period of David's history. He owed his safety to the forwarnings of danger which he obtained from the Lord, at one time through the prophet Gad; at other times through the priests with the linen ephod.——In the wilderness of Ziph Saul's host came so near to David that Jonathan made it convenient to have a personal interview with him, in which they entered again into solemn mutual covenant (vs. 16–18). Jonathan ere this had learned in some way that the Lord had designated David for the throne of Israel. It was his fond hope that himself might be second in authority under him. For some reason the Lord was not in this plan, and it failed.

Tidings that the Philistines had invaded the land recalled Saul and his army from this pursuit of David, and once more relieved him from impending peril.

These providental escapes from Saul are thought by many critics to have been the occasion of Ps. 31. See my Notes on this Psalm. While the allusions in this Psalm are so general that it may apply to far other circumstances than those of David, yet its application to these scenes of his history is natural and easy, and gives us a precious view of the fullness and strength of his trust in Israel's God. It is refreshing to read the Psalm in connection with these terribly trying scenes of David's life. Oh, the blessedness of having such a God for one's unfailing Friend, and such a faith in his loving and evermore protecting providence!

The special incident in chap. 24, is another march of Saul into the hill country of Judah with three thousand men in pursuit of David. Engedi, David's rock-fortress, overhangs the Dead Sea, about midway from end to end on its western shore. It is a point exceedingly difficult of access, and admirably chosen for David's purposes of concealment and safety. Here, through one of those divine providences which the Lord knows so well how to order, Saul turns aside for private purposes, alone, into the very cave in which David and his men lay secreted, and thus threw himself unwittingly into the hands of the man he was seeking to kill. David advanced and cut off the skirt of Saul's robe. Then, calling Saul's attention to the fact he made him see that he was truly his friend, and could not be induced by any consideration to take his life. For the moment, Saul's heart was touched by this magnanimity, and seems to have been grateful for the sparing of his life. Could it be possible that this David was indeed innocent, and that the charges brought against him were vilely slanderous and false?——Saul, apparently aware that David would one day be king, improved this opportunity for a covenant binding David to spare his family when he should be among the dead. Then Saul went home; but he did not invite David to resume his old place at his court; nor did David see any other path of safety for himself save with his warriors again in the strongholds of the hill country of Judah.

In connection with the scenes of this chapter 24, and with the analogous scenes of chap. 26, it were well to read Ps. 35—a noble Psalm, showing that David's lofty magnanimity in twice sparing the life of Saul interlinked itself with his piety toward God. The deepest sentiments of his soul held that "vengeance belongeth to the Lord," and that the highest human wisdom leaves it there for God to repay in his own time. He, therefore, said—let me never attempt to pluck from the Almighty hand this sublime prerogative! Trying, indeed, it is to be cruelly slandered—trying to have one's life hunted and imperiled for no fault; but God knows it all, and will right the wrongs of his waiting children according to his infinite wisdom and love.——See my Notes on Ps. 35.

Chap. 25 records (v. 1) the death of the prophet Samuel, and then recites the experiences of David with Nabal, a rich but crusty shepherd of Mt. Carmel, in south-eastern Judah. This contact resulted in developing Nabal's churlishness and folly, and, also the excellent good sense and wisdom of Abigail his wife, terminating ultimately in Nabal's death, and the marriage of David and Abigail. It is supposable—not certain—that this man Nabal suggested to David his Psalms 14 and 53, in both of which he draws the picture of the Hebrew "*nabal*"—the fool. See my Notes on Ps. 14. This man Nabal was wicked and mean enough to inspire in a soul noble as David's the utterances which appear in these kindred Psalms. The history shows that David's abhorrence of Nabal's character was keen and strong. Not unnaturally his subsequent reflections upon it led him to these generalizations upon human depravity.

In chap. 26, we find a series of events bearing a striking analogy with those recorded in chap. 24—alike in these points: that Saul is brought most completely into the power of David; that David's servants suggest and advise the taking of Saul's life, but he magnanimously refuses and will not harm a hair of his head; that he takes a tangible proof of these facts; that when the facts are brought before Saul, he is deeply affected, and even more fully than before, confesses his folly and sin toward David. These scenes, however, are unlike in too many points to admit the supposition that the basis of fact was only one and the same. The geographical localities are unlike; the first at Engedi—the second in the wilderness of Ziph: in the first Saul was alone; in the second he lay with his chief warriors about him: in the first he was not asleep—in the second he was: in the first, David's attendants are not named, but in the second, Abishai was with him: in the first, the thing taken away to certify to the fact was a part of the skirt of Saul's robe—in the second, Saul's spear and a cruse of water from his bolster: and, to mention no more, the reported conversations between David and Saul, though alike in general drift were quite unlike in the particulars.* It is also noticeable that in the last case Saul not only said, "I have sinned," but added—"Return, my son David, for I will no more do thee harm, because my soul [life] was precious in thine eyes this day; behold, I have played the fool and erred exceedingly" (v. 21). But David had known Saul too well to put confidence in him, or trust himself one day in his hands. Indeed the next chapter opens with words from David more despondent than we have elsewhere met with; "David said in his heart, I shall now perish one day by the hand of Saul." Consequently, this chapter 27, narrates his second flight to Achish king of Gath, to find refuge again among the Philistines. Sadly for David this course subjected him to the moral strain of an ever present temptation to

---

* In David's speech (v. 19) we read—"If the Lord have stirred thee up against me, let him accept an offering." But how could David speak thus of the Lord?——The answer is, in the same sense in which the evil spirit upon Saul is said to have come from the Lord—*i. e.*, by a simply permissive agency, and this at once retributive in view of Saul's great sin, and in harmony with the natural laws under which human depravity works in the case of hardened, desperate sinners. David's meaning, therefore, is—If thou hast provoked the Lord to give thee up to such madness of passion, repent and conciliate him with sacrifice and offering.

DAVID AND SAUL. 159

deception—as we shall see.——He and his 600 took their families and effects, and, therefore, naturally sought a city somewhat secluded for their residence. They were assigned to Ziklag, which had belonged to Judah; then to Simeon; then fell into Philistine hands; but from this time onward was a city of Judah.—— The passage (v. 6); "Wherefore Ziklag pertaineth unto the kings of Judah to this day," was manifestly written *after* Judah had kings of its own, commencing with Rehoboam; and *before* the captivity when their control ceased. But these words were probably introduced by some compiler, and are not from the original author of this book.

We notice (on v. 7) that David's stay in the country (the fields, not cities) of the Philistines was one year and four months—the first note of duration we have met with between David's anointing and Saul's death.

Why did David and his men invade the Geshurites and Amalekites (vs. 8–12)? Perhaps in self-defense; perhaps for subsistence, and because they were the national enemies of Israel. These tribes were on friendly terms with the Philistines, so that David finds it expedient to mislead Achish when he inquired upon whom he had been making an inroad.——In v. 11 we may omit the word "*tidings*," for which we have no equivalent in Hebrew, and read—David saved neither man nor woman alive to bring them to Gath, *i. e.*, as captives; lest they should tell too much, or their nationality be known. So Achish retained all confidence in David and was quite ready to take him and his band into the pending invasion of Israel—a fact which made the condition of David intensely critical. Shall he break friendship with Achish, or shall he go with him and fight against Saul and Israel? Unless God interpose to help in this dilemma, who can?

Chap. 27 opens with preparations among the Philistine lords for vigorous war upon Israel. Achish thinks highly of David as a warrior, and assures him that he and his men must go. David's reply is skillfully indefinite: "Surely thou shalt see what thy servant can do" (v. 2). Achish is so much pleased that he would fain make David and his band his own body-guard.—— In the sequel (chap. 29) the lords object so decidedly and so reasonably against David's going with them that he is dismissed, greatly to his relief no doubt, and fortunately, since it relieved him from the temptation to perpetual duplicity toward Achish.

At this point the history of this military expedition is suspended for the purpose of narrating the experiences of King Saul (28: 3–25).

The hosts of Philistia are much further north than usual—Shunem, the site of their camp, being within the tribal limits of Issachar, on the west point of Little Hermon, nearly four miles north from Jezreel. Saul mustered his army on the mountains of Gilboa which skirt the eastern portion of the great plain of Esdraelon —fifty miles north by east from Jerusalem. "Three miles north of them is the parallel chain of Little Hermon. These two heights mark the position of the two armies; Saul and his men on the western heights of Gilboa; the Philistines on those of Hermon. Endor is beyond Hermon on the northern slope. Saul, not without risk and toil, passes by night across the valley and over Hermon beyond the camp of the Philistines to consult the sorceress at Endor." *

The historian again reminds us that Samuel was dead (v. 3), and states that Saul had exterminated from the land those who had familiar spirits and the wizards. When he saw the immense and formidable hosts of the Philistines, "he was afraid, and his heart trembled" (v. 5). In his distress he sought counsel and help from the Lord, but found no answer, neither by dreams, nor by the Urim (the linen Ephod of the priest) nor by prophets—all these usual methods of obtaining answers from God failing him utterly.

In this emergency Saul determined to consult some woman " who had a familiar spirit," *i. e.*, who had some supposed spirit so under her control as to *come at her call*, even as the servants of a family come at the call of their master. The original Hebrew word is used for a *bottle*, the analogy being apparently this—that as a bottle supposes something contained within it, so the body of the sorceress is supposed to have some personal presence and force within, other than human. This analogy suggests ventriloquism as the art by which the sorceress practiced upon the credulity and superstition of the people; the pretense being that this other (ap-

---
* Coleman's Text Book and Atlas, p. 115.

SAUL AND THE WITCH AT ENDOR. 161

parent) voice is that of the spirit.——Saul said: Find me a *woman;* implying that this art was specially practiced by their sex. The narrative assumes that this sorceress of Endor pretended to call up the spirits of the dead—this power or skill being commonly styled "necromancy." By the art of ventriloquism sounds were produced which seemed to come up from the under world—out of caves or of deep recesses. Thus, naturally, necromancy and ventriloquism were twin arts, operated together, the one by means of the other.

The leading facts of this narrative (vs. 11–19) are clearly stated and easily understood. I take the most obvious sense to be the true one, and must believe, therefore, that the sorceress called for Samuel, and *that Samuel in fact came* and talked with Saul, uttering words most true and terribly appalling. Saul said (in substance): I have called thee up in this way because I could get no answer from God. I was in an agony of fear before the Philistines, and I felt that I must see thee.——Samuel replied: Why call me up from the state of the dead, seeing the Lord has departed from thee and become thine enemy? What have I ever done for thee—what can I ever do for thee, save to bring to thee the words of God? But now God has no more words for thee except these dreadful words of doom—that to-morrow thou and thy sons must go into the world of the dead; thy army be cut to pieces; thy camp seized and plundered, and thy kingdom subdued before the Philistine army. The Lord has taken the kingdom utterly from thee and from thy house, and given it to thy neighbor, even to David.——So much seems to be clearly affirmed, in words that will bear no other significance.

The more vital question yet remains. Was this success in evoking the dead from the under world ordinary or extraordinary? Was it an average illustration of the powers of sorcery as practiced in those ages, or was it an entirely exceptional case, permitted by God's special providence for rebuke and awful warning to Saul—rebuke for the sin of forsaking God and then seeking help in his distress otherwise than by repentance and by returning legitimately to the Lord;* and

---

* In this connection let note be taken of the comments on this transaction which appears in 1 Chron. 10: 13, 14: "So Saul died for

warning that should ring the death-knell of his doom before the final blow should fall? I answer most decidedly, the latter. Nothing can be inferred from this narrative in regard to the real powers of the sorceress of Endor. Her astonishment when she saw Samuel proves that this was entirely a new experience to her, all unknown before. She shrieked with amazement and fear. She said: "I saw God (elohim) ascending out of the earth." Her choice of the word "*elohim*" indicates mingled astonishment, surprise, and fear. She could think at the moment of nothing less than God— the awful God! Saul inquired—What is his form, his appearance, understanding her to speak not of many gods but of one; and she in reply gave an answer by which Saul recognized the person of Samuel.

As to the magic arts of this sorceress the original words used and the facts of the narrative prove only this: not that she ever on any other occasion called up the dead; not that she obtained audible reponses from the spirits of the dead, or knowledge in any way from such spirits; but only that she *pretended* to do these things, and made use of ventriloquism and perhaps other kindred arts to make people believe that she possessed and used these powers.*

One other question may perhaps arise, viz., In what sense could Samuel say to Saul—"To-morrow shalt thou and thy sons be with me?" (v. 19.)——I can only answer: The case does not require us to press the words beyond the sense of *being in the state of the dead*. There was no occasion then and there to indicate whether his condition in that state would be happy or miserable. Nor can we infer from this passage either that the Hebrews of that age did, or that they did not, know and believe in one place and state of existence for the righteous and another for the wicked. For aught that appears here they may or they may not have thought

---

his transgression which he committed against the Lord, even against the word of the Lord, which he kept not, and also for asking counsel of one that had a familiar spirit, to inquire of it; and inquired not of the Lord: therefore he slew him, and turned the kingdom unto David the son of Jesse."——This shows that one of the fatal sins of Saul was this resort to familiar spirits, instead of humbling himself before the Lord and seeking help from him only.

* See more on this subject of magic arts in my Pentatuech, pp. 276-279, and in my "Isaiah" pp. 66-69.

of one place and state exclusively for the righteous and another for the wicked dead. Samuel stopped short of any teaching on this subject. It was enough for his purpose then to apprise Saul that he and his sons must die on the morrow and pass into the state of the dead.——Samuel, however, did say enough to show that in his belief and certain knowledge, there could be neither fellowship nor sympathy in either this or any other world between such a spirit as that of Saul and his own.

Resuming the thread of the history, as in 1 Sam. 30, we note that the absence of David and his warriors from Ziklag for three days, accompanying the Philistines so long in their preparation and in the outset of their march upon Northern Palestine, exposed their wives, children, and cattle to capture by a band of Amalekites. Noticeably they sought spoil, not blood; and while they took away every living thing and burnt the city, "they slew none great or small." *——The return of David and his party to this scene of smoking ruins and utter desolation—wives, children, cattle, no longer there—was a moment of overwhelming trial. David's men seemed half maddened with grief. Surely, thought they, somebody must be to blame for this; it must be David. So "the people spake of stoning him, because the soul of all the people was grieved, every man for his sons and for his daughters" (v. 6).

How sublimely David rose above the depression, the distractions, the sadness of these surroundings is finely put in these words: "*But David encouraged himself in the Lord his God.*" Ah, he had no other friend who stood by him in this emergency; and fortunately he could endure without any other. It sufficed him that the infinite God stood by him, never more near and true; his manifested love never more consoling; his strong arm never more sustaining! Very rarely does David's historian turn from his narration of David's outer life to speak of his inner life—the sources of his hope, and courage, and strength; but this case is an exception. We are thankful for it. We are glad to know that in this hour of sorest earthly trial David looked upward;

---

* The sparing of all human life suggests that like the Ishmaelites and Midianites of old (Gen. 37: 27, 28), they were slave-traders and thought of marketing their slaves in Egypt.

and lo, God was near. He, too, had wives and perhaps little ones, and knew as little of their fortunes as his soldiers knew of the case of their wives and children. In his personal trials he might as reasonably look for their sympathy as they for his, and might as reasonably blame them as they him; but in the strength of his faith and piety, he rose above all these manifold, distracting trials and "*encouraged himself in the Lord his God.*" Let us be thankful for one such example of endurance and of victory through the strength of the Mighty One of Jacob.

David calls for Abiathar and the ephod, and through it inquires—"Shall I pursue after this troop? Shall I overtake them?" The answer brought the first external ray of light and hope:—"Yes, pursue;" "thou shalt surely overtake," and, better yet, "shalt without fail, recover all."——Did not they give chase with warm heart, and make good time?

The pillaging Amalekites seem to have had most of three days the start, but moved off slowly, incumbered with booty and slow traveling captives. When far enough away to feel safe, they gave themselves up to eating, drinking, dancing, and wild exultations over their spoil. While thus occupied David and the four hundred whose strength held out through this hot and long pursuit, fell furiously upon them and made one long day of terrible slaughter, recovering meantime all their stolen wives, children, and cattle, and in addition taking the other spoil which the marauding party had stolen and their own animals—an immense booty.——It was at once a case of David's forethoughtfulness and of God's nicely adjusting providence, that David, precisely at this juncture, having come into possession of such an amount of spoil, distributed it so liberally among the cities of Judah. It was the very time of all times to call their attention to him as the great warrior of the age; as their own tribal chieftain, and their devoted friend. Whether at the moment of this decision to dispose of his spoil in this way he had already heard of Saul's death, does not appear; but the Lord knew it, and his providences were competent to "time things," so that the presents were in season to pave the way for David to become king of Judah.

One other circumstance occurring in this scene, throws light on David's character. Two hundred of his six hundred warriors became too faint and weary to go further than the brook Besor (vs. 9, 10), and were left there in charge of their baggage. When the four hundred returned victorious to this company, David came near and saluted them, inquiring kindly for their welfare. The men of Belial who had, as they thought, done the severest marching and all the fighting, said—Give none of the spoil to those two hundred men; only restore to them their own wives and children. Not so, said David; they must share equally with the rest. The Lord has given us the victory and all this spoil; in gratitude to him let us not deal severely but generously with our brethren. So this became a statute and ordinance for Israel; those who guard the stuff share equally with those who go into the battle.

Death of Saul.

With chap. 31, we close the first book of Samuel and the record of Saul's life. In this great battle, Israel fled before the Philistines, and many fell slain on Mt. Gilboa. Saul and his sons and his armor-bearer were among the slain. In 1 Sam. 31: 5 it is said that Saul, having been severely wounded, put an end to his own life by falling upon his own sword. The account in 1 Chron. 10: 3–6 re-indorses this statement. But in 2 Sam. 1: 6–10 a certain Amalekite appears coming to David and saying, perhaps truly, yet it may have been falsely—" At Saul's request I slew him, and then took his crown and bracelets, and have brought them to David my lord."—This man of Amalek no doubt expected from David a liberal reward, but met, instead, his own death. The circumstance served to show that David was a sincere mourner over the death of Saul. The inhabitants of Jabesh-Gilead, remembering Saul's early kindness, sent their valiant men to recover his body and the bodies of his fallen sons and give them an honorable burial. They well deserved this honorable mention of their gratitude and valor.

David's Elegy upon the Slain.

The *song of lamentation or elegy*, composed by David upon occasion of the death of Saul and Jonathan (2 Sam. 1: 17-27) has been admired in all ages for its touching pathos and exquisite beauty. We can not afford to pass it without the respectful attention ever due to tender grief and sympathetic sorrow over the fallen dead.

"David lamented with this lamentation." He not only composed this elegy, but sung it; not only sung it himself, but gave command that it be taught to the sons and daughters of "Judah"—*of Judah* specially because they were of his own tribe; because then and for the ensuing seven years he was king of Judah only; and because his magnanimous soul discarded all tribal jealousies, and would have the men of Judah mourn for Saul no less than the men of Benjamin.—— "He bade them teach Judah"—not "the *use of* the bow," which would be utterly foreign from the sense; but "the *bow*," i. e., the *bow-song*—this very song in which "the bow of Jonathan" (v. 22) holds a sufficiently prominent position to supply a distinctive name for this song. The Hebrews were accustomed to designate their songs by some such catch-words, of which we have instances apparently in the Psalms. ——As we might expect, this beautiful poetic elegy found its congenial place in the "Book of Jasher"—a repository, as we have seen, of fugitive poems produced from time to time among the Hebrew people. See Josh. 10: 13.

Num. 21: 14-18 seems to indicate the same or a similar collection under the title—"The book of the wars of the Lord."

The poem opens with v. 19. "The beauty of Israel" —her warrior king and his noble sons—"are slain upon the high places of Israel" [Mount Gilboa]. The keynote of the song is in the refrain—"How are the mighty fallen!" repeated in vs. 25, 27. Such is our sense of death when brave and mighty men sink in one brief moment beneath his power.——"Tell it not in Gath"— for David had spent years in Gath, and knew but too well how its sons and daughters would catch up these tidings, and hasten to their idol temples with jubilant songs of triumph. He knew how the streets of Askelon would re-echo with rejoicings; and this thought was bitter to his soul.——"Ye mountains of Gilboa, let no dew or rain fall on you," henceforth forever! Let there be no fields, rich with products for sacrificial offerings. Let everlasting blight mar your former glory! It would be painfully incongruous to see those hill-tops smiling again in verdure and beauty after having been the theater of scenes so mournful. To the sad heart of mourners it seems some relief to imprecate desolation on the localities which have become associated with the death of the loved and the brave. All this is touchingly true to nature. These imprecations were felt to be the more appropriate, because on those heights the shield of the mighty was vilely cast away as if of one who had never been anointed king of Israel. Yet let it not be hastily assumed that Saul and Jonathan were not brave and successful warriors. The bow of Jonathan never turned back from before the mighty; the sword of Saul never returned from battle without being laden with trophies of the slain. Moreover, Saul and Jonathan were not only valiant in war; "they were lovely and pleasant in their lives." Of Jonathan's amiable and noble spirit, David never could say too much. He had profound reason to appreciate him, and he was of a nature too appreciative, too noble and magnanimous, not to reciprocate such love. As to Saul, David cherished a profound regard for him as his anointed sovereign, and, no doubt, saw much (in some aspects of his character) that he could both esteem and love; but Saul's manifestations were strangely mixed; and David leaves us a little in doubt how much of this touching elegy of Saul and Jonathan was indebted to Jonathan rather than to Saul for its tenderness and pathos, and its unsurpassed appreciation of amiable qualities. What this elegy would have been if Saul only had been its subject, we are not in a condition to judge.

In v. 24, Saul stands out in his distinctive personality as king of Israel. The daughters of the land might fitly bewail the death of their king, remembering how he had ministered to their adornment—the ruling passion in the oriental woman's heart being recognized here as in the song of Deborah (Judge 5: 30). But when the poet's thought turns to Jonathan (vs. 25, 26), his tones tremble with most touching pathos:—" I am distressed for thee, my brother Jonathan; very pleasant hast thou been to me; thy love to me was wonderful, passing the love of women." Thus the loving heart of David bewails what seemed to him the untimely death of his dearest friend. All his fond hopes that Jonathan might survive his father, and stand beside himself in the honors or the cares of Israel's throne, are dashed suddenly and forever. The joys of a friendship so deep, so self-sacrificing, so noble, and so pure—ah, how have they passed away, to return no more!

Saul's Character.

The whole of Saul's recorded life having now passed before us, it is pertinent at this point to review his character.

Physically, of commanding dignified person, he no doubt seemed to the people of Israel demanding a king, to fill their ideal admirably. Men who looked on the outward appearance, not on the heart, would reasonably ask nothing more. He reigned long enough to show that qualities lying deeper than the outward appearance were requisite for a wise and prosperous king on the throne of Israel. Unfortunately these physical qualities drew to him more or less homage and flattery, and so ministered to his pride and to his great fall.

Psychologically, Saul was dangerously impulsive in spirit, of strong emotions and terribly excitable temper. It was due to these qualities that he so readily felt the sympathetic influence of the music and the songs of those prophet-bands at Gibeah (1 Sam. 10: 10), and again at Ramah (1 Sam. 19: 22–26). But especially must we attribute to these qualities of his mind (in part at least) those fearful outbursts of jealousy and passion under which once and again he hurled his javelin at David, and also at his own noble son Jonathan. The narrative would justify us in ascribing these ebullitions of mad passion in part to an "evil spirit" that came upon him; yet not in any such sense as would rule out the normal working of his own impulses, and the natural development of his own mental qualities.

SAUL'S CHARACTER. 169

Saul's insanity was not of a sort which vacated his own moral responsibility. His real character shines out in all those words and deeds of violent passion. We must not attribute them to any foreign spirit in any such sense or degree as would remove them from the control of his own will or from the realm of his responsible activities.

The fatal defect in Saul was the want of true piety. Morally, his character lacked bottom. His will was not yielded implicitly and absolutely to the will of God. It was never the first law of his soul to obey God in every thing with no possible exception. In this point he was in utter contrast with David, whose whole soul went forth in the words: "O God, my heart is fixed." "I delight to do thy will, O God." If Saul had been true to God he would have obeyed the great test-command to exterminate Amalek, and never could have suffered himself to modify the divine directions. If his heart had been wholly right with God, he never would have apostatized and thus have made it a moral necessity for God to forsake him. The great moral lesson which Saul's history leaves for the instruction of mankind is, therefore, precisely this: That without true piety, the finest qualities of character and the highest position in society will fail utterly to make a true and noble man. If Saul's heart had been true to God he would have been one of the grandest specimens of humanity. But, lacking this true obedience to God, he made his life an utter failure, and his character a moral wreck. In his case the noblest physical and mental qualities are proved to be utterly weak to resist the temptations to pride, jealousy, passion, and madness, unless they are put under the keeping of grace divine and the soul be brought into harmony with the will of God.——Such help from God toward self-control and toward the formation of a noble character, Saul never sought. He was never a man of prayer. David was. In this one vital and fundamental respect they stand before us in total contrast with each other. True, Saul sought after the Lord in his great distress when overwhelmed with fear; but *never in other circumstances.* Consequently, it was all strange business to him. He had not made himself familiar with the way to the mercy-seat. His soul could not turn naturally to his God as to a well known and long tried friend. Oh, how did he feel the need of such a friend in that dreadful night when he threaded his desolate and perilous way, past the pickets of the Philistine host, to find the witch of Endor—only to learn there the more surely that God had utterly forsaken him; that terrible defeat, slaughter, and death lay but a few hours before!

Brief Review of David.

The first well-defined stage of David's public life closes with the death of Saul. Before we leave it to pass on, let us note his own review of it as it appears in his Ps. 18, and, with only slight variations, in 2 Sam. 22. This Psalm was written at a later period and contemplates his deliverance from other enemies as well as from Saul; but as is plainly indicated in the heading of Ps. 18, it looked toward Saul pre-eminently.—— This Psalm is sublimely *full of God*. "I will love thee, O Lord, my strength. The Lord is my rock and my fortress; my God in whom I will trust;"--such is its lofty strain. His salvation from all his enemies is from God alone. How grandly he accumulates epithets and symbols to set forth the interposing power of his Great Deliverer! How sublimely did his God appear for his help in every hour of his need! Conscious of personal innocence and integrity as to the great issue between himself and Saul, he had but to trust in the Holy One of Israel, and deliverance came at length!

CHAPTER VIII.

About to enter upon a new chapter of David's history —*David as king*—it is in place to refer to our sources of historical information, viz., 2 Sam. 2-24 to 1 Kings 2: 11; and co-ordinately with this, 1 Chron. 11-29 chapters—the former (2 Sam. and Kings) more full in matters pertaining to his political and military life; to his great sins and to his domestic trials; the latter (1 Chron. 11-29) more full on the points of his religious activities; his re-organization of the tabernacle worship, and his immense preparations for the temple. The course of David's history must be suspended here for a moment to introduce the reader to these very valuable books—viz., of Chronicles.

Author and Date of the Books of Chronicles.

Compared with Samuel and Kings, the Chronicles are a collateral history, going over to some extent the same ground. It is quite obvious that they were compiled from the same original sources, viz., the annals of the Hebrew people, written at or near the time of the events, and by a succession of prophets of whom some at least were Levites. From Moses onward, provision was made for a permanent record of all important events, to be kept in the national archives of the Hebrew people. To these original documents we find the compilers of these historical books continually refer for more full particulars.

The important questions as to these historical books are—*When were they compiled, and by whom?*——Neither date nor author are given in the books themselves, nor indeed in any records that have come down to us. We are left, therefore, to approximate the true answer to these questions as best we may by the study of the books themselves, comparing the adaptation of the points they make to the known case of the people in their subsequent history. For it is safe to assume that the books were compiled to answer a purpose. It can not be doubted that the books of Samuel and of Kings were compiled at an earlier date, and were, therefore, in the hands of him who compiled the Chronicles and of his contemplated first readers for whose use he made this compilation. He made up these books because in his view something of this sort was specially needed in his day.——We may therefore inquire:—Is any period of Hebrew history known to us in which the specialties of these books of Chronicles—the points in which they differ from the books of Samuel and of Kings—would be particularly pertinent and applicable? If so, then, with high probability, that was the period when these books were compiled.

In my view the times of the restoration—the age of Ezra and of Nehemiah—were such a period. If we study that age carefully as we have it in the historic books of those men, and then look thoroughly through the books of Chronicles, we shall be struck with the admirable adaptation of these books to those times. The points of history selected and the points omitted will combine to show a remarkable adjustment to the moral wants and demands of the restored people.——Thus in the times of Ezra and Nehemiah there was very great moral power *in the Hebrew genealogies.* Perhaps it was never before or since greater than then. It was vital to revive and to endear the memory of the fathers and patriarchs of the chosen people. The returned exiles had need of heroic endurance, to which nothing could minister more directly than a sense of their nationality —the power of the great names and noble spirit of the founders of Israel. It was, moreover, of some importance to weed out the adventurers—the men of mixed or unknown parentage.——Thus we see that both Ezra (chap. 2) and Nehemiah (chap. 7) gave special attention to enrollment, pedigree, nationality. Hence, the adaptation of the genealogical chapters 1 Chron. 1–9.

Next, observe that Saul's history had few moral lessons of special value for the returned exiles. So he is dismissed with one short chapter (10)—that of his death.——Of David's history, all those portions that precede the death of Saul are entirely omitted. His wars are touched briefly, those against Syria, Zobah, Moab, Ammon, and Edom coming under notice mainly to account for the immense spoils which they poured into David's hand and which he consecrated to the building of the great temple.——Under the head of matters omitted, nothing is more striking than the omission of the whole history of the ten tribes after the revolt under Jeroboam, except so far as they come into such contact with Judah as compelled some allusion to their history. This omission strikes out the history of Elijah and Elisha.

In the line of matters not omitted but embraced, we have a very full account of David's religious work for the nation—bringing back the ark; re-organizing the ritual worship; classifying the labors of priest and Levite; organizing the new department of sacred song; and making immense preparations for building the temple. All these were points of most vital interest to the men of the restoration. Precisely this was the sort of work which God was laying to their hand. They had just such an organization to effect; they had the great temple to rebuild. It was worth the whole labor and cost of writing these books of Chronicles, to bring down and utilize the example and the labors of David and his associates.——Further, the gifts of the people toward the temple-building—so spontaneous, so liberal, so enthusiastic (1 Chron. 28 and 29)—were of priceless moral value to the returned exiles. So also it was in place to tell them very particularly of the great work of Solomon in its erection, and of his wonderful consecration of the finished temple by prayer, and sacrifice, and song.

In selecting points of Jewish history, from the revolt to the captivity, the compiler dwelt with special minuteness on the great religious reformations wrought in the reigns of Jehoshaphat, Hezekiah, and Josiah. The wicked kings are passed with less detail—yet we may be thankful that having presented the great sins of Manasseh, he gave us (as the book of Kings does not) an account of his confession and repentance. Those great reformations were full of instruction, and of inspiring impulse to the men of Ezra's time.——If we were to examine in yet more detail the points omitted and not omitted, in these books, compared with the corresponding history in 2 Samuel and Kings, the comparison would be found to bear in the same direction, showing yet more clearly that the compiler of the Chronicles aimed to adapt his work to such a people as the returned exiles, and to such a state of things as then existed. There can, therefore, be no reasonable doubt that the books were compiled then and for an exigency then pending and pressing.

Equally clear is it that Ezra was the man to do this work, or at least to see that it was done and to supervise it. He was "a ready scribe in the law of Moses;" he "had prepared his heart to seek the law of the Lord, and to do it, and to teach in Israel statutes and judgments" (Ezra 7: 6–10). His soul breathes itself forth in Ps. 119: 97: "O how love I thy law; it is my meditation all the day." His spirit, therefore; his familiarity with the Hebrew Scriptures; his prominence as the religious instructor of the returned exiles, and his absorbing interest in this work, all conspire to designate him as the compiler of these books.——It may fitly be added that Jewish tradition attributes to him the great work of revising the Hebrew Scriptures then extant—a work to which the compilation of Chronicles bears no little analogy.

It remains to refer in a word to certain points of internal evidence which indicate with high probability the *date* of compilation of the books of Chronicles;— viz., (a.) Its genealogical records seem to come down to the captivity; *e. g.*, 1 Chron. 5: 22: "They dwelt in their stead until the captivity;"—1 Chron. 6: 15: "Jehozadak went into captivity when the Lord carried away Judah and Jerusalem by the hand of Nebuchadnezzar;"—and 9: 1: "So all Israel were reckoned by genealogies. Behold, they were written in the books of Israel and Judah, who were carried away to Babylon for their transgression."——(b.) Of perhaps yet more decisive bearing toward the same conclusion is the fact that at its close—(viz., 2 Chron. 36: 20–23) the history actually shades off into the history of Ezra itself, giving us (as the history of 2 Kings does not) the duration of the exile—viz., "till the reign of the kingdom of Persia;" *i. e.*, until Babylon fell into their hands, and their empire was located centrally in Babylon itself— closing with the edict of Cyrus for the restoration of the Jews—a paragraph, which, as it ends this book of Chronicles, so does it also begin the book of Ezra—a method of connection which we have already noticed where the book of Judges resumes and continues the history of the book of Joshua.

David as King.

Since the hour when, by the hand of the prophet Samuel, the Lord designated David as prospective king of Israel, and poured on his head the consecrating oil (1 Sam. 16), the thread of the historic narrative has run along the line of his life. We have had Saul only because of his relations to David. Saul being now dead, we shall see David in new relations.

Comprehensively, the future history of David will embrace these leading events.

I. The steps to the throne, first of Judah; ultimately of all Israel.

II. Jerusalem wrested from the Jebusites; built up and made his capital.

III. The ark located at Jerusalem; a special tabernacle prepared for it, and this city made the great religious center.

IV. The tabernacle worship fully reorganized, with the important accompaniment of sacred song.

V. The great promise made to David that his posterity should fill the throne of Israel indefinitely, including and terminating in the great Messiah.

VI. David's wars; the subjugation of the Philistines, of Zobah, Syria, Moab, Ammon, and Edom.

VII. His great sins in the matter of Bathsheba and Uriah.

VIII. His domestic calamities consequent upon these sins, involving the history of Amnon and of Absalom.

IX. His sin of numbering the people—which resulted in fixing the site of the temple.

X. David's work of preparation for the temple.

XI. Arrangements for the succession; conspiracy of Adonijah; Solomon.

XII. David's last words and character.

Following the order of topics above indicated, we note,

I. *The steps to the throne, first of Judah; ultimately of all Israel.* Tidings of Saul's death reached David at Ziklag where he lay with his trusty six hundred. This death put a new face upon his circumstances; opened to him new possibilities; and naturally raised in his mind the inquiry—What is to be done next? Shall he make any movement looking toward his elevation to the throne? Judah was his own tribe; his few adherents were chiefly of that tribe: his sympathies lay there and his hopes also; therefore, true to the impulses of his religious character and life, he brings before the Lord this first great question— Shall I go up to any of the cities of Judah? The Lord answered, Go: and to his next question—To which? The Lord replied, To Hebron. This city had been conquered by Caleb and made his inheritance (Josh. 14: 12–15); was centrally located for the tribe of Judah; was a strong city and in friendly relations to David; was hallowed, moreover, with interesting associations as the burial-place of Abraham and Sarah (Gen. 25: 9, 10, and 23: 19, 20); and if Caleb's posterity inherited the spirit of their father it must have had in it some excellent material. It was twenty miles south of Jerusalem. Thither the men of Judah came and there they anointed David to be their king.

David would naturally expect efforts to secure the succession to the line of Saul; and hence saw the wisdom of carefully conciliating the good-will of the nation by manifestations of sympathy and kindness toward Saul's family and friends. Out of his wisdom, therefore, and probably out of his heart as well, he sent messengers to express his sympathy and good-will to the men of Jabesh-Gilead for the honor they paid to the remains of their king.* For similar reasons at a later period he rewarded the assassins of Ishbosheth, Saul's son and successor, by ordering their immediate execution (2 Sam. 4: 12).

Abner, Saul's captain-general, had placed Ishbosheth on the throne made vacant by Saul's death. First, he took him across the Jordan to Mahanaim and put him over all Gilead; † subsequently (perhaps in the order narrated in 2 Sam. 2: 9), "over Asher, Jezreel, Ephraim, Benjamin, and all Israel."——The historian narrates (2 Sam. 2: 12–32) the scenes of a battle fought at Gibeon, between Joab, commanding David's men, and Abner, at

* The Hebrew word (2 Sam. 2: 6) signifies, not "requite," but to manifest kindness and sympathy.

† The reasons for selecting Gilead and the trans-Jordanic tribes as the starting point may probably be found in the special sympathy felt for Saul in Jabesh-Gilead and in the reasons for it as suggested above in remarks on 1 Sam. 11 and 31.

the head of the warriors of Ishbosheth—the salient points of which were first, a bloody conflict between twelve chosen warriors from each army, in which every man seems to have fallen; and next a general fight in which Asahel, brother of Joab and Abishai was slain by Abner,* the battle ultimately closing with the fitting appeal of Abner to Joab—"Shall the sword devour forever? Knowest thou not that it will be bitterness in the latter end? How long shall it be ere thou bid the people return from following their brethren?" Thus better counsels prevailed; the mutual slaughter of brethren ceased — the counted dead numbering of David's men twenty, but of Abner's men three hundred and sixty. This is the only battle on record between the parties contending for the succession to the throne of Israel. David wisely adopted the policy of conciliation and "masterly inactivity," waiting, as he had trained himself to wait during the life of Saul, for the slow movements of God's providence to seat him in his own time on the throne over the whole people.——In the sequel of this struggle, Ishbosheth gave offense to his captain, Abner, whereupon the latter, in retaliation or from better motives (2 Sam. 3: 17, 18), laid his plans to bring all the tribes over to David. Ere they were fully carried out he was foully assassinated by Joab in revenge for the death of his brother Asahel. David promptly did his utmost to protest against this murder, to avert the displeasure of the people, and to conciliate their good-will.

Chap. 4 records the assassination of Ishbosheth by men who manifestly thought to please David, but who met his pronounced displeasure and their own exemplary death. This brought matters to a crisis. The head men of the opposition to David were in their graves; his prudence had won the good-will of the nation. It only remained to convene the representatives of all the tribes and place him triumphantly on the throne of Israel. They came to David at Hebron; "there David made a league with them before the Lord," analogous to the written charter under which Saul

* The Hebrew—" smote him under the fifth rib " means, and should be read—*in the abdomen*—through the bowels. The same emendation of our English version is called for in 2 Sam. 3: 27, and 4: 6, and 20: 10.

"took the kingdom" (1 Sam. 10: 25), and "they anointed David king over Israel" (2 Sam. 5: 30). David was thirty years old when made king over Judah; reigned seven and a half years over that tribe only, and thirty years over all Israel.

The author of 1 Chronicles gives in chaps. 11 and 12 a very particular account of the valiant men who had previously attached themselves to David, some at least of whom came to him at Ziklag before the death of Saul (1 Chron. 12: 1); men who had wrought signal exploits of heroism and power and were thoroughly prepared to lead the armies of Israel. This passage records, statistically, the large accessions to David's host that came in from the several tribes, among whom special mention is made of the Gadites (1 Chron. 12: 8–18). The figures in several cases seem very large. The small number relatively from Judah is surprising, not to say, incredible;—of Judah, only 6,800, while the very small tribe of Simeon counts up 7,100; the half tribe of Manasseh, 18,000; Ephraim, 20,800; Zebulon, 50,000; Dan, a tribe signally diminutive and almost unknown, 28,600; but, strangest of all, from the two and a half tribes east of Jordan, 120,000. The numbers from the powerful tribe of Judah sink into insignificance when placed by the side of other and much less populous tribes. We seem compelled to suspend judgment on the point of the accuracy of these numbers.

II. The kingdom being secured to David, his first work is to locate, build, and fortify his capital. For this purpose *Jerusalem is wrested from the Jebusites.* There were good reasons for the choice of this site. Hebron, though central for the tribe of Judah, was very remote from the center of Israel. The capital of the nation should be further north. Jerusalem fell within the original limits of Benjamin, so that the choice of this location might conciliate the good-will of the tribe which had furnished Saul for the first king. Moreover, the beauty of its site and its great natural strength (for war) were points by no means insignificant. David's eye was quick to note these attractions. Jerusalem must become his great city.* Probably some at least of

* Its site is thirty-two miles from the Mediterranean; eighteen (Coleman says twenty-four) from the Jordan; twenty miles north of Hebron; thirty-six miles south from Samaria.

THE ARK LOCATED IN JERUSALEM. 179

the immense hosts (put at 280,000 men) who gathered for his coronation remained to assist in the subjugation of this stronghold of the Jebusites.——The references to "the blind and the lame" (in 2 Sam. 5: 6, 8) are not very clear in our accepted version. In v. 6 we may translate: "The Jebusites spake to David, saying: Thou shalt not come in hither, for the blind and the lame shall keep thee off (*i. e.*, prevent thy coming in). So great was their confidence in the natural strength of their citadel that they believed the blind and lame of their number were adequate for its defense. Subsequently these words passed into a proverb: Because of the blind and the lame, he shall not enter the house; or as given by Perowne: "The blind and the lame are there; let him enter if he can."——The allusion to the blind and the lame as "the hated of David's soul," indicates how deeply this taunt had stirred his sensibilities.——According to 1 Chron. 11: 6, Joab was the first to master the ascent and thus secure the honor of being David's chief captain. The reference to "the gutter" (2 Sam. 5: 8) suggests that the ascent was made through some water-worn passage, which very possibly had been overlooked by the Jebusites.——The citadel once mastered, David proceeded to enlarge the area of this lofty summit and to strengthen its fortifications.——Thus Jerusalem was *the* city of David, born to greatness in the first year of his reign over all Israel. In the result it came to be more richly embalmed in sacred song and hallowed with more sweet associations and blessed memories than any other city brought before us in the holy Scriptures; indeed, we might say, above any other city known to history.

III. The next great event of David's reign was the location of the ark in his royal city. (See 2 Sam. 6, and 1 Chron. 13, and 15, and 16.) The narrative is most full in 1 Chron., especially as to the provision made for sacred song on this memorable occasion. Indeed, we find here the very song of praise which "David delivered into the hand of Asaph and his brethren on that day"—a song which re-appears in the Psalter, part of it (viz., 1 Chron. 17: 8–22) in Ps. 105: 1–15, and vs. 23–33 in Ps. 96: the concluding verses in Ps. 106: 1, 47, etc. The occasion was one of thrilling interest and lofty enthusiasm, David being manifestly the leading spirit. His heart was thoroughly in it. He began with "consulting the captains of thousands and hundreds and every leader" (1 Chron. 13: 1); proposed to send abroad over all the land to call a real mass meeting, but especially all the priests and Levites. The measure was "right in the eyes of all the people," and they marched forth to bring up the ark of God from Kirjath-jearim.*——One only circumstance occurred to mar the joy of this occasion—the death of Uzza who put forth his hand to the ark when "the oxen shook it."† The sin of Uzza was rashness and irreverence for things sacred; and the divine purpose in this fearful death was manifestly to impress the sacredness of this special symbol of Jehovah's presence among his people. It should be remembered that the transportation of the ark by means of a cart and oxen was all irregular—the law having specially provided that it should be borne only by human hands—those of consecrated Levites.——This blow stunned and perplexed David. Afraid to go on, he halted the procession and placed the ark in charge of Obed-edom. During its stay of three months there, the Lord signally blessed that house—a fact which reassured David and encouraged him to a second and successful attempt to locate it in his royal city in a special tent which he had provided for it. Perhaps this success was the more joyous for the previous failure. The ark—borne this time by Levites—was brought in with shouting and sound of trumpet, David, girded with a linen ephod, "dancing before the Lord with all his might." His wife Michal, Saul's daughter, was not in sympathy, but as she saw him through her lattice, "despised him in her heart." On his return "to bless his household," she taunted him with the insinuation that his exposure of person was vulgar and undignified if not even immodest. David's noble reply was—I did it in honor of Israel's God who chose me before thy father and before all his house to appoint me ruler over all Israel; and if this be vile and base, I glory in being yet more so in

* See notes above on 1 Sam. 7.

† So the passage stands in 2 Sam. 6: 6; but the translators of 1 Chron. 13: 9, render the same Hebrew word "stumbled." Gesenius gives the word the sense, *kicked;* Fuerst, "threw down." The attractions of the threshing-floor may have been the occasion of their lurching.

THE ARK LOCATED IN JERUSALEM.

honor of my God. Michal was barren thereafter to her death; and David showed himself to be the "man after God's own heart."

In this connection no one should fail to read Ps. 24 and 15, both having the same key-note; "Who shall ascend into the hill of the Lord? Who shall stand in his holy place?" Since the Great and Holy Lord God has deigned to make this holy hill his visible abode, who, of all living men, shall have the honor of dwelling here so very near to God?——Each of these Psalms gives essentially the same answer—the man of genuine integrity, of clean hands, and of pure heart; he shall receive blessing from the Lord.——The closing verses of Ps. 24 give us obviously the very words chanted by the vast choir when the curtains ["gates"] were lifted and the ark passed in to its inner sanctuary, the symbol of "the King of Glory"—"the Lord strong and mighty; the Lord mighty in battle." (See Notes on these Psalms).

It is in place here to call the reader's attention to the fact that David prepared a special tabernacle for the ark. The original tabernacle, built under the hand of Moses, and borne through all their wilderness journeyings was at this time on the high place of Gibeon, and remained there at least till into the reign of Solomon. The books of Chronicles are definite on this point (*e. g.*, 2 Chron. 1: 3, 4); "Solomon and all the congregation with him went to the high place that was at Gibeon, for there was the tabernacle of the congregation of God, which Moses the servant of the Lord had made in the wilderness. But the ark of God had David brought up from Kirjath-jearim to the place which David had prepared for it, for he had pitched a tent for it at Jerusalem." The same facts are certified to in 1 Chron. 21: 29, and are implied in 1 Chron. 16: 39.——No reason is given for leaving the tabernacle at Gibeon, subjecting the nation to the evils of having two holy places instead of one; but we may suppose the delicate relations of David to the tribe of Benjamin and to the friends of Saul were prominent among them. It may have been a concession made in the interests of peace and of tribal good feeling, of such sort as no prophet of God was ever sent to rebuke.

IV. *The tabernacle worship re-organized, with the very important accompaniment of sacred song.* The development of this subject is found almost exclusively in the books of Chronicles. The history of David as in 2 Samuel makes only the slightest allusion to it.——In 1 Chronicles the important passages are chaps. 6, and 9: 10-34, and 15 and 16, and 23-26.——In 2 Chonicles much light may be found in the history of the great reformations—that under Jehoshaphat (2 Chron. 17); that under Hezekiah (chaps. 29-31), and that under Josiah (chaps. 34 and 35.)

Whoever shall study carefully the passages referred to in 1 Chron., will see that David was a great *organizer.* He knew the worth of system and how to secure it. The vital points in his system were—(a.) A complete classification of the things to be done; (b.) The assignment of these several departments of work to special classes, made responsible for doing each their own business.——(c.) In at least several of these departments there was a further subdivision of the employees into twenty-four "courses," acting as relays, *i. e.*, taking up the work in succession. But how long each party served is not explicity stated.

Here, it should be said that David did not work out this system altogether alone. The narrative intimates that he had the counsel of Samuel, and also of the prophets Nathan and Gad. See 1 Chron. 9: 22, and 2 Chron. 29: 25.

In general the work to be done and the assignment of their duties respectively to the priests and to the Levites followed the law of Moses. David had very little occasion to modify the service of the priests. Then, as before, by the Mosiac law, they bore the highest responsibilities in the Mosaic ritual; ministered nearest the sanctuary; led in the offering of sacrifice and incense, and in the services of the great day of atonement. As expressed here (1 Chron. 23: 13): "Aaron was separated that he should sanctify the most holy things, he and his sons forever, to burn incense before the Lord, to minister unto him and to bless in his name forever." (See also 1 Chron. 6: 49).——The great improvement in the organization effected by David related to the Levites. He made their former duties more definite; divided them into

PUBLIC WORSHIP RE-ORGANIZED, WITH SACRED SONG. 183

classes, assigning to each its service; and he very considerably enlarged the field of their labors. They were relieved of their original task of *carriers*—bearers of the tabernacle and all its utensils; and therefore could take on other services in place of those. (1 Chron. 23: 25, 26). They were still employed as before to wait on the priests and perform multitudinous services in purifying, cleansing, removing filth, etc.; also in preparing the shew-bread and the materials for meat offerings, etc., as we see in 1 Chron. 23: 28–32. They were also employed as porters, having charge of the gates; as scribes and recorders; and, not least, as treasurers—an important function after the large accession of consecrated wealth which came in from the spoils of war. See 1 Chron. 26: 20–28.——The directions in which their service was greatly enlarged were chiefly these three: the service of instruction; the service of civil officers and judges; and the service of song. Very distinct reference to their service as teachers among the people appears in the history of the reformation under Jehoshaphat (2 Chron. 17: 9); also under Hezekiah (2 Chron. 30: 22); and under Josiah (2 Chron. 35: 3). Very probably this branch of their duties was a growth, advancing from the time of David onward.——Much the same may be said of their functions as civil judges, this service, like that of public instruction, resulting from the fact that they were by profession devoted largely to the study of the Hebrew law. We read (1 Chron. 26: 29) that David assigned "Chenaiah and his sons for the outward business over Israel, for officers and judges." Jehoshaphat made them prominent in the capacity of judges (2 Chron. 19: 8–11).

But by far the most important change made by David in the service of the Levites lay in the direction of sacred song. So far as appears this was chiefly if not entirely a new service—a new appendage to the religious worship at the tabernacle. The provisions made for it were at once systematic and ample. Heman, Asaph, and Jeduthun (or Ethan) and their families were specially set apart to lead in this service. The arrangements for music were prominent in the removal of the ark from the house of Obed-edom to Jerusalem, and seem to have continued from that point onward. We read: "These are they whom David set over the service of song in the house of the Lord, *after that the ark had rest.* And they ministered before the dwelling-place of the tabernacle of the congregation with singing until Solomon had built the house of the Lord in Jerusalem; and then they waited on their office according to their order" (1 Chron. 6: 31, 32). On occasion of removing the ark David spake to the chief of the Levites to appoint their brethren to be singers with instruments of music, psalteries, and harps, and cymbals, sounding by lifting up the voice with joy. So the Levites appointed Heman, Asaph, and Ethan, and others "to sound with cymbals of brass:" "so all Israel brought up the ark of the covenant of the Lord with shouting and with sound of the cornet, and with trumpet, and with cymbals, making a noise with psalteries and harps" (1 Chron. 15: 16, 17, 19, 28).—— On this whole subject the passage (1 Chron. 25: 1–7) is classic, showing that those men were not mere *performers*—professional yet heartless singers and players on instruments; but they poured their souls forth in sacred song; "*prophesied*" the phrase is—"prophesied with a harp to give thanks and to praise the Lord." Due training in music was not neglected, for we read that they were *instructed* in the songs of the Lord, even all that were skillful—in number, 288.——It is noticeable that this service of song was not merely occasional (as seems to have been the case before David) but was constant, for after locating the ark in its sacred tent, they "left there before the ark, Asaph and his brethren, to *minister before the ark continually* as every day's work required" (1 Chron. 16: 37).——Another allusion (1 Chron. 23: 30) speaks of the office of these Levite singers "to stand every morning to thank and praise the Lord, and likewise at even."——In the standard passages in 1 Chronicles which describe David's reorganization of the tabernacle worship and the introduction of music, we are not informed definitely at what stage in the course of sacrificial worship music and song were introduced—whether they preceded the offering of sacrifice, followed, or accompanied simultaneously. But in the historical account of the great passover under Hezekiah, the desired information appears in full. Having put the Levite choir in position with the orchestra also (instruments) "Hezekiah commanded to proceed with the burnt-offering; and, *when the burnt-offering began*, the song of the Lord *began also* with the trumpets and with the instruments ordained by David king of Israel. And all the congregation worshiped, and the singers sang, and the trumpeters sounded; and *all this continued until the burnt-offering was finished.* And when they had made an end of offering, the king and all that were present with him bowed themselves and worshiped" (2 Chron. 29; 25-30). Thus sacred song strictly *accompanied* the service of the burnt-offering till it was ended; after which, all, king and people, reverently bowed themselves and worshiped.

We are not informed whether the reading of the law formed a part of these services of worship; nor, if so, how large a part and where introduced. It is highly probable that portions of the law were read in connection with some at least of these seasons of tabernacle worship, the considerations in support of this view being these: That the Lord through Moses prescribed the reading of the law entire on the feast of tabernacles; that the Levites were expected to go round among the people and teach them out of the law— much more, therefore, should we expect the law to be read in the great worshiping congregation at the tabernacle; and, finally, that after the captivity the fact comes to light unmistakably that Ezra the scribe and his associates "read in the book of the law of God distinctly and gave the sense, and caused them to understand the reading" (Neh. 8: 1-8). It is not hinted that this reading of the law was an innovation—a practice unknown before, but it is implied that the *exposition*—the giving of the sense—was new, the necessity for it being that the people, long resident in Chaldea, had become unfamiliar with the original Hebrew and needed some aid in the way of translation into their Chaldee dialect.——Moreover, the subject-matter of the Hebrew psalmody, as it appears in the Psalms they sung, is so imbedded in the earlier Hebrew Scriptures —the Pentateuch and the subsequent historical books— that there must have been some reading of those antecedent scriptures to revive in the minds of the people the themes of those hallowed songs.

In this whole matter of sacred song as related to the

tabernacle worship, David bore a leading part. He not only played the harp himself with such skill as gave him a national reputation, but he invented other instruments of music, to which fact we find allusions in 1 Chron. 23: 5, and Amos 6: 5. "Four thousand praised the Lord with the instruments which I made, said David, to praise therewith."——It follows almost of course that he composed music—as he certainly wrote in part and at first in large part, the Psalms that were sung. The first book of the Psalter (Ps. 1–41) is on good ground ascribed exclusively to David. Is is also noticeable that several Psalms which immediately follow Ps. 24—the location of the ark on Mt. Zion—were manifestly composed shortly after that event—upon the spur of that most inspiring occasion, and obviously in order to provide at once a sufficient variety of songs to meet the wants of a standing perpetual service.

Whether the music of that age would be pronounced "classic" in our own, we have absolutely no means of deciding. It is hopelessly lost, nor have we any power to reproduce with certainty even one of their numerous musical instruments. Yet of this we may be certain, it was *music*. It had in it some of the harmony of sweet sounds; it had the power to lift up human souls to a true devotional enthusiasm. It bore on high the outgoings of devout thanksgiving, praise, and adoration; it stirred pious souls to their depths of love and grateful trust; and, best of all, was well pleasing to God.—— Of the poetry of those songs, we fortunately have ample means of judging. If the music was worthy of the poetry—equal to it in beauty and in power, we can afford to wish it had come down to our age in all its glory. That it made the tabernacle worship attractive, inspiring, impressive—a most effective means of reviving true piety in Israel, there can be no manner of doubt. Such hallowed songs, embodying and impressing such lofty sentiments, bringing God so near to men and lifting men so near to God; and all this backed up by the earnest example and the noble enthusiasm of a king whom to know was to esteem and to honor—these influences and impulses must have wrought a great reviving in the piety of the Hebrew people. It is refreshing to contemplate such an advance in the agencies for the religious life, and to think of the fruits borne to the peace and piety of Israel and to the honor of Israel's God.

V. *The promise made to David that his posterity should fill the throne of Israel indefinitely—including and terminating in the Great Messiah.* The passages referred to are 2 Sam. 7, and 1 Chron. 17, which with slight variations are essentially parallel.——The precise date during his reign is not given. The allusions to other events before and after (2 Sam. 7: 1, and 8: 1) show that David's own palace was already built; that the ark had been previously brought into Jerusalem, and located in its tent there; and that some of David's wars preceded, while some followed. This was a period of rest from war.

The scope of the passage is on this wise. David sat in his house in meditation. His thought turned on the magnificence of his own palace in contrast with the very humble dwelling-place of Jehovah, God of Israel—a house of cedars against a tent of curtains. It struck him as being the very reverse of what it should be; for certainly God should have a temple of unequaled splendor, and David, the humble, unostentatious dwelling-place. The purpose sprang up at once in his heart: I will build a temple worthy of God for his earthly abode. ——He made this suggestion to the prophet Nathan. It seems to have struck his mind very favorably. Go on, said he, do all that is in thine heart; for surely the Lord is with thee; this good thought must have come from him, and he will bless thee in the work.——But in the visions of the following night the Lord gave Nathan the special message for David which embosoms the prophecy of this passage. Go and say to him—The building of my temple is not assigned to thee. Never since I brought Israel from Egypt have I spoken a word to any of her tribes or princes, as to building a temple for my abode. I took thee from thy shepherd life; have borne thee on victoriously, and placed thee securely on the throne of Israel, yet, with never a word to thee expressing command or even desire that thou shouldest build me an house. But when thou shalt sleep with thy fathers, thy son shall build me an house, and I will establish his kingdom forever. My mercy shall not depart from him as I took it from Saul; but thine house, thy kingdom, and thy throne shall be established forever.

THE GREAT MESSIANIC PROMISE.

We now reach the great and vital question of this passage: *Is the Messiah here?* Does this promise reach beyond the merely human kings of David's line—say beyond Zedekiah, under whom the kingdom of Judah fell before the Chaldean power? If it does, it includes Jesus the Messiah; if it does not, then there is no Messiah here.

That this promise to David does include the Messiah, and, indeed, does look very specially to him, is amply supported by the following considerations:

1. The impression it made on David's mind—so deep and almost overpowering—indicates that he took, not the narrow, limited view of its significance, but the very broadest view.

2. The great emphasis laid upon the point of *time* bears most conclusively in the same direction. This is by no means a merely incidental and subordinate point, but is, of all, the most prominent;—that, under David's Greater Son, his throne and his kingdom should " be *established forever.*" This cardinal point is affirmed four times, as if to call special attention to it as the main feature of this promise. It was this point, especially, which made so deep an impression upon David: "Thou hast spoken of thy servant's house for a great while to come." For this, especially, he prays: "Let it please thee to bless the house of thy servant that it may *continue before thee forever.*"——No adequate sense of these words can be cramped into the period between David and Zedekiah. Their proper significance bears us far on beyond the fall of the last lineal earthly king in David's line.

3. Looking for a moment into New Testament authority we note the testimony of Peter, given under the special inspiration of the great day of Pentecost (Acts 2: 30): "David, being a prophet, and knowing that God had sworn with an oath unto him that of the fruit of his loins, according to the flesh, he *would raise up Christ* to sit on his throne," etc. There seems to be no room to doubt that Peter refers to this passage in 2 Sam. 7, for there is no other promise of God to David on record to which he can refer. Peter inferred (very justly) that the promise of an *eternal* throne to one who was a descendant of David must assume and imply his *resurrection*, and an immortal life beyond. So David, under

the spirit of prophecy, understood it, and, consequently, foretold the resurrection of Christ in Ps. 16: 9-11.

Hence Peter's inspired interpretation of this passage makes it a very special and undeniable prophecy of Christ.

4. The way is now open to say that this is a germinal or seed prophecy—a standard prediction which leads the thought of numerous subsequent prophecies, and which furnishes largely the current phraseology— the symbols and terms in which later prophecies of the Messiah were clothed.——Both the meaning and the force of this general statement will be better appreciated if it be made somewhat definite by analysis. I therefore suggest that it may be studied in these three points:——(a.) The Messiah was subsequently presented very generally as a *King*—a king after the type of David, with a kingdom analogous to his.

(b.) Also as a successor to David, on his throne.

(c.) Also as bearing in prophecy the name, David. The latter point is the more conclusive because he was never known by this name during his incarnation. Among many names given him, this is never one. It appears in prophecy only, and, therefore, has the more unquestionable allusion to this great germinal prophecy.

The Messianic Psalms, especially those written by David himself, must be high authority on this point, since they reveal his own conceptions of the promised Messiah. If he saw the Messiah here, his prophetic Psalms should see him in the same general character and from the same stand-point; and, *vice versa*, if these prophetic Psalms give us a Messiah who is king on the throne of David, then they interpret for us this leading promise, and prove its reference to Christ.

——Remarkably these Psalms do everywhere represent the Messiah *as King* (*e. g.* Ps. 2): "The kings of the earth set themselves against Jehovah and against his anointed" [King]; "Yet have I set *my King* upon my holy hill of Zion" [of course a successor of David]. "I will give thee the nations for thine inheritance"—making him king of all the earth.——In Ps. 110 (from David) the leading conception is that of a king: "Sit thou at my right hand until I make thine enemies thy footstool;" yet here he is also "a priest forever after the order of Melchisedek" who was both king and priest.—Of great though secondary value to this point are Ps. 45, written by the sons of Korah, and Ps. 72, by Solomon; the former speaking of "the things I have made *touching the King*"— whom "God hath *blessed forever*," *i. e.*, with a throne established forever. The latter presents throughout a King who reigns in justice and righteousness, with a dominion universal as to extent and eternal in duration.

Whoever will carefully compare these four Psalms with the passage 2 Sam. 7, can be at no loss to trace in them the development of the great germinal idea of this antecedent promise. In these Psalms the Messiah is precisely *a King*, God's own anointed. With the exception of the single reference to Melchisedek (Ps. 110,) the Messiah is a king only—no other aspect of his character is brought to view at all. True, David wrote other Psalms in which he prophetically sees a suffering Messiah—to which, however, there is no occasion here to refer. They by no means conflict with his predictions of the Messiah as King. David himself was a tried and afflicted sufferer before he reached his throne—and so became a more complete type of his greater Son.

The Messiah, as seen by the prophet Isaiah, is in several visions a King, and, what is more, a King on the throne of David (*e. g.*, 9: 6, 7); "For unto us a child is born; unto us a son is given (born in David's line); the government shall be upon his shoulders;" "his name shall be the Prince of Peace. Of the increase of his government and peace there shall be no end" (the very point made so emphatic in 2 Sam. 7)—"upon the *throne* of David and upon his kingdom to order it and to establish it with judgment and with justice from henceforth even forever." "Establish"—the very word coming from 2 Sam. 7. The strain of this passage, moreover, is an epitome of Ps. 72.——Isa. 11 : 1–10, follows a similar line of thought. One who is a root-shoot from Jesse; *i. e.*, a son and successor of David, reigns with perfect righteousness and glorious prosperity, and the nations bow joyfully to his scepter to the result of their own purity and blessedness.——In Isa. 55: 3 the phrase "the sure mercies of David," looks toward this very passage

THE GREAT MESSIANIC PROMISE. 191

(2 Sam. 7) as embodying and embosoming in itself the fullness of Messianic promise—the great idea of divine mercy to a lost world.

It can scarcely be necessary to follow this argument through the Messianic prophecies of the other prophets. I might cite from Jeremiah (23: 5): "I will raise unto David a righteous Branch, and a King shall reign and prosper, and shall execute judgment and justice in the earth" etc., or from Ezekiel 34: 23, 24, and 36: 24, 25, and Hos. 3: 5, where the Messiah appears under the very name David; or from the visions of Daniel (*e. g.*, 2: 44) in which the idea of a kingdom underlies his entire symbolism; "The God of heaven shall set up a kingdom which shall never be destroyed," etc.; or from Zech. 9: 9, 10: "Shout, O daughter of Jerusalem; behold, thy King cometh to thee; he is just and having salvation; lowly, and riding upon an ass; he shall speak peace to the nations, and his dominion shall be from sea to sea," etc.——But we ought not to overlook the sublime strains of those latest prophets who, standing in the presence of the infant Jesus, foresaw his future triumphs and gave their interpretation of these earliest promises made to David. The angel Gabriel brought down these words prophetic of Jesus: "The Lord God shall give unto him the throne of his father David, and he shall reign over the house of Jacob forever and ever, and of his kingdom there shall be no end" (Luke 1: 32, 33)—the whole costume—every figure and allusion, coming from our passage (2 Sam. 7), and from later prophecies which run in the same strain. So Zacharias, filled with the Holy Ghost: "Blessed be the Lord God of Israel for having raised up an horn of Salvation" (a powerful Savior) for us in the house of his servant David, under whom we shall be saved from our enemies," etc.—he being a real *king* over his people.

Let us close with the testimony of Paul, from whose sermon at Antioch (Acts 13: 22, 23), we may read—" I have found David the Son of Jesse, a man after mine own heart; of this man's seed hath God *according to his promise*, raised unto Israel a Savior, Jesus "—the promise referred to being none other than this in 2 Sam. 7.——These citations and allusions will suffice for specimens of the prophecies which follow the general line of thought in our passage, and show that inspired prophets, both of the Old Testament and of the New, saw in it the promised Messiah and borrowed from it more or less fully the figures and conceptions under which most commonly they thought and spoke of him.

It is no objection to the reference of this prophecy in part to the Messiah that it also refers in part to Solomon. Solomon stood in the nearer future; Jesus, in the more remote: Solomon the first in this line of succession from David; Jesus, the last. Of Solomon it is said (2 Sam. 7: 13) "He shall build a house for my name." To him specially does this apply: "If he commit iniquity, I will chasten him with the rod of men and with the stripes of the children of men," *i. e.*, with chastisement such in general character as fathers administer to their wayward sons for their moral good. Some readers are in danger of overlooking the antithesis here between Solomon and Saul. From the former God would not take away his mercy; from the latter he did: the former he would chasten as a father the son in whom he delighted and whom it is the purpose of his heart to save; the latter God abandoned to his deserved doom with no corrective discipline, for whom the Lord loveth he chasteneth. Hence, Saul was lost; but Solomon, though at one time sadly apostate, was brought back by God's good chastisement and saved. David's heart might well have comfort in these promises concerning Solomon; far more in the greater promises in regard to his far greater Son in whom only could the promise of a throne and kingdom established forever find their fulfilment.

We have frequently found the history of David as given in the historical books supplemented by the Psalms written under the first impressions of those historic events. In the case before us, (this first great promise in 2 Sam. 7, and 1 Chron. 17), it is very obvious that David's prophetic Psalms (*e. g.*, Ps. 2 and 110) were an outgrowth and fuller development of the germinal idea given him here. But, not to dwell more at length on these prophetic Psalms, let us note especially the remarkable coincidence in spirit and sentiment between the David whom we see here (2 Sam. 7: 18, 19), saying: "Who am I, O Lord God, and what is mine house that thou hast brought me hitherto?"—and the David whom we hear in Ps. 8, saying: "What is man that thou art mindful of him and the son of man that thou visitest him? for thou hast made him only a little lower than God (so the Heb.), and hast crowned him with glory and honor." Paraphrasing the former passage, we might put it: Who am I, and what is my house that thou hast brought us to this high honor of being the ancestors of the Great Messiah, holding a throne that is to be perpetuated through indefinite ages —to become the joy of the whole earth and to reveal forevermore the good-will of God to men?——In like manner, paraphrasing the latter, we might give it: What is man, frail, weak man, that thou shouldest be so lovingly mindful of him and shouldest visit him *so*, coming down to dwell incarnate with him in the person of thine only Son, and shouldest make man only so little less than God by thus lifting him into wonderfully mysterious alliance with divinity; and then shouldest crown him with glory and honor by making Jesus, that great divine man, born of woman, absolutely *Lord of all!*——In this construction of Ps. 8, we find a line of thought and state of feeling remarkably similar to that which was awakened by this first great promise.——As to the soundness of this construction of Ps. 8, see my notes upon it, p. 37.

VI. The next point in David's history is *his wars of defense and of conquest*. The battle in which Saul fell left Israel prostrate; the Philistines entirely in the ascendant. So long as David reigned over Judah only, they seem to have made no new aggressions; but when they heard of his inauguration over all Israel, they feared the loss of their supremacy. They had known David as warrior and commander, and thought it best to strike before he could consolidate his empire. So they gathered for war; "came and spread themselves in the valley of Rephaim"—the great plain which stretches toward the south-west from Jerusalem. From this position they could menace both Jerusalem and also Bethlehem and the strongholds of Judah. By the counsel of the Lord David went forth and smote them, sweeping them as the mighty waters breach their dam and sweep the land with desolation. So hasty was their flight, they even left their god-images. David and his men burned them—fit retribution for the sacrilege of the Philistines against the ark of God. Soon they rallied and came up again, taking the same military position in the valley of Rephaim. In reply to David's inquiry for direction, the Lord said: Go not out to attack them in front, but "fetch a compass behind them and come upon them over against the mulberry trees." Wait then till thou shalt hear the sound as of one moving in the tops of those trees; then strike, for this is the Lord going forth before thee to smite the host of the Philistines. Done; the Lord was there indeed, and victory was complete. David drove them from Geba (near Gibeah of Benjamin) to Gazer—*i. e.*, through the pass of Bethhoron into their own country and almost to the Mediterranean.——The point of special interest here is that God made his coming and presence audible—"the sound of a going in the tops of the trees," and made this their signal for the assault upon the Philistines. So the Lord is sometimes pleased to make his spiritual presence manifest to the joy of his waiting people, indicating in modes which need not be mistaken that their time for assault upon the powers of darkness has fully come.

These wars which repelled the incursions of the Philistines, and broke the prestige of their power are probably recorded in their chronological place—soon after David became king over Israel and before he brought up the ark to Jerusalem; also before the great promise made to him in 2 Sam. 7. Other wars against the Philistines followed these events (2 Sam. 8: 1).

At this point we may probably locate Ps. 9. (See my Notes upon this Psalm.) It meets the circumstances of David, after some great victories, yet while other enemies are still in force. "Thou hast rebuked the heathen;" "Arise, O Lord, let not man prevail; let the heathen be judged in thy sight." In David's thought all his victories were of God through the might of his arm. All his hopes for the future rested on the Lord alone. Why, then, should he not exultingly sing Jehovah's praises for his help, and pour out his prayer for blessings needed yet and evermore?

The great wars of David with powers other than the Philistines, viz., the great kingdoms on the north, east, and south-east of Israel, are recorded only in the most general terms (2 Sam 8 and 10, and 12: 26–31; also in 1 Chron. 18–20). Moab and Edom were brought into the relation of vassals—"became David's servants and brought gifts." Ammon, more abusive and cruel, hired a strong force of Syrians and made a formidable stand against Israel—only to be overwhelmed, and its great city, Rabbah, ultimately stormed and pillaged. Zobah, then a strong military power, lay between Damascus and the Euphrates, and was subdued by the arms of David.——By these conquests David extended the borders of his subject territory even to the Euphrates—the extreme boundary given in the original promise to Abraham (Gen. 15: 18).——Another important result of these wars was the accumulation of an immense spoil—gold, silver, brass, in royal abundance. The officers of Hadadezer, king of Zobah, are said to have borne shields of gold. Toi, king of Hamath, a friend, brought David as presents, " vessels of silver, of gold, and of brass." Thus from these two sources—the spoils of conquest, and the presents of friendly or tributary powers—David enriched his treasury immensely, and dedicated it to the Lord, chiefly for future use in the erection and adornment of the temple.

As usual, the spirit of these great wars of David appears, not in the history only (*e. g.*, 1 Chron. 19: 13), but in the Psalms, which bear traces of having been composed and sung in this connection. Such with high probability are Ps. 20, and 21, and 68. (See my Notes on these Psalms.) Bearing in mind that these foreign powers were strong and formidable beyond any others known to David's history, we shall see the fitness of Ps. 20—one continuous strain of prayer for the help of God, and of unfaltering trust in his name. Ps. 21 comes in as the song of grateful thanksgiving for victory, making this definite point of identification: " Thou settest a crown of pure gold upon his [our king's] head " (Ps. 21 : 3). The historic fact appears (1 Chron. 20: 2) : "David took the crown of their king from off his head and found it to weigh a talent of gold; and there were precious stones in it; and it was set upon David's head."——Ps. 68 is entirely adapted for the occasion of the last recorded war of conquest—that in which Ammon and its strong city, Rabbah, fell before the arms of David. Its key-note rings with exultant, overflowing praises to the Mighty One of Israel.

VII. *David's great sins in the matter of Bathsheba and Uriah.* Chronologically, these events fall within the period of David's last great war—that against Ammon and Rabbah.

This one sin of David's known life is recognized by the sacred historian (1 Kings 15: 5) as so far surpassing all his other sins in enormity that it might be said he did that which was right in all else, "turning not aside from the things commanded of God, *save only* in the matter of Uriah the Hittite."

This great sin had in it almost every possible element of aggravation. It was flagrant adultery, for David already had, not one wife only, but many; and Bathsheba had a husband—one of the noblest of men, whose record as a brave, patriotic, self-denying warrior, is pre-eminently spotless and grand. David's sin included, not adultery alone, but *murder*—the deliberate murder of this heroic and self-sacrificing man, Uriah the Hittite. One sin naturally leads on to more sinning. Thus David sought first and desperately to cover his iniquity. Could he not bring Uriah, the husband, home to his own house and bed? He orders him sent back from the field of war; converses with him as if no dreadful guilt lay heavy on his soul; and then dismisses him to his home. "There followed him a mess of meat from the king." Surely (thought David) he will carry that home to his wife. No; the warrior slept with David's servants at the palace gate, ready for the stern duties of the soldier's life. But David can not afford to be baffled, and, therefore, summons Uriah to his presence again and urges him to go to his home, but with the result only of bringing out more strongly the heroic spirit of the true warrior. "My Lord Joab and the servants of my king camp in the open fields;" my country calls me to like sacrifices; and so long as she does, no home attractions can be heeded.——Then it occurs to David that this heroic spirit may be overcome by wine. He, therefore, tempted him to eat and drink, "and made him drunk." Even then he failed of his purpose. ——In the next stage David rushed to the horrid purpose to take Uriah's life—for how could he meet the disclosure of his guilty connection with Uriah's wife, especially since Uriah himself is a man so noble, of a nature so pure and lofty?——Did he let Joab into this guilty secret? He found him in this case a ready instrument for his purpose—viz., to put Uriah into the

DAVID'S GREAT SINS. 197

hottest of the fight, and then retire the supporting column and let him fall in battle. This letter of instructions to Joab, he sent by the hand of Uriah with no fear that he would break the seal and come at the awful secret. And he knew Uriah too well to fear that he would retreat before the foe even if all others did. Thus David slew Uriah by the sword of the warriors of Ammon.

Some of the points of peculiar aggravation in this double sin of David are presented tersely and with telling force in the supposed case by which the prophet Nathan introduces his rebuke of his king. The poor man's one lamb—his household pet; nursed in his bosom; fed at his table; to him as a daughter—this lamb is torn away by his rich neighbor who had lambs enough and to spare—the heartless tyrant! The case kindled David's indignation; but, oh, how did the application of it—" *Thou art the man*," pierce his soul with daggers of self-condemnation ! He felt every word as a burning arrow. Conviction brought forth confession, penitent grief, and imploring cries for mercy.

Now let it be distinctly noted: these sins not only had their aggravating circumstances, but *the inspired pen records them*. Not one is withheld. Not only is the crime charged upon David, but its points of special enormity are thoroughly unfolded. There is no attempt to suppress a single fact bearing upon the aggravation and guilt of these sins.——Moreover, there is no concealment or suppression of the fact that these great sins were utterly displeasing to God. He did, indeed, forgive the royal penitent; but he took care that these dreadful sins should be rebuked over and over again; brought up to David's sad remembrance; brought out in sunlight before the nation and before the world. First, the babe is smitten, and after seven days of lingering life and prolonged suffering—David meanwhile on the ground, weeping, fasting, praying—the child dies. Then came those dreadful scenes of lust and murder among his own sons and daughters—Tamar ravished; the guilty Amnon, David's first born, murdered by his brother Absalom :—how terribly suggestive of his own example before these very children! How hot with scorching rebuke! What griefs harrowed his sensitive spirit when it became known to him and to all Israel that Absalom had outraged his father's bed! Then he drove that father from his palace, city, and throne. Bitterest of all, Absalom dies in his sins! David could bear the vilest indignities; the basest ingratitude toward himself; the foulest treason; the sadness of enforced exile; but oh! when the tidings came that Absalom was dead—his own guilty son dead—gone—lost, amid the horrors of unpardoned sin—alas, this filled his cup of woe! Did he not then recall his own sin in the matter of Bathsheba and Uriah the Hittite? Alas! how does God bring the sins of men to their remembrance, and make them feel in the depth of their souls that it is a fearful thing to sin!

Another line of thought and feeling is fitly awakened by these scenes in the life of David. We can not think of him as if he were one of the fallen angels—a junior brother of Satan or of Moloch. He was one of our own fallen race, a brother to our very selves. If he had passions tempting him into awful sin, so have we. If he could so far forget his manhood, his piety, his obligations to his Infinite Benefactor, his relations to the noble warriors in the field and to their virtuous wives at home, as to fall into these most grievous sins, so, alas, may we. This fearful record lies against our own fallen nature. If we, personally, have been kept from sins so great and aggravated, let us rather honor the grace that has saved than plume ourselves on the assumption of better self-control and purer virtue.——We have, then, a real though sad interest in the most tragic and painful scenes of human sinning. It were well if this interest shall move us to such a study of David's case as will be morally wholesome. It stands on the scripture record for the sake of its great moral lessons.

We have followed the thread of the narrative, noting the circumstances of these sins and the suggestive providences with which the Lord followed them through most of the remaining years of David's life.——Besides these records, we have two Psalms bearing very directly upon the experiences of this sinning man. Ps. 51 reveals David's heart at the point where the friendly, faithful hand of Nathan held up before him the aggravation of his sin, and gave him God's view of it. We hear him crying out for mercy in the bitterness of his pangs. He seems to lose sight of every thing else but God. His sins are seen as if committed against God only. Oh, can he ever be forgiven? And if forgiven, can he hope to be so washed and cleansed and lifted above temptation's power that he shall never fall again?——These are the words of his prayer. Never were fitter words poured forth from a penitent soul. It is refreshing to think how often they have come to the thought and to the lips of other smitten, consciously guilty souls, and have helped to bear up to God the broken-hearted sighs and struggling prayers of men longing for pardon and salvation.——There is yet another Psalm which manifestly pertains to David's experience in this great sin, viz., Ps. 32. It seems to have been written a little later than Ps. 51, and yet to record in part his earlier experience. It is well to consider that an interval of some time—some weeks or months at least—occurred between David's sin and his repentance. What of his state of mind then? Was all well within? Did the light of the Lord shine sweetly on his soul? Was he resting calmly on the everlasting promises?——This Ps. 32 has some words bearing to these points: "When I kept silence, my bones waxed old through my roaring all the day long. For day and night thy hand was heavy upon me; my moisture was turned into the drought of summer."——Ah, what sadness of woe! What a withering of all the juices of the soul's life! What a living death! ——So it was, long as the sinner kept silence. No relief came until he acknowledged his sin unto God and confessed all his transgressions. Then there came the first gleam of hope and joy:—"Thou forgavest the iniquity of my sin."——This is the key-note of the Psalm: Oh, the blessedness of the sense of pardon! Oh, the rest, the peace, the strange transition from the agony of the unrepentant soul to the repose, the mellowness, the very tears of joy which come with a sense of being indeed forgiven!——It is precious to have David's testimony to these experiences of his once sinning and then penitent heart. It came of God's good providence and of his guiding Spirit that these great sins of the good king of Israel should be utilized to some such fruits of instruction for the ages that were to come after.

VIII. *David's domestic calamities, subsequent to his great sins.* These have been alluded to briefly above. A somewhat more detailed account should be presented.

The record is found in 2 Samuel 13–20. The books of Chronicles omit these portions of David's history.

In these events Amnon, Tamar, and Absalom, children of David, are prominent. Amnon was his first-born (2 Sam. 3: 2). Absalom and Tamar were not on the mother's side of Hebrew parentage, their mother Maachah being a daughter of Talmai, king of Geshur (2 Sam. 3: 3). This petty kingdom lay on the N. E. border of Palestine in the vicinity of Bashan.——Such a marriage was condemned by both the letter and the spirit of the Hebrew law. In the present case it was prolific only of evil to David and to his house. What inducements—whether political or personal—led him into this marriage connection do not appear in the record. Both Absalom and Tamar are spoken of as beautiful in person. As to Absalom, no other good qualities, if he had any, come to light. He brought sorrow and little else into the household and to the heart of his father.

Amnon appears badly; with no redeeming features in his character. That his love of Tamar turned so suddenly and so meanly to hate—what shall we say of it less than to call it unutterable vileness! But let all whom it may concern take notice that ungoverned lust will naturally dislodge and expel from human souls all that is noble, and leave scope only for what is ineffably base and mean. This hatred in Amnon's soul suggests that worst law of sinning natures, which in a sort compels the sinner to hate whom he harms, and to hate most those he has most cruelly wronged. If any element of human sinning is more Satanic than this, we may be thankful that the resraints upon sin in our world suffice commonly to keep it under.——If any body mourned the death of Amnon greatly, the record omits it. It was more sad that there should be such a son in the family of David than that he should come to an end so untimely by fraternal hands. Incidentally these events were among the fruits of polygamy—the children of envious and rival mothers having the same father were not wont to waste much love upon each other.

Absalom, vain of his personal attractions and lost to all proper regard for his aged father, set his eye upon the throne, and did not shrink from striking for it, though at the cost of his father's blood. The history (2 Sam. 15: 1–6) recites the arts of the arch conspirator and demagogue—an imposing, magnificent retinue; a very complaisant and winning address; becoming every body's most special friend; supremely desirous to subserve every man's particular interests——"So Absalom stole the hearts of the men of Israel." Moreover, he was young and handsome, and did not scruple to suggest that the king was getting too old to fill the throne to the best purpose. Would not a young man do much better?

In v. 7, "after forty years," should be—after *four* years; or (as Maurer) after forty *days*;* for so long, Absalom had been pushing this enterprise, ingratiating himself into the good graces of the men of Israel; making special friends in every city of the land, who when the opportune moment should at length arrive, and the trump of rebellion should sound, would be ready to swell the cry—"Absalom reigneth in Hebron" (v. 10).——To blind the eyes of his father, he becomes very religious, begging leave of absence to go to Hebron to pay a vow made during his three years' stay in Geshur (13: 38)—put in his own words thus: "If the Lord shall bring me again indeed to Jerusalem, then I will serve the Lord." At Hebron a great feast was provided and special friends invited, his purpose being to make this the head-center of the conspiracy. Under the impulses of feasting and wine, all disguises were to be dropped off, and the cry, "*Absalom reigneth*," was to ring out over all the land. Ahithophel, the life-long counselor and supposed friend of David was invited. It is reasonably certain that in this case Absalom knew his man. It has been conjectured that this shrewd counselor whose wisdom had given him a national reputation (16: 23) and whose lapse to the party of Absalom touched the heart of David most keenly (15: 31), had become disaffected toward David because of his relations to Bath-

---

* The nature of the case forbids the period of *forty* years. Josephus, and also the Syriac and Arabic versions, have it *four* years. Two ancient manuscripts have it, not "years," but *days*—in which case it may date from Absalom's kind reception home by his father.

sheba who seems to have been his grand-daughter.*
Thus that great sin was still working out its fruits of
retributive ill.

From this stage of the proceedings, the historian
turns our thought to David (15: 13 and onward). The
whole country is rising to hail Absalom king, and to
swell the hosts of his armed followers. Perils thicken
fearfully about David's path. Expecting an immediate
assault upon Jerusalem, and reluctant, it would seem,
to expose this city and its sanctuary to siege or storm.
David proposes flight, and straightway makes his
escape eastward, over Mt. Olivet and across the Jordan,
taking his stand finally at Mahanaim. Naturally, he
deems it vital to keep himself fully posted as to the
plans and movements of Absalom, and not beneath his
attention to throw some influence if possible, into those
plans. He knew full well that Ahithophel would counsel wisely for Absalom: Could he in any way counteract
his counsels? He will try. So he sends back Hushai,
a real friend, to match his sagacity against that of
Ahithophel. It proved an over-match. Ahithophel,
chagrined by the rejection of his advice, and probably
foreseeing the failure of Absalom's entire scheme, put
an end to his own life. Whether remorse for his
treachery were another Judas element in his doom is
not said. In answer (perhaps) to David's prayer (15:
31) God's hand was against Ahithophel as well as
against Absalom. Ahithophel, doubtless, gave the best
advice for Absalom's success. If it had been followed,
David could scarcely have escaped. But Hushai knew
Absalom's weak point—vanity and passion for a grand
display. Therefore, adjusting his scheme accordingly,
he at once pleased Absalom and ruined him.

The narrative of David's flight from his royal city
(2 Sam. 15: 13, to the end of chap. 17) will awaken
tender sympathy for the aged king, exiled from his
home, his city, and his throne by a heartless, ambitious,
wicked son. With what noble self-forgetfulness and interest in others' welfare rather than his own, does he
debate with Ittai the Gittite (15: 19–22) the question
of his going, or returning.——Shall the ark of God be

* For, according to 2 Sam. 11: 3 Bathsheba's father bore the name
Eliam; and by 2 Sam. 23: 34, Eliam was the son of Ahithophel the
Gilonite.

taken with him in this flight? Nay; let it remain; "if the Lord be pleased to bring me back, well; if otherwise, let him do as seemeth good to him."——See the noble king ascending Mt. Olivet, not as ever before, but weeping, with head covered, feet bare, and many a sad thought of the throne of his kingdom, and the house of his God, and the dear memories of the past;—and with thoughts yet more sad of those great sins which his righteous God must needs call to his remembrance. With the things visible and outward, there were many among his people to sympathize. Hence we read (v. 30); "All the people with him covered every man his head, and went up weeping as they went;" and also, when they crossed the Kidron, "all the country wept with a loud voice" (v. 23). But those deeper griefs that come of the sad memories of sinning—alas, they are for the sufferer's heart to bear alone. That these were the most bitter ingredients in David's cup may be readily seen. For, the fortitude of the soldier's heart was almost second nature to David. He was not at all the man to pale before scenes of martial conflict or the agonies of wounds and death. But here are far other ingredients of grief and woe. Note how he receives the cursings of Shimei: "So let him curse, because the Lord hath said unto him, curse David. Who then shall say, Wherefore hast thou done so?" (16: 10). David saw in this cursing, and, indeed, in this whole conspiracy, the Lord's rebuke of his own great sins. He could bear any and every trial involved in it save this one—the frown of his own holy Lord God!

We see yet more of David's heart in those Psalms (42 and 43) which obviously relate to this period of his history. These Psalms and this history are at one in the points of enforced exile from the place of hallowed worship; of the location of their respective events—viz., in the land beyond the Jordan—that of "the Hermonites;" and of crossing that river where "deep called unto deep at the noise of its water-courses," suggesting in sad symbol, the waves of deep sorrow that dashed over his soul; and, not least, of the almost insupportable sense of depression and discouragement against which his soul is perpetually struggling and which it tasks the utmost energy of his will to withstand: "Why art thou cast down Oh, my soul? Hope thou in God, for I shall yet have cause to praise him for the help of his countenance" and the joy of his salvation.

That David had sorrow and trial in this war which Joab and the warriors of Joab's cast of character could by no means appreciate is obvious in his military orders to spare the life of Absalom, and in his agony of grief under the tidings of his death. Ah, it was unutterably sad to be driven into war against a beloved though wayward son—a son as to whom the father is so painfully conscious that his own example has not been faultless— a son whom God is using as his own instrument of rebuke and chastisement for those terrible sins which David can never forget, and which, while he lives, God will never let him quite forget!

The death of Absalom was not only tragic as related to the agony it brought upon the heart of the father, but it was suggestive and even retributive as related to his personal vanity and proud ambition. The mule on which he was riding we may suppose to have been the royal animal—"the king's mule" (1 Kings 1: 33, 38) which he had seized as one of the perquisites of the throne. His hair was of so much importance in his eyes as to have the honor of a special mention in his history. (2 Sam. 14: 26). Whether his horsemanship was unequal to its task, or whether the shock of battle unnerved him or his beast, so it happened that his furious riding brought his disshevelled locks into contact with the pendant boughs of a terebinth tree and held him fast while the beast dashed away and left him in mid-air suspended. Joab was only true to his own instincts and principles when he sprang to the occasion for smiting down this rebellion by hurling three javelins through the heart of Absalom. Little thought or cared he for the grief of the father when in his view the life of the nation was at stake.

The battle was fought on ground known as "the wood of Ephraim;" but manifestly on the east and not the west side of the Jordan. Why it bore this name does not appear.——It proved a perfectly decisive battle. The generalship and discipline were chiefly on one side; while the weight of numbers was on the other. Absalom and his hastily mustered, undisciplined horde were no match against the old warrior Joab and his trained heroes of countless battles.

A period of not many days sufficed to restore David to his royal city and to his former throne. The uprising of Sheba, a Benjaminite, (20 : 1-22) was but a ripple on the general surface of that quiet into which the kingdom settled down after the death of Absalom.——The same Shimei who was first to curse David when he was fleeing in sadness from his city hastens to be among the first to meet him with apologies and confessions on his return toward his vacant throne (19 : 16-23). The spirit manifested by Shimei and Sheba indicated that there was yet some jealous, tribal feeling in Benjamin that could not forgive David for supplanting the family of their hero, the first king of Israel. The points charged by Shimei (16: 8), were utter slanders—such slanders as testify to the spirit that begets them, and not to any facts of the sort assumed.

Let us not go past these scenes of David's trial with Absalom without special reference to yet other Psalms from David's pen, expressive of his experiences under these trials. Such are Psalms 61, 63, 64, and 65. Several distinct points of coincidence in circumstances as well as special adaptation render it nearly certain that these Psalms were written under the fresh impression of those scenes. Instead of recurring to those proofs or to the spirit of those Psalms as illustrating the heart of David, I must refer the reader to my Notes on those Psalms.

IX. *The sin of David in numbering the people*, which in its result fixed the site of Solomon's temple. A narrative of these scenes appears in both 2 Sam. 24, and 1 Chron. 21.——In Samuel we read: "And again (the former case being recorded 2 Sam. 21 : 1-14) the anger of the Lord was kindled against Israel, and he moved David against them to say, Go, number Israel and Judah." In Chronicles (somewhat differently)—" and Satan stood up against Israel, and provoked David to number Israel."——The same Hebrew word rendered "moved" in Samuel is rendered "provoked" in Chronicles. The agent is said in Samuel to be the Lord, but in Chronicles, Satan, or, as some suppose, not the prince of evil spirits—the well known individual Satan, but, taking it as a common, not a proper, noun (it being without the article), an adversary—*some* adversary, undefined. The Speaker's Commentary accepts this absence of the article as proof of reference to some other than Satan. Bertheau and others make the word refer to the prince of evil spirits—which is more probable.

A group of questions is here sprung upon us; *e. g.* (a.) Wherein lay this sin of numbering the people?—— (b.) *What* tempted David to order this numbering, and who was his tempter?——(c.) Was the anger of the Lord previously kindled against Israel for some other cause, and if so, for what?

(a.) Did it necessarily become a sin to attempt to number the people because God had virtually promised Abraham that they should be innumerable? (Gen. 13: 16, and 15: 5).——Perhaps not *necessarily*, yet there might arise from that fact a temptation to try it inquisitively.——The passage (Ex. 30: 12) should be noticed: "When thou takest the sum of the children of Israel after their number, then shall they give every man a ransom for his soul unto the Lord, when thou numberest them; *that there be no plague among them when thou numberest them.*" This "ransom" was the half shekel (a poll-tax), "offered unto the Lord to make an atonement for your souls" (Ex. 30: 15, 16). That is, numbering the people was admissible *if done for good cause*—this assessment of the half shekel being such cause. Moreover, the charge of this tax upon every man would naturally obviate the feeling of national pride in their great numbers. The language here seems to imply a certain danger or liability to sin from numbering the people—to be obviated by the assessment of this tax.——It appears that the good sense of Joab gave him an instinctive apprehension of this danger. See 2 Sam. 24: 3; and yet more strongly in 1 Chron. 21: 3—"Why doth my lord require this thing? Why will he be a *cause of trespass to Israel?*"—— Perhaps, also, a hint is suggested in 1 Chron. 27: 33: "David took not the number under twenty years old, because the Lord had said he would increase Israel like to the stars of the heaven." But David may have thought he had good reason for enumerating the men of war, and might, therefore, venture to go so far.

Opinions as to the nature of this sin fall into two classes.——(1.) That it lay in the line of pride over the great prosperity, and the vast number of the people. (2.) In the line of an unauthorized poll tax upon those

DAVID'S SIN OF NUMBERING THE PEOPLE. 207

of military age. The former, it seems to me, has the greater probability.

(b.) As to the question, *What* tempted David? if the view above given be the true one, the answer is—That old enemy of human well-being—pride of heart, the passion for self-aggrandizement and display—such as would whisper into David's ear—Who but I among all the great nations? Where can be found a nation so prosperous and so populous?

As to the agent in this temptation, it was God only in the permissive sense; Satan in the personal and positive sense, permitted of God, and by his very nature, wanting nothing more than the barest permission to give scope to the Satanic malice of his heart, and involve both David and the Lord's people in terrible calamities.——It may, perhaps, be put to the account of "progress of doctrine" that in the later book (Chronicles) this agency is ascribed to Satan, while in the book of Samuel, neither his name nor his agency appears.

(c.) As to any previous enkindling of the Lord's anger against Israel, or any special cause for anger which became in some measure an inducement to permit this sin and its punishment, we can only say—The narrative gives us no light, so that we must be content *not* to know.

Despite of Joab's protest, David persisted, and the numbering proceeded. Returns (incomplete) were made after nine months and twenty days (2 Sam. 21: 8). The results are stated variously in the two accounts. No great reliance can be placed upon the accuracy of this census; the command itself "was abominable to Joab." David's heart smote him after the numbers came in. It does not certainly appear whether this conviction of his sin *preceded* the Lord's manifestations of displeasure: the account in Chronicles seems to make it subsequent. David's penitence was apparently deep and humble (1 Sam. 21: 10). The morning after this penitent prayer the Lord sent the prophet Gad to propose to his choice one of three plagues:—Three years' famine (probably *three* as in Chronicles rather than *seven* as in Samuel); or three months *driven* before national enemies; or three days' pestilence. The latter seemed to David to come most directly from the Lord; so he chose it, reasoning thus:

"Let us fall into the hand of the Lord, for his mercies are great; and let me not fall into the hand of man." Whether this pestilence filled out three days is not certain—the phrase, "from the morning even to the time appointed," most naturally implies this, though the Speaker's Commentary favors the sense—even to the time of the evening sacrifice; *i. e.*, one day only.
—— Both accounts concur to make the number that perished in this pestilence 70,000. It extended over the whole country from Dan to Beersheba. When it first reached Jerusalem the destroying angel became visible—drawn sword in hand, standing at the threshing-floor of Araunah the Jebusite. David besought the Lord to spare the people and bring this judgment upon himself only—the guilty man. The Lord bade the angel stay his hand and bade David build an altar on the spot indicated by the visible presence of the destroying angel. Noticeably David insisted on buying the site for the altar and paying in full for the animals sacrificed—a fact which shows that the cost of the Mosaic sacrifices was one element of their moral value.

This site became memorable as that of the future temple on Mt. Moriah as we learn (2 Chron. 3: 1): "Solomon began to build the house of the Lord at Jerusalem in Mt. Moriah *where the Lord appeared unto David his father*, in the place that David had prepared in the threshing-floor of Araunah the Jebusite."

Comparing the two accounts of this sin and of the judgment sent because of it (2 Sam. 24, and 1 Chron. 21), we find the diversities somewhat numerous; the real discrepancies few; from which the inference seems warranted that these authors drew from different original sources and not from one and the same. There is not the least difficulty in assuming that the contemporary annals of Israel were written by more hands than one; *e. g.*, "the acts of David the king, first and last, in the book of Samuel the seer, and in the book of Nathan the prophet, and in the book of Gad the seer," as we read 1 Chron. 29: 29. In the ultimate compilation of the books we have (*e. g.*, 2 Sam. and 1 Chron.) the compiler of the former may have had one or two of these original documents; the compiler of the latter, the remaining one; or if each had them all, he may have found slight differences; possibly some discrepancies—and would dispose of these according to his own judgment or upon traditionary data.——I have rarely thought it desirable to discuss these diversities or even the slight discrepancies—they being of the sort which are passed over very lightly in all history as simply inevitable under the necessary imperfections of the most careful annalists. Critical labors upon the historical books of the Old Testament are frequently embarrassed by obvious imperfections in the Masoretic text—as to which it is our misfortune that the critical helps for its correction are few, and those few imperfect. There is one redeeming consideration. These imperfections in the text very rarely, if ever, affect any vital event of the history, or any important doctrine. In view of this fact, all those who candidly read and sincerely believe and obey the revealed word will be—on the moral side—grateful to God; and on the critical, satisfied, despite of such imperfections.

We will not pass on from the scenes of these two chapters—the sin, and the pestilence which was arrested by means of prayer—without referring to Ps. 30, which, on the strength of its internal testimony and its heading, must pertain to these facts. These points are discussed in my Introduction to Ps. 30. The course of thought throughout this Psalm is entirely appropriate to this occasion.

X. *David's work for the temple.* The record of this work appears mostly in 1 Chronicles. The compiler of these books (supposing him to have been Ezra) had special inducements to bring out David's example in this matter, and that of his officers and people, with great fullness and force. It would bear with wholesome moral power upon the men of his own generation —in the age of the second temple. We can afford to be grateful to him for the service thus rendered to all future ages by the record of this munificent and full-souled example of giving unto the Lord. Let us study it.

In 1 Chron. 18 : 7–11, we read that David consecrated to the future temple the spoils of war and the royal gifts poured into his lap by friendly kings.——1 Chron. 22 recites with some detail his immense gifts of brass, iron, cedar, building-stone, precious stones, gold and silver—

the amount of gold being put at 100,000 talents, and the silver at 1,000,000. The data furnished in the account of the poll-tax assessed upon the male adults of Israel in the wilderness (Ex. 30: 13, and 38: 25, 26) show that the talent was equal to 3000 shekels. These data are (1). The number of males who paid, viz., 603,-550; (2). The sum paid by each—one-half shekel; (3). The total amount thus assessed and paid, viz., 100 talents, plus 1775 shekels. From these data we find that 600,000 half shekels were equal to 100 talents, *i. e.*, 3000 shekels to one talent. The best authorities make the shekel equal to 274 Parisian grains.——But probably the mass of readers will best appreciate the vast amounts named in 1 Chron. 22: 14, if they estimate it as if raised by the poll-tax of the time of Moses. One hundred talents for 600,000 men is in the ratio of 1,000,000 talents to 6,000,000,000 of men. If we estimate the total population of our earth to-day at 1,000,000,000, it would require six worlds of the same population with ours to raise the silver which David is said here to have furnished to Solomon's temple. And the gold was even greater in value though one tenth less in weight—gold being to silver as one to seventeen.

The immense amounts here indicated raise very grave doubts as to the correctness of these figures—doubts which are not a little strengthened by a comparison of these with other sums estimated in talents which appear in this history. Thus Solomon's annual income (considered immense) is put (1 Kings 10: 14) at 666 talents of gold per annum—(estimated equal to three millions of pounds sterling). In 1 Chron. 29: 3, 4, David's contributions to the temple out of his personal estate are put at 3,000 talents of gold and 7,000 talents of silver; the contributions of all his princes (in mass) at 5,000 talents and 5,000 drams of gold, and 10,000 talents of silver (1 Chron. 29: 6, 7). The queen of Sheba gave Solomon 120 talents of gold (1 Kings 10: 10) and King Hiram of Tyre, the same amount (1 Kings 9: 14). These were princely gifts (equal each to £540,-540). Placed by the side of the amounts named in the text of 1 Chron. 22: 14, they suggest either some error in the text, or a grave doubt whether they are to be taken as precise arithmetical amounts, rather than general expressions for a *very great* quantity. Beyond all question the amount realized for the temple from the spoils of war—chiefly from the wars of David—was very great; not improbably so great as to make an accurate computation and an exact arithmetical expression of it very difficult to the Hebrew historian.

David did more for the temple than merely to heap up gold, brass, and cedars. He charged his noblest son with the responsibility of pushing the enterprise to its completion. More than this, he breathed the lofty enthusiasm of his own great soul into his officers and princes. To Solomon he said (in substance): My son, it was an object dear to my heart to build an house unto the name of the Lord my God. But the Lord said to me: "Thou hast been a man of war and blood, and mayest not build it; I will give thee a son, a man of peace and rest; he shall build the house." Now, my son, the Lord has given thee this high honor; be strong and of good courage; arise, and be doing, and the Lord be with thee.——His words to his princes, exhorting them to aid Solomon, are full of vigorous inspiration: "Is not the Lord your God with you? Hath he not given you rest on every side? Now set your heart and your soul to seek the Lord your God. Arise, therefore, and build ye the sanctuary of the Lord God to bring the ark of the covenant of the Lord and the holy vessels of God into the house that is to be built to the name of the Lord" (1 Chron. 22: 17-19).——An incidental allusion to the public treasurer (1 Chron. 26: 26-28) shows that a fund consecrated to the future temple had been accumulating since the days of Samuel the seer, his name and the names of Saul, Abner, and Joab being mentioned as contributing—the three latter probably from the spoils of war.

1 Chron. 28 and 29 are full of this inspiring theme. David convenes his princes and officers, military and civil; declares to them his own strong desire to build a temple for God; rehearses the words of the Lord to him denying him this privilege, but not debarring him from the honor and joy of making immense provisions for it. He commits the work to his son Solomon. Then turning to Solomon, he exhorts him in their presence to seek the will of God with all diligence; to know the God of his fathers, and serve him with a perfect heart and a willing mind—for the Lord would surely know

whether his heart were sincere inasmuch as he searches all hearts, and understands all the imaginations of the thoughts. "If" (said he) "thou seek him, he will be found of thee; if thou forsake him, he will cast thee off forever." He then proceeded to give him the pattern of the house which he had received from the Spirit of God, even to very minute specifications, not only of the house itself, but of its sacred furniture.——In commending his son to the sympathy and aid of his numerous officers, he takes occasion to refer to the immense stores which he had accumulated and consecrated to this great work of which much had been drawn from his own private fortune (1 Chron. 29: 2–5); and then makes his warm appeal to them for their benefactions: "Who then is willing to consecrate his service this day unto the Lord?" The chief officers, the princes, captains, and men in authority, responded promptly and nobly. As the record has it, "they offered willingly;" and more than this—they gave till the joy of giving became a thrilling luxury:—"Then the people rejoiced for that they offered willingly to the Lord; and David the king also rejoiced with great joy (v. 9).—— Such an inspiration of giving brought God very near both to David and to his people, so that David's soul poured itself forth spontaneously in one of the most remarkable thanksgiving prayers on record—thus:

10. Blessed be thou, Lord God of Israel our father, forever and ever.

11. Thine, O LORD, *is* the greatness, and the power, and the glory, and the victory, and the majesty: for all *that is* in the heaven and in the earth *is thine;* thine *is* the kingdom, O LORD, and thou art exalted as head above all.

12. Both riches and honor *come* of thee, and thou reignest over all; and in thine hand *is* power and might; and in thine hand *it is* to make great, and to give strength unto all.

13. Now, therefore, our God, we thank thee, and praise thy glorious name.

14. But who *am* I, and what *is* my people, that we should be able to offer so willingly after this sort? for all things *come* of thee, and of thine own have we given thee.

15. For we *are* strangers before thee, and sojourners as *were* all our fathers: our days on the earth *are* as a shadow, and *there is* none abiding.

16. O LORD our God, all this store that we have prepared to build thee a house for thine holy name *cometh* of thine hand, and *is* all thine own.

17. I know also, my God, that thou triest the heart, and hast pleas-

ure in uprightness. As for me, in the uprightness of mine heart I have willingly offered all these things: and now have I seen with joy thy people, which are present here, to offer willingly unto thee.

18. O Lord God of Abraham, Isaac, and of Israel, our fathers, keep this forever in the imagination of the thoughts of the heart of thy people, and prepare their heart unto thee:

19. And give unto Solomon my son a perfect heart, to keep thy commandments, thy testimonies, and thy statutes, and to do all *these things*, and to build the palace, *for* the which I have made provision.

Then a response from the people was in place. David said to all the congregation; "Now bless the Lord your God;" and all the congregation blessed the Lord God of their fathers and bowed down their heads and worshiped the Lord.

Giving careful attention to this thanksgiving prayer we shall readily note the deep sense it expresses of God's greatness and excellent glory; the transition from this to the littleness of man and of themselves; their appreciation of the high honor granted them to have and to know such a God and to feel that all their good comes from him; the joy of their hearts in giving back so much of their treasure to build an house for his name —all they have being truly his own; and coupled with this a rich, refreshing sense of having consecrated this wealth to God with an honest and willing mind.

Noticeably it did not abate from the joy of this consecration and thanksgiving prayer to think that this God to whom they offer both their gold and their prayer knows all hearts and will witness to their sincerity. The climax of their joy seems to lie in this deep consciousness of being whole-hearted and thoroughly sincere in this entire service.——Fitly this prayer closed with the petition—May God's grace perpetuate this spirit of consecration forever! "O Lord, keep this forever in the imagination of the thoughts of the heart of thy people, and hold their hearts steadfast to thyself, and give to Solomon my son a perfect heart to keep thy commandments and to build the palace for which I have made provision" (vs. 18, 19.)

This was one of the last great efforts of the aged king, before he should lay down his earthly work to die, and one of the noblest. A grander example of munificent benefaction—of giving with the whole heart, when has the world ever seen?

XI. *Arrangements for the succession to the throne. Conspiracy of Adonijah.* If David had any son other than Solomon, worthy to succeed him on the throne, the history gives no hint of it—no light as to his name or character. Both Absalom and Adonijah thought themselves worthy: it is doubtless well that the Lord thought otherwise. The succession fell to Solomon, probably as being prospectively the fit man, and possibly by virtue of some divinely manifested choice. In his early years he did indeed appear exceedingly well, as we shall see.

Adonijah, a younger brother of Absalom, missed the lessons of wisdom which he ought to have learned from the failure of his brother's conspiracy for the throne. Probably he relied upon the extreme age of his father and the youthfulness of Solomon; and, not least, upon the momentum which his movement would receive from the prestige of Joab's name and influence. But the sins of earlier years lay heavy upon Joab. Neither David nor the Lord could forget them; and probably his standing before the people suffered in consequence. Adonijah's real strength, therefore, was never great.——Following close in the foot-steps of Absalom, he affected royal display; chariots, horses, fifty men to run before him, and, to crown all, a great feast under the inspiration of which the trumpet was to ring out its blast with the proclamation—"Adonijah reigneth;" "God save king Adonijah!"——Nathan the prophet is prominent in counteracting this conspiracy. Hastening to Bathsheba, the queen mother, in few words he puts before her mind the pending danger both to herself and to her son and to the whole realm; She brings the case before the aged king. He rouses himself to one last effort; under the solemn oath confirms the kingdom to Solomon, and directs the steps to be taken to secure the succession to him. Under the leadership of Nathan the prophet, Zadok the priest, and Benaiah, now captain-general of the army in place of Joab, Solomon is re-anointed and the proclamation thereof goes abroad over the city in the joyful acclamations of the people. The conspiracy of Adonijah is squelched without a blow. His guests were about to close their long feasting and revelry when the quick ear of Joab caught the trumpet blast and he started up, inquiring, "Wherefore is this noise of the city being in an uproar?" (1 Kings 1: 41). At this juncture, Jonathan, son of Abiathar arrives, fully able to explain it. Hearing his story "all the guests that were with Adonijah were afraid, and rose up, and went every man his way"—and nobody said any more that Adonijah was king. Quietly, peacefully, without bloodshed, or further delay, Solomon was firmly seated on the throne of his father. Some old political offenders—Joab, Shimei, and this Adonijah, were one by one disposed of—Joab with no conditions and no interposition of clemency; the other two under conditions which might have saved them from death for their political crimes. Joab was a hard man, born to rule; of stern and resolute will; a veteran and able warrior and little else; a man who subserved the purposes of his king in many very important respects, yet who, compared with David, lacked most if not all of his softer, nobler qualities—whom David never could love, though he could use him because he must, and though he feared him for his dangerous rashness and reckless violation of David's known commands and wishes. As a representative man Joab belonged to an age which in David's time was passing away, and with the advent of Solomon, had passed altogether.

Abiathar deserved his penalty—that of being displaced from the high priesthood—the last incumbent in the line of Eli, in whom the judgment, passed two generations before upon Eli and his house, received its consummating fulfillment.

The tone of the narrative (1 Kings 1 and 2) does not give indications that this uprising of Adonijah was specially grave in character or grievous to the aged king. But it may have been more so than appears at first view. David was an old man, passing that stage of this earthly life when "the grasshopper is a burden." His vital forces were extremely low; "he gat no heat." Disease was upon him. Old friends from whom he had a right to expect better fidelity were turning against him. And this second conspiracy of a son, even though not specially formidable, was yet painfully suggestive, and to a father so near the last days of life, must have been cruelly afflictive.——These considerations will show the adaptation of two separate groups of Psalms to these scenes of his life; viz., Ps. 38-41, and Ps. 69-71. To the careful reader of these Psalms it will be entirely obvious that they give the experience of the Psalmist in extreme old age, and under the weight, not of years only, but of infirmities and of sickness. Each of these groups stands at or near the close of one of the originally distinct books of the Psalter—the first book closing with Ps. 41; the second with Ps. 72.——I need not repeat here the various considerations which sustain this view of their application to these last trials of David. The reader is referred to my Notes on these Psalms. They have special interest as being the latest utterances of that voice which sang the high praises of God so sweetly in early life, and which seems to have missed no opportunity to bear its testimony to a heart warm with the love of God; for the most part constant and abiding in its trust and true to the high mission of service for God and God's people to which the Spirit had called him.

XII. *David's last words and character.* The passage 2 Sam. 23: 1-7, the translators of our version took to be "the last words of David." The original might be translated either the later or the latest; meaning, therefore, either words later than the preceding song, or the latest of all. There can be no special objection to the sense, latest, last.

The passage has the distinctive features of Hebrew poetry—the repetitious parallelism and the exuberant imagery. It is also very terse; consequently elliptical, and sometimes in a measure obscure.——To give the greater force to the few special points he has to make, he states in the outset who he is and under what authority he speaks. "The man raised up on high"—taken from following the flock of Jesse and exalted to be the Lord's Anointed over his chosen people.——" The sweet Psalmist of Israel "—literally, he who is sweet, delightful as to the songs of Israel; *i. e.*, whose sacred songs are charming, mellifluous, precious to the ear and to the soul.——In four-fold phrase; in four diverse forms of expression he affirms that he spake under inspiration of God. "The Spirit spake by me;" it was *his* word that fell from my tongue; "the God of Israel said;" "the Rock of Israel spake to me," thus :—and this is the first and main sentiment of this song: "He that ruleth over men must be *just*, ruling in the fear of God." Inasmuch as he is set to act *for* God and *under* God, let him be true to God's high behest; let him fairly represent his own Infinite King and Lord. God ordains human government only for the ends of justice and righteousness. Men who rule for other ends and unto other intended results are an utter abomination before him.——V. 4 makes prominent the blessings which attend just and upright ruling. Such a ruler is to his people as the light of morning when the sun rises, even a cloudless morning; and as the grass which springs up under clear light (sun-shine) after rain.——V. 5 is difficult, the choice of constructions lying between the interrogative and the affirmative; the former thus: For is not my house *so* with God (*i. e.*, like these figurative representations)? For he has made with me an everlasting covenant, ordered in all respects and sure (faithfully kept); for this is all my salvation and all my desire; shall it not therefore prosper?——With this construction the sense is unexceptionable, but the original lacks the usual particle of interrogation, and, therefore, leaves some doubt as to the soundness of this construction.—— The second (the affirmative) construction admits in its first clause and in its last that the then present indications in David's house were less propitious than one might expect. Yet the Psalmist declares his unfaltering faith in God notwithstanding—thus: Though my house be not (just at present) so blessed of God; yet his covenant with me is everlasting—is well-ordered and kept; and my heart is wholly in it with my utmost longing desire, although for a season now there may seem to be no visible progress.——The sense under this construction is by no means bad. There were dark things in the house [family] of David as he neared the close of his life; was it not therefore pertinent that he should take note of them as things to be thought and spoken of in this song of last words, yet giving the world his grounds of consolation and hope; viz., in the fact that God's covenant with him is everlasting—is well arranged and ultimately sure; and that in the end his Great Anointed would come to a throne analogous to his own and rule in righteousness and with transcendent glory.

Over against the prosperity of the just and honest ruler, the sons of Belial—wicked, unjust men—shall be as thorns all thrust away; not to be touched by the hand; but the man who has occasion to touch them must be armed with iron and wood like the shaft of a spear. Then let them all be burned where they lie, or (as some take the last word)—for their utter end, destruction. Wicked rulers come to an end of unmitigated ruin. Thorns they are, torn out by their roots; handled with instruments of wood and iron and without mercy; then fired and burned till they are no more. The fruits of good and just ruling are cheering as the light of the new day; grateful and welcome as the fresh vegetation of grass and flower under sunshine after rain. Extreme and utter is the contrast under the reign of the sons of Belial. This sentiment is worthy to be the last thought of King David—worthy to be embalmed in the poetic strains of his latest inspired song.

The Character of David.

There is the less occasion to comment at any considerable length upon David's character, because throughout his history it is remarkably *transparent*. The attentive reader sees the real David everywhere in his full and distinct proportions. Nobody can doubt his sincerity, his great simplicity of character, his affectionate disposition, his proclivity toward strong and ardent friendships, his magnanimity as we see it continually evinced toward Saul, and, indeed, toward Absalom—his two sorest enemies. That he had personal courage, who can fail to see? So also he had rare power as a leader of men, whether in war or in peace—a large measure of that cool, independent, self-reliant judgment, which made his intuitions so safe, and his success so nearly universal. This class of qualities alone would suffice to place him among the world's greatest men.

In respect to gifts of mind in the special sense he was thoroughly a musician and a poet. Through native endowment he took in readily these great arts—poetry and song. By means of these gifts, and their early and never neglected culture, he was prepared of God to inaugurate that wonderful institution of sacred song in Israel which ministered so richly during his reign to the attractions and to the moral power of the sanctuary worship, and which has sent down through all future ages its legacy of blessings.——But the best thing to be said of David is that from early age to his death, he was a servant, a worshiper, and a friend of God. There have been other men of equal native endowments who yet have failed to fill any worthy sphere of service for God or for man, through lack of this steadfast relationship to God. David was a great success in life, because he lived and walked with God. We may omit at this stage the one great sin of his life, counting that a mournful exception to the otherwise pure and steadfast current of his history.——Yet while this great sin and the manifold evils in his family are before our mind, let it be said, not by any means as an apology morally, but somewhat as an explanation philosophically—that it was David's misfortune to live in an age of polygamy, and, moreover, an age when current sentiment made polygamy specially incumbent upon kings. It made his family troubles still greater that he went to a heathen land for at least one of his wives—viz., to Tolmai, king of Geshur—the marriage which brought into his family both Absalom and Adonijah. How many of his wives were selected for their personal virtues and real worth we can not well judge. The evidence scarcely extends beyond a solitary one (1 Sam. 25). It is sad to notice that while there was at least one (2 Sam. 6: 16, 20) who could taunt him for his noble enthusiasm while the ark was coming into his royal city, we lack the evidence that any one of them ever sympathized with him in his great afflictions, or helped him in his struggles of agonizing prayer, or bore with him the burden of training wisely his numerous sons and daughters. Oh, how blessed his lot had been with but *one wife*, and that one worthy of his own noble heart —provided, also, there had been no current sentiment or usage, according a certain license to kings for the violation of their marriage vows! But David was human, and, therefore, not altogether above the influence of the pernicious sentiments and usages of his time. To those sentiments and usages as occasions and temptations we trace his great sin, and more than a few of the saddest calamities and sorrows of his life.

Passing these sins, every thing else testifies that he walked with God. If we read his Psalms in connection with the leading events of his historic life, we see the evidence that his prayer and communion with God kept the Holy One of Israel ever before him; that he sought and found help under all the changes and extremest exigencies of a most eventful life; that during those years of perpetual trial from Saul, his soul was evermore steadied and stayed on the Lord his God; that under the glory of a prosperous throne he did not become giddy and vain, but bore his honors meekly and sought to acquit himself rather to God than to men. It is wonderful how such fear and love of God give to the great men of earth the ballast they so much need. How safely they outride the storms of life with God at the helm! A sense of his presence impresses just views of responsibility, brings conscious help in every need, and precious consolation, though every other source thereof should fail.——We may, therefore, think of David as setting before the kings of the earth, and, indeed, before all men holding positions of responsibility, an illustrious example of the priceless value of true piety, showing how it comes in to *make* a noble character and to insure the best success in human endeavor; how it shields from peril and guides in wisdom; how it ministers consolation where every human heart needs it, and glorifies man by keeping him evermore beneath the shadow of the Almighty.

Mutual Relations of the Hebrews to other known Historic Nations.

Before we take our leave of David, let our attention be turned a moment to the connection of the Hebrew people with other nations known to history.

With their Exodus from Egypt, the Hebrews severed themselves for a long time from all historic connection with Egypt. Amalek, Midian, Edom, Moab, Ammon, and the Amorites of great Arabia; the Canaanites, Hittites, and Philistines of Palestine; have none of them sent down to our time any historic records of date anterior to Solomon. Whatever records (if any) they may have had have long since perished. Egypt, during most or all of this period—from the Exodus to Solomon—was comparatively inactive; Assyria was yet undeveloped.——That the Hebrew people came into no collision of arms with either Egypt or Egypt's old enemies of Western Asia, peopling the valleys of the Orontes and the Euphrates, may perhaps be due to the fact that they did not hold the coast line of the Mediterranean—the well-known thoroughfare of armies —Egyptian or Asiatic—in their hostile demonstrations. May it not have been of God's wise providence to leave this coast line through so many centuries in the hands of the Philistines, and thus exempt the Hebrews from all contact with the movements of hostile armies threading that great route of travel from Egypt to Western Asia? Remembering how it befell King Josiah (2 Chron. 35: 20-24) when he came into collision with Pharaoh Necho, hurling his chariots and horsemen upon the rising empire of Chaldea, we may readily apprehend the possibilities of this danger. Until the reign of David they did not practically occupy that coast line—the western margin belt of Palestine.

Thus it came to pass that during the entire period from Moses to David, including the administrations of Joshua, the Judges, Samuel and Saul, all the foreign powers with whom the Hebrews came into contact have passed into oblivion, leaving no historic records behind them.

With David a new era in this respect opened. When he pushed his victorious armies into the valley of the Euphrates and smote the king of Zobah (2 Sam. 8: 3-8) and also the Syrians of Damascus who were called in to their help, he came politically into contact with nations of whose history some fragments have survived to our times. *Are those fragments in harmony with the history which appears in our sacred books?*

This war is mentioned by Eupolemus [*] in a fragment preserved to us by Eusebius, thus: "David discomfited the Syrians who dwelt by the river Euphrates, and subdued Commagene, and the Assyrians and Phenicians of Gadalene. He also made expedi-

[*] A great historic writer, of the age shortly before the Christian era.

tions against the Idumeans, and Ammonites, and Moabites, and Itureans, and Nabateans, and Nabdeans."——
Nicolas of Damascus (of the age of Augustus Cæsar) is believed to have drawn his information from the records or traditions of his own country. He wrote: "After this there was a certain Hadad, a native Syrian, who had great power. He ruled over Damascus and all Syria except Phenicia. He likewise undertook a war with David, the king of Judea, and contended with him in many battles. In the last of them all, which was by the river Euphrates and in which he suffered defeat, he yet showed himself a prince of the greatest courage and prowess."——
That Nicolas speaks of David as "king of Judea" is due to the date of his writing (within the century before the Christian era) when that country was known under no other name. That he eulogizes Hadad, though recording his signal defeat before David, may be ascribed to merit or to national feeling. The salient points in this fragment indicate its authenticity.

According to the sacred narrative David came into special relations with Tyre and her king Hiram. (See 2 Sam. 5: 11, and 1 Kings 5: 1, and 1 Chron. 14: 1.) These points are made historically probable by the following considerations: That Tyre, Sidon, and Phenicia, in general, led the civilized world in the line of commerce and architecture; that after David obtained control of the great commercial thoroughfare from the Mediterranean to the Euphrates, it became vital to their commerce to be on friendly terms with him; that the natural trade with David's country was of priceless value to those cities—they giving cedars and skilled mechanical labor, and getting bread-stuffs in exchange. Hence, most naturally, "Hiram became ever a lover of David" (1 Kings 5: 1).

Direct confirmation of the sacred history appears in the fact that the name of Hiram as the king of Tyre at this period comes to us certified upon an Assyrian inscription; also in the testimony of Menander preserved by Josephus, of Herodotus, and also of Dius. Dius and Menander were Phenician historians.*

* See more at length on these confirmations in Rawlinson's Bampton Lectures, pages 89–92, and 304–308.

Special confirmation appears also in the nicely accurate references in Scripture to Sidon and to Tyre—the former in most ancient times the leading city; but the latter taking the lead in the time of David and ever after. Testimonies from the oldest profane records are remarkably in accord with this change in the relative importance of these cities. While Sidon occurs in Scripture even before Abraham Gen. 10: 15, 19; in the benedictions of Jacob, Gen. 49: 13; and as "great Zidon," Josh. 11: 8, and 19: 28, Tyre comes first to view (Josh. 19: 29). So, in profane authorities, Homer speaks of Sidon often; but of Tyre never.

Thus our scriptural history of David receives all the confirmation from profane sources which the present state of those records allows us to expect. As we come down to later periods and as profane records multiply, the points of confirmation will be correspondingly more numerous.

CHAPTER IX.

Introduction to the Books of Kings.

As has been said already, the two books of Samuel were originally one; also the two books of Kings and the two of Chronicles. The oldest Hebrew manuscripts and other authorities are unanimous to this point.—— Josephus counts the books of the old Testament canon as *twenty-two* on this method. The fact has some importance for its bearing on our questions of author and date of compilation. Examined and judged of in the light of internal tests of authorship, the two books of Samuel might be assigned to one and the same hand; so also the two books of Kings to one author; and likewise the two of Chronicles; while under the same tests we should assign the books of Kings to one author; the books of Chronicles to another and later hand; and the books of Samuel to yet another but earlier. The author of Samuel never refers us to any original sources; does not say: "The rest of the acts of Saul, first and last, lo they are written in the books of the

Chronicles of the kings of Israel." It would seem that in his day the prophet-annalist was but beginning his professional service of making permanent record of the great historic events of Israel. It may be noted, also, that the author of Samuel gives but very few points of chronology—few compared with either the author of Kings or the author of Chronicles. If (as is generally supposed) the books of Samuel were begun by Samuel the prophet, and continued by his successors, *e. g.*, Gad and Nathan, the latter followed closely in the steps of their prophet-father. Manifestly, the same general methods of composition continue throughout these books.

The books of Kings exhibit unity of purpose and method to such an extent as strongly favors the supposition of one and the same author. He refers us to his original sources systematically, from Solomon to Josiah inclusive—but no further. For what follows Josiah, he may be presumed to have drawn from his personal knowledge. This is one among several circumstances which strongly favors the opinion that Jeremiah was the author of these books of Kings. Other circumstances are the marked similarity between the history of Josiah's sons, of the conquest of Judah and destruction of Jerusalem as given respectively in the prophecy of Jeremiah and in 2 Kings; also the similar moral purpose which underlies both books. Prominently under this head we shall note the references to idolatry as the great national sin and the ground cause of her ruin, and a like familiarity with "the book of the law," especially with the judgments threatened against apostate Israel in Leviticus and Deuteronomy.

Comparing Kings with Chronicles, we shall see that the latter brings the history down to a later point, even to the restoration from captivity in Babylon; also that its author gives credit in the same way for his original authorities, referring the reader to them for "the rest of the acts" of all his prominent kings; moreover, that he either had access to other and different authorities from those used by the compiler of Kings, or at least made in some cases fuller extracts from them. We find that he often gives us new matter; *e. g.*, in regard to King Asa, compare 2 Chron. 14–16 with 1 Kings 15; also to Manasseh's captivity and repentance (2 Chron.

INTRODUCTION TO THE BOOK OF KINGS. 225

33: 11-19 with 2 Kings 21: 1-18); and in general the author of Chronicles gives a much more full account of the great reformations under the reigns respectively of Jehoshaphat, Hezekiah, and Josiah; while, on the other hand, the author of Kings gives much more real history of the kings of Israel and of those prophets, *e. g.*, Elijah and Elisha, whose labors were chiefly among the ten tribes. Fortunately these books serve largely to supplement each other. They also stand in the relation of independent witnesses.

Recurring to the hypothesis that Jeremiah was (supposably) the author of Kings (as I have assumed Ezra to be of Chronicles), it is well to say definitely that I do not claim for these positions any direct historic evidence. No such evidence exists. Both books appear without name of author. But in the absence of the highest and only absolute evidence, it may be at once pleasant and useful to approximate toward a satisfactory theory as to the author of each of these books.

On the point of Jeremiah's authorship of Kings, it may suggest itself as a strong objection that his own book of prophecy comes down to us with less of order and method in its arrangement than any other book of the Bible. It is singularly disconnected and fragmentary, indicating that its author either had little command of his time, or that he lacked a proper appreciation of order. The former is almost without doubt the true explanation of this disorder in the prophecies of Jeremiah. Now, therefore, if Jeremiah, either for lack of leisure, or because of the unrest, imprisonment, persecution, suffering, of his lot, could not put together a connected series of his own prophecies, how (it may be asked) could he write out such a history as appears in these books of Kings?

The answer is at hand. The books of Kings were written at an earlier date than the body of his prophecies. Nearly all his successive prophecies date after the death of Josiah, during the reigns of his godless sons. Then Jeremiah was subject to harassing persecutions— almost never at rest sufficiently for quiet authorship. But his earlier life was passed under totally different circumstances. Beginning his prophetic work in Josiah's thirteenth year, he had eighteen years of unbroken quiet before Josiah's death. Nothing in his known circumstances forbids the supposition that during this period wrote the book of Kings.——We may go further. Not only does nothing forbid this supposition; there is every thing to favor it. At the commencement of Jeremiah's prophetic life Josiah was entering upon a great religious reformation. For the promotion of this reform, he and his people needed precisely such a power as this book of Kings would supply. Every word in these two books (or one) bears with telling force to promote the moral impression which such a reform demanded as its very ground-work. These two books give prominence to the history and work of the prophets, *e. g.*, Elijah and Elisha. At this juncture it was every thing to utilize the labors of all the previous prophets and bring them to bear with concentrated force upon the hearts of the people.——The author of Kings omits no historic fact which would legitimately show that the idolatrous kings of Israel brought down upon themselves, their dynasty, and their realm terrific judgments from the Almighty. His selection of matter witnesses that God evermore promised blessings to his people and their sovereign when obedient, and that his mercies were exceedingly great to those who humbly sought him and penitently turned from their evil ways. Thus blending mercies to the penitent and prayerful with judgments on the prayerless and idol-worshiping, these books brought the maximum of moral power to bear toward that last great reform in which the Lord sought to pluck his people from the ruin then imminently impending.——Thus do all internal testimonies combine to sustain and render highly probable the hypothesis that Jeremiah was the author of the books of Kings.

On the subject of chronology there is no lack of statements in either Kings or Chronicles. Both authors usually state how old each king was when he began to reign, and how many years he reigned. While the author of Kings is carrying along co-ordinately the contemporary reigns in the two kingdoms, he is wont to note in what year of the reigning monarch in one kingdom a new king came to the throne in the rival kingdom. Dating from a fixed epoch, *e. g.*, from the division into two kingdoms at the accession of Rehoboam, or from the dedication of the temple, seems not to have been thought of. This improved method of chronology has been a thing of later times.

It is the affliction of all critics that these chronological notices are decidedly imperfect. It is generally agreed that these imperfections are to be attributed variously to the following causes:——(a.) The use of Hebrew letters for numbers—these letters being liable to be mistaken by copyists one for another.——(b.) The practice of using abbreviations to some extent, thus increasing the liability of mistake.——(c.) The practice by the earlier scribes or revisors, of suggesting corrections on the margin, which, by some later hand were introduced into the text.——(d.) The attempt of some professed chronologist to carry out his preconceived system at the expense of modifying dates and numbers to make them conform to his ideas.——(e.) In the series of kings of Israel it is probable there were some periods of anarchy or of foreign rule, not definitely indicated. This may account for the fact that the total years of her kings from Jeroboam I, to the ninth year of Hoshea (the end of the northern kingdom) is less by twenty years than the corresponding sum of Judah's kings from Rehoboam to the sixth year of Hezekiah.

Under influences coming in from one or another of these several sources it must be conceded that the chronological numbers in both Kings and Chronicles are as a whole quite unsatisfactory. No critical labors have hitherto been able to solve all the difficulties.—— The purpose and plan of this volume do not provide for extended discussion of these points. The figures which I give may be considered as in the main only approximations to perfect accuracy. It is fortunate that these imperfections of the Hebrew text are mostly restricted to numbers and dates, and do not affect vital facts; much less, important doctrines.*

Solomon.

The main points of his history may be arranged thus:

* For convenience to the reader I place in the appendix to this volume a chronological table of the kings of Judah and of Israel, and also of the prophets according to what are regarded as the best authorities accessible.

I. *His early promise.*

II. *His dream at Gibeon: God's word to him and his choice.*

III. *His wisdom and knowledge, and his literary works.*

IV. *His great wealth and royal state.*

V. *His building of the temple and its consecration.*

VI. *The second vision at Gibeon.*

VII. *His foreign relations;* political, commercial, social, domestic.

VIII. *His apostasy from God; its antecedents and occasions.*

IX. *His repentance; the evidence in the case.*

X. *The influence of this reign upon the moral and religious state of Israel.*

XI. *Points of contact with profane history.*

I. *Solomon's early promise.* In common with Saul, Israel's first king, Solomon, at least in his early life, was modest and humble, neither self-conceited nor vain. Both had at first a reasonably just sense of the great responsibilities of a king. This is more apparent in Solomon than ever in Saul, and constituted one of the brightest token of his future promise. His strong desire to rule well, coupled with a sense of personal obligation to God, which was evinced in his devotion to religious duties, must have inspired large expectations in the hearts of the sagacious elders of Israel, and if evinced fully to David before his death, must have been exceedingly gratifying to him. The record in 1 Chron. 28: 9–10, 20, 21, gives very fully the warm parental exhortations with which David devolved upon his hopeful son these great responsibilities, but drops not a word of reply from Solomon; nothing to indicate the spirit with which he received these exhortations. But when he entered upon his royal duties his spirit became at once apparent, giving the best of testimony that the counsels of his dying father had gone to his heart. Such regard for wise parental counsels is in any young man among the brightest and best elements of future promise.

II. *Solomon's dream at Gibeon: God's word to him and his choice.* Of this great event the staple facts are given in both Kings and Chronicles (1 Kings 3: 4–15, and 2 Chron. 1: 2–12), but most fully in Kings, although the antecedent circumstances are stated more at length in Chronicles. The two accounts are manifestly independent of each other.——The author of Chronicles states that Solomon spake to all Israel—officers of every grade and people—to go with him to Gibeon, and explains the reason for assembling at that place, viz., because the tabernacle built by Moses was still there, although the ark had long been in Jerusalem in a tent specially provided for it by David. The brazen altar built originally in the wilderness was also there. Thither Solomon and all the congregation resorted, and there he offered a thousand burnt-offerings. On the night following the Lord appeared to Solomon in a dream, and said—" Ask what I shall give thee." From this point we have the more expanded statements in Kings. The answer of Solomon expatiates upon God's great mercies to his father, culminating in the gift of a son sitting upon his own throne over so great a people; expresses his deep sense of personal weakness—" I am but a little child, and I know not how to go out or come in;" and then makes his great request: "Give thy servant, therefore, an understanding heart to judge thy people that I may discern between good and bad; for who is able to judge this thy so great people?"—— It pleased the Lord that Solomon had asked this thing, and as if to testify at once to this pleasure in Solomon's choice, and to his glorious munificence in giving blessings to the humble and pure-minded, he said: "Because thou hast asked this thing, and not the lower, selfish good of long life, or riches, or the life of thine enemies; Behold, I have done according to thy word, and have given thee wisdom, never surpassed among mortals, and never to be; and I have also given thee that which thou hast not asked—both riches and honor. On one special condition, viz., "If thou shalt walk in my ways and keep my statutes as David thy father did, then I will lengthen thy days."——The historian adds: " Then Solomon awoke, and behold it was a dream." But, manifestly, this was no mere fancy, and can by no means be classed with ordinary, average human dreaming, under the normal action of mind in sleep. It is extraordinary and special, like the vision of Jacob at Bethel —produced by most impressive manifestations of God's presence to the human soul, awakening its powers to their highest activity. The moral power of the will is by no means suspended, but rather intensified. Solomon's choice was, therefore, most entirely moral and responsible, and God so regarded it. This case seems to be closely analogous to prophetic vision which is frequently spoken of as a "dream," and which stood in some undefined relation to sleep—a relation of which we can get no absolute knowledge without personal experience—perhaps not even with it.

We may notice that while the promises of great wisdom and great wealth were absolute (without conditions), the promise of long life was made upon conditions, viz., of his steadfastness in the ways of his father David. In this point Solomon sadly failed, and consequently failed to realize the long life conditionally promised. He is supposed to have ascended the throne at an age not exceeding twenty. Having reigned forty, he died at the age of sixty—not by any means an old man.

The moral lessons of this dream at Gibeon are richly suggestive and instructive. It suggests that, practically, in view of the youthful vigor normally accorded to virtuous young men, and the possibilities that lie within the grasp of earnest, persevering endeavor, God says to every young man as he said to Solomon—"*Ask what I shall give thee.*" Make choice of the ends you would accomplish in life. If they are worthy ends my blessing shall be upon you. According to your faith it shall be done. Any young man can choose as Solomon did to "*serve his generation according to the will of God*"—to do the very duties which God in providence lays before his hand, and to do those duties in the best manner possible to him with his powers and opportunities. This virtuous noble purpose is one of the first and best possibilities of every young man. He *can* be, in this highest sense, *good*. He can consecrate to the service of God in the line of labor for human well-being whatever powers God gives him. So doing he may be confident of two things: (a.) that his choice will please God; (b.) that God will give him success—most surely of all, success in his endeavors to please God truly and serve him faithfully—than which no other success can be greater or better. If he shall not become as wise or as wealthy as Solomon, he can, at least, please God *as well*—can fill his measure of responsibility as honestly and as acceptably to God, and can make it most sure that his life shall not be a failure.

Again: the case as presented here, is good both for proof and for illustration of the principle that when men "covet earnestly" and supremely the best gifts, God loves not only to give these best things thus preferably and supremely sought, but to throw in the lesser things as unasked gratuities—in business phrase —"into the bargain." God gave Solomon not only the wise and understanding heart to rule well—that which he specially sought; but also great wisdom in other directions; immense riches, moreover, and unsurpassed honors. It seems to have been very easy for the Lord to throw in all these lesser things, and make no particular account of them. They were so much extra—a kind of bonus, which signifies the rich munificence of the Giver, and the gushing fullness of his heart toward that unselfish virtue which is so like God, and which he so naturally enjoys when he sees in his creatures.——Moreover, this case suggests the general law as propounded by Jesus in his great sermon; "Seek ye first the kingdom of God and his righteousness, and all these things"—food, raiment, these lower blessings—"shall be added unto you." They shall be thrown in, almost without your asking. Give your full heart and chief endeavor to seeking the kingdom of God and his righteousness, and God will see to the filling of your cup with earthly good as may be best for you in his sight.——Hence we may conclude that the principle on which God blessed Solomon was not exceptional but general. Any body can have blessings from God on the same principle— good blessings—the Lord himself being judge as to what is really good for any one of us personally to have. "Godliness hath the promise of the life that now is," and in no trivial sense.

III. *Solomon's great wisdom and knowledge; his literary works.* The special type of wisdom which Solomon asked—"an understanding heart to judge thy people, that I may discern between good and bad" (1 Kings 3: 9); "wisdom and knowledge that I may go out and come in before this people" (2 Chron. 1: 10)—was that sagacity, that intuitive apprehension of character and conduct, coupled with an unfailing sense of equity as

between man and man which he needed as the supreme
judge of Israel. His thought was specially upon the
civil administration of law. In its external relations
the realm was at peace with all the nations of the earth.
But internally, human depravity must needs be cared
for; controversies would perpetually arise; here, therefore, this profound sagacity of the discerning unbiased
judge would be the first qualification in Israel's king.

——Noticeably, the author of Kings proceeds at once to
give an illustrative case in proof that God did really
endow Solomon with unsurpassed gifts in this special
direction. The story is told with beautiful simplicity
(1 Kings 3: 16-28). Two women ("harlots" they are
called), living in the same house, each became a mother
nearly at the same time. One of them overlaid her little
son by night and caused his death, and then slyly placed
the dead infant in the bosom of her sister harlot and took
thence the living boy for hers. In the morning this
second mother arose to nurse her child, and lo, it was
dead! But what mother does not know her own infant
from a thousand? She saw that this dead infant was
not her own dear boy. Now there is a fierce dispute
and contention for the living babe—a case which none
of the lower courts availed to solve—so it came before
Solomon.——His decision has been admired in all ages
as a perfect model of human sagacity. Look at the case.
Here was the conflicting testimony of these two women,
one swearing point blank against the other. The circumstances ruled out the possibility of any extraneous
testimony; they were the only witnesses. It would
probably have been impossible to go further back with
the inquiry, which of these two women sustained previously the best reputation for truth and veracity. In
such inquiries. the acutest judges often find it requires
little short of omniscience to sift and weigh the conflicting testimony. Solomon attempted no such thing.
But Solomon looked into human nature. He knew the
heart of a real mother. So he said, "Bring me a sword."
Now "divide the living child and give each of these
claimants one half." This was not ordered in pettish
mood, as if he were fretted and disgusted with their persistent demand for the living treasure. No, indeed; all
he wanted was to see whose maternal heart would quiver
at the thought of that sword passing through the body

SOLOMON'S WISDOM AND WRITINGS. 233

of her own dear babe. This was the revelation which he sought, and which he gained. The mother of the living child cried out, *no, no;* give her the living child, and by no means slay it. Let me have the dead—but, Oh, spare the living one! The other acquiesced, alas, but too readily in the king's decision—the heartless wretch! Now Solomon understands the case perfectly. His verdict comes: That mother whose bowels yearn over the living child is the rightful claimant; give her the living child.——We may hope he punished the false claimant for her group of horrid crimes—stealing a living babe and putting her dead one in its place; persistent perjury, and horrible inhumanity. But on this point the record is silent. His decision on the main question made a profound impression as it went forth over all Israel. "They saw that the wisdom of God was in him to do judgment."

According to God's promise the wisdom and knowledge which he aided Solomon to obtain took a wide range and covered far other ground than what is strictly and technically judicial science. As the author of Kings has it (1 Kings 4: 29), "God gave Solomon wisdom and understanding exceeding much, and *largeness of heart* even as the sand which is on the sea shore." "Largeness of heart" is *breadth of understanding*—a wide range of knowledge; treasures of science and wisdom, at once minute and comprehensive, covering many spacious fields of human thought. The specifications which appear in the record lead us definitely toward two departments of human knowledge:——(1.) Natural history, of both animals and plants; for "he spake of trees, from the cedar tree that is in Lebanon even to the hyssop that springeth out of the wall; he spake also of beast and of fowl, and of creeping things and of fishes."——And (2.) A department which we have no precisely equivalent term to indicate, but which may be defined as human knowledge expressed in proverbs and cultivated in the framing and solving of "hard questions." It made itself at home in the science of ethics, but was free to go abroad quite beyond this territory. Of the "three thousand proverbs" which Solomon spake we have doubtless a specimen in the book of "Proverbs" which bears his name. If we had also some of those "hard questions" which the Queen of

Sheba brought to "prove him with" (1 Kings 10: 1) and which profane history refers to as the past-time and wit-sharpener of Solomon and of Hiram of Tyre and his savans, we might better comprehend the drift of curious inquisitive thought in that age. It was, doubtless, oriental, but whether Samson's riddles or the grander questions of Job and his three friends, or the current strain of the book of Proverbs, would best represent it, we have not all the means of knowing that we might desire. The historian states, however, very explicitly that Solomon exceeded all the kings of the earth in wisdom as well as in riches, and that all the earth sought to Solomon to hear his wisdom which God had put in his heart (1 Kings 10; 23, 24); and yet more specifically, that his wisdom exceeded the wisdom of all the children of the east country and all the wisdom of Egypt, for he was wiser than all men—than Ethan, Heman, etc.—names which appear among the authors of the Psalms and the leaders in the music of the sanctuary.——Solomon cultivated poetry also, for "his songs were one thousand and five"—of which one only remains to our time, and that the superlative one— "the song of songs." Of this we need only say here that considered simply as poetry, it combines warmth and purity of social affection with an exquisite sense of beauty in nature, in a degree rarely if ever surpassed.——Of his literary works nothing remains to us save his three well-known books: Proverbs, Ecclesiastes, and the Song; and two Psalms ascribed to him, viz., 72 and 127.

IV. The great wealth and royal state of Solomon are the leading themes of two chapters, viz., 1 Kings 4 and 10. We shall pass this point with only a brief notice. ——The method and order in matters political, introduced and perfected under David, continued under Solomon. The spirit of this system was carried by Solomon into his domestic establishment, the magnificence of which was very far beyond any thing before known in Israel. It was the special admiration of the Queen of Sheba (1 Kings 10: 4, 5).——Of his splendid buildings what shall we say? In addition to the glorious temple, a palace for himself; another for Pharaoh's daughter— the first wife of Solomon brought to our notice (1 Kings 3: 1); "the house of the forest of Lebanon" (1 Kings 7:

THE BUILDING AND CONSECRATION OF THE TEMPLE. 235

2, and 2 Chron. 9 : 16); various cities in his own country; the great and long famous Tadmor in the wilderness; navies and ports for the commerce of the Mediterranean Sea and of the Indian Ocean—where was the limit of his magnificent works in this line?

V. *The building of the temple and its consecration* demand somewhat special notice.

Of its plan nothing more need be said than that it followed the model of the tabernacle built by Moses in the wilderness. Having the same objects in view, constructed to subserve the same system of worship,—its compartments on the ground floor were identically the same. Every thing was on a larger yet corresponding scale; the same altars; the same courts; the same holy place, and the same holy of holies, enshrouded in the thick darkness.

As to dimensions the record is—sixty cubits in length by twenty in breadth; proximately 90 feet by 30—double the corresponding dimensions of the tabernacle. But within these relatively small dimensions, what an amount of magnificence and splendor were compressed! The most superb textile fabrics; the most exquisite carved work, and the immense amount of surface overlaid with gold, placed this structure in point of cost, beauty, and magnificence, greatly in advance of any structure known in ancient times. It was seven years in building. The skilled laborers were largely Phenician, supplied by Hiram king of Tyre. The unskilled men for the immense labor of transportation were mainly from the subject races of foreign birth living among the Israelites. 1 Kings 5 gives ample details as to the levies of men, their duties, the associated labors of Tyrians and Hebrews; the materials of cedar, fir, and stone, obtained in Phenicia but transported by water to Joppa and thence overland to Jerusalem. Every stone being cut in its quarry, all materials of wood being prepared (framed and dressed) before being shipped from Tyre, two valuable results were obtained; there was no waste of power in transportation; and in the holy city the great temple rose solemnly, in comparatively quiet stillness—from those immense foundation stones now being laid bare, to the top-stone, laid at last " with shoutings of grace, grace unto it."

The antecedent correspondence between Solomon and

Hiram of Tyre (given more in brief 1 Kings 5; but more in full, 2 Chron. 2), sets forth with delightful recognition of the true God, the plans of Solomon and his propositions to the king of Tyre; the occasion for a temple; the uses it should subserve; and his reasons for making it supremely magnificent. "The house which I build is great, for great is our God above all gods. But who is able to build him an house, seeing the heavens and the heaven of heavens can not contain him? Who am I that I should build him an house, save only to burn sacrifice before him?" (2 Chron. 2: 5, 6)——Hiram's answer has some remarkable words for an idol-worshiping king. This is said to have been sent in writing:—"Because the Lord [Jehovah] hath loved his people, he hath made thee king over them. Blessed be the Lord God of Israel, who made heaven and earth, who hath given unto David the king a wise son, endued with prudence and understanding, who might build an house for the Lord and an house for his kingdom."——Was this the complaisance of shrewd diplomacy, or the utterance of honest convictions? If the latter, why did not king Hiram cast his idol gods to the moles and to the bats, and give his own heart's honest worship to "the God who made heaven and earth?"

But a far more profound religious interest gathers about the scenes of the dedication of this temple. Both our authors (*i. e.*, of Kings and of Chronicles) give the details of this service, and with little variation and in very considerable fullness, narrating the sacrifices that preceded and that followed; the introductory address of Solomon to the assembled people (1 Kings 8: 12–21), and then the consecrating prayer (vs. 22–53), and the closing benediction upon the people (vs. 54–61). The service must have been in the highest degree impressive and sublime. Every word seems to be perfect in adaptation to the great purpose and the grand occasion. We can scarcely forbear to ask (mentally)—Were these words altogether original with Solomon, or was the hand of Nathan or of Zadok, or of some other leading religious spirit, in them? The question is of value mainly as bearing somewhat upon our estimate of Solomon. But we are left with no hint of other hand in the responsibilities of this service save his own. Accounting it as his we have here a very gratifying testimony that he well conceived the relation sustained by the Hebrew people toward the God of their covenant, and that he had ideas at once just and grand of the purpose of this temple as a house of prayer—a place honored of God with the symbol of his presence, toward which his worshipers were to turn in their offerings of prayer and of praise to the glorious God whose throne filled the highest heavens, yet who had deigned to manifest his presence among his worshiping people in this earthly temple.

The tone of this consecration contemplates this temple as designed for *national* and *public* worship—for the prayers of the whole people rather than for individuals.

Among the special points of this consecrating prayer were—its prominent recognition of David and of God's promise to him; and its numerous specifications of the peculiar circumstances under which, supposably, the Lord's people in their various need might address their supplications to God as in symbol dwelling in this temple to hear their prayers. The sublime grandeur of the thought that the Great God should condescend so low is put impressively: "But will God in very deed dwell with men on the earth? Behold, the heaven and the heaven of heavens can not contain thee; how much less this house that I have built?"——So also the culmination of the prayer by invoking the entrance of Jehovah with the ark of his strength: "Now, therefore, arise, O Lord, into thy resting-place, thou, and the ark of thy strength; let thy priests, O Lord God, be clothed with salvation and let thy saints rejoice in goodness. O Lord God, turn not away the face of thine anointed; remember the mercies of David thy servant" [mercies *promised* to David].——Then the visible answer to this wonderful prayer: "Fire came down from heaven and consumed the burnt-offering and the sacrifice; and the glory of the Lord" [that visible halo and effulgence of brightness] "filled the house." "All Israel saw this, and bowing themselves with their faces to the ground upon the pavement, worshiped and praised the Lord, saying—For he is good; for his mercy endureth forever."

The correlation between the material and the moral grandeur of this closing scene is put with equal beauty and force by Dean Milman (History of the Jews I: p. 318): "As the king concluded, the cloud which had rested over the holy of holies grew brighter and more dazzling; fire broke out and consumed all the sacrifices (2 Chron. 7: 1); the priests stood without, awestruck by the insupportable splendor; the whole people fell on their faces, and worshiped and praised the Lord, '*for he is good, for his mercy is forever.*' Which was the greater, the external magnificence or the moral sublimity of this scene? Was it the temple, situated on its commanding eminence, with all its courts, the dazzling splendor of its materials, the innumerable multitudes, the priests in their gorgeous attire, the king with all the insignia of royalty on his throne of burnished brass, the music, the radiant cloud filling the temple, the sudden fire flashing upon the altar, the whole nation upon their knees? Was it not rather the religious grandeur of the hymns and of the prayer; the exalted and rational views of the divine nature; the union of a whole people in the adoration of the one Great, Incomprehensible, Almighty, Everlasting Creator?"

VI. *The dream of Gibeon repeated: the Lord appearing to Solomon the second time.* Both our histories narrate this second appearance (1 Kings 9: 2–9, and 2 Chron. 7: 12–22)—the author of Chronicles most fully, but only the author of Kings compares it specially with the dream at Gibeon. It followed the dedication of the temple, and was manifestly designed to deepen moral impressions, and perhaps to warn specially against spiritual dangers already foreshadowed. In substance the Lord said—I have heard thy prayer in the dedication of this temple, and have accepted it. If now thou wilt walk before me with perfect heart as thy father David did, the throne of thy kingdom over Israel shall be established forever: but if thou turn aside after other gods, then will I cut off Israel from this glorious land of promise, and this consecrated temple shall be no protection against retributive judgments, for its ruin shall be as signal as its magnificence is now glorious.——Oh, had these words of warning been duly remembered and diligently regarded!

VII. *Solomon's foreign relations—political, commercial, social, and domestic.* In the outset it may be assumed that in a civilized world, international commerce implies the existence of pacific political relations, defined by treaties expressed or implied. Trade is peaceful by nature. Applying this law of civilized national life we may notice that the history speaks more distinctly and fully of Solomon's commercial than of his political relationships. But where there was national commerce, we may assume national peace on some well understood basis.

With Egypt Solomon established the closest relations possible at a very early period in his reign. "He made affinity with Pharaoh king of Egypt and took Pharaoh's daughter" in marriage (1 Kings 3: 1). This domestic union implied peaceful relations between these two kingdoms, and opened the way for the unrestricted commerce of which we read subsequently (1 Kings 10: 28, 29), in which Solomon imported from Egypt "horses, chariots, and linen yarn," not merely for home consumption, but for export and sale to supply "all the kings of the Hittites and for the kings of Syria."——To his relations with Tyre the whole record testifies. These relations were of course necessarily political; they were definitely and intensely commercial—bread-stuffs in exchange for building materials and skilled labor; besides the co-operative trade which Solomon and Hiram carried on jointly through their commercial navies and seafaring men across the great Mediterranean with North-western Africa and South-western Europe—in Hebrew phrase, "with Tarshish" and "ships of Tarshish." The imports of this trade were gold and silver, ivory, apes, and peacocks" (1 Kings 10: 22, and 2 Chron. 9: 21).—— Moreover, having built Ezion-Geber on the eastern arm of the Red Sea for their port, they drove a very considerable trade with the southern coast region of Arabia and probably with India and Africa. The precise location of Ophir—the land of gold—is still an unsettled question, opinions being divided between Arabia and India, with much to be said for either theory. The products of this traffic were gold (principally), yet also "almug (or algum) trees and precious stones" (2 Chron. 9: 10, and 1 Kings 10: 11).——With the Queen of Sheba and her kingdom, located, as is supposed, in South-west Arabia, Solomon opened a regular traffic; and not with her kingdom only among the numerous principalities of great Arabia, but "with all those kings." To the statements made 1 Kings 10: 14, 15 as to the annual receipts of Solomon in gold, put at 666 talents, it is added: "Besides what he had of the merchant men and of the traffic of the spice merchants, and of all the kings of Arabia, and of the governors of the country."

Solomon pushed his overland commerce in still another direction, viz., toward the Euphrates—that land of immense wealth and resources. To facilitate this traffic, he built Tadmor in the wilderness, otherwise called Palmyra, both names signifying the palm-land (2 Chron. 8: 4). This great city was practically a halfway house between Damascus and the Euphrates, about 120 miles from each. Much of the country to be traversed on this route was a desert. The magnificent ruins of this once splendid city are among the wonders of the Eastern world.

This geographical survey of Solomon's commercial relations will suffice to show that in his age the land of Israel was central to the commerce of the civilized world, and that under his influence his kingdom, in conjunction with Tyre, became an immense emporium for the traffic of all civilized countries. This traffic brought into Israel, or at least, it brought *to the* king of Israel, great wealth; but it brought also great perils—great temptations, and, apparently, great decline in her religious life.——The danger to Solomon was immensely greater from the fact that, according to the usages of his age, these intimate political and commercial relationships carried with them social and domestic relations also. Beginning with Egypt, Solomon made affinity with Pharaoh, and took his daughter to wife. Polygamy among the oriental kings of that age being the rule, not the exception, Solomon took other wives—as the sad record in 1 Kings 11: 1–8 puts it: "King Solomon loved many strange [foreign] women besides the daughter of Pharaoh—women of the Moabites, Ammonites, Edomites, Zidonians, and Hittites." The numbers given are startling—not to say almost incredible; "seven hundred wives, princesses, and three hundred concubines." These numbers may, perhaps, be erroneously large; but the real number was doubtless great. The usages of kings wrought powerfully in this direction; political and business interests favored, and, perhaps we might say, seemed to demand continual enlargement of the royal harem.

VIII. *Solomon's apostasy from God; its antecedents and occasions.* The history ascribes this apostasy to his ungodly, idolatrous wives. "He clave to them in love," and by natural consequence "they turned away his heart" from God.——They did not come over to his religion and to the sincere worship of his God; but they brought their own religion, their own idol gods, with themselves into Israel. Gradually (we may presume), little by little, they drew him into their own practices of worship. It was when he was old, says the historian, when the ardor of his youthful devotion had sadly waned; when wealth and luxury had induced effeminacy, and after unbounded admiration and high position had stealthily undermined his piety—it was upon a heart long exposed to these subtle influences that the social power of so many wives—princesses of leading influence, of high culture, and commanding social position—was brought to bear upon him to his sad fall. Many of them—we know not definitely how many—came with the prestige of royalty, representing the dignity of courts and kingdoms. Shall not the king of Israel receive them with all the honors due to the kingdoms and thrones which they represent? Shall he not respect the religions they severally profess? Politeness, complaisance, the demands of civilized society, the interests of international peace and commerce—all concur in demanding unrestricted toleration of their idolatrous worship. [So it would *seem;* so, but for the higher claims of God, and of truth, and of his holy covenant, it would be].——When to these demands of worldly sort we add the fact that Solomon clave to these wives and concubines in love—that his sensitive nature yielded to such powerful attractions— we have no need to go further to seek the occasion of Solomon's relapse into great sin. He became an idolater. "His wives turned away his heart after other gods;" "his heart was no longer perfect with the Lord his God as the heart of David his father." Specifically it is stated that Solomon went after Ashtoreth, the goddess of the Zidonians, and after Milcom, the abomination of the Ammonites. He also built high places and furnished every facility for the worship of these gods—the abominations of Moab and Ammon.——The author of Kings, who alone gives us these sad facts, is careful to remind us that these marriages with foreign idolaters were strictly forbidden by the divine law. Solomon must have known that the God of Israel forbade his taking many wives—forbade his taking even one who was an idolater—a "strange," *i. e.*, a foreign woman, still adhering to her national idolatry. It was a fearful stride in the downward road when Solomon broke over the safeguards of this prohibition, and took his first heathen wife. What could save him when he lost respect for this law of God, and pushed on accumulating foreign idolatrous wives, perhaps, by hundreds? It was, indeed, a sad and terrible fall!

IX. *His repentance; the evidence in the case.* On the question of Solomon's repentance we have to deal with probabilities, not with absolute certainties. The Scriptures neither explicitly affirm nor deny. Arguments are sometimes built upon the silence of Scripture; but manifestly such arguing should proceed very cautiously. The author of Chronicles is silent as to Solomon's apostasy; but it would not be safe to infer from his silence, either that Solomon never did apostatize, or that this author could not have known it.

The author of Kings who has spoken with sufficient plainness of his apostasy has said nothing as to his repentance; yet let no one infer from this silence that Solomon never repented. The Lord may have had reasons for leaving this fact with no explicit affirmation—perhaps to make the moral warning from his fall the more impressive.

My reasons for the hope and for a certain amount of belief that Solomon repented of his great sin before he died, come from these two considerations:——(1.) The tenor of God's promise to David in respect to this very point, as it appears in 2 Sam. 7: 12-16. Beyond all doubt this passage has special reference to Solomon: "When thou shalt sleep with thy fathers, I will set up thy seed after thee who shall proceed out of thy bowels" (applicable specially to Solomon); "he shall build an house for my name" (Solomon only); "If he commit iniquity" (which he did) "I will chasten him with the rod of men" (it was Solomon who wrote—"Whom the Lord loveth he correcteth, even as a father the son in whom he delighteth" Prov. 3: 12): "But my mercy *shall not depart away from him* as I took it from Saul whom I put away from before thee." Saul was abandoned of God and never brought to repentance. God "took his mercy away from him" in that awful sense of giving him over to his righteous doom. But the Lord distinctly declares that he will not in this special sense take his mercy away from Solomon. Upon Solomon he will still hold fast and restore him to repentance—to his ultimate salvation.——I do not see how the contrast between Saul and Solomon, indicated in this promise, can mean less than a pledge on the part of God to bring Solomon to repentance after his committing iniquity.

(2.) My second argument comes from the book of Ecclesiastes. This book bears ample evidence of having been written by Solomon—late in his life. He is no longer a young man. He has lived long enough to have given all forms of worldly pleasure a full trial and to have proved their utter vanity. He has thought over his guilty life of pleasure-loving and pleasure-seeking until he not only sees its folly but feels it. He sees that such a life is inconsistent with fearing God and keeping his commandments; and he most unequivocally declares that such fear of God and such obedience are the supreme duty of mortals.——These points in this book of Ecclesiastes afford strong proof of his real repentance—much the more strong when seen in the light of the special design of this book, viz., written for those who had admired his pleasure-loving life, and intended as his protest and warning against the very life he had lived before them which they had so much admired. [For a more full presentation of the design and scope of this book of Ecclesiastes, see my Introduction to it.]——The book should be taken as Solomon's testimony to the grand mistake of his life and as the warning of a penitent man against what he then saw to have been his great life-sin.——That the argument of Ecclesiastes is made against worldliness, and not specifically against idolatry, may be due to one or both of these reasons:—
(a) That his philosophical mind deemed it better to

strike at the root-sin than at its branches, his own experience having shown him that apostasy began with the love of the world; or (b) That inasmuch as those foreigners for whom especially he wrote this book were born into idolatry and begirt on every side with its surroundings, he had most hope of doing them good by approaching them in the line of the great principle or law of man's relations as a sentient and moral being to God his Maker and Father. If they could be made to see and feel that the fear of the Lord is the beginning of all wisdom and that man's passion for pleasure should be subordinated to the demands of his higher moral nature and to the known will of God, the question of worshiping idols would subsequently dispose of itself. Hence, I infer that the silence of Ecclesiastes on the subject of idol-worship can not be held to disprove his real repentance of his own idolatry. The drift of this book does signify that in his view his own fearful apostasy began in his supreme devotion to worldly pleasure.

X. *The influence of this reign upon the moral and religious state of Israel.* Neither of the authors of our two histories (Kings; Chronicles) has made it a special point to answer this question. Consequently, we are left to inferences from the nature of the case, and from such facts as they narrate, bearing incidentally upon it.

It scarcely need be said, that, the human mind being what it is, royalty is always a great power. The manifest spirit and known life of kings have weight with their people. The force of this common law of mind is in the present case augmented by the fact that in the previous reign, religion in Israel had been greatly revived under the influence of David. During most of his reign he had powerfully sustained the worship of the sanctuary, giving it the full weight of his personal attendance, and, yet more, the power of his warm, earnest soul, and, more yet, the words of his own poetic genius, and the attractions of his own music. All these elements of influence were then combined with his royal example to tone up the religious life of the nation. The people had been under training, therefore, in the line of being influenced by the king toward vital godliness.——To this we may add that the first years of Solomon led off in the same direction. Apparently, during all the time of the temple-building until its solemn dedication, the royal influence of Solomon was conducive to the sound religious life of his people. All the more fearful, therefore, must the revulsion have been when they saw their king trampling under foot the great law of God by which he held his throne—multiplying wives to himself; taking them from the idolatrous nations on every side; building idol temples and altars for those wives, and, at last, himself joining with them in their abominable idol-worship. We are not told whether he forsook his own temple, and the worship of the God of his own covenant; and, in fact, it is of the least possible account, whether he did or did not. If he did not in form, he certainly did in spirit, for none can serve both God and Mammon—both Jehovah and idol gods. If he attempted it, his example could scarcely be less pernicious than if he had utterly deserted his magnificent temple. In either case his moral power must have gone solid against real religion —against the true worship of the holy God. The contrast between Solomon on his knees before all the assembled thousands of Israel in his prayer consecrating the new temple, and this same Solomon, going with his scores or hundreds of heathen wives to worship their gods on the high places of the land, must have been terribly impressive—to all pious hearts sad, not to say revolting; but to the masses, we have reason to fear, seductive toward the same idol worship. So much we must infer from the well known laws of the human mind, and from the relations of the throne to the people under the religious system of Israel.

In addition to this inferential testimony, we have the evidence of historic fact; as, for example—that when Jeroboam raised the standard of revolt and drew around himself ten out of the twelve tribes, and set up golden calves in Bethel and in Dan for the people to worship, there was not apparently one note of remonstrance from the people; not a word of protest appears upon the pages of their history from any pious worshiper in those ten tribes against their national apostasy. Alas, how fallen already from the spirit of the reign of David and from the institutions of Moses! What a change apparently since the dedication of Solomon's temple! Either the apparent worship of the thousands of rulers and people on that august occasion was utterly shallow and superficial, or the new generation which the lapse of only twenty-nine years has brought upon the stage has degenerated wofully. [Solomon reigned forty years, and the temple was begun in his fourth year and finished in his eleventh.]

The question of the influence of Solomon's reign upon Israel should take a wider range than merely the attendance upon the temple worship, or even the spirit of that worship. The court, the family residence, and the entire surroundings of Solomon rose almost at one bound from the severe but noble simplicity of the reign of David to the highest style of luxury and splendor known to the most cultivated and wealthy nations of the age. Nay more; for Solomon had the honor before the sovereigns of Tyre, Egypt, and Sheba, of having surpassed them all in taste and splendor, inventing and perfecting new appliances for all earthly delights. The barriers set up in the Mosaic law against conformity to outside luxury and pomp were suddenly swept away: no court on the face of the earth surpassed or even equaled Solomon's in its magnificence. He led; they only followed.——What was the influence of all this upon the masses of the people? Was there not a quickening passion for horses and chariots; for palaces and equipage; for luxuries of the table, and for ornamentation in dress? If not, there must have been a marvelous virtue among the masses, or a strange suspension of the normal laws of human nature.—— To what extent the immense influx of wealth to the throne by commerce and otherwise, reached the people, giving them facilities for its accumulation, it may be difficult for us to determine absolutely. It is, however, safe enough to infer that there was a great body of men not enriched and not elevated in point of style, or even of the comforts of life, by the new influences which were bringing such wealth to their king. There was an immense demand for hard work, and Solomon drew heavily upon the solid muscle of thousands and tens of thousands of men drafted into this service. It would be very like all other workings of human nature if, having the power to coerce such labor, he did not pay wages enough to improve the condition of these laboring classes. The fact comes out very clearly after his death that the people had felt the burden of these levies for service and of their government taxes, and were quite ready for revolution if their request for relief were denied. The state of the working men—the millions—of Israel was therefore not improved but deteriorated by the influences of Solomon's reign. This deterioration was by no means favorable to either the religious or the social and general culture of the people.

The history (1 Kings 11: 14–40) appends to its sad account of Solomon's apostasy the fact that in the latter years of his reign, Solomon had more or less annoyance, not to say political trouble, from personal enemies. Hadad, representing the royal house of Edom, had found great favor in the court of Egypt; Rezon, from the kingdom of Zobah, had found a home in Damascus, and became the head of a powerful band. Both became declared enemies of Solomon and disturbed the otherwise mostly unbroken peace of his realm. In the same connection we have the early history of Jeroboam—a bright, active young man, whom at first Solomon promoted to responsibilities because of his manifest energy and efficiency. The Lord by his prophet designated him as the future king of ten of the tribes. It seems that this revelation came to the knowledge of Solomon, who sought, unsuccessfully, to defeat it by taking Jeroboam's life. Jeroboam fled to Egypt, and was ready for his place when the tribes broke with Rehoboam. These persons became God's instruments to disturb the peace of Solomon's reign— not to say, also, to scourge him for his great apostasy. These facts bear strongly upon the political—perhaps not specially upon the religious—condition of Solomon's kingdom.

There is yet another point on which all thoughtful minds will be moved to inquire, viz., the influence for good or for ill of the unsurpassed magnificence of Solomon's temple. During the twenty-nine years (the maximum) intervening between its dedication and Solomon's death, this temple stood in all its glory; the impressions made by it, then fresh and new, were in their fullest strength;—what was the result?

Under David the Mosaic Institutions had manifestly developed an immense power. The worship at the one place; the daily morning and evening sacrifice; the new moons; the great day of atonement, and the three great annual festivals—these normal seasons of public worship, enlivened and enforced by the thrilling service of sacred song—not to say, also, by the constant and devout attendance of their beloved king David, must have made the tabernacle worship a powerful agency for religious culture in Israel. It is safe to assume that these seasons of national worship were well attended during the greater part of David's reign. "The tribes went up"—the masses of the people thronged to the sacred city. The social and religious forces of their sacred institutions were in full operation—were, we may probably say, in their glory.

Under Solomon's reign the public worship at the sanctuary opened with the quickening inspirations of that mighty movement for temple-building. Immense contributions of gold, silver, treasure—the presence of materials borne laboriously from Joppa to Jerusalem and piled up there year after year, stone upon stone, as the building advanced, in growing magnificence;—these seven years of previously unknown experience among this people were crowned at length by the unsurpassed solemnity of its dedication when God came down in fire and in the visible glory of the Shechinah and took possession—all constituting an era in their national history rarely surpassed in its interest and its promise.

As Christian philosophers, it behooves us to put and press the question: *What were the results?* Was religion mightily revived, and were its sweet, hallowed influences for the religious culture and for the moral life of the people, powerfully sustained? Did the magnificence of this temple take hold with transforming power upon the heart of the masses and elevate them in piety and purity? And specially to our purpose in view of the great national temptation of the age—Did this gorgeous temple plant itself as a breast-work of protection against idolatry?

I am aware that it may be said, The problem is not before us in its simple, unmixed elements, because the influence of the king and his court became so entirely adverse, and interposed so much counteraction.——But why should we not reckon in the power of this temple upon king as well as upon people? Did the magnificent temple conduce toward the piety and stability of Solomon himself? Did it hold his court with a strong grasp to the steadfast service and worship of the God of Israel? Did the esthetic power of architecture, ornamentation, and magnificence, grasp the souls of either the cultured or the uncultured Hebrews, and did these elements extend their influence to the foreigners who gathered to the great city and to the royal court, so as to move them all effectively toward the true worship of Israel's God?——It was a great experiment; it was novel—altogether untried before. What contribution does it supply to our wisdom and knowledge on these great points?

In reply, a few things may be safely said—as thus: ——(a) There is no evidence that this temple, after its dedication, improved the tone of the religious life of Israel; in other words, that it promoted a real revival of pure religion.——(b) It is quite certain that it did not avail to counteract the various tendencies which came in powerfully upon the nation in the age of Solomon toward idolatry.——(c) It is therefore quite certain that too much may be expected of religious architecture and of the esthetic influence of the place and surroundings of public worship.——(d) While this case of Solomon's temple may be quite too much mixed to justify the conclusion that its influence was evil rather than good; while under all the circumstances it might be quite illogical to infer that it brought no blessings to the people; yet surely the case must suffice to prove that these external influences are far less than omnipotent; that too much may be expected of them, and that "the excellency of the power" that saves men from sin and builds up real holiness in human souls must come more directly from God than this.

XI. Some points exhibiting *contact of sacred with profane history* during Solomon's reign demand brief attention.

It was very early in the reign of Solomon, before he had finished his own palace or even the temple, that he "made affinity with Pharaoh of Egypt" by marrying his daughter (1 Kings 3: 1). Most chronologists concur in locating this Pharaoh in the 21st dynasty. A very common opinion makes his name Psusennes II,—the last king of his dynasty. The authorities, however, for these names are somewhat discordant, and no absolutely sure conclusion can yet be reached. For our present purpose of confirming sacred history by the authority of profane it must suffice to say that Egyptian dates, independent of the Scriptures, place the close of this dynasty within the reign of Solomon; and that all concur that Shishak, who comes to view before the death of Solomon (1 Kings 11 : 40), and specially in the fifth year of Rehoboam, (1 Kings 14: 25, and 2 Chron. 12: 2), as an enemy, was the first king of a new dynasty, the 22d; a new king, who had no sympathies in common with the family of Solomon.*

Turning to Tyre we find confirming testimony yet more abundant than in the reign of David. The Phenician historians, Dius and Menander, not only give the name Hiram as that of some Tyrian king, but as the name of that very king who was in league with Solomon. In extracts which come down to us through Josephus they both speak of "hard questions," passing reciprocally between these kings to be solved for a wager; and curiously (whether in the interests of truth, or of national vanity) represent that one Abdemon, a man of Tyre, solved the riddles sent by Solomon, and sent back others which Solomon could not solve.†

Again, Menander states that Hiram gave his daughter in marriage to Solomon—a statement the more probable because the sacred records speaks of his taking wives, princesses, from the Zidonians (1 Kings 11: 1).

Coincidences in the line of comprehensive and general facts (rather than specific) are given very forcibly by Rawlinson thus:—(1.) The kind of empire ascribed in Scripture to David and to Solomon, stretching from the Mediterranean to the Euphrates, is that which was common in those ages throughout Western Asia—one great central power, holding numerous petty tribes and kingdoms in a tributary relation. Assyria rose soon after to a similar prominence; and, next after it, Chaldea.—— (2.) The great buildings of Solomon, somewhat minutely

---

* See Rawlinson's Historical Evidences, pp. 93, 94.
† Rawlinson, pp. 307, 308.

described in the Scriptures, are shown to be remarkably in harmony with the taste and style of the age. The ruins of Nineveh, Susa, and Persepolis, extensively disclosed during the present century, are found to be in a similar style of architecture and ornamentation with the great structures of Solomon. We may make these special points: Immense pillars or columns of cedar; the copious use of gold and of ivory; figures of the lion about the throne, and gigantic sculptures.——
(3.) The relative prominence of the Phenician cities above, not the Hebrews only, but the whole world then known, in the arts, in navigation, and in commerce. This superiority of theirs is implied throughout the Scriptures; it is the testimony of all the most ancient history.

Thus the Hebrew history of the age of Solomon is in accord with the little we know of the Egyptain records of that age; yet more clearly so, with the Phenician annals; with the traditions of the Syrians of Damascus, and of Western Asia in general. We have here reached a point where confirming testimony begins to come in from the Assyrian inscriptions; from the ruins of Assyrian and Persian palaces; from Phenician coins, and histories, and from the earliest Greek poetry.*

* Rawlinson, p. 99.

CHAPTER X.

The Revolt.

The kingdom as left by Solomon is rent asunder; ten tribes organize under Jeroboam, bearing henceforward the name Israel: only two tribes, Judah and Benjamin, yet bearing the name Judah, remain to Rehoboam, son and successor of Solomon.

This great historic event is dated B. C. 975. It became an important epoch in Hebrew history, the more so because this separation was permanent, no reunion being ever effected; and because it severed the new, the Northern, kingdom from the influences of the sanctuary, divorced them from the one place of national worship, and practically drifted them off into idolatry, and consequent degeneracy and corruption—political, religious, and moral.

Both our histories give essentially the same account of the negotiations which resulted in rupture between the ten tribes and Rehoboam—the author of Kings having, however, given a much more full account of the early history of Jeroboam. The point of grievance with the people was excessive taxation. The luxury and cost of Solomon's court, *i. e.*, his family establishment, his harem, and his political relationships, had become simply enormous. Whether the profits of his foreign trade brought in less supply to his treasury, or whether the tribute paid by subject kings fell off in the latter years of his reign, it is quite plain that he levied unsparingly upon his people. It had become so severe that the masses were at one in demanding relief from Rehoboam as the condition of their allegiance.

Rehoboam met this demand as a grave question; deferred his answer for three days, and sought advice. The older counselors—as usual the wiser—advised him to make concessions. The young men * brought up

---

* As to the age of Rehoboam at his accession, put at forty-one, (1 Kings 14: 21, and 2 Chron. 12: 13) there are strong reasons for assuming this to be an error of some copyist for twenty-one. He was manifestly associated in education and age with the young men (1

with himself in luxury and self-indulgence, with never a taste of what labor means, and having not the least sympathy with the toiling millions, advised a defiant answer, threatening heavier burdens. This latter advice met the views of Rehoboam. It was of the Lord that he should be left to play the fool; so he gave the people this reply: "My little finger shall be thicker than my father's loins. My father chastised you with whips; I will chastise you with scorpions." Defiance begat defiance; the people answered: "What portion have we in David, neither have we inheritance in the son of Jesse: To your tents, O Israel: now see to thine own house, David." "So the people departed to their tents;" and the kingdom was rent asunder—never to be reunited.——To put this movement to the test, Rehoboam sent out his tax-gatherer, Adoniram "who was over the tribute." "The people stoned him with stones that he died." Then Rehoboam, and his tribe Judah, thought to rush to arms to subdue this rebellion, but God sent his prophet Shemaiah to forbid the attempt; and they desisted. The ten tribes called Jeroboam for their king, and both kingdoms naturally turned their attention to military defenses—standing armies and fortifications. Everybody saw war in the future of these kingdoms. The problem of "balance of power" became intensely critical.

From this point onward we have two kingdoms to study in place of one. It becomes a practical question —shall we attempt to carry forward these histories co-ordinately, passing often from one to the other; or shall we take one of them through its entire career, making its history the leading thread and touching the rival kingdom only for its relations to the one first presented; and then in like manner make the second kingdom the leading theme till its history is told? I judge the latter method will best avoid confusion and conduce to a clear and well-defined conception of the history of both kingdoms; and propose to treat first in order of *the kingdom of Israel*.

Kings 12: 10). If really forty-one, he must have been born one year before Solomon came to his throne, and of an Ammonite mother —a thing highly improbable. Much later in life Solomon married women of the Ammonites; but not (we may strongly presume) before the death of David.

Our sources of information are mainly the books of Kings and of Chronicles. These two books differ on the point last spoken of, viz., the method of treating the co-ordinate histories of the two kingdoms. The author of Kings carries both kingdoms on together, passing from one to the other very frequently, yet aiming, so far as could well be done, to keep them both before the mind continually. He gives all the kings in both lines; usually their age when they began to reign; always the number of years they reigned, and ordinarily the year of the reigning monarch in the other kingdom when each king began. It is not easy to say whether he gives disproportionate attention to Israel; but it may certainly be said that, compared with his brother, the author of Chronicles, he presents the Northern kingdom much more fully and the Southern much less fully.——On the other hand, the author of Chronicles gives all the kings of Judah, but not all—not more than half the names even —of the kings of Israel; gives as to the kings of Judah the years they severally reigned, and commonly their age when they respectively began to reign; but never tells us in what year of the rival monarch any one of them began. Indeed he makes no attempt to present the history of the kings of Israel. He refers to those kings only in order to write out more fully the kings of Judah. The latter are always the leading theme. The kings of Israel come in only incidentally. The author of Chronicles had a different purpose in his history from that of his brother, the author of Kings—as has been suggested above in the introduction to Chronicles, viz., to bring out specially the history of the good kings and of their great revivals; and in general whatever might bear with wholesome force upon the then present duties, responsibilities, hopes, and faith, of the returned exiles. ——The author of Kings wrote as we should expect Jeremiah to write; selected his matter as if he were Jeremiah, aiming every-where to show how idolatry worked out every form of ruin; how God labored through his prophets and by means of varied discipline and judgment to recall his wandering people to himself; how—as he often puts it—"the Lord sent to them all his prophets, rising up early and sending"; but the people would not hear, and could not be saved.——This purpose held him to a close and continuous history of the Northern kingdom, down to its final and speedy fall. Illustrations of the same principle occur not infrequently in Judah; he gives them due attention in their place.——The author of Kings does not assume that Chronicles is already extant; but the author of Chronicles does assume that the book of Kings may be before his readers, so that he can refer readily to the kings of Israel without formally introducing them to his readers.——Sketching the history of Israel first in order, we shall naturally follow for the most part the thread of the narrative as in Kings.

Jeroboam.*

The first king of Israel had shown himself active, shrewd, capable; one of those men who are born to do something in the world, and are ready upon occasion to step into any position of high responsibility. His keen eye saw at once that the religious element in man's nature is a great power, to be taken into account in politics. If his people continued to go up three times a year to Jerusalem for their religious worship, how could he trust them to be true to his throne? Yet they would not be satisfied without some religion—so he projected a new system. In this system it was vital that the localities of worship should be within the bounds of his own kingdom. He did not care to bring all the people to *one* place; he consulted their convenience and perhaps other objects by fixing upon two—one at Dan, in his extreme northern limit, where idolatry seems never to have lost its foot-hold since the age of the Judges; and the

* The Septuagint, compared with the Hebrew text, gives a quite different history of Jeroboam's antecedents—a history not merely supplementary, but in many points radically unlike. Some critics (*e. g.*, Stanley, as in Smith's Bible Dictionary—"Jeroboam") adopt the Septuagint in preference to the Hebrew text—attracted by its minuteness of detail, and by what is taken for verisimilitude.——It is not claimed that the Hebrew text is lame, apparently deficient, or lacking self-consistency. I see therefore no sufficient reason to discredit it as compared with the Septuagint. The additions in the latter are in my view to be classed with its additions to the book of Esther and to the book of Daniel as representing Hebrew tradition at the time of its translation.

other at Bethel—far toward its southern border. We read of "an house of high places"—probably a temporary and inferior structure of the sort common on the hill-tops—consecrated to idol-worship; and also of an altar upon which offerings were made and incense burned (1 Kings 12: 31, 33). More surprising than all else is the fact that he made two golden calves, and in the very words used by Aaron in his scene of calf-worship (Ex. 32: 4, 8) proclaimed, "Behold thy gods, O Israel, which brought thee up out of the land of Egypt." The most astounding thing here is that the people could so readily relapse into that form of idolatry which brought upon their nation God's fearful rebuke in the wilderness. As to Jeroboam, we may remember that he was fresh from Egypt, and, naturally enough, brought back with him this Egyptian worship; but how could the people endure it? It was, perhaps, less revolting at first view because, *professedly*, the calf was not to be itself the object of worship as if itself *a God;* but rather *represented* the true God. Egypt paid high honors to the cow as one of the most useful of animals, so that those philosophic minds who rose from the creature up to the Creator may have regarded the honors paid the calf as being virtually paid to its Maker. This process of thought, though too refined and abstruse for the masses, may yet have smoothed the descent downward to this form of idol-worship. The people of Israel at this time accepted it but too readily, no remonstrance appearing on the pages of this history.*

Jeroboam made two other changes: (1.) Of the stated times for worship; not three times a year, but only once; and this not in the first month, which might (undesirably to him) remind the people of the Passover; and not on the seventh, which would be associated with the feast of tabernacles; but on the eighth, which would be associated with nothing in Hebrew history.——(2.) Next, he ruled out the entire body of

* It should be said, however, on the authority of Chronicles, that "such as set their heart to seek the Lord God of Israel came to Jerusalem to sacrifice unto the God of their fathers"—thus quietly protesting against Jeroboam's calf-worship. It seems to be implied in this connection (2 Chron. 11: 13–17) that they not only came to Jerusalem to worship, but removed their residence and citizenship, thus strengthening Rehoboam's kingdom.

priests and Levites as knowing too much and having too much personal character; and, therefore, not sufficiently tractable for his purpose. In their place he put the lowest of the people, his new religion having no sympathy with intelligence or moral stamina of character.——Religiously his kingdom is now (as he hopes) on a footing of stability. The priests and Levites being thus thrust out of service and honor and robbed of bread, emigrated into Judah, carrying out of one kingdom into the other, not numerical force only, but the better elements of religious character.

The Agency of God's prophets in Israel.

It should be specially noticed that as Israel was cut loose by the policy of Jeroboam from the religious influences of the Mosaic Institutions, the Lord sought to supplement that lack in a measure by employing prophets. In the outset, Ahijah of Shiloh, in promising Jeroboam ten tribes, assigned the idolatry of Solomon as the reason for taking these tribes from his son, and promised Jeroboam a sure house—*i. e.*, a permanent throne for himself and posterity, on condition of his faithful allegiance to Jehovah (1 Kings 11: 31–39). Nothing in the history indicates that Jeroboam gave this proposition even his respectful attention. It is quite plain that he did not shape his national policy to meet this divine proposal.

In 1 Kings 14 we see Jeroboam again in contact with this aged prophet, Ahijah of Shiloh. He had a favorite son, Abijah, severely sick. Probably he hoped for some help from the prophet, or from the Lord through his prophet, though the ostensible errand was only to inquire what shall become of the child. Well aware that his record as king would bear greatly if not fatally against his success, he sends his wife (did he trust to a mother's power to move human sympathy?)—sends her *disguised*, but liberally laden with presents for the old prophet. ——Ahijah had lost his eye-sight, so that the deception might have been successful, save that the eyes of the Lord were there. When the sound of her feet on his threshold fell on the old prophet's ear, how was she astounded with his greeting: "Come in, thou wife of Jeroboam; why feignest thou thyself to be another?

for I am sent to thee with heavy tidings."——The prophet prefaced these tidings with an allusion to the Lord's original proposal to Jeroboam of a sure throne if he would rule righteously for the God of Israel; arraigned him for his utter failure to meet these conditions; charged him with open, outrageous idolatry; and closed with the doom of swift extinction to his royal house, and with the announcement to Jeroboam's wife: "When thy feet shall enter the city, the child shall die." So it came to pass.——This prophetic message also announced the rooting up of Israel from her goodly land, and her dispersion in captivity beyond the great Euphrates—as God's ultimate judgment for her persistent idolatry.

In 1 Kings 13 appears a very remarkable narrative of the mission of a prophet from Judah (name suppressed)—sent to meet King Jeroboam at his idol altar in Bethel. We may suppose it to have been on the day of Jeroboam's annual feast in the eighth month. He stood by the altar to burn incense. The prophet cried against the altar at the word of the Lord, declaring that a child should be born to the house of David who should offer on that altar the very priests of the high places that burn incense there, and should burn upon it dead men's bones to defile it. This prophecy beyond question referred to King Josiah.*

When Jeroboam heard these words from the prophet he put forth his hand to seize him, and also commanded the bystanders—"Lay hold on him." Instantly that outstretched hand withered, and the king "could not pull it in again" to its normal position. The prophet had given a sign that should verify his prediction, viz., "The altar shall be rent, and the ashes upon it

* The text as we have it has the phrase, "Josiah by name"—which, however, some critics suppose to be spurious—but only upon internal, not external grounds. They urge that it is not common that prophecy should be so minute as to give names so long in advance of fulfillment; that such minuteness has no worthy object, and that in the narrative of its fulfillment (2 Kings 23: 15–20) it is not intimated that Josiah's name had been given in the prophecy then being fulfilled.——I fail to see any special force in these objections. It is barely possible that the phrase may have been introduced by some subsequent compiler as an explanation; but a bare possibility can never justify a violent change of the sacred text, for which change we have no important reasons.

shall be poured out."——To make the king's consternation the more complete this sign forthwith took place; the altar was rent, and the ashes scattered abroad. Jeroboam begged for the prophet's prayers, and for his hand to be restored to its normal power. The prophet prayed and God restored the withered hand.——Suddenly the king's tactics were changed. Instead of violent arrest, he said to the old prophet—Now be so good as to go home with me to dinner, "and refresh thyself, and I will give thee a reward."——Never, answered the prophet; my orders are not to eat bread nor drink water in this desecrated place, and not to return by the same way that I came.——So far this prophet is true to his commission, and all has passed off well. The moral trial under which he fell now opens—on this wise.

There lived an old prophet at Bethel (was he ever a good man?)—whose sons seem to have witnessed the scene at the Bethel altar. Returning home they rehearse the story to their father. Forthwith he orders his ass saddled; pursues and overtakes the old prophet of Judah, and invites him to his own home to eat bread. The prophet answers—No; my orders explicity forbid it.——But, rejoins the old man of Bethel, "I am a prophet as thou art, and an angel spake unto me by the word of the Lord, saying, "Bring him back with thee into thine house that he may eat bread and drink water." "But" (adds the record) "he lied unto him."——This was the point of stern temptation. He is weary, we may presume, and hungry, so, with quite too little thought, he concludes that, perhaps, the Lord had changed his mind and given his consent that his prophet might take some refreshment even in this wicked Bethel.——While they sat at the table a message really from the Lord (not a lie as the former) came to this Bethel prophet for his guest: "Thou hast disobeyed the word of the Lord to thee; thy carcass shall never go to the grave of thy fathers." The prophet of Judah started for his home; a lion met him in the way and slew him.

These are the staple facts of the record: What is their explanation, and what are the lessons they were intended to teach?

An era of prophetic missions to the ten tribes in revolt was now opening. The reception given to this prophet from Judah by Jeroboam was quite in point to show how delicate and critical such prophetic missions were likely to be, and how vital to their success it was that the prophets should not only understand their messages, but have supreme, unlimited confidence that the messages given them were really from God. For all along through this era of prophetic missions in Israel, the devil would be working his system of false, lying prophets to counteract as best he could the influence of God's true prophets. It was vital, therefore, to forewarn God's prophets to be on their guard against the devil's prophets and against his lies. Jeremiah had this fearful battle to fight to the bitter end. No prophet whose history is known to us came into contact with false prophets so often and so fiercely as he. Such a case as this in 1 Kings 13 finds a place naturally, therefore, in this history, assuming it to have been written by Jeremiah.

As to the moral character of this old prophet of Bethel, it is not perhaps competent for us to pass upon it absolutely. The only point of difficulty is this: how, if he were a prophet of God, he could lie so to the prophet of Judah, and, on the other hand, how, if he were a prophet of the devil, the Lord should have spoken through his lips there at the table, dining with his guest. Perhaps it may relieve us on either horn of this dilemma if we consider, (a) That a man, normally good, may sometimes sin—as in this case, may be left of God to lie:—— and (b) That a bad man may be used of God, as Balaam was, to make prophetic communications, though only in rare, exceptional cases.

Recurring to the moral purpose of God in permitting such a trial to come upon one of his prophets and really seduce him into sin, to his sad but exemplary death, we may suggest that it was supplemented not long after by the case of Jonah, which, being put on permanent record by his own pen, bears a similar warning to all prophets of the Lord to execute with unswerving fidelity their divine commission. These prophets were human; only mere men of flesh and blood, and accessible, therefore, to those various temptations which more or less encompass all the saints of God in their earthly life. The solemn functions of the prophet brought his soul into peculiarly near relations to the Great God; but

JEROBOAM OF ISRAEL AND ABIJAM OF JUDAH. 261

even this did not lift him above all approaches of temptation; did not quench utterly those susceptibilities upon which temptation works—to the result sometimes of sorrowful sinning.

In the subsequent history of this Northern kingdom, we shall frequently meet with the Lord's prophets. A few of them appear without name. It is certain that there were some there to whom no allusion is made in either of our historic books. Their presence and labors there come down to us only in their own prophetic books; *e. g.*, Hosea, Amos, Micah. Of those prophets who ministered in Israel, some left no prophetic writings, and are known to us only through the historic books; *e. g.*, Elijah and Elisha; Jehu, son of Hanani. Another class named in these histories are yet best known through their preserved writings—the books designated as "The Prophets;" *e. g.*, Isaiah, Jeremiah, Jonah.

Returning to Jeroboam, we note that the historian touches but briefly upon the political events of his reign. When Rehoboam sprang to arms to repress the revolt, the Lord peremptorily forbade it; and he desisted. Apparently no great battle was fought between these two kings during their respective reigns, though a state of hostility was chronic: "There was war between Rehoboam and Jeroboam all their days" (1 Kings 14: 30, and 15: 6); "wars between Rehoboam and Jeroboam continually" (2 Chron. 12: 15).

As Jeroboam reigned twenty-two years and Rehoboam but seventeen, Abijam, son and successor of Rehoboam, filled out three years on his throne alongside of Jeroboam. The author of Kings says briefly: "There was war between Abijam and Jeroboam;" but the author of Chronicles devotes most of one chapter (2 Chron. 13: 1–20) to a very remarkable and most bloody battle between them. Opening with a proclamation by King Abijam, setting forth the claims of David's posterity to the throne over all Israel; the apostasy and idolatry of Jeroboam; and, on the other hand, the adherence of Judah to the established worship at the temple; and, placing himself publicly under the protection of the Lord God of their fathers, he exhorted his enemy in arms to forbear to fight against God.——Jeroboam with 800,000 warriors was in the field against Abijam, with only half that number. To his advantage in superior numbers Jeroboam sought to add that of ambushment. With his immense masses of men he quite surrounded his enemy.

When Judah saw their foe before and behind, they cried to the Lord; the priests sounded with their trumpets; the men of Judah gave their terrible war-shout; at that moment God smote Jeroboam and all Israel before Abijam and Judah. The record is that there fell slain of Israel 500,000—a half million of men. The historian's brief comment is: "Thus the children of Israel were brought under at that time, and the children of Judah prevailed because they relied upon the Lord God of their fathers." Abijam followed up his victory; took various cities, Bethel included. "Neither did Jeroboam recover strength again in the days of Abijam, and the Lord struck him and he died."——His reign, commencing with some vigor, became morally more and more rotten, and ended in political weakness and dishonor.——His son Nadab reigned but two years, then fell by a conspiracy which extinguished the royal line and the entire family of Jeroboam.

Baasha, of little known but humble antecedents, was the head conspirator. He seems to have gained control of the army then besieging Gibbethon in war against the Philistines. This done, he slew Nadab, and all survivors of the line of Jeroboam; then seated himself on the vacant throne—only to reign yet more wickedly. Beginning in the third year of Asa (of Judah), and reigning twenty-four years, his history hands down only these facts—that he was in hostile attitude toward Asa all his days; and that at some period he began to fortify Ramah, "that he might not suffer any to go out or to come in to Asa king of Judah" (1 Kings 15: 17, and 2 Chron. 16: 1). Ramah held a commanding military position on the great road from Jerusalem northward, and but five miles distant. A strong garrison there would prevent good men of the Northern kingdom from going to Jerusalem, or emigrating into Judah, and might sharply menace Asa's capital. To compel Baasha to desist from this enterprise, King Asa hired Benhadad of Syria to attack the northern cities of Baasha's kingdom—with the desired result. For this reliance on a foreign heathen power, Hanani, the prophet, is sent to rebuke Asa: "Thou shouldest have relied on the Lord thy God"—always able to save his trustful people; who had previously saved thee from the mighty host of the Ethiopians, and would have saved thee at this time. "In this thing thou hast done foolishly; from henceforth thou shalt have wars."*

After Baasha, his son Elah reigned two years; then fell by conspiracy (headed by Zimri, captain of half his chariots) while he was ingloriously drinking himself drunk in the house of his steward. Zimri proceeded at once to exterminate the whole house of Baasha, as the Lord had said by Jehu the prophet— the penalty for having utterly failed to rule righteously in the fear of God and to put down idolatry.—— Another dynasty is blotted out from Israel.

This conspirator Zimri reigned but seven days. ("Had Zimri peace who slew his master?" 2 Kings 9: 31). The army again besieging Gibbethon—where twenty-six years before Baasha struck for the throne— hearing that Zimri had slain the king, chose to put Omri, then captain-general of the army, on the throne. They soon disposed of Zimri. Another competitor, Tibni, was ultimately slain, and Omri reigned, no one disputing the throne. For six years he held the old capital Tirzah, (a beautiful city of Ephraim, just north from Mt. Ebal, and identified by Dr. Robinson); and then built Samaria—thenceforward the nation's capital to the fall of the kingdom.——Morally and religiously, Omri is no improvement upon his predecessors, "walking in all the ways of Jeroboam wherewith he made Israel to sin to provoke the God of Israel to anger with their vanities" (1 Kings 16: 26). Omri will be most remembered as the father of Ahab.

* As to the date of these transactions, the author of Kings give no figures; the author of Chronicles gives figures (2 Chron. 15: 19, and 16: 1), which must be in error, since they would place these events eight or nine years after Baasha's death. For Baasha began to reign in the third year of Asa; died, therefore, after a reign of twenty-four years, in Asa's twenty-seventh year; but here the figures are in Asa's thirty-fifth and thirty-sixth year.——Among various proposed methods of correction, the best dates, not from Asa's accession, but from the revolt—twenty years further back.

Ahab, and Elijah the Tishbite.

Three great historic facts make the name of Ahab conspicuous: (a.) His marriage to Jezebel, daughter of Ethbaal, king of the Zidonians; and its consequences; ——(b.) His relations to Elijah the prophet;——(c.) His affinity with the otherwise good Jehoshaphat, and the evils entailed upon Judah through this connection.

(a.) Jezebel, a born idolater, of indomitable spirit and energy, equal to any wickedness which her proud aspirations might prompt her to commit, brought into Israel the whole system of Baal-worship; sustained it by importing or raising up in Israel hundreds of Baal-prophets, and by the utmost exertion of her personal and political power. She appears every-where as Ahab's counselor and instigator to wickedness. Her plot to murder Naboth for his vineyard; to cut off the prophets of the Lord *en masse;* and, finally, to revenge herself on Elijah by taking his life, are at once cases in point and illustrations of her influence. The power of such a queen opened a new era in the kingdom of Israel. It took a long stride in the downward road toward national reprobation and ruin; brought a new strain of moral trial upon the religious people still surviving in that kingdom; and called forth fresh interpositions of that redemptive force which God had provided through his prophets.

We are but barely introduced to the wicked Ahab and his more wicked Jezebel (1 Kings 16: 29–33), when all suddenly (1 Kings 17: 1) Elijah the Tishbite bursts upon our view. Probably "Tishbite" indicates the city from which he came,—of which nothing is certainly known; Gilead, east of the Jordan, the country where he had been a sojourner, yet apparently, not a native. Beyond this we inquire for his antecedents in vain. Was he of the schools of the prophets—a pupil trained under some earlier men of God? Had he been in prophetic service before this mission to Ahab? Or was he only a rude mountaineer, of rough, stern culture; trained through years of solitude and prayer into devout communion with God and unblenching firmness of obedience to God's high behests?——Ah, indeed, we seem to know nothing where our curiosity instinctively asks so much. It is doubtless safe to say that the Lord had had the training of his servant Elijah for precisely such an emergency as the reign of Ahab and the sway of Jezebel had created; so that it only remained at this juncture to summon him forth from the mountains of Gilead for his work.

His first message to Ahab was put in few but most telling words: "As the Lord God of Israel liveth, there shall not be dew nor rain these years, but according to my word." So much; no more; and Elijah disappears as abruptly as he came. The word of the Lord bade him "hide himself by the brook Cherith that is before Jordan."* There the Lord commanded the ravens † to bring him bread and flesh morning and evening; and he drank of the brook until under the severity of the drought the fountain failed.——His next location is outside the limits of Israel, with a widow-woman of Zarephath (the Zarepta of Luke 4 :,26) "which belongeth unto Zidon." He finds her gathering a few sticks for (as she supposed) her last cooking fire, for she had come down to the last handful of meal and the last running of her oil. Elijah is hungry, and presses his request for a meal even of this starving family; but his employer will provide; and authorizes him to say to this woman— Go on; fear not; but make me a little cake first, and then make for thyself and son—for the Lord God of Israel saith, "The barrel of meal shall not waste, nor shall the cruse of oil fail until the day that the Lord sendeth rain upon the earth." So the supply held out and the board of Elijah and of his hostess was provided, for many days.—— According to the narrative, the closing scene of Elijah's stay in the house of this widow was the raising of her son to life. The woman seemed to assume that her son's death was in some way the result of Elijah's presence there, for she said to him, "What have I to do with thee, Oh thou man of God?"

---

* This brook emptied into the Jordan, but on which side of it, and which of many it was, must probably remain unknown.

† All attempts to change these ravens (exegetically) into Arabs or merchants or Orbites seem to fall short of even probability. Concealment from Ahab was a prime object which none of these proposed amendments provides for. Moreover, if human hands brought this bread and flesh, why should they have come twice every day?—— We have no occasion to miss the exquisite beauty and fitness of the case as in our version—God using the ravens to feed his prophet.

What is there between me and thee that my child must die? "Art thou come unto me to call my sin to remembrance and to slay my son?"——Elijah took the dead boy to his own prophet-chamber and laid him upon his own bed. Then he gave himself to prayer— "Oh Lord my God, hast thou also brought evil upon the widow with whom I sojourn by slaying her son?"—— We need not construe the spirit of this prayer as captious, nor as inquisitive for the reasons, nor further as inquiring whether God's purpose was real *death* with no restoration: Perhaps it simply brought up the case before the Lord preparatory to the supplication which he proceeded to make;—"Oh Lord God, I pray thee let this child's soul come into him again." The Lord heard this prayer; the child lived again. That the prophet stretched himself upon the child three times is said, yet with no hint as to the object or the reason for this act. We must suppose the prophet did so in obedience to intimations made to him of God's will; but we ask in vain for the reasons.——The results of this miracle were at least these two; (a) It convinced the mother (so she said) that Elijah was a man of God, and that the word of the Lord in his mouth was God's truth; and (b) It gave Elijah a fresh experience—by no means out of place at that time—that God hears prayer, and that he might depend on other answers in his time of need.

Elijah, Ahab, and Rain.

The scenes of the memorable chap. 18 (1 Kings) open here. It is a great crisis in Israel. The heaven shut up to the extent of neither dew or rain for three and a half years; the fountains and streams dry; the cattle perishing with thirst; famine confronting every household; suffering and solicitude every-where.——Such was the state of the nation when the Lord said to Elijah, "Go, show thyself to Ahab; for I will send rain upon the earth." Ahab, it seems, had remembered the conditions—" No dew or rain these years save according to my word;" so that since the drought had become a terrible reality, he probably believed that he must have Elijah's hand before he could have rain. Long before this, therefore, he had been searching for the missing prophet far and near. It comes to light here through Obadiah that he had not only searched his own kingdom from end to end, but other kingdoms and nations also, even taking of them their oath that they could not find him.—— The head steward of Ahab (it so happened) was not only a trusty man, but one "who feared the Lord greatly"—of which he had given proof by secreting and feeding 100 of the Lord's prophets by fifties in two caves, at his own expense and personal peril. The occasion for this was Jezebel's effort to cut off all the Lord's prophets. How many she actually murdered we know not. Through Obadiah the Lord saved this 100. For them he had work in Israel.

Ahab and Obadiah were both out on a common mission, though in different directions, in a desperate effort to find water and herbage somewhere to save their horses and mules alive. While on this mission Obadiah met Elijah and recognized him. "Go," said Elijah, "tell thy master, Behold, Elijah is here." Obadiah hesitates. Remembering what pains the king has taken for so many months to find Elijah, and how marvelously he had seemed to be spirited away, Obadiah finds it hard to believe the prophet's word, and fears he shall get into personal trouble with Ahab. Elijah is in earnest: "As the Lord liveth before whom I stand, I will surely show myself to him to-day." So Obadiah informs Ahab, and Ahab meets Elijah. The words that pass reveal the men. With strangest moral perverseness Ahab would hold Elijah responsible for all the mischiefs of this terrible drought: "Art thou he that troubleth Israel?*——At once fearless and true to the facts, Elijah replies: "I have not troubled Israel; but thou, and thy father's house, in that ye have forsaken the commandments of the Lord, and thou hast followed Baalim." Doubtless, he made the word "*thou*" emphatic, for this would express only the simple truth. Ahab had followed Baalim above all who had gone before him. He had brought all this trouble upon Israel.——Both these men were squarely outspoken; Ahab certainly was not restrained by any special respect for the man of God; and Elijah, how muchsoever he might honor the king, as in his duty bound, could not

* The verb he used would suggest Achan, to whom it was linked by historic association. Ahab charged Elijah with being to Israel a second Achan.

forget that himself was the messenger of the King of kings, and was commissioned just then to confront this guilty rebel against Jehovah.——Whether it were due to his sense of truth, to the power of his conscience, or to something in Elijah's manner which he knew not how to meet, Ahab made no further reply. Plainly, Elijah rises at once into the place of power, and puts things his own way. With wonderful boldness he proceeds to give command: "Now, therefore," thou king Ahab, "send and gather to me all Israel to Mt. Carmel, and the prophets of Baal 450, and the prophets of Asherah * 400, who eat at Jezebel's table.

Ahab obeys this behest. Did he ask, what for? There is no hint that he raised any question. The hand of the Lord in it was a power he could not withstand. How it happened that Jezebel was not there does not appear. It was enough that all her prophets came.——The place for this great transaction was of Elijah's selection. Mt. Carmel is a lofty mountain ridge, stretching about twelve miles from N. N. W. to S. S. E., terminating at the north in a bold headland which looks out upon the great sea; and at the south, in a projecting point which, overlooking the plain of Esdraelon and the city of Jezreel, met all the desired conditions of outlook and natural grandeur for transactions so sublime as these. Some point near this southern extremity of the Carmel ridge is believed to have been the exact site of this transaction †—a place contiguous to a living fountain, which might supply the water necessary, and where the wood for the altar was at hand.

In due time the people *en masse* were there, and also the prophets of Baal and Asherah. Ahab also was there, yet during most of this day, Elijah seems to ignore his presence and address himself only to the people and to the idol-prophets;—first to the people, in the words as in our version: "How long halt ye between two opinions?" To the word "halt," we must not give the sense—linger or pause as if through indecision and consequent inability to act; but pre-

* Asherah (Heb.) was the corresponding female goddess, always matched with Baal.

† See Bib. Sacra, Oct., 1873, p. 672: "El Mohrakah, or the place of Elijah's Sacrifice."

cisely that of walking, as one with legs of unequal length, swaying the body, therefore, to and fro, pitching now this way and now that—in most ungraceful, not to say painful or revolting motion. Herein lies the pungency of Elijah's appeal: How long do ye vacillate between these two diverse opinions as to the God ye will worship? How long will ye swing, pendulum-like, from one God to the other—now borne by your nobler convictions toward the true God; anon seduced back to Baal by your lusts? He appeals to their sense of fitness and right: "If the Lord, your nation's own Jehovah, be God, follow him; but if Baal be really the supreme, almighty God, then follow him."—This appeal probably carried conviction; yet the people answer him not a word. It was a moment of crisis. Elijah was equal to the emergency. The people were there; the work in their souls is begun. Baal's priests are there also—for some foreordained purpose. The great question at issue is—which God, Jehovah or Baal, shall have the homage of all hearts. Elijah has put the case upon its reasons; the people have nothing to say against his logic; but still seem to be too feebly impressed to make a bold and firm decision.—The prophet's next step therefore is a test. Let us see who is the true God. We will invoke him to reveal himself by fire, each upon his own altar. The circumstances shall be such as to preclude all mistake and all deception: then the answer will be open to every eye, and all may know absolutely whether Jehovah or Baal be the true God.——The God of Israel had given this sort of demonstration more than once before. Perhaps some of the people might remember to have heard of the original consecration of the priests, as in Lev. 9: 23, 24; or the case of Gideon and the angel's staff, touching the offering upon his altar (Judg. 6: 21); or the sacrifice of David at Araunah's threshing-floor (1 Chron. 21: 26); or the descending fire when Solomon's prayer consecrated the temple (2 Chron. 7: 1).——As to Baal, moreover, since he claimed to represent more or less the great powers of nature, it was certainly not unreasonable to ask him to send down (if he would or could) a flash of lightning, and consume the animal sacrifice on his own altar. The proposition of Elijah was, therefore, obviously a fair one. The people at once responded, "It is well spoken;" (Heb.—that's a good word.)

Turning to the prophets of Baal, Elijah said: Ye are many, and I stand on my side alone; go on, therefore, first in order; choose your bullock; slay, cut up, and place in order upon your altar, only put no fire under; and then call upon your god to answer by fire and consume your sacrifice. When you have made your trial, I will take my turn.——They commenced operations quite early in the day; for, having slain their bullock, dressed and placed it on the altar, "they called on the name of Baal from morning even until noon; O Baal, hear us." But there was no replying voice; no token of his having heard a word of their prayer. As their agony increased, they proceeded—not to "leap upon the altar" as the English version puts it, but to *dance* around it—such "bodily exercise" being in natural sympathy with their intense mental excitement. Elijah looked on quietly and patiently until noon, and then, for the people's sake, began to make suggestions. If these were sarcastic, keen, taunting, the occasion justified him. The people needed to see the facts in this strong light. "Cry louder," said Elijah, "for Baal is doubtless a god, and you will make him hear by and by; he may be in deep meditation, engrossed in some thoughts of his own; or he may have retired to his private apartment upon a call of nature; or he may have a journey on hand; or perhaps just now he may be asleep and you will have to wake him—so cry yet a little louder!——And they did cry a little louder; and not only so, they cut themselves with knives and lances (the war-weapon; not the surgeon's), drawing blood freely—as if to make appeal to the sympathy of their inattentive, sleepy god. So they held on from morning till noon, and from noon till the middle of the afternoon—the hour when the evening sacrifice began; but there came no voice; no answering response; no fire; no sign of recognition from the heavens above or from the earth beneath.——Elijah has now waited long enough. Addressing himself to the people, he cried: "Come near to me;" it is my turn now. The people gathered about him. He repaired the broken altar of Jehovah with twelve stones, reminding them of the twelve tribes and ignoring the unsanctioned rending of the kingdom. He then prepared a trench around the altar for water; put his wood in order and his slain bullock upon the wood; and then bade the bystanders bring on water. Again and again, even to the third time they brought their vessels (not "barrels," but more nearly buckets) full of water till the whole altar, wood and bullock, were saturated, and the very trench around was more than full. There must be no room for suspicion of concealed fire beneath.——Now is the time for prayer—one short but fervent prayer: "Lord God of Abraham, Isaac and Jacob, let it be known this day that thou art God in Israel, and that I am thy servant, and that I have done all these things at thy word. Hear me, O Lord, hear me that this people may know that thou art the Lord God, and that thou art turning their heart back to thyself again." There was no need of vain repetition; the prayer was heard. All suddenly the fire of the Lord fell. In the sight of all those gathered thousands it gleamed down from on high; it "consumed the sacrifice and the wood, and the stones" of which the altar was built, "and the dust" (the earth which occupied the center), "and licked up the water which filled the trench." When the people saw this they could be silent no longer, but fell on their faces and cried aloud: "Jehovah, he is the God; Jehovah, he is the God."

It was a thrilling scene. The impulses of such a moment must not be lost. Elijah cried aloud in tones of command: "Seize the prophets of Baal; let not a man of them escape. By the law of God they must be slain." Elijah brought them (so is the record) down to the brook Kishon which flows out of the valley of Esdraelon to the great sea, past the high peak of Carmel where they were, and slew them there. The overawed people are ready for this measure as one of the natural and righteous results of the great decision that Baal is not God and that Jehovah is; so they doubtless aided in this slaughter of Baal's priests. What Ahab thought of it the record saith not. He either had no heart or no power to resist.

At this point Ahab appears in the narrative. "Elijah said to Ahab, Get thee up (*i. e.*, from the brook Kishon where Baal's priests were slain) to the top of Carmel where thy supper is in waiting; eat and drink with glad heart, " for there is a sound of abundance of rain." Either Ahab had not much laid to heart in sorrow the slaughter of Jezebel's priests, or he felt the spell of Elijah's power, or his other excitements gave place to joy as he heard of the coming rain—for he was ready for his refreshment and " went up to eat and to drink."

——Elijah had other responsibilities. As the rain had been withheld three and a half years in answer to his prayer, so it was to come again at length through prayer. Elijah with only his servant went up to "the top of Carmel." There he "cast himself upon the earth and put his face between his knees"—his chosen attitude for this great struggle of prayer. Go, said he to his servant, and look toward the sea; watch for the first gathering cloud. He goes, but soon returns—there is nothing. Go again—the prophet meantime praying and waiting, and the servant going and returning, with the same result till the seventh time. Then he brought back the thrilling word: "Behold, there riseth a little cloud out of the sea, like a man's hand." Instantly Elijah understood it;—"Go, tell Ahab;" "Prepare thy chariot; descend from this mountain that the rain stop thee not." The heavens are black with clouds and wind; the mighty rain breaks forth from those surging clouds in torrents. Ahab's chariot drove swiftly toward his palace in Jezreel, sixteen miles distant. Elijah girded up his loins, and happy to serve as footman for his king ran with the agility of a trained mountaineer before this flying chariot to the very entrance of Jezreel. It is not said that he went into the city; the presumption is that he did not. After a long day of such intense excitement and exhaustive labor did he not need retirement, food, and rest?

What was the out-come of this momentous day—of these demonstrations that Jehovah is *the God;* of this breaking down of Baal-power; of this slaughter of Baal's priests; and, to crown all, of this glorious rain?——Let us follow Elijah yet a little further, and then return to consider more fully the results that came of that day, and also the results that seemed hopeful and possible, but yet failed of realization.

There were a great many vacant seats at Jezebel's supper table that evening. Can Ahab give any account of their absence to his inquiring, perhaps anxious Jezebel? "He told her all that Elijah had done"—all about the test by fire—the astounding decision in favor of Jehovah against Baal; and "withal how he had slain all the prophets of Baal with the sword."——Was Jezebel appalled? Not for a moment. But her wrath kindled into fury. Too much excited to lay plans for his arrest, or possibly thinking it wiser to frighten him from the country, she sent a messenger to Elijah to say—"So let the gods do to me and more also, if I make not thy life as the life of one of them by this hour to-morrow."—— We must take the record as we find it, hard as it may be to account for the statement. Elijah was afraid of Jezebel, and fled for his life. The man who but yesterday seemed as one who never had a fear—facing 850 Baal-men; commanding and aiding to execute their wholesale slaughter; standing alone for God before his idol-worshiping king and the assembled thousands of Israel; so near to God moreover in heart and in faith and so prevalent in prayer—ah, but what of him now? ——"He saw" [the various reading has it, he was afraid]; he fled for his life, alone save his one servant; he stayed not his flight till he reached Beersheba, on the extreme southern border of Judah, estimated to be ninety-five miles from Jezreel. There he left his servant (who perhaps was unable to go further), but pushed on himself yet one whole day's journey into the wilderness—so far before he felt himself safe from the wrath of Jezebel. Here "he sat down under a juniper tree"* and begged that he might die! † Alas, the flesh is weak; he is utterly exhausted. Was human endurance ever tasked more fearfully? After such a day on Mt. Carmel, such a foot race to Jezreel, and such a flight for life; breadless, sleepless, two or three days and nights at least—no wonder his spirits sink within him; no wonder he feels that it would be sweet to die!——God's "kind restorer, balmy sleep," came to his relief; and yet, more, after he had slept, we know not how long, the Lord sent his angel to touch him, and call him up to eat. Lo, this angel had

---

* Understood to be a species of broom, common in the deserts of Arabia, of size sufficient to afford agreeable shade.

† Was it not a wonderful case of forgiving mercy that God not only passed over this impatient outcry, but exempted him from ever dying!

placed at his pillow there in the wilderness a traveler's cake already baked, and a cruse of water. The prophet ate and drank, and lay down again to sleep. Again, the angel waked him to a second meal—wonderfully sympathetic and appreciative—"because the journey is too much for thee." Now, somewhat rested and refreshed, he traveled on forty days and nights, sustained by that great hand Divine to Mt. Horeb. There he turned into a cave for his home and place of rest. Here the first word of gentle rebuke came to him:—"What doest thou here, Elijah?" Who sent thee here, and on what errand? Is this the place to fight the battle for truth and for Israel's God against Baal, and against apostate Ahab and his seducer Jezebel?——Remarkably Elijah's answer gives mostly the dark side and not the bright; one set of facts, and not the other. "I have been very jealous for the Lord of Hosts" (so far, true); "for the children of Israel have forsaken thy covenant—[but they had with one loud voice declared for Jehovah—"he is the God"]; "they have thrown down thine altars, and slain thy prophets with the sword" [yet Obadiah had secreted and saved a full hundred]—"and I, even I only, am left, and they seek my life to take it away." He did not mention that Baal's prophets were all cut off too, not one of them being left; nor that, through the good hand of the Lord upon him, he had seen the Lord answering by fire and mightily convincing the assembled thousands of Israel that Jehovah and not Baal is the Supreme God, and compelling their unanimous consent. These great facts so grand, and, withal, so recent, Elijah fails to mention. There are depressed moods of mind that have a natural sympathy with the darker side of things, and this law of human frailty the Lord is not wont to ignore.——In this case he comes yet nearer to his servant for a more full and impressive manifestation. "Go forth," said he, "and stand upon the mount before the Lord." We read—"Behold, the Lord passed by, and a great and strong wind rent the mountain, and brake in pieces the rocks before the Lord; but the Lord was not in the wind; and after the wind an earthquake; but the Lord was not in the earthquake; and after the earthquake a fire; but the Lord was not in the fire; and after the fire a still small voice," (Heb. a voice of whispering stillness). "And it was so that when Elijah heard this, he wrapped his face in his mantle" (conscious that God was, indeed, there), "and went out and stood at the entrance of the cave." Then the same word as before came to him again: "What doest thou here, Elijah?" To which he gave the same answer.——That God came in these gentlest manifestations—not in those most appalling—is due, we may assume, to the tenderness of his sympathy and pity for human infirmity. Elijah must be rebuked, yet there were redeeming features, and circumstances of apologetic bearing, such as the Lord never ignores.——It is, moreover, supposable, and by no means improbable, that the Lord intended a still further significance in the gentle voice, contrasted with the tempest, the earthquake, and the fire; viz., to suggest to his prophet the higher modes of spiritual power. Perhaps, Elijah estimated above its relative value the influence of judgment, fiery zeal, blood, and carnage; and had yet to learn that God's gentler ways reach men's hearts to better purpose—as rocks are better melted than shattered to fragments.

We have now before us the staple facts of Elijah's experience and life from Carmel to Horeb. We ought not to pass them without patient reflection.

That day on Carmel—the sun has risen and set on few like it. I do not care to call special attention to the external grandeur and sublimity of those transactions; nor to the religious heroism of God's one only prophet; nor to the masterly powers of mind wielded under God by this one man over almost a thousand of Baal's men, and over the many thousands of assembled Israelites;—but I call attention to the scenes of Carmel as being *supremely auspicious for a grand moral and religious reformation.* What external circumstances could ever be more so?——(1) Note that most impressive demonstration of the true God made by descending fire upon the altar. Think how it impressed those admiring thousands! Was not that a good beginning toward a radical change in their allegiance from Baal to Jehovah?——(2) Scarcely less propitious and impressive was the second great demonstration of a present God— that *by water*—by that mighty, glorious rain. Especially was this of priceless value, because it came in answer to prayer. It lifted up its witnessing voice before the nation, testifying that God hears and answers prayer. Usually God's judgments upon Israel had been removed only on condition of their national repentance and of *their* uplifted cry for mercy. Here the people had professed their acceptance of Jehovah as their God. It seems to have been upon the basis of this acknowledgment that God returned to them in this great mercy of rain.——The rain was, moreover, so great a mercy, it could scarcely fail to put their hearts into a favorable attitude for moral and religious impression.——(3) To these elements of general influence must be added whatever had been gained upon the heart of Ahab—an amount which (had Jezebel been out of the account) might have been very considerable: ——and (4) The positive gain secured by the sudden removal of every Baal-prophet from the land.

Was not this, therefore, a grand opportunity for pushing a general and radical reform throughout the Northern kingdom? How shall we adjust ourselves to the disappointment as we see this sublimely grand opportunity mostly lost? A work so great and so hopeful—begun so auspiciously—what shall we say when we see it suddenly arrested and find it hard to discern even so much as dim traces of resulting good?——Were not the people expecting that Elijah would be their great leader in the re-establishment of Jehovah's worship and the utter expulsion of Baal-worship from the land? And how could they be expected to declare every-where for Jehovah and against Baal in the face of Jezebel's fury when even Elijah had fled before her threats and nobody knew whither he had gone?

It will not be wholesome to pass judgment severely upon the course of Elijah on the days next after Carmel; but we may suggest:——What if, on hearing the threat of angry Jezebel, he had lifted up his prayer to God— "What wilt thou have me do? How shall I sustain and carry on to final triumph the great work which thine own strong hand but yesterday began?"—What if he had said with Nehemiah—"Shall such a man as I flee?" What if he had given himself anew to the Lord his God, saying—Here is my life, if thou dost call for the sacrifice; or if it please thee, let the life of Jezebel, like the lives of her prophets, be taken out of the way and thy work go on, no such adversaries opposing.

It is not permitted us to go back into the eternal counsels of God and ask—Why did he permit such a failure in a work so dear to his heart and so auspiciously begun? Why did he let Elijah lose heart so sadly, and place such a contrast before the world between the sublime heroism of one day and the (apparently) inglorious flight of the next?——We will not attempt to push questions of this sort. Let us rather suggest that this is one of the sad experiences to which the Lord's cause has been subjected all down the ages—viz., set back (as men view things) by the human infirmity of his servants. It is humiliating, and perhaps should teach us to beware of too much confidence in great men.

Again, let it be suggested as at least supposable that magnificent success, close on the heel of those scenes of Carmel, and coming apparently as their result, would have witnessed that God was in the tempest, the earthquake, and the fire, rather than in the still, small voice; and so might have tended to misrepresent Jehovah's spiritual power. True, the time had not come to bring forth before the world the peculiar power of tenderness, and tears, and pitying love; but the Lord might have deemed it unwise to accumulate testimonies and illustrations of an entirely different, not to say opposite, character and bearing.

Let it be suggested also, that such a case as this affords a very special lesson on prayer, teaching not merely that God hears prayer; not merely that, despite of the so-called "scientific" objections, he can hear prayer about rain—to the extent of arresting the entire rain-fall in Israel for three and a half years, and then bringing it down in torrents, in answer to one man's prayer, but specially this lesson—that this praying prophet was "a man *subject to like passions as we are.*" The case as here put before us is a touching comment on this very practical point. "Of like passions as we." Not a man lifted above the infirmities of human flesh; not a man of nervous organism equal to unlimited endurance, but perhaps rather specially subject to terrible depression after the exhaustive strain of immense and protracted excitement;—a man who, after having his prayers answered so wonderfully one day, seems to have almost forgotten, the next day, to lift up the simplest of all prayer—Lord, teach me how to order myself in this emergency.——Well, it was surely very gracious in our Heavenly Father to give us such a lesson, showing that he can hear the prayers of men of like passions with ourselves, and can hear *us*, although compassed about with manifold infirmities.

I suggest only one point more in quite another line of thought. This history may well astound us with its illustrations of the terrible influence of *one bad woman*. What Satanic energy of will! What bold ingenuity! What seductive power over her husband toward wickedness! We might have supposed that no mind less mighty than Satan's could throw itself into the face of such a movement as that inaugurated on Mt. Carmel and block it utterly;—but apparently Jezebel was equal to it—and did it! May the Lord spare the world from other such!

Resuming the history of Elijah, we note that the Lord had more service for him yet; viz., to go back to the upper Jordan valley—a district somewhat remote from Jezebel's home; and in due time call into the Lord's service Hazael to be king of Syria; Jehu to be king of Israel—both to serve as executioners of his judgments on Ahab and his kingdom; and also, Elisha, to be his associate and successor, a prophet in Elijah's room. Subsequent history shows that these words said to Elijah were rather a general outline of the divine policy than a specific programme for his own work, for the anointing of Jehu took place some time after his translation, and was done under Elisha's direction by an unnamed "son of the prophets;" and there is no intimation that Elijah went in person to anoint Hazael. It only appears (2 Kings 8: 7-15) that Elisha, some time after Elijah's translation, said to Hazael: "I know the evil that thou wilt do to the children of Israel," etc. ——Elijah did call Elisha personally, as we read 1 Kings 19: 19-21—a scene which suggests the manner in which our divine Lord often called his disciples suddenly away from their fishing nets or from their custom-house office; and yet this call is singularly colored with those shadings of wild Arab life which rarely fail to appear in Elijah the Tishbite.——At Abel-Meholah—some place in the Jordan valley (not at present identified) he found Elisha plowing, in care of twelve teams and plows—himself with the twelfth—a farmer of very considerable responsibilities and probably of wealth. As he passed along he threw his mantle over him and silently went on. A few moment's reflection suggested to Elisha the import of this mantle-call; so he left his oxen in the furrow and ran to overtake Elijah, crying out: Grant me time to go home and give my farewell kiss to my aged father and mother. Then I will follow thee. "Go back," said Elijah, "for what have I done to thee?"——This seems rather curt, with an undertone of rebuke, as if he would say: "If thou art not ready to forsake father and mother to follow me, I have no service for thee: do as you like." The thing Elisha actually did may have been a kind of compromise between his first thought and Elijah's demand. He seems to have omitted the going home for the farewell kiss to father and mother whom he might never see again; but he made a sort of farewell sacrifice to his farm and to his workmen. His own yoke of oxen are slaughtered and boiled—his yoke and plow being the fuel. This is the end of his personal farming—this farewell feast to his laborers. This done, he follows Elijah as his servant.

To encourage Elijah—perhaps to rebuke his dark-sided view of things—the Lord said to him: Thou art not by any means the only man in Israel who remains true to Jehovah and against Baal; for I have seven thousand men yet left me of whom not a knee has ever bowed to Baal, nor has a tongue kissed him. Elijah needed some inspirations of hope and of numbers, and God kindly gave them. The time had come, moreover, when a true-hearted and sympathizing companion and servant—such as Elisha became—of younger blood, and perhaps of steadier nerve, might be at once a comfort and a help; so the Lord provided him.

The History of Ahab Resumed and Concluded.

Three chapters remain in 1 Kings (20–22) in all which the leading thread runs on the line of Ahab's life. The prophets of God appear in every important transaction, yet not the same prophet, for the Lord had several in his service, and work for all.——Chap. 20 narrates various war-scenes between Ahab and Ben-hadad of

Syria in which a prophet appears in v. 13; the same one reappears in v. 22, recognized here as "*the* prophet" (the article of renewed mention); but in v. 28 there appears another prophet, as we may infer from his different designation—"there came a man of God;" and from his different geographical locality, this being east of the Jordan.——Again, in v. 35, we find yet another description: "A certain man of the sons of the prophets"—who is probably yet another and a third prophet appearing in the scenes of this one chapter. ——In the scenes of chap. 21 (of Ahab and Naboth) Elijah bears God's message to the guilty king; while in chap. 22—the history of Ahab and Jehoshaphat going in alliance against Ramoth-gilead and the Syrians—the Lord's messages are given through Micaiah, son of Imlah.

In the history in chap. 20, Ben-hadad, king of Syria, besieged Samaria with an immense armament. Having reached a point where he felt sure of the city, he sent messengers to Ahab to say—all your treasures, all your wives and children, are mine. It was understood on both sides that the surrender of these was the condition proposed by Ben-hadad himself for sparing the city and going home. Though these conditions were hard, Ahab accepted them. But this concession came so easily, it encouraged Ben-hadad to make a larger grab, and withal to satisfy the grasping spirit of his servants, and, moreover, to make the terms yet more humiliating. So he sent messengers again to say— although I made thee a proposition so and so, yet I want more. "I will send my servants to thee, and they shall search thy house, and the houses of thy servants; and it shall be that whatsoever is pleasant in thine [*their*] eyes, they shall put it in their hand, and take it away." No wonder this roused Ahab's indignation. He brought the case before the elders and people, and they indignantly said, *No!* Ahab replied to Ben-hadad, *No*, and received in return the hardest sort of threatening. Ahab answered with one of the wisest sayings of his on record: — "Tell him, Let not him that girdeth on his harness, boast himself as he that putteth it off."——Ben-hadad said to himself, We shall see, and to his officers, then carousing with him over his wine, "Up and make ready"—to storm the city.

HISTORY OF AHAB. 281

———Just in that critical juncture there came a prophet of the Lord to Ahab with a message which ought to have been thrice welcome:—"Hast thou seen all this great multitude? Behold, I will deliver it into thy hand this day; and thou shalt know that I am the Lord."———Surely, this was mercy—help, unasked, and undeserved, but in his deepest need. Ahab very sensibly inquired, "By whom" wilt thou send this deliverance? To which the Lord answers—"By the young men of the princes of the provinces," *i. e.*, by the servants, attending the governors of adjacent districts or principalities who seem to have fled to Samaria before these invading Syrian hosts. In the line of war-power, these young men were neither numerous nor formidable. It was found they numbered, all told, 232—less than the reduced band led on by Gideon.

Besides these, the children of Israel mustered for active service 7,000. Ahab asked a second question—Who shall order the battle? and God answered, Thou.

———They made the sally out from Samaria at noon—Ben-hadad's dinner hour—he and his thirty captains drinking themselves drunk in their royal tent. These young men (232) took the front. When it was reported to Ben-hadad that a squad of men were seen coming out of Samaria, he simply replied, "Whether they come out for peace or for war, take them alive." But they were in for deadly fight; they slew every one his man; the Syrians fled; Israel pursued, and "slew the Syrians with great slaughter." Samaria was free; the Syrians scattered and fled to their homes. Ben-hadad hardly escaped on a horse with the horsemen.

The same prophet then warned Ahab to make his position strong, for this enemy would come back at the same time next year. The historian put on record the reasonings of the defeated Syrians as they con over the causes of their failure, and their new schemes for future success—thus: The gods of that people are gods of the hills; therefore, they beat us on the hills; we can beat them on the plains. Another change also we will make: discharge, those thirty-two kings—(they dont fight well)—and put military captains—men trained for war, in their stead. Then muster another army of the same number, man for man, horse for horse, and

13

chariot for chariot; so we shall have the victory.——
The children of Israel drawn up against them seemed
(says the historian) like two little flocks of kids, while
the Syrians filled the country—an immense host, for,
according to the figures given in the sequel, 127,000
men never returned to their homes. A few thousand
should be added to this number for those who did.

Their proud reasonings about the weakness of Israel's
God on the plains proved the salvation of Israel. To
vindicate his own glorious name and his power in arms,
which must not be reproached with impunity, the Lord
interposed and went down himself into this fight. A
new prophet came and said to Ahab—"Because the
Syrians have said, Jehovah is the God of the hills but
not of the valleys, I will deliver all this host into thy
hands, and ye shall know that I am the Lord."——
Seven days in succession these armies—the great one
and the little—faced and menaced each other. (Did
Ahab's faith hold out? Why this delay to join issue?
On these points the record is silent). On the seventh
day the battle was joined, and "Israel slew of the
Syrians 100,000 footmen in one day." The rest fled to
Aphek, in the plain of Esdraelon at the southern base
of Little Hermon. There the city wall fell upon 27,000
men, to their death. Ben-hadad fled into the city and
secreted himself in a private chamber.

In the ensuing negotiations Ben-hadad proved himself adroit and Ahab unaccountably weak-minded and
vain. He seems to have had no conception of the
dangerous qualities of his great national adversary.
Perhaps he felt flattered by the proposed alliance with
such a king. The Lord rebuked this folly; "Because
thou hast let go out of thine hand a man whom I had
appointed to utter destruction, therefore thy life shall
go for his life, and thy people for his people" (1 Kings
20: 42). The event fulfilled this word; Ahab fell before
the Syrians in battle, and his nation was scourged fearfully by that formidable power.——From this great
victory and God's disapproval of his treaty policy, Ahab
went home to his capital heavy and displeased—not
quite happy with himself, and very far from being
happy in God. The fatal lack in his character was—
no harmony of will with Jehovah; no living faith; no
sincere prayer for divine guidance. How abundantly

God would have blessed him if only he had been in a state fit to be blessed?

Ahab, Jezebel, and Naboth.

In 1 Kings 21 we have the story in which these three were the prominent actors. Naboth had inherited a vineyard in Jezreel. Ahab built his palace quite near. Fixing his eye on this vineyard, he said, That would be nice for a vegetable garden, and I want it. With a sense of justice that does him honor he said to Naboth: Your vineyard plat is exceedingly convenient for my use; I will give you a better vineyard for it; or I will pay its value in money. Naboth replied: God forbid that I should alienate the inheritance of my fathers. For long succeeding generations my father's fathers have held it; by the law of Moses it must go down to my children's children: no money can buy it.——Ahab's will had rarely been crossed, and he lacked both the grace and the manhood to bear this refusal. He even threw himself upon his bed, averted his face and would not eat. Jezebel must know what the matter is, and he told her the story.——Jezebel had no sense of justice standing in her way. She believed in the right of kings to do their own pleasure and to have all their heart's desire. First, she taunted her royal husband: "Dost thou govern the kingdom of Israel?" This does not look much like being a king! Put the matter into my hands and then see. I will give thee that vineyard of Naboth.——She wrote letters in the king's name; summoned a court of mock justice, and arraigned Naboth before it; suborned false witnesses to swear upon him the crime of blaspheming God and his king; and enjoined them to execute the penalty for this offense; viz., to hustle the criminal out of the city and stone him to death. It was done; and then she reported the matter to Ahab and told him to go and take the vineyard of the murdered Naboth.——It is sad that we must say, Ahab neither objected to this use of his royal name and seal, nor to taking possession of an estate obtained by such high-handed crime. He set off—shall we say with light heart—to take possession. Ah, but just then, he met Elijah—the last man he would wish to see. The Lord had noticed what was going on under Jezebel's management, and had singled out Elijah as the fit man to confront Ahab again. Ahab's first words reveal his heart toward the venerable "man of God:" "Hast thou found me, O mine enemy?"—found me once more in sin; found me when I had fondly hoped God would for this once let me alone?—found me to act against me the part of an enemy? Must I be forever annoyed by such men as you, coming across my path to block my way with those awful words of Jehovah?——As usual, Elijah has his answer ready: Yes, indeed, I have found thee, and this is the reason why: "Because thou hast sold thyself to work what is evil in the sight of the Lord." My message is short: "God will cut off thy life and the life of thy posterity, sparing not a man, and the dogs shall eat Jezebel by the wall of Jezreel."——The historian sums up his estimate of the character of Ahab in the words: "But there was none like Ahab who did sell himself to work wickedness in the sight of the Lord, whom Jezebel his wife stirred up. He did very abominably in following idols in all things as the Amorite nations whom the Lord drove out of Canaan for their abominations."——Yet it is added in the close of this narrative that when Ahab heard these terrible maledictions, he stood appalled with fear; he humbled himself; rent his clothes; put on sack-cloth; fasted and went softly [what did Jezebel say to this?] —so that the Lord modified his pronounced doom by deferring certain portions of it till after his death, to be consummated upon his posterity.

In the record of Jezebel, not one redeeming feature anywhere appears. Her character bears the stamp of unmixed wickedness—pure and utter depravity. We should think much better of her if she had hired an assassin to waylay Naboth and hurl a javelin through his heart. It was doubly horrible to prostitute the sacred forms of justice to the purposes of such foul murder and wrong. Perhaps she thought to conceal crime under such a covering; but God abhors such concealments, and has ways to blast such schemes. All in all, the character of Jezebel is drawn—to be execrated. There could be no other worthy object in delineating such ineffable meanness and wickedness. True, she had a most indomitable will: so has Satan

—and both are the more to be execrated. True, her character is self-consistent—of one piece and one stripe throughout; and so is Satan's—both simply and supremely wicked—than which what worse thing can be said of any moral being?

Thus far in the life of Ahab, we have found his history in the book of Kings only. What we read in the ensuing chapter (1 Kings 22) occurs with only slight variations in Chronicles also (2 Chron. 18).

Ahab, Jehoshaphat, and Ramoth-Gilead.

Here for the first time we find relations of alliance—political fraternity—between the usually rival kingdoms of Israel and Judah. The author of Chronicles indicates the particular form of this alliance; "Jehoshaphat joined affinity with Ahab," asking and taking Ahab's daughter for the wife of his son Jehoram, heir-apparent to his throne (2 Chron. 18: 1, and 21: 6).——This affinity is the more astounding because Jehoshaphat was in the main a good man and a real reformer, while Ahab was wicked, and Jezebel notoriously and fearfully so. What Jehoshaphat's inducements were the record does not clearly indicate. The author of Chronicles puts things in this order: "Now Jehoshaphat had riches and honor in abundance; and joined affinity with Ahab." This author not seldom gives indications of a philosophic turn of mind; so that we probably do no violence to his words if we introduce the logical connective—"And *consequently*" joined affinity with Ahab. It would not be the first or the last time in which riches and honor have opened the door and led the way to affinities which *morally* should have been revolting. The question has an interest for us, far more and higher than merely speculative;——How so good a man could make so bad a blunder and involve himself in perils so great, and his family in a ruin so fearful:—for other men of our race—not to say ourselves—may fall before like temptations.——Jehoshaphat had riches and honor in abundance; enough to make affinity with his family more than acceptable to Ahab and Jezebel. Ahab had put himself in affinity with the royal and wealthy house of Tyre—a step upward, probably, in the eye of the civilized world of that age; and if Jehoshaphat looked at things merely as the world looks at them—why should not he think so too? And why should it not seem to him a ready way to put himself in strong, sustaining relations to the great political powers nearest at hand—to join affinity at once with Ahab and Jezebel and Jezebel's royal father? This might seem the more desirable on account of the growing political power of Syria—so near, and naturally so hostile.——The capital mistake of Jehoshaphat lay in leaving God out of the account. In his estimate of political forces and national strength, the God of his fathers seems to have been sadly, sinfully omitted.

In process of time this family affinity led to a family visit. "Jehoshaphat went down to Ahab in Samaria." The author of Chronicles, and he only gives the social side: "Ahab killed sheep and oxen for him in abundance, and for the people he had with him"—his royal retinue—perhaps a military guard, so strong as to suggest to Ahab the proposal he proceeds to make. Ahab held a council of war with his servants; "Know ye not that Ramoth in Gilead is ours; and yet we have been tamely inactive and we take it not out of the hand of the king of Syria." Turning to his royal guest he said, "Wilt thou go with me to battle to Ramoth-Gilead?"——With no hesitation apparent on the face of the record, he answered, Aye; count my people as thy people and my horses as thine.——But Jehoshaphat has been in the habit, on the question of war, of asking counsel of God through his prophets, and his second thought (if not his first) was that in a matter so grave as this might prove to be, it would be well. So he said to Ahab, "Inquire, I pray thee, at the word of the Lord to-day." Ahab at once gathered 400 of his prophets.——What kind of prophets were these? Has Jezebel already replaced the Baal-prophets who fell on Carmel? Or were these ostensibly prophets of Jehovah? Or were they the religious officials of Jeroboam's system—those meanest of the people whom he made his priests?——The first alternative is scarcely probable so soon; the second is quite improbable; the third encounters least difficulty. It is plain they are low and mean enough—sufficiently reckless of truth and subservient to the known wishes of their monarch. They knew what answer Ahab wanted; and they gave it: "Go up, for

God will deliver it into thy hand."——Jehoshaphat was impressed unfavorably by the look and tone of these prophets; their answer was to him by no means satisfactory. "Is there not here," said he, "a prophet of the Lord besides, that we may inquire of him?" Rather reluctantly, Ahab answers: "There is yet one man, Micaiah son of Imlah; but I hate him; for he doth not prophesy good for me, but evil." Jehoshaphat dislikes the tone of this remark:—"Let not the king say so."—— Politeness to his guest had its claims on Ahab; so he hastened off a messenger for this Micaiah.——Meantime the 400 prophets were entirely harmonious and emphatic in their assurance of success in this expedition. Ahab's messenger suggested to Micaiah that this great troop of prophets were all of one voice, and that if he could bring himself to express the same opinion, it would be exceedingly agreeable to King Ahab. Micaiah was not the man to listen for a moment to such considerations. He spoke warmly: "As the Lord liveth, what the Lord saith unto me that will I speak."——Brought before Ahab, and the great question put to him:— "Shall we go up to Ramoth-Gilead, or shall we forbear?" he answered in a way which made his words signify one thing, and his tone and manner another. It was equivalent to this: If you want an answer to please yourselves, that is one thing: if you want the answer that God gives, it is quite a different thing. Even Ahab caught this distinction, and somewhat resenting it, replies:—"How many times shall I adjure thee that thou tell me nothing but that which is true in the name of the Lord?"—Oh, if you want what is true in the name of the Lord (said Micaiah), I will give it. The scene presented to my prophetic eye was this: —"All Israel scattered upon the hills as sheep that have no shepherd: and the Lord said unto me; These have no master; let them return every man to his house in peace."——The import of this could not be misunderstood. The king fallen; his army smitten and disorganized under the usual cry—"Ho, every man to his tents!" ——Ahab turned to Jehoshaphat to say—"Did I not tell thee so? He never prophesies any good for me, but only evil." Micaiah notwithstanding, resumes, to describe another prophetic scene—a kind of cabinet council (of course this is drapery), location not given, to debate the question how to allure Ahab up to Ramoth-Gilead to fall there in battle. The scheme of false, lying prophets is agreed on and put in execution.——In respect to the morality of this transaction as related to the Lord, it meets no other difficulty than is involved in every case of God's providential agency in the existence of sin—which agency is not a license for sinning— is never the employing of his moral subjects to do the sinning; but is simply leaving the wicked to commit sin of their own free will, his shaping hand being interposed only to turn it to best moral account.

The narrative relates that Zedekiah, the spokesman of the four hundred, fired up at the intimation about lying spirits; and that Ahab ordered Micaiah back to the custody of the governor of the city—an order which seems to imply a previous imprisonment. "Keep him there on bread of affliction and water of affliction [the coarsest fare], till I return again in peace." "If thou return at all in peace," (responded Micaiah), "then the Lord hath not spoken by me;" and he cried aloud to call the attention of the whole people to his words. A staunch man is he, swerving never a hair's breadth from the rough line of duty as the Lord's prophet. No conciliating words has he to say, bearing never so little upon his personal liberty or his hardships in prison.

The views of the prophets are now all in, and the hour for decision has come. What does Jehoshaphat think of the answer from the only real prophet of the Lord? He does not appear as well at the end of this consultation with prophets as at the beginning. We must probably conclude that Ahab and Jezebel are the leading master minds of the group, and that Jehoshaphat succumbs and really sacrifices his own convictions to his desire to please his host and stand to his original assent to go.——They are off for the war—and about to go into battle. Ahab may have had some intimation that he would be the special target for the arrows of the Syrian host; and, therefore, (not quite honorably) he proposed to Jehoshaphat—"Let me go into battle in disguise; but put thou on thy robes." With no remonstrance Jehoshaphat consented; but when the battle concentrated hotly upon his royal chariot and his conspicuous robes, he cried out, and his enemies turned back from pursuing him.* Ahab, attracting no special attention, escaped this concentrated fire; but some unknown Syrian archer drew his bow at a venture [Heb. 'in his simplicity; with no particular intent or aim] and this arrow took Ahab between the joints of his coat of mail and his breast-plate, and proved his death-wound. The king had himself supported upright in his chariot till night-fall that the conflict might not be arrested by his withdrawal from the field, and then fell, to rise no more. The blood ran from his wound into the bottom of his chariot; the washing was done at the pool of Samaria; there the dogs licked up that blood; and there the harlots bathed themselves in that bloody pool [So the Heb., and certainly the Septuagint seems to mean]—a divine and predicted retribution for the blood of Naboth—the beginning of this retribution, but not the end thereof. The after-part came from the Lord by the hand of Jehu, and involved the blood of Jezebel and of Ahab's second son and second successor, Joram—first wounded in battle with the Syrians; but ultimately slain by Jehu (2 Kings 9: 24 –37).——Thus closed the life of Ahab, after a reign of twenty years in consummate wickedness.

Of Jehoshaphat we shall see much more when we study him in his place in the line of Judah's kings. Yet let it be said here that this affinity with Ahab brought upon him the divine rebuke as the author of Chronicles is careful to say;—" When he returned in peace to his house in Jerusalem, Jehu, son of Hanani the seer, went out to meet him, saying, Shouldest thou help the ungodly, and love them that hate the Lord? Therefore, is wrath upon thee from before the Lord. Nevertheless, there are good things found in thee in that thou hast taken away the groves out of the land, and hast prepared thine heart to seek God."

The author of Chronicles, with his eye on the history of Jehoshaphat and with a kindly view of his character, made the hand of God specially prominent here: " When the captains of the chariots saw Jehoshaphat they said—It is the king of Israel, and they compassed about him to fight; but Jehoshaphat *cried out* and the *Lord helped him*, and God moved them to depart from him."

Ahaziah of Israel and Elijah. (2 Kings 1.)

Ahaziah, son and immediate successor of Ahab, was morally worse than even Ahab, and not unnaturally so, as the mother has more absolute power in forming character than the wife. What ought to be expected of a son, born of Jezebel -nursed, molded, made, by her hand?——Ahaziah comes to view first, hurt by a fall, and sending messengers to inquire of Baal-zebub,* god of Ekron, if he should recover. The Lord sent Elijah to meet those messengers and to say—Do ye not assume that there is no God in Israel when ye go to inquire of Baal-zebub, god of Ekron? "Thus saith the Lord to your king; Thou shalt not come down from that bed, but shalt surely die." They reported back this answer. The king was inquisitive to know who said those words, and obtained from them this description:—"A hairy man and girt with a girdle of leather about his loins." "That, said he, is Elijah the Tishbite." Forthwith, the king sent fifty men under their captain to bring Elijah before him. It is not explicitly said, but yet is certainly to be inferred, that the king's purpose was to put Elijah to death.——This band of soldiers found Elijah sitting on the top of a hill, and accosting him, "Thou man of God," ordered him in the king's name to come down. Elijah answered: "If I be a man of God, let fire come down from heaven and consume thee and thy fifty." The fire fell and consumed them. The king sent a second company with the same result; and then sent a third; but this third captain begged that the life of his company might be spared. The angel of the Lord bade Elijah go down, fearing nothing. Elijah came before Ahaziah, and delivered to him in person the original message. Ahaziah died as the Lord had said. The significance of these facts seems to be that King Ahaziah had determined to take the life of Elijah, but was frustrated in this purpose, and met his own death instead. That the spirit of persecution against Elijah had reached the point of plotting his death, is a fact bearing upon his translation which shortly ensued.

* Baal-zebub, god of flies, was (probably) supposed to protect his worshipers against this oriental annoyance.

Elijah's Translation. (2 Kings 2.)

So far as is known to us, Elijah is the only man after Enoch, exempted from the otherwise universal law of mortality—transferred to the blessedness of heaven without death. If we ask—why was Elijah selected to this high honor rather than any other holy man of God, the utmost we can say is that God had given him the honor of confronting Jezebel and Baal on the high places of Israel; of imperiling his life in this conflict; of concentrating upon himself at once the wrath of the wicked men of his generation and the gaze of the whole Hebrew people; so that if the Lord were to make any signal demonstration of his power to lift his imperiled saints out of danger, and even from earth to heaven, Elijah was naturally the candidate.——If we ask, Why should the Lord ever make an exception like this to the great law of human mortality, taking a man up from human view in a chariot of fire, the answer might take a somewhat wider range, for we might suggest—not merely to confound wicked persecutors; not merely to show himself the Almighty Protector and Friend of his persecuted people; but to prove to skeptical mortals that heaven has both *reality* and *place ;* that there is a home for the righteous beyond the life that is of earth; and practically to bring that heavenly home nearer to human thought and motive. One such translation, well certified, might spread its influence over vast countries, and send it down through long succeeding ages. How grand and yet how specific the testimony it bears to the resurrection of the righteous dead! How it must awaken thought and inquiry! For it could not be supposed that the blessed home for God's saints in his presence could be for Enoch and Elijah only; it could not be assumed that those two human bodies and those only among all the saved would find place before the throne of God. Certainly, men must infer that the bodies of other saints—nay of all the saints—must reach that blessed world, as well as theirs, in God's due time, and in his ordained method.——It scarcely need be suggested that in an age, drifting like that of Elijah so fearfully away from the true God into Baal-worship, the call for such a demonstration of the future life would be urgent, and the scope for its influence vast.

As to the immediate antecedents of this translation, it is noticeable that Elijah, Elisha also, and even all the "sons of the prophets"—those well filled schools then flourishing at Gilgal, Bethel, and Jericho—had pre-intimations of the event. There was no effort to draw together a crowd of witnesses; nor, on the other hand, was there any special effort to exclude all witnesses, and have it take place before no human eye. Elisha felt that he could not forego the spectacle. Elijah's attitude on this point seems to have been—If you care enough about it to go anywhere and stay anywhere with me, you will see it; otherwise, not.——Note that when Elijah was shown that his time was near, he moved on toward the designated place, touching successively at Gilgal, Bethel, and Jericho—*i. e.*, at all the locations of prophet-colleges—at least, all in that vicinity. Need we ask for what purpose? Perhaps he had some farewell benediction or some word of encouragement as to the work of God which he must so soon transfer from his own hand to theirs. Be this as it may, this last call must have fixed attention most intensely on the scene so near at hand when "the Lord would (as to Elisha) take away his master from his head" (2 Kings 2: 7).

Elijah and Elisha, journeying on, had crossed the Jordan, the stroke of Elijah's mantle parting asunder the waters at their feet. Elijah had said to his servant: What last keepsake shall I give thee? and had been answered: "A double portion of thy spirit to be with me;" when, all suddenly, as they were in conversation (was it upon those visions of glory then just ready to burst upon Elijah's eye?) there appeared a "chariot of fire and horses of fire, and parted them both asunder, and Elijah went up by a whirlwind into heaven." Elisha's eye was clear; he saw it, and took in its grand significance; for he cried: "My father! my father! the chariots of Israel and the horsemen thereof!" It was a moment for only exclamations in briefest words. Apparently his thought was—My father! the chariot of the God of Israel has taken him; he is gone! Or possibly this: My father—he who is more and mightier to Israel than chariots and horsemen!

The sequel is of minor importance. Elisha caught the falling mantle of his prophet-father; smote and parted the Jordan waters therewith; touched at Jericho where the sons of the prophets met him and proposed to send fifty strong men to see if Elijah had not been dropped on some mountain or in some valley;—against which Elisha protested till his protest availed nothing. Fifty men searched three fruitless days and then returned. Let us hope this result helped them to loftier and more just views of what Elijah's translation signified. It is surprising that they should think of this as even possibly an expedient to get Elijah out of present danger, or away into some remoter field of prophetic service.

We must note that Elisha shortly after touched at Bethel—the site of one of the prophet-schools, but (at least since Jeroboam) a wicked city. There the ascension of Elijah was known, not in the college only, but on the street; for, as Elisha was passing along, there came forth boys (small young men, the Heb. signifies), and mocked him with the challenge: "Go up too, thou baldhead;" ascend after thy master, old bald-head! This insult to age; this shocking impiety toward the God of the holy prophets; this inexpressibly awful hardihood in joking thus upon the chariot and horses of fire which swept Elijah up to heaven—what shall we say or think of it? We are not surprised that a divine impulse moved Elisha to curse them, and that God made them examples of swift and terrible retribution.

King Jehoram, the Second Son of Ahab.

The dynasty which began with Omri, which was made notorious by Ahab, whose general character was perpetuated by his immediate successor, Ahaziah, terminated with the death of his second son, Jehoram. Contemporary with Ahab and Ahaziah, as we have seen, was the prophet Elijah. Elisha, his servant and successor, came often into contact with Jehoram, but lived far into the dynasty which began with Jehu; *i. e.*, through the reign of Jehu, twenty-eight years; through the reign of his son Jehoahaz, sixteen years; into the reign of Jehu's grandson, Joash, when his long and eventful life closed.

After following out briefly the thread of Jehoram's reign to the close of the Omri-Ahab dynasty, it will be in place to give our special attention to the recorded incidents which cluster round the prophetic life of Elisha.

Of Jehoram's religious life, the record is that he did *not* follow his father nor his mother in the worship of Baal, for he put away the images of Baal that his father Ahab had made. He did, however, maintain the calf-worship instituted by Jeroboam.

2 Kings 3 narrates a notable military expedition, in which Israel, Judah, and Edom were in alliance against Mesha, king of Moab. It was made at the instance of Jehoram of Israel, to whose throne Moab had been tributary since the days of Omri; but near this time (2 Kings 1: 1) rebelled and withheld the customary tribute. It is stated here that Mesha, king of Moab, was a sheep-master—a royal shepherd on a large scale—his annual tribute to Israel having been the wool of 100,000 lambs and 100,000 rams. The A. V. (accepted version) means to say that this tribute included the animals as well as the wool. The Heb. says: He returned these lambs and rams *as to* the wool, or simply *wool;* but not "*with* the wool." It is certainly supposable, and on the whole probable, that the wool was the only tribute rendered. (So Keil.)

In this expedition the allied armies, instead of taking the more natural and usual route to Moab, across the Jordan, and thence southward down the eastern shore of the Dead Sea, kept down on the western shore, to pass its southern extremity, and so strike Moab on its southern border. This was a wild, mountainous, seven-days' route; the army found itself entirely without water. Jehoram was utterly discouraged; "Alas, that the Lord hath called these three kings together to deliver them into the hand of Moab." Jehoshaphat, having more faith in God, was not so easily broken down. "Is there not here, said he, a prophet of the Lord that we may inquire of the Lord by him?" How Elisha happened to be there we are not told; but he was near at hand. A servant of the king of Israel knew the fact and reported it. His description is worthy of notice: "Here is Elisha who poured water on the hands of Elijah." Was this service analogous to the washing of feet in the time of our Lord? It could scarcely have been due to the infirmities of feeble old age; for Elijah was a vigorous pedestrian up to the hour of his ascension.——The three kings, instead of summoning Elisha before them, "went to him." Elisha had some respect for Jehoshaphat; none at all for Jehoram; and thought proper to say so. "What have I to do with thee! Get thee to the prophets of thy father, and to the prophets of thy mother." For Jehoshaphat's sake, however, he consented to ask counsel of the Lord in their behalf.——But first Elisha called for a minstrel—a player on stringed instruments. While the minstrel was playing, the hand of the Lord came upon Elisha, bringing the prophetic vision he sought.——Was this connection between music and prophecy normal, or only occasional and special? There being no other allusion save this to the presence of a minstrel in the prophetic life of Elisha, it would be gratuitous to infer from this one case that he never prophesied without such aid. Was it that his mind had been disturbed by his thought of Jehoram, Ahab, and Jezebel, and that, therefore, he needed the soothing influence of music?

His message bade them "make that valley full of ditches;" promised them that without seeing wind or rain, they should yet see that valley filled with water in ample supply; and further, that the Lord would give the Moabites into their hand. As the next day opened, and while the morning sacrifice was in progress, the water came from the mountains of Edom. We are left to suppose that a great rain fell on those mountains—a miracle in the not infrequent sense—the Lord's hand wielding the agencies of nature for his own special purposes.——A two-fold result followed. The water saved the army; the appearance of it as seen at sunrise by the Moabites—red as blood, filling those ditches—suggested to them that their enemies had fallen out with each other, and that mutual slaughter had filled the valley with blood. Rushing, therefore, in reckless disorder upon the hoped-for spoil, they fell upon hosts of men in arms, and were fearfully cut to pieces. The fleeing remnant was closely besieged in Kirhareseth—supposed to be the modern Kerak—a place of immense natural strength. The narrative sets forth that the king of Moab, finding his last sally with 700 swords-men to break through to the king of Edom ineffectual, took his eldest son, heir-apparent to his throne, and offered him for a burnt-offering upon the city wall; *i. e.*, in full view of the besieging army. The author then closes with the statement—not altogether lucid—"And there was great indignation against Israel, and they departed from him, and returned to their own land!" What was the ground of this great indignation? Who felt it; and had it any connection with raising the siege, and with the return of the allied armies to their homes? I see no explanation of the case more obvious and probable than that this horrid spectacle impressed the besiegers with the severe and terrible straits to which the king of Moab was reduced; awakened pity and sympathy in his behalf, and corresponding indignation against the king of Israel, at whose instance this war on Moab was waged—under which sentiments the allied armies desisted from such horrid war and went home. Humanity forcing its way to power amid the horrors of barbarism!

Reverting to the mercy shown to Jehoram and to the allied armies through Elisha and the miracle of water, we may class it with many others in this age, designed to show apostate Israel that her God was mighty to save, and that, if the king and his people would indeed return to him, and be true to their covenant, they would ensure the very highest prosperity. Jehoram ought to have been a better man after that great relief brought to him through this divine mercy. It was one of the great and wise efforts of the God of Israel to call him back to a better mind.

Mesha, king of Moab, and the Moabite stone.

The historic connections of Mesha, king of Moab, with Israel have received recently a most remarkable confirmation by the discovery in 1868 of what is coming to be generally known as "*the Moabite Stone.*" This is a pillar or monumental stone about three feet nine inches in length, two feet four inches in breadth, and one foot two inches in thickness. It is undoubtedly an official monument commemorating the emancipation of Moab from an oppressive subjection during about forty years to the kings of Israel. The language is fundamentally Hebrew, no word occurring of which the root does not exist in the Hebrew Scriptures. "It reads (says M. de Vogue) like a page of the Hebrew Scriptures." "The form of the letters is the oldest known to any written language. The Pentateuch was no doubt written in such letters in the time of Moses; Solomon and Hiram corresponded with each other in such characters." At the time it was copied enough was still legible to show that Moab had been in subjection to Israel, and had achieved her independence; and that the reigning monarch under whom her independence was achieved bore the name *Mesha*. It began thus:

"I, Mesha, am son of Chemosh-gad king of Moab, the Dibonite. My father reigned over Moab thirty years, and I reigned after my father. And I erected this stone to Chemosh at Karcha [a stone of] salvation, for he saved me from all despoilers and let me see my desire upon all my enemies, and Omri, king of Israel, who oppressed Moab many days, for Chemosh was angry with his land. His son succeeded him and he also said, I will oppress Moab."

Its tone throughout is remarkably religious—in the sense of recognizing the fortunes of his kingdom, good or ill, as determined by his national god Chemosh. It is chiefly occupied with his special exploits in war and in the rebuilding of cities. A large number of proper names, *i. e.*, of great kings and of cities, appear on this stone—names which occur also in the Hebrew Scriptures—the number supposed to be satisfactorily identified being twenty-three, and conjecturally, some others. ——It is generally admitted that this Moabite stone brings to light the oldest extant specimen of alphabetic writing. It records the military achievements of Mesha, king of Moab, for a period of forty years or more, from about B. C. 925. This would fix the date of this writing not later than B. C. 885—contemporary with the accession of Jehu, the death of Ahaziah, king of Judah, and of Jehoram, of Israel.——Explorations in these ancient lands are now in somewhat active progress, stimulated by this signal discovery.

The Prophet Elisha.

Both Elijah and Elisha fulfilled their prophetic mission in the kingdom of the ten tribes. The only exception to this general statement which appears in the history is a letter from Elijah to Jehoram, king of

Judah, son of Jehoshaphat (2 Chron. 21: 12-15), sharply rebuking him for not following his father Jehoshaphat, and grandfather Asa, but instead, his father-in-law Ahab: also for murdering all the brothers in his father's family—denouncing for these great sins this fearful punishment: "Behold, with a great plague will the Lord smite thy people and thy children and thy wives and all thy gods; and thou shalt have great sickness by disease of thy bowels, until thy bowels fall out by reason of the sickness day by day."——This apostasy and these great judgments, though in the kingdom of Judah, yet came within the purview of Elijah as being the fruits of the seed-sowing of Ahab and Jezebel.——This letter from Elijah is the only notice of him which appears in the books of Chronicles. Elisha's name is not in these books at all—his prophetic life being entirely restricted to the kingdom of Israel.

In speaking of the schools of the prophets (pp. 115, 117-122) I referred to some incidents in the prophetic life of Elisha. We reach the record of them in 2 Kings, commencing from the ascension of Elijah. Truly a double portion of Elijah's miracle-working power rested on Elisha. First at Jericho, he restored the waters to salubrity and the land to fertility by the application of salt. The record is—"So the waters were healed unto this day, according to the saying of Elisha which he spake" (2 Kings. 2: 22).——Next in order stands the case of the impoverished widow of one of the sons of the prophets (2 Kings 4: 1-7) (presented back on p. 119). This miracle is of the same class with the feeding of five thousand with five loaves and two small fishes—God's mighty hand and loving heart ministering to human want otherwise than through the ordinary laws of the material world. A widow in straits learns that the God of Israel remembers the poor, and has resources in plenty for their help.——Next Elisha makes the acquaintance of a prominent woman of Shunem.* He found in her house a warm welcome and a free outgushing hospitality. In fact she was so impressed that he was a man of God, she induced her husband to fit up a prophet-

---

* On the western extremity of Little Hermon, and four miles N. of Jezreel.

chamber for his lodging whenever he might drop in from his missionary travels. [Shunem lay on his ofttraveled route between Carmel on the north and his prophet-colleges (Bethel, Jericho, Gilgal) on the south.] The historian narrates that a son was promised to this good woman of Shunem, previously childless; that this son fell sick (a case of sun-stroke), and died; that her heart turned at once to the man of God (her frequent guest Elisha), and she hasted to lay this burden of her heart before him; that she found him in Carmel, and told him of her affliction. The prayer of faith raised this dead child to life. In this case the restoration was preceded by what may possibly have been instrumental means, and yet the means were such that we can not be certain of any natural connection with the miraculous result. The prophet stretched himself upon the child, mouth to mouth, eyes to eyes, hand to hand, and the child's flesh waxed warm. Then he rose and walked the room and repeated this process until at length life returned. The reason, if any, for blending natural agencies (if they were *agencies*) with miracles, is not apparent. The reason for some *doings* which may test the faith of the party interested is "not far to seek."——This case is brought to view again (2 Kings 8: 1–6) some years afterward. Elisha had advised her to leave the country on account of a seven years' famine then impending. She went into the country of the Philistines. When she returned she found that her homestead had been appropriated, and she was compelled to apply to the king to recover it. By a special providence the king was just at that moment in conversation with Gehazi (Elisha's servant), inquiring about the great things that Elisha had done. The servant had reached the story of this raising of the Shunemmite's son—when lo! the woman herself appeared, crying to the king for her house and for her land. His interest in her case was so thoroughly awakened that she obtained her rights at once.

Resuming the history of Elisha, we find him on his mission tours, stopping at Gilgal, one of the prophet-colleges which was apparently under his care. Here again is dearth and famine; even the coarsest vegetables were scarcely to be had. In the search an unknown herb was found and brought in, which proved poisonous; yet the poison was neutralized by meal cast into the pot by the prophet's direction—a case which natural law fails to account for, and in which we must assume the supernatural.

In close connection with this stands yet another case of the miraculous increase of a small stock to a large supply—apparently at this Gilgal College. This man from Baal-shalisha, bringing in some of the first-fruits of his harvest, is a sample case, showing how, in part, the prophet-schools were fed. The benefactions of kind, religious friends were in this case eked out by that sort of miracle which multiplies little into much.

Naaman, the Syrian Captain-General.

This story (2 Kings 5) abounds in suggestive and practical points. Naaman, chief captain of the Syrian army, a mighty man of valor, successful, much esteemed by his king, was yet a leper. A little captive maid from Israel waited on Naaman's wife, and expressed her sympathy with Naaman's great affliction by saying: "Would God my lord were with the prophet that is in Samaria! for he would recover him of his leprosy." [Elisha's fame as a prophet and a worker of miracles must have reached the remote northern districts of the kingdom.] The king of Syria and his court had some faith in the miraculous powers of *the* great prophet of Israel (doubtless they had heard of him before). It is, therefore, concluded to send Naaman to the king of Israel, for he is assumed to be on intimate terms with such a prophet. The king of Syria gave him a letter of introduction, and a very liberal present besides. The letter to Israel's king read: "I have sent Naaman my servant to thee that thou mayest recover him of his leprosy." The king of Israel knew far less than he ought to have known about Elisha, and not dreaming that this application had grown out of his fame, was first astonished and then suspicious of foul play. Fortunately—*i. e.*, providentially—Elisha heard of the agitation and trouble of his king, and sent him this very sensible message: "Why hast thou rent thy clothes? Let Naaman come now to me, and he shall know that there is a prophet in Israel."——Naaman came in royal state with horses and chariots, and halted this brilliant body-guard before the humble door of the prophet. Elisha did not come forth to pay his respects to this royal troop, but quietly sent out a messenger to say: "Go and wash in Jordan seven times, and thy flesh shall come again and thou shalt be clean."——This sort of reception was entirely unexpected and seemed to Naaman even disrespectful. Moreover, the means for the cure were exceedingly cheap, not to say that he thought them disparaging to the noble rivers and pure waters of his own country. " I had supposed, said he, that the prophet would surely come out to see and to honor duly the captain-general of the great Syrian army; but he only sends out a messenger! I thought he would stand over me and call on the name of the Lord his God, and then wave his hand over the most diseased portions and so recover me of my leprosy. Does he think I shall condescend to be healed in this undignified way?"——Style and rank and pride were badly offended; Naaman was really wroth; "he turned and went away in a rage." Fortunately, he had with him servants more sensible than himself. One of them very quietly and respectfully suggested—" If the prophet had bid thee do some great thing, wouldest thou not have done it? How much rather then when he saith unto thee, Wash and be clean?"——This appeared sensible; so he went to the Jordan, dipped himself seven times in its waters, and was clean of his leprosy.

Let us turn back a moment to ask, Was not Elisha a little disrespectful, rather bluff, and deficient in true Christian politeness? Perhaps some one will ask: Did Jesus treat men and women so when they came to him to be healed?——To meet this case fairly it should be premised that we have no means of knowing how far Elisha's reception of Naaman was dictated by the divine monition within him, and how much by his own knowledge of human nature and sense of fitness; but it is safe to assume that his bearing in this case was not displeasing to God. Next, let it be said, The cases on record of Christ's miracles of healing fail of analogy with this, for he never had a Naaman halting his chariot at his door in all the royal state, and pomp, and pride of a Syrian captain-general. We remember that Jesus did say: "Whosoever shall not receive the kingdom of God as a little child shall not enter therein"—a principle which Elisha's bearing toward Naaman was well adapted, not to say intended, to exemplify. "The High and lofty One who inhabiteth eternity" has unutterable tenderness toward the lowly; but "the proud he knoweth afar off."

Naaman's sense of self-consequence had almost proved fatal to him, as it has to thousands of sinners who come to God for blessings with no true conception of ill desert and no real cry for mercy. Their inward thought is to be treated with all due deference and appropriate recognition of their various good qualities and doings.

When Naaman came up from the Jordan consciously made whole, he did not lay his course at once for home. With nobler impulses he said, I must go back to that "man of God" with two things to say to him: (1) That now I know there is no God in all the earth but in Israel, and that I will henceforth offer neither burnt-offering nor sacrifice unto other gods, but unto Jehovah:—(2) That I am ready to *pay well* for the healing I have found:—"Therefore, I pray thee take a blessing from thy servant." This the prophet peremptorily and persistently refused. It would not be wholesome to let Naaman think that such blessings were on sale or could be remunerated with money.——Then Naaman begs to take two mule-loads of Israelite earth with which to build an altar in his own country, assuming some special sanctity in the very soil of a land in which there dwelt a God having such power to save.——But it then occurred to him that his proposed worship of Jehovah only will need to be somewhat qualified; for his master, the king of Syria, worships the god Rimmon, and expects his servant Naaman to be present that he may lean upon his hand, and to bow himself also when his master bows himself before this idol-god. For this exception to the general law of worshiping Jehovah only, Naaman begs pardon, hoping it will not be too great an indulgence to ask: "The Lord pardon thy servant, I pray, in this thing."——Thus, though some great truths are forcing themselves in upon his mind, yet still he gropes along but slowly out of his pagan idolatrous darkness. It will be readily seen that

THE PROPHET ELISHA. 303

Naaman's case is a real specimen of human nature.——
If any would ask whether he carried out successfully
and to the divine acceptance his declared purpose to
sacrifice to Jehovah alone with only the one specified
exception, the answer can be given with unerring certainty: By no means. No man ever yet succeeded in
worshiping both the idol Rimmon and the true God,
Jehovah. "Ye can not serve God and Mammon."
Never so little worship of Mammon vitiates all the professed worship of Jehovah. We know this of Naaman
as well without any historic record of his future life as
with it.

In the sequel of this story of Naaman, Elisha's servant Gehazi put himself on record to illustrate that
"the love of money is the root of all evil." He did not
comprehend how Elisha could be willing to miss so fine
a chance to make money. Therefore when he saw that
money going away, yet in hands that were so willing
just then to give it, he said, "As the Lord liveth"
(what a place for such an oath!) "I will run after him
and take somewhat of him." He made up a story to
tell to Naaman, and succeeded in getting two talents of
silver and two changes of raiment. Having secreted it,
he took his place again before Elisha as if nothing had
happened. "Gehazi," said the prophet, "whence comest
thou?" Where hast thou been? He tried another
falsehood to hide his crime, but had to bear the curse
of Naaman's leprosy through his remaining life.

The fragment of prophet-college history which we
have in 2 Kings 6: 1–7, touching the enlargement of their
buildings, probably at Gilgal or Jericho, has been under
consideration in our sketch of those schools (page 119).

Next (2 Kings 6: 8–33, and 7) we see Elisha in
scenes of war with Syria in the siege of Samaria; in the
consequent severe famine and the ensuing relief.
These scenes illustrate the remarkable variety of
miraculous powers accorded by the Lord to his prophet
and the means employed in God's providence to bring
them in clear and strong light before the king, his
royal capital, and the whole kingdom.

The king of Syria "warred against Israel" (6: 8),
here not in regular warfare with large army, but in
predatory bands of guerrilla character. In councils of
war, plans had been laid repeatedly to waylay the king

of Israel at particular points; but Elisha forewarned his king of the danger and saved him every time. The king of Syria was greatly troubled, being sure there must be some traitor among his cabinet officers. At length some one explained the mystery: "Elisha, the prophet, tells his king what thou speakest in thy bed-chamber." Then, said the king, we must arrest that prophet. Where is he? At Dothan.* Forthwith a large force, including chariots and horsemen, invested the city by night, ready to seize the prophet at the opening of day. The prophet's servant, perhaps aware of danger, went out at day-break to reconnoiter, and came back in great alarm: "Alas, my master; how shall we do?" Our enemies have surrounded the city! Elisha replied calmly: "There are more with us than with them." Did he remember the double camps of God's hosts (Gen. 32: 2) whom Jacob saw about him at Mahanaim? He knows that "the angel of the Lord encampeth round about them that fear him and delivereth them" (Ps. 34: 7). To beget like faith in his servant, Elisha prayed: "Lord, open his eyes"—his spiritual eye—"that he may see." The Lord answered this prayer instantly, and the servant saw, indeed, that "the mountain was full of horses and chariots of fire round about Elisha"—God's angelic host marshaled for the protection of his servant.——The Syrian forces close in upon the prophet. He is moved of God to pray: "Smite them, O Lord, with blindness." Done; and then Elisha in the guise of a friendly guide, said: "This is not the way nor the city; follow me, and I will lead you to the man ye seek"—a species of deception against an enemy in arms which moralists almost universally defend as no violation of the principles of truth. The prophet led them twelve miles, into Samaria; and there in answer to his second prayer, the Lord opened their eyes.——The current explanation of this form of blindness is that they were not made absolutely sightless, but that their eyes were holden only so far forth as the object in view required. They were unable to recognize their surroundings so as to understand where they were, though they still had vision enough to march after their leader.——The king of

---

* The same place which appears in the story of Joseph (Gen. 37: 17) near Shechem, about twelve miles north of Samaria.

Israel woke suddenly to find this host of his Syrian enemies at his mercy, and cried out to Elisha: "My father, shall I smite them?" Elisha answered: By no means; but feed them bountifully and send them home. This was done accordingly—a sort of peace policy which worked admirably, for we read that "the bands of Syria came no more into the land of Israel." This predatory guerrilla warfare was resumed no more. The siege of Samaria, narrated in the remaining part of this chapter, seems to have occurred, not soon, but long afterward.——In v. 22 the clause translated—"Wouldest thou smite those whom thou hast taken captive with thy sword?" is constructed variously by critics, some approving the English version, and others taking the passage affirmatively; smite your captives taken by force of arms (if you will), but not those who have been thrown into your power by God's miraculous hand. The Hebrew text favors the English version and so does the nature of the case, if it be true that ordinary captives in war were spared from violent death.

Samaria Straitly Besieged, and the Ensuing Deliverance. (2 Kings 6: 24-33 and 7).

This siege brought on extreme famine. Affecting evidence of its severity came to the king's knowledge as he was going the rounds upon his city walls where his defensive army was stationed. A woman cried out to him for help. Her story ran thus: By agreement with this woman we were to boil and eat my child the first day and her child the next. Mine was given up according to agreement; killed, boiled and eaten; but when the next day, I said to her, "Now give thy son that we may eat him," she had hidden him. The king felt the horrors of the case; saw the severity of this dreadful famine; rent his clothes and put on sackcloth. His first impulse was to cast the blame on Elisha, either as having sent this famine, or as being able but not willing to relieve it. So he vowed solemnly to take off his head that very day, and started off a messenger—a state executioner—for this purpose. Elisha knew from the Lord who was coming, and bade his friends shut and hold fast the door, for the king himself was close behind. It seems that the king's second thought was a better one; so he hastily followed the executioner; for the last words of v. 33, are manifestly his:. "Behold this evil is of the Lord" (not of Elisha, as I at first assumed); yet how can we endure it even from the Lord any longer? He seems to be in despair of help in waiting on God.

The next chapter (2 Kings 7) continues the narrative without interruption:—Banish, said Elisha, your despondent fears. Hear ye this word of the Lord: "Tomorrow about this time shall a measure of fine flour be sold for a shekel, and two measures of barley for a shekel in the gate (the market-place) of Samaria." We are not told whether the king believed the prophet's word; but a lord on whose hand the king leaned —one of his high officers, answered the prophet with sarcastic contempt:—"See! the Lord will make windows (sluices, flood-gates) in the sky to rain down bread upon us, and so this thing shall be!" This seems the more exact sense of the Hebrew word; "Behold," see how this thing shall be done—said in most utter unbelief. This language comes from the story of the deluge. God will open the flood-gates in the sky now as then, raining bread now as then he rained water.——Elisha simply answered, "Behold"—repeating the first word of that unbelieving taunt; there is another "*behold:*" "behold, *thou* shalt see this overflowing abundance with thine eyes, but shalt not eat thereof."

In the event the Lord caused the Syrians to hear a noise as of horses, chariots, and a mighty host, and they said—Israel must have hired the kings of the Hittites and Egyptians to come upon us: let every man flee for dear life. Leaving every tent standing; their animals tethered; their baggage and provisions all as they were, they fled in the evening twilight and made fast time toward their homes.——The fact was first discovered by four lepers, staying just outside the city gates, excluded from the city—their disease being accounted unclean, and, perhaps, contagious. They had started out at dusk, saying, we may as well die by the Syrians there as by the famine here. To their great surprise they found the first tent unoccupied, and the next also, and so on; food and stores of every sort plenty, but not a man. They ate awhile as famishing men would; but they soon thought—this is too good a thing to be withheld from our friends in the city; so hastening in they reported it. The cautious king at first saw in it a stratagem, and sent out a small exploring party. Joy and plenty ensue, the prophet's words are all fulfilled. Even that unbelieving lord lived to see those grand supplies of bread brought into the city, but not to taste of it; for, being put in charge of one of the gates, the rush out and in was so great that they trod him under foot—to his death. Unbelief, ripened to the point of insult and scorn was too reproachful to God to be borne with impunity.——Thus again the prophetic words of Elisha were fulfilled in the most public manner, in modes best adapted to fix the attention of the whole people, and to produce the best possible moral impression. It was a divine movement to recall the people of Israel from their Baal and calf-worship to a solid faith in their own Jehovah; and to save the nation from drifting utterly into idolatry and political ruin.

2 Kings 8 opens with the sequel to the history of the wealthy and worthy woman of Shunem. Elisha had apprised her of a seven years' famine, and suggested that she seek a home elsewhere. She went among the Philistines. This sequel is of interest as showing incidentally that the king (Jehoram, second son of Ahab) thought enough of Elisha to ask Gehazi to tell him all the great things his master had done. By God's providence it happened that Gehazi had just told the story of his raising to life the Shunemmite's son, when, lo, she came in, crying to the king for her land. The Lord thus prepared the way for the easy success of her plea.

The narrative next traces Elisha to Damascus—sent there of God, it would seem, to fulfill a part of the mission committed to Elijah at Horeb; viz., to anoint Hazael* to his work as a scourge upon the family of Ahab.

---

* The names of Hazael and Ben-hadad have been recognized in the Assyrian monuments. They occur in the inscription on the black obelisk now in the British Museum. Both are mentioned as kings of Damascus who contended with a certain Shalmanezer, king of Assyria, and suffered defeat at his hands. In one of the battles between this king and Ben-hadad, "Ahab of Jezreel" is mentioned

This chapter closes with a historic grouping of the leading points in the royal succession of kings on the now related thrones of Israel and Judah; viz., of Ahab's second son, Jehoram—wounded by the Syrians in battle, and returning to be healed of his wounds in Jezreel; of Ahaziah of Judah, grandson of Jehoshaphat and son of Jehoram, whose reign of but one year closed at the same time with that of Jehoram of Israel, both dying under Jehu's hand. Lest these similar names in these two dynasties confuse us, it should be borne in mind that the two immediate successors of Jehoshaphat in Judah were his son Jehoram and his grandson Ahaziah; while the two immediate successors of Ahab were first, Ahaziah, his eldest son, two years; and then Jehoram, his second son, twelve years. The same names are wont to reappear in closely related families.

Jehu, son of Nimshi, and his dynasty.

2 Kings 9 introduces a new dynasty in Israel, inaugurated by the anointing of Jehu—a high officer in the army. He was raised to the throne to be the scourge of God upon the whole family of Ahab, including the then related dynasty of Judah, both dynasties being at that time descendants of Jezebel.

An unnamed "son of the prophets" was sent (doubtless under direction of Elisha) to anoint Jehu. This also as well as Elisha's tour to Damascus to see Hazael was included in the special mission assigned to Elijah at Horeb when the Lord sent him back to his work in Israel. He transmitted these responsibilities to his successor Elisha.

Jehu was little else than God's messenger of terrible retribution—first on Joram [Jehoram], king of Israel, whom he shot through the heart; next, on Jezebel, Joram's mother, upon whom full vials of righteous judgment were poured out—in place and circumstance suggestive of her part in Naboth's murder; and then upon Ahaziah, king of Judah, son-in-law of this same

among the allies of the latter. This same Shalmanezer took tribute from Jehu. This is the point at which the Assyrian records first come into direct contact with those of Jews." (Speaker's Commentary pp. 37, 38.)

JEHU AND HIS WORK. 309

Jezebel; and, last, upon all the descendants of Jezebel and Ahab from the least to the greatest.

In the brief record of Jezebel's last hour we may note (2 Kings 9 : 30) the lofty spirit displayed in her manifest purpose to die like a queen. When she heard that Jehu had come to Jezreel, instantly forecasting the issue, she painted her eye-lids—the upper and the under—with a pigment of antimony to give the eye an unnatural brilliancy,* and also wreathed a royal tiara about her head, and then placed herself at the window.—— That dogs should eat the flesh of Jezebel in Jezreel where she had shed Naboth's blood was at once the fulfillment of a definite prediction of her doom, and the most revolting end, in the view of the ancients, to which any human being could come. Goliath, we may remember, could denounce no lower doom on the stripling David, than to say, "I will give thy flesh to the fowls of the air and to the beasts of the field." But the oriental dog is of all beasts at the lowest depth of meanness.

Over the few remaining fragments of Jezebel's bones (2 Kings 9 : 35) which the dogs had not had time or taste to devour, we may well pause awhile—not to drop any tears over fallen greatness, but to give thought to the solemn though tardy retribution which she had so long dared the God of heaven to send, and which she had so richly deserved. Since the death of Ahab (fourteen years) her name has not come upon the page of sacred history, but her baleful power had been felt in Israel, blocking every effort of prophet or other good men toward reform; filling Israel again with hundreds of Baal's prophets and priests for Jehu to slaughter by wholesale, even as Elijah had done at the foot of Carmel. We must doubtless ascribe it largely to her that Elijah's influence on Ahaziah (2 Kings 1) was so inappreciable; that the glorious testimony of his ascension fell powerless on the royal court, on Samaria, Jezreel, and Bethel; and that Elisha's long succession of miracles turned to so little account as a means of impressing the nation and witnessing to the true God in Israel. That she was gifted with qualities of most com-

---

* This practice of painting about the eyes is alluded to in Jer. 4 : 30, and Ezek. 23 : 40. Noticeably the Assyrian sculptures afford representations of eyes thus painted.

manding sort, such as we should profoundly honor if they were sanctified by goodness, there is no occasion to deny; but goodness seems to have been utterly foreign from her character. She was no less wicked than great; no less base than proud, persistent, and heroic. When it shall be suitable to do homage to Satan, we may afford to place on the same roll of honor this historic Jezebel.

In the passage (2 Kings 9: 11) which narrates the return of Jehu to his military comrades after his anointing by the young prophet, we read, "One said to him, Wherefore came this *mad fellow* unto thee?" Some reader may inquire, How came it that this young prophet made an impression so unfortunate upon these military men?——I answer, "The word 'mad' is stronger than the Hebrew term it should represent: 'fellow' is not in the Hebrew at all. The fact undoubtedly was that a peculiar excitement, a bearing of earnest enthusiasm, normally accompanied the prophetic spirit. This young man may have been unusually agitated, for he was young: a total stranger to this imposing company, all unused to military scenes and surroundings, and withal quite aware of the possible perils of anointing a new king and inaugurating a political revolution. We need not assume or admit any other symptoms of madness than these circumstances account for.

While Jehu was dashing from one scene of slaughter to another, fulfilling his high behest of terrible retribution upon Ahab's house, he fell in with Jehonadab [or Jonadab], son of Rechab, one of the noble reformers of the age; greeted him joyfully, and seemed to be almost overjoyed to have his favoring presence and approbation. (See 2 Kings 10: 15, 16.) Jonadab's aid was specially valuable in sifting out all the true friends of God from the Baal-prophets and priests whom Jehu had summoned together for slaughter. After Jehu had sifted them as carefully as possible by the terms of his call, he still felt the importance of being very sure that no servant of God should be inadvertently among them. Jonadab, familiar with the good men of the land, walked carefully through this gathered house-full in company with Jehu, to make it doubly sure that no servant of the Lord should be there.*

* This Jonadab, son of Rechab, comes to light historically in Jer

JEHU AND HIS DYNASTY. 311

In this history Jehu presents a somewhat striking contrast of physical vigor against moral weakness. Under the latter, I refer not altogether to his frequent deceptions, for it might be a question how far the exigencies of his bloody mission might apologize for or justify those; but to the fact that whereas he had a grand opportunity to bring back the nation to the worship of the true God, he missed this high privilege and opportunity most entirely. He rooted out Baal, but kept the calves of Jeroboam, and "took no heed to walk in the law of the Lord God of Israel with all his heart" (2 Kings 10: 29–31).——For the good he did the Lord pledged to him four successive generations upon the throne of Israel, but because of his manifold short-comings, morally and religiously, God gave him the throne of Israel no longer.*

Of the other kings in Jehu's dynasty only brief notices appear. His son Jehoahaz reigned seventeen years; had wars with Syria, for awhile disastrous, destructive; but subsequently, when he besought the Lord for help, he found deliverance and peace (2 Kings 13: 3–5, 22, 23). It fell to his son Joash to stand and weep over the aged prophet Elisha in his last sickness,† and to give utterance to his emotions in words borrowed from Elisha's own lips as he saw Elijah ascend: "O, my father, my father, the chariot of Israel and the horsemen thereof."——The dying prophet aroused himself sufficiently to give the king some prophetic announcements bearing on the then pending issues of his wars with Syria, in which the measure of the king's success turned upon the reach and compass of his faith.

At this point the historian records that the bones of

---

35. To my sketch of his history and that of his family—both ancestors and descendants—as given there, the reader is referred.

* At this stage of the history in 2 Kings we find a digression to the affairs of the kingdom of Judah (filling chap. 11 and 12) to give the history of Athaliah and of Joash;—of Athaliah, a daughter and genuine successor of Jezebel, coming in here by natural association with Jezebel and Jehu, and of Joash, rescued from her murderous hand by special providence, and, of course, linked in the history with his grandmother Athaliah. We shall give them further notice in their place among the monarchs of Judah.

† Supposed to have reached the age of ninety, for full sixty-three years had passed since his call into the prophetic office.

Elisha imparted life to a dead body thrown in hastily upon them (2 Kings 13: 20)—so wonderfully was the miraculous element blended with his whole life, extending even to his decaying bones. The demand for miracles, *resulting from the great decline of faith*, especially in the kingdom of the ten tribes, is a point worthy of special notice. The ministry of prophets, and particularly of the miracle-working prophets, Elijah and Elisha, was the chief agency employed of God to resist and eradicate Baal-worship from the land and to bring the people back to a living faith in Israel's God. Other prophets in considerable number had important work to do in this special field; but miraculous agency seems to have been chiefly limited to these two men.

Two prophets whose writings have come down to us, Hosea and Amos, fall within the long reign (41 years) of Jeroboam II, son and successor of this Joash who stood by the dying Elisha. Their writings show how solemnly they expostulated with and how earnestly they rebuked both the people and their king for their sins; how tenderly they entreated them to turn to their compassionate Father to find mercy; and yet with how little avail. If these written exhortations fairly represent the oral preaching of the prophets in Israel, it must have been wonderfully pungent, searching, thrilling,—and ought to have been full of moral power.

Physically, Jeroboam's long reign was vigorous; "He restored the coast of Israel from the entering of Hamath unto the sea of the plain (the Dead Sea).* The political power of Israel had fallen very low, but was revived for a season through divine compassion under this Jeroboam II.†

With his son and successor Zachariah reigning but six months, this dynasty of Jehu terminated, and the kingdom declined thenceforward rapidly to its final fall.——One Shallum reached the throne by conspiracy and by the murder of Zachariah—to hold it but one month, and then give place to another conspirator,

---

* This had been predicted by the prophet Jonah, although this prophecy does not appear in the Scriptures (2 Kings 14: 25).

† Between Jeroboam II and his son some annalists find an interregnum of eleven years, resting upon a comparison of 2 Kings 14: 2, 17, 23, and 2 Kings 15: 1, 8. If the figures in these texts are correct this interregnum must be assumed. If incorrect, we are in great chronological darkness.

MENAHEM AND PUL OF ASSYRIA. 313

Menahem, who took at once his life and his throne—to hold it ingloriously ten years. His only recorded achievement is that, when attacked by Pul, king of Assyria, he hired him to "confirm the kingdom in his hand" for the price of 1,000 talents of silver. This money he exacted from his wealthy citizens, assessing them fifty shekels each. The talent of silver being equal to 3,000 shekels, each talent was divided among sixty men, and the whole among 60,000.——The Northern kingdom had no rich temple-treasury to drain on such occasions. It was doubtless politic in Menahem to throw this burden upon his richest men.

Reverting at this point to the connections between sacred history and profane, we have here the first notice of an Assyrian king forcibly invading either of these Hebrew kingdoms. Assyria, with Nineveh for its center, had been rising in power a full century and pushing its conquests toward the west and south-west. Yet, on the authority of Geo. Rawlinson (Speaker's Commentary on 2 Kings 15: 19) "the name of Pu. does not appear among the Assyrian monumental kings. It is even absent from the copies of the Assyrian Canon which profess to give the entire list of monarchs from about B. C. 910 to B. C. 670." Assyria proper seems to have been in a depressed state for some forty years before Tiglath Pileser—the period within which this expedition must fall. Berosus, who mentions Pul, calls him a Chaldean and not an Assyrian king. These circumstances are thought to favor the assumption that in the struggle for ascendancy between Babylon and Nineveh, here was a period in which the former was in the ascendant, and that Pul was one of her kings—then recognized, however, by remote western nations as essentially of the Assyrian line.—— The Assyrian inscriptions show that Menahem was subsequently subdued by Tiglath Pileser, who made an expedition into Syria early in his reign—an expedition not noticed in the Scriptures. He sat on the throne of Assyria proper, at Nineveh, a monarch of great vigor. From this time onward the Assyrian kings bear relations of most vital moment toward both these Hebrew kingdoms, subduing and uprooting the northern (as we shall see), but most signally failing to crush out the southern.

The short reign (two years) of Pekahiah, son and successor of Menahem, ended with conspiracy and his violent death—one Pekah, son of Remaliah, a captain of his, being the successful usurper. During his reign of twenty years—religiously like his predecessors, doing only evil — Tiglath-Pileser came up against him, dismembering his kingdom by wresting from it the region of Naphtali, including several important cities (mentioned 2 Kings 15: 29).——This Pekah became prominent, associated with Rezin, king of Syria, in wars with Ahaz, king of Judah, with various success; besieging Jerusalem unsuccessfully (2 Kings 16: 5), but smiting the army of Ahaz with immense slaughter (according to 2 Chron. 28: 5–8). To these events we must refer more in detail in tracing the history of Judah.

After Pekah, the narrative puts Hoshea, who reached the throne by conspiracy and the murder of Pekah. The chronological figures are extremely confused and conflicting—2 Kings 15: 30 placing this event in Jotham's twentieth year; v. 33, following, giving Jotham's reign a total of only sixteen years; and 2 Kings 17: 1 bringing Hoshea to the throne in the twelfth year of Ahaz, Jotham's successor. It is at least difficult, if not impossible, to decide which figures are correct and which in error. Some annalists locate an interregnum of nine years between Pekah and Hoshea. If this were the case we must assume that his first efforts to gain the throne were unsuccessful. The kingdom was fast verging toward utter ruin.

The End of the Kingdom of Israel. (2 Kings 17 and 18: 9–12.)

The events of Hoshea's reign of nine years decided the fate of the kingdom. The wickedness of the nation had culminated and become unendurable before God. Practically, reform was hopeless; destruction and captivity, therefore, alone remained to close the scene.

Shalmanezer and the Assyrian power became the Lord's instruments for this result. First, he placed Hoshea under tribute. After Hoshea had paid tribute for a period (not exceeding six years) he revolted and sought aid from So, king of Egypt, in sustaining himself against Shalmanezer. This bad faith brought upon him the vengeance of Shalmanezer, who at once laid siege to Samaria. After a siege of three years the city fell, and its surviving population were borne away into captivity—placed in Halah and by Habor, the river of Gozan,* and in the cities of the Medes.——This proved to be their final captivity. These tribes never returned to their native land. The kingdom was extinguished forever.

The historian proceeds immediately (vs. 7-23) to assign the moral grounds for the hopeless captivity of the ten tribes. They had gone into idolatry. They had practiced it secretly; they had practiced it openly. They had adopted the idols and the idol-worshiping usages of all the nations round about them, and had done this despite of most stringent prohibitions from their God; despite of repeated warnings; and of oft recurring judgments. In these moral efforts to save them God had sent his prophets often and long, but they would not hear. They had hardened their necks and would not believe God. They had utterly broken his covenant, and so had forfeited all the protection and blessings which in that covenant were pledged to the obedient. Sinking themselves down to the very depths of the abominations of idol-worship, they had not only made and worshiped golden calves, but they had worshiped the host of heaven; they had served Baal; and had even burned alive their sons and daughters; had used divination and enchantments;—in short had gone into the extremest forms of idol-worship and debased themselves with all its attendant pollutions and abominations. Hence the Lord "cast them utterly out of his sight." The goodly land of promise had been made his abode—his chosen dwelling-place. Consequently, when he utterly rejected these tribes, it was fitting that they should be driven from this land—"out of his sight"—in the expressive and repeated language of the historian (vs. 18, 20, 23).

The king of Assyria filled these emptied cities and fields with another population, gathered up from Babylon, Cuthah, Ava, Hamath, and Sepharvaim (v. 24)—

---

* This is the correct translation: "In Halah [a country], upon Habor, the great river of [the country] Gozan. This Habor, often spelled Chabour, is one of the largest tributaries of the Euphrates from the west, draining the entire province of Gozan [Gauzanitis.]

idolaters all, each class introducing and worshiping its own idol gods at its option. Remarkably it is said that "because they feared not the Lord, he sent lions among them who slew some of them"—whereupon, according to the current notion that each country has its own special gods whose protection must be sought by worship acceptable to them, these colonists report to the Assyrian king that they can not live there unless they are taught how to worship the gods of that land, and that he then sent back to them one of the priests taken away from the country. He came and dwelt in Bethel—probably his old home—and taught them how they should "fear the Lord" (v. 28). The historian is careful to say, however, that they kept up their old idol-worship none the less. This priest, being of Jeroboam's sort, had, we may presume, no higher ideas. The Samaritan population, occupying the territory held by the ten tribes, come to light historically in connection with the restored Jews in the age of Ezra, and also in long subsequent ages, *e. g.*, in the time of our Lord, and even down to our own times; but how much their religious character after Ezra—their Samaritan worship and Samaritan Pentateuch—stand related to this original priest (2 Kings 17: 27) sent back by the king of Assyria is one of the very doubtful historic questions. The subject will come up again in the history of Nehemiah's expulsion of an apostate priest who had married into the family of Sanballat the Horonite (Neh. 13: 28.)

It is in place here to speak briefly of the *confirmations of sacred history* which come in from profane sources during the separate existence of Israel and Judah—*i. e.*, from Jeroboam I (B. C. 975) to Hoshea's death and the captivity of the ten tribes (B. C. 722). This confirming testimony may be conveniently arranged under these heads, showing:

1. That during the duration of the Northern kingdom, Egypt, Moab, Syria (with Damascus for its capital) and Assyria (with Nineveh for its capital) were contemporary powers.

2. That at the points where the Scripture record presents those powers in war with Israel or Judah, they were in fact vigorous, warlike, aggressive; *i. e.*, sustaining such a character as is implied in the sacred record. This, it will be noticed, is an advance upon the

preceding point; for those kingdoms were subject to great variation in these respects—were sometimes relatively weak; again, relatively strong; were at some periods able or disposed to act only on the defensive; at other periods, they were vigorous and terribly aggressive.

3. That the coincidences between the sacred history on the one hand and the profane historians and monuments on the other, extend even to the *names* of prominent kings on both sides; some names of Hebrew kings as given in Scripture being found on the monuments of these foreign kingdoms; and, on the other hand, the names of their own kings as on their monuments being found in the Hebrew Scriptures.

4. Not only are many important names found in both histories—the sacred and the profane; but they are found as contemporaries—chronologically coincident.

These points taken in connection seem to me to complete the confirmation which we desire, being all that truth need to seek, or its friends to require. We take up these foreign kingdoms separately.

Of *Moab*, nothing more need be said than has been already presented in our notice of the "Moabite stone" and of King Mesha on page 296.

Egypt comes into view politically but thrice. First is the invasion of Judah by Shishak, a case of great interest and value, presented in our history of Rehoboam and Judah.——Next is the invasion of Judah in the reign of Asa by Zerah the Ethiopian, to be considered under our notice of Asa.——The third occurs in the brief record of Hoshea's negotiations with So, king of Egypt, for help against Shalmanezer, king of Assyria (2 Kings 17: 4). "He had sent messengers to So, king of Egypt, and brought no presents to the king of Assyria, as he had done year by year."

Who was this "So?"—A slight disagreement exists among even able critics, the difference lying between Sabaco and Sevechus, *i. e.*, between the first king and the second, of the 25th Egyptian dynasty, which was of Ethiopian origin. Geo. Rawlinson, Usher, Hitzig, favor the former; Gesenius, Fuerst, Kiel, the latter.—— The letters of this Hebrew name* are most easily iden-

---

* סוא

tified with Sevechus.* The date of his reign corresponds with these years of Hoshea. Fuerst says he sat on the throne about B. C. 728, which would be six years before the fall of Samaria.

That Egypt should be in hostile attitude toward Assyria, is of course to be assumed. Historically, we might say she was never otherwise. Their interests were always antagonistic, so that the question of war or no war as between them was only a question of power to wage it. This Ethiopian dynasty brought to the throne of Egypt an immense accession of Ethiopian allies—rude men, and but rudely trained in the military science of the age; yet with their aid, Egypt might dare to put herself in antagonism against Assyria. At a point a few years later than this, we shall see Tirhakah, immediate successor of Sevechus (So), threatening the Assyrian armies in Palestine (2 Kings 19 : 9).

Syria (its head Damascus) became a very positive factor in the political and military relations of these two Hebrew kingdoms from Ahab (1 Kings 20) to Ahaz of Judah (2 Kings 16). Something is known of the Syria of this age through its own historian, Nicolas of Damascus; but as yet no important monumental inscriptions—such as have been found in the ruins of Nineveh—have come to light. The Assyrian inscriptions, however, throw some light on Damascene Syria.
——All foreign sources of historic knowledge concur with the sacred Scriptures in the general character and relations of Syria during the ninth century B. C. She was then a vigorous power, having in her vicinity the kingdom of Hamath; the kings of the Hittites and of Phenicia—herself the most powerful among them, and often in alliance with some or all of them. Her war-force lay chiefly in her infantry and in chariots, with relatively very few horsemen. Moreover, all accounts, sacred and profane, concur on the point that during this period the great eastern empire of Assyria lay unaggressively upon their eastern border, occupied with internal dissensions, or for other reasons, making no warlike demonstrations westward.†

* Some acquaintance with the Hebrew alphabet and its relations to the Greek (Sevechus), and also to the hieroglyphic characters, would be necessary in order to trace the identity of So with its Greek or Egyptian equivalent.

† See Rawlinson's Historical Illustrations, 128, 129.

The memorial stone known as "the Black Obelisk," now in the British Museum, speaks of " Ahab of Jezreel" as joining in a league of kings against the Assyrians, and furnishing ten thousand footmen and two thousand chariots. Among the confederate monarchs was Ben-hadad, who appears in the Scriptures as Ahab's contemporary. According to our Scriptures Ben-hadad had wars with Ahab, yet there was at least one period—three years in duration—of peace (1 Kings 22: 1). The special interest manifested by Ahab in fostering friendly relations with his "brother Benhadad" (1 Kings 20: 31–38) finds, perhaps, its explanation in the fact that they both had great reason to fear the growing power of Assyria, and saw that naturally their common interests demanded of them alliance and not hostility.——Moreover, the Black Obelisk bears the name of Jehu, called, however, "son of Omri," perhaps because they knew the kingdom of Israel as attaining its celebrity under Omri the builder of its capital; also of Hazael who succeeded Ben-hadad. Hazael appears there as the chief antagonist of the Assyrian invaders of Syria, and as successor to Ben-hadad. Jehu (or, as some think, Ahab, really the son of Omri) is on the Obelisk as sending ambassadors to the Assyrian capital with presents or tribute.*

The ancient Syrian histories are in accord with Scripture in its account of Ahab's marriage with Jezebel, daughter of Ethbaal, king of the Zidonians (1 Kings 16: 31). Dius and Menander give the name of this king Eithobalus. They make him the sixth king after that Hiram with whom David was in league. The interval between Hiram and this king they make fifty years. Assigning to him a reign of thirty-two years, they make him contemporary with Ahab. They state also that Eithobalus was the high priest of Astarte [otherwise Ashtaroth]—a fact which may account for the religious fanaticism of his daughter.

With *Assyria*, the points of contact are somewhat numerous, and will become more so at periods yet later. ——Of Pul, the first king named as being of Assyria, and of his relations to Menahem, king of Israel, I have spoken.

* Historical Illustrations, p. 127.

Tiglath-Pileser who ascended the throne of Assyria, B. C. 747, came into collision of arms with Azariah, and with Ahaz, kings of Judah (of which more notice will be taken in our review of Judah); also with Pekah and Hoshea, kings of Israel. From the latter he exacted tribute.*

Shalmanezer commenced the siege of Samaria. Sargon, his successor, claims to have taken the city in the first year of his reign. The Scripture records are so shaped that they do not conflict with this claim. While it is said definitely that Shalmanezer laid siege to Samaria, the name of the king who took it is not given. "They" (the Assyrian forces) "took it" (2 Kings 18 : 10). According to the Assyrian documents Sargon came to the throne B. C. 721 or 722. Scripture chronologists had already, on independent grounds, fixed upon these as the alternative years.

The coincidences between the history of Assyria and that of Judah and her kings, both before and after the fall of Samaria, will be treated in their place.

The History of the Ten Tribes Reviewed in its Moral Aspects.

Morally considered, the fall of this northern kingdom is one of the great events of Hebrew history.——The revolt of ten tribes from Rehoboam rent asunder the kingdom as it stood in its greatness under David and Solomon. Their continual, persistent decline—religious, moral, and, therefore, political—wrought their ruin. It was only after they had thoroughly proved themselves faithless to God and incorrigibly so that they were given over of him to their righteous doom.

Let it be remembered this doom of national destruction had been predicted long before, even by Moses (Lev. 26, and Deut. 28), and this prediction the Lord through his prophets missed no good opportunity to reaffirm.——Note also that whereas, under the national policy of Jeroboam, they had in the outset severed themselves from the Mosaic Institutions, especially the temple worship and the national festivals—a step which seemed to Jeroboam a necessity of their separate national existence—the Lord graciously sought to supply this lack by a specially vigorous development of

---

* Historical Illustrations, 135, 136.

religious agency through the prophets. In very many respects this seems to have been a really higher agency —at least, one more directly religious and spiritual. It was sustained remarkably by miracle, as we have seen particularly in the case of Elijah and Elisha; also by wonderful interpositions of God by means of drought and famine; also by various national events—wars, deliverances. These were of a sort admirably adapted to impress, not only the king and his court, but the whole people, with a due sense of their obligation to Jehovah, and of the supreme wisdom of banishing all idols, and of giving their worship and service exclusively to their own Almighty God.

To all this we must add the labors of those prophets who not only spake but wrote, putting their messages in permanent written form and scattering them we know not how widely among the people. Of these, we have among the northern tribes Hosea and Amos certainly; and Micah seems to have some reference to this kingdom. It was only after all these efforts had proved unavailing that the Lord at length gave them up— Hosea indicates in more passages than one with what wonderful tenderness of emotion and after what touching admonitions and warnings. It was through his lips and pen that the Lord said: "How shall I give thee up, Ephraim? How shall I deliver thee, Israel? How shall I make thee as Admah? How shall I set thee as Zeboim? My heart is turned within me; my repentings are kindled together" (Hos. 11: 8).

The fall of the northern kingdom was purposely made admonitory to the southern. It could not be otherwise than a solemn warning to Judah. We can not say definitely how powerful the influence of this final fall and captivity of Samaria was upon the people of Judah in promoting the great reform wrought by Hezekiah. This reform he commenced in his first year, six years before the final conquest; but continued it with efforts more or less vigorous throughout his reign of twenty-nine years. Consequently, under the "logic of events" the great fact was bearing upon his people of God's exterminating judgments upon that apostate nation. It was of yet more value to them because its date (after this great reform commenced) gave them the opportunity to invite their brethren of the north to come in and join them in this general turning to the Lord. In our study of that reform we shall see how intimately they must have become acquainted with the religious state of the northern kingdom; how clearly they must have seen and felt their fearful apostasy from God, and the incorrigible hardness of the masses; and how powerfully this must have augmented the moral effect of that terrific judgment, which, almost before this great reform had culminated, became a fearful fact before their eyes.

After the fall of the northern kingdom prophets became more conspicuous in Judah. Released from service in the north, they concentrated their labors upon the only remaining kingdom, uniting in one grand effort to save Judah from the same threatening doom. We meet no further notice of the prophet-colleges at Bethel, Gilgal, and Jericho. They may or they may not have continued in operation. Those localities were not remote from Jerusalem, but no historic allusions to their work or even to their existence have come down to us.

CHAPTER XI.

History of the Kingdom of Judah.

From Rehoboam (B. C. 975) to Zedekiah (B. C. 588) the sacred history appears chiefly in 2 Chron. chaps. 10–36; but partly in the book of Kings—for the period prior to the fall of the northern kingdom in 1 Kings 12–22, and 2 Kings 1–17; and subsequently to Hoshea, in chaps. 18–25.

Both our histories (Kings and Chronicles) recite the grounds of the secession of the ten tribes; state that Rehoboam at first summoned his whole army to compel submission; but that God's prophet forbade it. Beyond this the author of Kings gives few particulars, save that Rehoboam and his people "did evil before the Lord;" built the high places for idol-worship, and practiced the abominations of the heathen. For these sins the Lord sent upon them Shishak, king of Egypt, who came to Jerusalem and robbed the temple of its treasures, and especially of the shields of gold which Solomon had made.

The author of Chronicles adds many more particulars; *e. g.*, that after the revolt Rehoboam set himself to building and fortifying cities (2 Chron. 11 : 5–10); that the priests and Levites came to him from all Israel; and besides these, all who sought the Lord and were unwilling to forego the national worship of their fathers' God at Jerusalem. These classes were the best elements of the nation's strength, and added greatly to the resources and stability of Rehoboam's kingdom. Particularly it is said "they made him strong three years; for three years they walked in the ways of David and Solomon."——Subsequently under a false sense of strength, Rehoboam forsook the law of the Lord and all the people with him. For this apostasy the Lord sent upon him Shishak with 1200 chariots; 60,000 horsemen; and infantry without number. They took all the fortified cities of Judah. At this point the tone of the narrative (2 Chron. 12 : 4–12) implies that although Shishak carried the other strong cities by storm or siege, yet the Lord spared Jerusalem the horrors of both siege and storm, because Rehoboam and his princes, admonished by the prophet Shemaiah, humbled themselves before the Lord. "God's wrath was not poured out upon Jerusalem by the hand of Shishak." He only came into the city and pillaged the temple. The author of Chronicles labors to make the point very clear that it was only because of their repentance and humiliation before God that he softened the severity of this punishment. It was while Rehoboam and his princes were holding a council of war over this invasion that Shemaiah the prophet brought the Lord's message of rebuke: "Ye have forsaken me; therefore have I left you in the hand of Shishak." Whereupon they humbled themselves and said, "The Lord is righteous." When the Lord saw this, he relaxed the severity of this scourge. "The wrath of the Lord turned from Rehoboam that he would not destroy him altogether; also in Judah, things went well." So evermore in God's government over nations, guilt, persisted in, measures retribution accurately; but repentance and humiliation never pass unnoticed—always bring some relaxation; often the full arrest of punishment.

At this point the coincidence of sacred history with profane—Rehoboam's fifth year, with this invasion of Shishak, king of Egypt—demands special attention.

In the Scriptures Shishak appears first in 1 Kings 11 : 40, as then the king of Egypt to whom Jeroboam fled for protection from Solomon. This fact indicates a decisive change in the policy of the Egyptian court since Solomon took to wife the daughter of the reigning monarch. It suggests another dynasty, of other, not to say opposite, sympathies and policy. In harmony with this we find that Shishak (the Sheshonk of the Egyptian monuments) was the founder of a new dynasty, the 22d. He was not on the best terms with Solomon and readily took Jeroboam into his confidence and friendship. Naturally, therefore, he only waited for the favorable moment to make this formidable military campaign into Palestine in the interests of his friend Jeroboam.

Early in the present century during the exploration of Egyptian ruins which commenced with Napoleon's occupation of the country, the monumental record of this identical invasion of Palestine by Shishak was discovered, sculptured upon the walls of the great temple of Karnak. "It was a list of the countries, cities, and tribes, conquered or ruled by him or tributary to him." This list as copied in Smith's Bible Dictionary (Shishak) runs up to 133, of which No. 29 was at first read and believed to be—*The kingdom of Judah.* Subsequent studies of the hieroglyphic alphabet have created a measure of doubt as to the correctness of this rendering of the name. But these doubts can in no wise weaken the evidence that this inscription gives the monumental history of this very invasion by Shishak. A large number of the cities of Palestine are unquestionably identified. Egyptologists were at first surprised to find many cities on this list that were known to be located within the ten tribes, and therefore were assumed to belong to Jeroboam. How, it was asked, is this, that Shishak assaults and captures the cities of his old friend? At length Dr. Brugsch noticed that these were all cities either of the Levites or of the old Canaanites; —the former in well known sympathy with Rehoboam, and the latter perhaps had not yet given in their allegiance to Jeroboam. What had before seemed inexplicable now became clear. Shishak was fulfilling the double purpose—first of fattening his army on the pillage of cities; and second, of bringing those cities into subjection to Jeroboam.

ASA, KING OF JUDAH.

Chronologically, this invasion is generally supposed to have been made in the twentieth year of Shishak, which corresponds with the fifth of Rehoboam. Some uncertainty hangs over all the chronology of this period, Hebrew or Egyptian; but this coincidence is as well established as any point in that age of the world.

The history of *Abijah, king of Judah*, (called Abijam in the book of Kings) has been fully presented above (pages 261, 262).

After his reign of three years, his son *Asa* succeeded him with a reign of 41 years. The author of Kings (as noticed above), relates that Asa ruled for the most part righteously; removed the queen-mother "because she had made an idol in a grove;" hired Ben-hadad to attack the northern cities of Baasha in order to compel him to desist from fortifying Ramah.——At this point the author of Kings drops his history; but the author of Chronicles continues it, informing us that the Lord sent Hanani the seer to rebuke him for relying on the king of Syria and not upon his own Jehovah. In this expostulation, the seer refers to a great victory which God had previously given Asa over an immense host of Ethiopians and Lubims under Zerah. "Because thou didst rely on Jehovah, he delivered them into thine hand. For the eyes of the Lord run to and fro throughout the whole earth to show himself strong in behalf of him whose heart is perfect toward him. Herein (*i. e.*, in going for help to Ben-hadad and not to Jehovah) thou hast done foolishly; therefore from henceforth thou shalt have wars."——It was a sad infirmity in so good a man—a great sin indeed—for we can not say less of it—that "Asa was wroth with this prophet, and put him in a prison-house; for he was in a rage with him because of this." This double sin—rebelling against God, and punishing God's prophet, as if he and not God was responsible for this message, manifestly brought upon him a painful disease in his feet—under which, it is said, "he sought help, not from the Lord, but from his physicians." Alas, the folly and the sin! Did he die at last under this scourge; and worse yet—with his heart still in rebellion against God? The vail of silence (on this point) drops over him. He was buried with most ample earthly honors; fragrant spices were burned over his mortal remains; but the fragrance of penitent tears on his sick-bed would have improved this record immensely. As it is, we get from it a solemn admonition against clouding the close of a historic life, in many respects brilliant and worthy, with such proofs of a rebellious spirit against God and God's honest servants.

We turn back to note more particularly the great events of his life, the record of which we find, not in Kings but in Chronicles. (See 2 Chron. 14: 9 and 15): The first was an invasion of his kingdom by Zerah, the Ethiopian, leading a host of a million of men with three hundred war-chariots. The location of the great battle, in the valley of Zephathah, at or near Mareshah, far in the south-west districts of Judah, shows that Zerah entered Palestine from the south-west, and was still in the plains, yet just on the border of the hill country of Judah. The prayer of Asa in the face of this great battle is here on record (2 Chron. 14: 11)—every thought and sentiment in it most admirable—thus: "Lord, it is nothing with thee to help, whether with many, or with them that have no power; help us, O Lord our God; for we rest on thee, and in thy name we go against this multitude. O Lord, thou art God; let not man prevail against thee."——This prayer put the king and his people under the protection of the Almighty, and brought forth his uplifted arm in their behalf. *How*, by what special agencies, the half million men of Asa's army (v. 8), supposing them all present, drove, routed, and almost utterly annihilated this million of enemies —we are not told. It is only said that "the Lord smote the Ethiopians before Asa and before Judah, and the Ethiopians fled." The victorious host pursued the fleeing to Gerar, full twenty miles, and took immense spoil. The victory was most decisive: it broke the arm of Egypt's strength for a full generation.

This Zerah is usually identified with Usarken II, fourth king of the twenty-second Egyptian dynasty,* who is supposed to have been by birth an Ethiopian, and to have held the throne of Egypt on the double ground of an alliance between the two kingdoms, and

---

* Poole in Smith's Bible Dictionary ["Zerah"] expresses doubt between Usarken I, and Usarken II; the former the second, and the latter the fourth king of this dynasty; but on the whole favors the latter.

by right of his wife, the lineal heir to the Egyptian throne. Chronologically there is accord between the sacred dates and the Egyptian—the battle having occurred about the fourteenth year of Asa, *i. e.*, B. C. 940.

The impulses of this wonderful victory were wisely turned to account in promoting religious reform in Judah. "The Spirit of the Lord came upon Azariah, son of Oded (this Oded being perhaps but a different form of the name Iddo), and he went forth to meet Asa, returning under the yet fresh impressions of this great deliverance. "Hear ye me," said he, "Asa and all Judah and Benjamin. The Lord is with you while ye be with him; and if ye seek him, he will be found of you; but if ye forsake him, he will forsake you."——How briefly and yet how truthfully put!——He proceeded to speak of the many seasons of religious declension occurring in their past history. In v. 3, "Now for a long season" should rather be—*at many seasons*—referring to the period of the Judges, as well as other seasons subsequent. In these declensions there was no teaching of God by priests or by the written law, and there was the greatest insecurity of life and instability of thrones. He exhorted them to be strong in faith and full of courage and confidence in God. This must of course be understood to imply that they purge away all vestiges of idolatry and give their heart and worship to the true God only.——To this reform Asa and his people set themselves earnestly. All who had faith in Israel's God gathered together, not from Judah and Benjamin only, but "the strangers with them out of Ephraim and Manasseh and out of Samaria; for they fell to him out of Israel in abundance when they saw that the Lord his God was with him."

They renewed their covenant to seek the God of their fathers with all their heart and with all their soul, confirming it with the solemn oath, and with trumpets, and with cymbals:—a thrilling scene indeed, of apparently most hearty and joyous consecration. "All Judah rejoiced at the oath, for they had sworn with all their heart, and sought him with their whole desire, and he was found of them. And the Lord gave them rest round about."——It is pleasant to think of this revival as thoroughly *national*, seizing upon the awakened souls of the whole people under the impulses of this wonderful victory, and bearing all hearts in unison back to the God of their fathers in solemn and most joyful consecration.——It is to be hoped that this reform was followed up with better religious instruction of the whole people, and with more or less enduring results of improved religious life.

Jehoshaphat.

The author of Chronicles devotes four chapters (2 Chron. 17–20) to this good king, of which chap. 18 appears substantially in 1 Kings 22. The historical matter in the other chapters is chiefly new—not found in Kings. ——As the most exceptionable points of his life grew out of his affinity with Ahab, it results naturally that the author of Kings, writing up Ahab fully, gives the darker side of Jehoshaphat. The new matter which comes in 2 Chron. presents the better side, viz., his noble endeavors in the very beginning of his reign to revive religious instruction in his kingdom (chap. 17: 3–9); his effort, after the failure of his campaign with Ahab, to reorganize and purify the judiciary system (chap. 19); and the great victory through prayer and song which the Lord gave him over the combined forces of Moab, Ammon, and Edom (chap. 20).

Reviewing briefly these staple facts of his history, I note the remark (17: 3) that "he walked *in the first ways* of his father David,"—which some critics would amend by striking out *David*, thus making the passage refer to his father Asa whose first ways were better than his last. But the same might be said (qualifiedly) of David. His first ways were without blemish; but not so his last. The true principle of textual criticism is, never to change the text arbitrarily where it gives a fairly tolerable sense as it stands.——In v. 6, we read that "his heart was *lifted up* in the ways of the Lord" —not, however, as this verb often means, *in pride*, but in strength, in true dignity, in moral heroism.——In vs. 7–9, it should be noticed that the king sent out on this missionary tour of public religious instruction five princes, laymen; nine Levites, and two priests. Some critics are perplexed over the question—What had these laymen to do in this work? Surely (say they) it can not be that this good king sent them *to teach*. But this

JEHOSHAPHAT, AND HIS REFORMS. 329

is the very thing the author says. And they may have been very capable. Their presence, doubtless, gave prestige and influence to this mission. Let it be hoped that this noble king was not trammeled by any restrictive scruples about the right or even the propriety of putting laymen into this service—so be it they were capable and worthy.——Noticeably, "they taught in Judah, and had the book of the law with them, and went about throughout all the cities of Judah and taught the people." This "book of the law" could not have included less than the five books of Moses. Had they each a copy? Or was this whole mission of sixteen men subdivided into several, with one or more copies to each party?——How often and in what way did they convene the people? On Sabbaths only? Or did their days of public service include others—say the semi-sacred days of the Hebrew system — the new moons, and the protracted seasons of their three great religious festivals? Or did they hold protracted meetings consecutively, up to the measure of their strength, on the modern missionary touring system? These points of detail are left unrecorded. We may be sure it was a grand and noble enterprise, and may trust that it bore along with it waves of the waters of salvation.

During this religious instruction of the people, the fear of the Lord fell on all adjacent kingdoms, restraining them from war upon Judah. Some of the Philistines brought Jehoshaphat presents, and a large amount of silver. [The word used, v. 11, seems to mean, not tribute-silver, but *burdens* of silver]. Arabian tribes also brought him sheep and he-goats in large numbers, here specified.——The statements given here of the size of his standing army stagger belief, and compel us to assume an error of some copyist. Here are five divisions of the army—three from Judah, and two from Benjamin—who waited on the king, besides his garrisons in the fortified cities of Judah. Noticeably, the total is precisely double the army of King Asa as in 2 Chron. 14: 8.——The Speaker's Commentary estimates that such an army implies a maximum population of 1480 to the square mile—fully three times as dense as in any known country of our age.

Jehoshaphat's second branch of reform (2 Chron. 19)
15

had special reference to the administration of law—the judiciary system. We read—"He went out again through the people from Beersheba to Mt. Ephraim and brought them back to the Lord God of their fathers" (v. 4). "And he set judges in the land throughout all the fenced [fortified] cities of Judah city by city." Apparently the king with his cabinet made the tour of the whole land, and reorganized the judiciary under their own personal inspection; for the last clause of v. 8, records their return to Jerusalem—a clause which is but imperfectly translated and unfortunately arranged in the division into verses. It should be the first clause of v. 9; "And then they (the king and his attendants) returned to Jerusalem."——It is not entirely clear whether this reform introduced a new system, or merely modified an old one—reënforcing it with better men, under rules more fully defined, and with fresh impulses toward justice and righteousness. The principles he laid down are admirable—a fine model for an upright judiciary in whatever age of the world and for whatever people.

Judah Invaded by the Allied Armies of Moab, Ammon, and Edom. (2 Chron. 20.)

The salient points of this invasion and its results are striking and richly instructive. It was an immense army; they advanced upon Jerusalem from the south, having organized at the south end of the Dead Sea and marched northward along its western shore. They had already reached Engedi, some twenty-five miles from Jerusalem, when the movement was fully reported to Jehoshaphat. He saw the danger and set himself to seek the Lord earnestly by prayer and a day of national fasting. The nation gathered together for prayer, Jehoshaphat leading them in words here on record. Alluding to Solomon's prayer at the dedication of the temple, he assumes that this is a case in point—"evil coming upon the land"—in this case the sword; "the people standing in this house," the temple "in thy presence" (for thy name is in this house) "crying unto thee in our affliction; thou wilt hear and help." He cries to God to look upon their enemies, coming up to drive them out from the land God had given them, and prays—"O our God, wilt thou not judge them? for we have no might against this great company that cometh against us, neither know we what to do; but our eyes are unto thee."——Such an appeal God never fails to hear. In this case he answered by sending his Spirit mightily upon one of his prophets—Jahaziel—who said—"Be not afraid nor dismayed by reason of this great multitude; for the battle is not yours but God's. To-morrow go ye down against them, but ye shall not need to fight in this battle: set yourselves; stand ye still and see the salvation of the Lord with you, for the Lord will be with you."——Jehoshaphat bowed to the earth in grateful, joyful assent; all Jerusalem fell before the Lord in worship; the Levites stood up to praise the Lord God of Israel with loud voice on high. As the army marched forth Jehoshaphat gave them his military orders: "Believe in the Lord your God, so shall ye be established: believe his prophets, so shall ye prosper." In the forefront of his men of war marched the great choir, "praising the beauty of holiness," singing in vast chorus: "Praise ye the Lord, for his mercy endureth forever." "When they began to sing and to praise, the Lord set ambushments."——We must pause a moment here to ask the meaning of these words. The sense of the Hebrew word for "ambushments" is clear—viz., liers in wait; but who were they? Not men of Judah—for two reasons: (a.) They were not to fight but to stand still and see God's salvation. (b.) They had not yet reached the scene of the battle and did not reach it till their enemies lay strown in death over all that bloody field.——As the Lord was by promise to bear a direct hand in that fighting, we must accept the ancient interpretation—viz., that these liers in wait were God's angel-hosts, commencing the fight by surprising and smiting with panic; then, perhaps, leaving those allied armies to devour one another—first, Moab and Ammon against Seir till Seir was utterly cut in pieces; then Moab against Ammon till they were in turn destroyed. When the men of Judah had reached the high lands which overlooked this battle-field, lo, their vast hosts were dead bodies fallen to the earth, and none escaped. ——Of course the spoil was immense—work for three days' gathering.——But more to our purpose is the grateful recognition of God's mercy made by the army of Judah in the valley of Berachah—this name being significant of *blessing*—a name which the place bears to this day. If we would like to see the song they sung, we may be gratified; for there can be scarcely the least doubt that it is preserved to us in Psalm 47—every word, sentiment, and allusion of which meets the circumstances of this case to perfection. We may almost hear the glorious shout of that army-host: "O clap your hands, all ye people; shout unto God with the voice of triumph. For the Lord Most High is terrible; he is a Great King over all the earth." (Had he not been proving this before their very eyes?) "He shall choose our inheritance for us." (Jehoshaphat's prayer suggested that their enemies meant to root them out; their song glorifies God for renewing to them his grant of Canaan.) "God is gone up with a shout; the Lord with the sound of a trumpet." (Having been down into the fight and utterly vanquished his foes, what remained but that he should go up with the victor's song of triumph?) And so the Psalm closes with a call for loudest praises to the God of their salvation. [See my notes on Psalm 47.]

Still onward we read that [without the loss of a man] they "returned, every man of Judah and Jerusalem, with Jehoshaphat in the forefront of them to go again to Jerusalem with joy." . . . . . "And they came to Jerusalem with psalteries and harps and trumpets unto the house of the Lord." Here there was yet more song, not of instruments alone, but of voices also, and with fitting words. Psalm 48 [the next in order] meets this occasion so perfectly as to identify it beyond reasonable question. "Great is the Lord and greatly to be praised in the city of our God, in the mountain of his holiness. Beautiful for situation, the joy of the whole earth is Mt. Zion on the sides of the north—the city of the Great King." Never before was Jerusalem more beautiful in their eyes, standing unharmed, its dangers passed away; its palaces in all their splendor; its temple radiant with glory. God had made himself known there for a refuge. True, the kings [of the south] had been assembled against her; but "trouble came upon them and they hasted away."——How beautifully they sing: "We have thought of thy loving kindness, O God, in the midst of thy temple. Let Mt. Zion rejoice;

let the daughters of Judah be glad because of thy judgments." [Was there not joy among those saved sons and daughters?] "Walk about Zion; mark ye well her bulwarks; consider her palaces"—and think that he who hath saved all these to us is still our God forever and ever; he will be our Guide evermore.——So in this national song this redeemed people celebrated the loving kindness and ever-enduring faithfulness of their nation's God.——We need not wonder that (as the historian testifies) "the fear of God was on all the kingdoms of those countries when they heard that Jehovah fought against the enemies of Israel." "The realm of Jehoshaphat was quiet, for the Lord gave him rest round about." *

The passage (2 Chron. 20: 35-37) is manifestly out of its chronological order here. This event occurred within one or at most two years after Ahab's death (Ahaziah his successor having reigned less than two years); consequently about the seventeenth year of Jehoshaphat—eight years before his death. Hence the words "after this" can not mean, after the great victory recorded in this chapter.——With this passage compare 1 Kings 22: 48, 49. Ezion-geber being a port on the Elanitic branch of the Red Sea, these ships were for the Indian, not the Mediterranean trade, and were therefore called "ships of Tarshish" only in the sense of being ships of the largest size—"East Indiamen." Or possibly some place in those waters bore this name "Tarshish."——The Lord wisely baffled this commercial enterprise; for it was not well for Jehoshaphat to be in intimate relations to this godless Ahaziah.

Jehoram.

This eldest son of Jehoshaphat succeeded him with a very wicked and inglorious reign of eight years. The most striking fact of his reign was the perpetual curse brought upon himself, his family and his kingdom, through the influence of Jezebel whose daughter Athaliah became his wife. As might have been expected Athaliah was a second Jezebel. Her pernicious influence was felt in Judah to the day of her death.——

* Psalm 83 may be read usefully in this connection, since it was probably prepared for this occasion; certainly for *such* an occasion.

Jehoram had six brothers. Their father gave them riches, and the control of certain fortified cities of his kingdom. It is supposable that Jehoram thought their power dangerous to his throne, yet the historian makes no apology on this ground, or any other, for his heartless murder of them all as soon as he had become established in regal power. Inasmuch as his widow Athaliah pursued the same bloody policy as soon as her son Ahaziah was slain by Jehu, it is safe to assume that the practice was Phenician—brought into Israel with Jezebel and the worship of Baal.——Jehoram introduced into Judah Baal worship, denoted by the word "fornication" (2 Chron. 21: 11), it being spiritual adultery toward Jehovah to whom the people stood in a covenant relation, analogous to that of marriage. It is even said that the king compelled his people to this worship.—— To him Elijah sent the letter already referred to above, setting forth his great sins and denouncing fearful judgments, both personal and domestic. The Philistines and Arabians became God's instruments to plunder his palace, take into captivity his wives and all his sons save the youngest; while God's own hand inflicted the terrible and fatal scourge of disease of the bowels. The historian writes his epitaph in few words: "He passed off *with no desire:*" nobody cared to have him live; nobody lost a tear for his death. Supremely selfish and utterly wicked, the world felt relieved when he breathed no longer. The historian intimates that whatever good survived to his kingdom was due to his parents and not to any good qualities of his own. "The Lord would not destroy the house of David, because of the covenant he had made with David, as he had promised to give a light to him and to his sons forever" (21: 7). Otherwise, so much wickedness might have sunk the nation.

Ahaziah.

This only surviving son of Jehoram, called Jehoahaz (21: 17), and probably, by an error of the transcribers, Azariah in 22: 6, succeeded his father and reigned one year only. He met his death at the hand of Jehu while himself on a visit to his cousins of Ahab's line in Jezreel, where Jehu was fulfilling his divine commission against the house of Ahab. His record is brief but only bad—doing evil and evil only—"his mother Athaliah being his counselor to do wickedly" (2 Chron. 22: 3). The author of Chronicles, one of the most profoundly philosophical historians, evermore tracing events to their ultimate cause, suggests that the destruction of Ahaziah was of God by coming to Joram (king of Israel at Jezreel); for when he was come, he went out with Joram against Jehu son of Nimshi, whom the Lord had anointed to cut off the house of Ahab (2 Chron. 22: 7). Caught among the wicked from whom he had inherited his wickedness; caught there just when the bolts of heaven's vengeance were smiting them; why should they not smite him also?

Athaliah.

We have seen this bad woman already. We shall remember her as the daughter of Jezebel, the wife of Jehoram eldest son of Jehoshaphat, and mother of Ahaziah his successor. The only woman who ever sat on the throne of Judah, she made her name forever notorious (I will not say immortal) by the meanness and heartless inhumanity of her wickedness. As surviving queen-mother, it was her responsibility to bring forward her eldest son to the throne. Instead of of this she murdered "all the seed royal," including all her sons upon whom she could lay her hand; and then mounted the throne herself. Only God's special providence enabled one of her daughters (probably a step-daughter), Jehoshabeath, to rescue Joash, the youngest son—then an infant in the hands of his nurse—from the jaws of this woman-demon. Athaliah held the throne six years, and then met the violent death she had so long and so richly deserved—reigning only wickedly, and dying, we may be sure, unwept. The historian briefly—we may say, suggestively—remarks: "All the people of the land rejoiced, and the city was quiet after they had slain Athaliah with the sword." Nothing is recorded of her except crimes. It is reasonably safe to infer that there was nothing better or else to record.

Jehoiada and Joash.*

The name Jehoiada brings to view a venerable High Priest, husband of that Jehoshabeath who saved the infant Joash from the jaws of Athaliah, and who became God's instrument to rid the world and especially the throne of Judah of Queen Athaliah. When Joash attained the age of seven years, Jehoiada convened his friends from the whole country in council. It was concluded that the nation had borne the curse of such a queen full long. They concerted measures to inaugurate Joash the rightful heir as king, and to dispose of Athaliah. The boy had been secreted in the recesses of the temple—a place which Athaliah was not wont to visit. Jehoiada had charge there. It was the custom for the Levites, organized in several divisions, to stand guard over the temple in succession; so that it was necessary only to strengthen these guards by large accessions from the whole country, arming them from the arsenal of King David. Silently they had filed in and taken their posts till the military force was deemed sufficient; then on a given signal, the young king was brought forth, anointed, inaugurated;—and Jehoiada virtually made regent. Athaliah heard the trumpet-blast and the joyous acclamations as they rang out through the city—only to throw up her hands in horror, shouting, Treason!—to be hustled out of the temple and then cut down by the sword of avenging justice. The nation breathed freely once more; idolatry and cruel inhumanity had fallen together, and a righteous administration took their place.

Legitimately, the next step was the solemn ratification of a covenant in which, as said in 2 Kings 11: 17, the contracting parties were—the Lord, the king, and the people; also "between the king and the people." † After the extreme apostasy of the previous reigns nothing could be more appropriate than this renewal of covenant with God and his king.——As the next

---

* This history appears substantially in both Kings and Chronicles; viz., 2 Kings 11 and 12, and 2 Chron. 22–24; most fully in the latter.

† Noticeably the author of Chronicles (23: 16) puts it—"between him (Jehoiada), all the people and the king, that they should be the Lord's people." Jehoiada being High Priest, may be thought of here as *representing* the Lord in this three-fold covenant.

step in the same direction, "all the people went into the house" [temple] "of Baal; broke it down; broke in pieces his altars and his images, and slew Mattan, the priest of Baal, before the altar." Then the way was prepared to reorganize the worship of the temple after the Mosaic order, which was done apparently with a hearty will and a noble enthusiasm (2 Chron. 23: 18–21).——Next came the great work of repairing the temple. The need of this appears from the recorded fact that "the sons of Athaliah, that wicked woman, had broken into the house of God, and all the dedicated things of the house of God they had bestowed upon Baalim" (2 Chron. 24: 7). How extensive and fundamental these repairs were and needed to be is indicated by the original word used for repair, which (in 2 Chron. 24: 4) means to *make new;* in v. 5, to *make strong;* and in 24: 27, has the sense of *founding, laying foundations.* ——It seems that the young king entered into this work with youthful ardor if we may accept the most obvious sense of v. 6 which represents him as calling for Jehoiada and (apparently) chiding him for tardiness in that he had not pressed forward the Levites to bring in the collections from the people.——In the result the work was done nobly and no inconsiderable reform was achieved in the nation.

During the regency at least, and apparently during all the remaining life of Jehoiada, the worship of the true God was sustained with a fair degree of efficiency. But the best of men become old and die. "Jehoiada" (we read 2 Chron. 24: 15) "waxed old and was full of days when he died: 130 years old was he when he died." *

* The number 130 I am constrained to think is an error—on these grounds:——(a) It is almost double the duration of life of the old men of that period.——(b) Placing him in years by the side of Joash, who reigned 40 years, we should make Jehoiada 90 at his inauguration, yet then manifestly in his vigor if not in his prime; and this too on the supposition that they both died in the same year. But Joash survived the aged priest some years—suppose five. On this supposition Jehoiada was 95 at his inauguration.——(c) More still; the great work of repairing the temple was not done till after the 23d year of King Joash (2 Kings 12: 6), which on the supposition made above was only twelve years before the death of Jehoiada;—but he is then in active life—at 118.——(d) According to the total years of life as given (Jehoiada 130; Joash 47) the former was 83 at the birth of Joash, and yet married his sister. We must of course assume that Jehoshabeath was older than

After the good man had gone, the princes of Judah came to the king very complaisantly and gained his ear. Their purpose in coming is not stated definitely, but is readily inferred, for we read immediately: "They left the house of the God of their fathers and served groves and idols; and wrath came upon Judah and Jerusalem for this their trespass" (2 Chron. 24: 17, 18). They had become weary of the temple worship, and gave up their hearts to the fascinations of the sensuous, lustful orgies of heathen abominations.——"The Lord sent prophets to them to bring them back again to Jehovah, but they would not give ear." Then the spirit of the Lord came mightily upon Zachariah, son of the late aged Jehoiada. He addressed the assembled people: "Why transgress ye the commandments of the Lord, and why will ye not prosper?"—assuming in the last question that they must know that only disaster could result from such a course. How can ye be so infatuated that ye do not even *wish* to prosper? Already these results of ruin were apparent: "Because ye have forsaken the Lord, he also hath forsaken you."——The sad record follows: "They conspired against him and stoned him with stones *at the commandment of the king*, in the court of the house of the Lord."——Upon this horrible deed the historian (a thing very unusual) allowed himself to comment (v. 22), expressing his sense of its ingratitude to his venerable benefactor: "Thus Joash the king remembered not the kindness which Jehoiada (the father of the murdered prophet) had done to him, but slew his son. And when he died he said, The Lord look upon it, and require it."*——God heard this imprecation. The bolts of retribution fell thick and fast. Within one year a small band of Syrians came upon Judah, and the Lord delivered a great host of

her infant brother when she rescued him from death; but the disparity of 60 or 65 years between herself and her husband amounts to a stubborn improbability.——It has been suggested that the correct figures would be, not 130, but 103 or 83—the exigencies of the case favoring the lesser figure.

* This is that Zacharias to whom our Lord refers (Matt. 23: 35) as slain between the altar and the temple. According to the Talmud a horror of this impious deed long possessed the Jews. They believed that this blood was not to be effaced, but continued to bubble on the stones of the court like blood newly shed, until the temple was entered just prior to its destruction by Nebuzaradan.

Jews—forsaken of God—into their hand. They destroyed all the princes of the people—those apostates who instigated this apostacy; pillaged the country generally; and executed God's judgments upon Joash. God smote the king with sore diseases: his servants (named here) conspired against him and slew him on his bed—a woful end to a reign and a life so auspiciously begun. God's lessons of providential retribution are given with unlimited variety, if so be they may be made effective upon the hard and blind hearts of sinful men.*

Amaziah.

This son of Joash reigned twenty-nine years, with various fortunes, good or ill, corresponding to the various phases of his religious life—blessed so far as he walked with God; afflicted, dishonored, blighted, according as he forsook the Lord. His record appears in 2 Kings 14: 1-20, and more fully in 2 Chron. 25.—— We are told that he punished with death the murderers of his father—the men themselves, but not their children, following in this the law of Moses: "The fathers shall not die for the children, neither shall the children die for the fathers; but every man shall die for his own sin." This reference shows incidentally that "the law of Moses" was in the hands of the king, as according to that law it should be.

Of the two great wars of his reign, the first was against Edom. In this he captured Selah, its noted capital; slew ten thousand men, and hurled as many more, whom he had taken captive, from the top of the city rocks. No reason is assigned for this barbarous treatment of prisoners.——The author of Chronicles records two facts not found in the other history; viz., that Amaziah hired 100,000 men of Israel for one hundred talents of silver; but there came "a man of God" to him to forbid their going; and that, though reluctant to lose his money, he yet sent them home. They took this as an affront, and made reprisals by pillaging cities on

---

* In v. 27 the word "burden" should be taken not in the physical but in the prophetic sense—predictions of sore calamity. The sense here is: "Concerning the greatness of the burdens of predicted calamity uttered against him, see what is written in the story of the book of the Kings."

their way.——Next, that having conquered the Edomites, he was silly and senseless enough to bring home their gods and set them up for his own; bow and burn incense before them. The Lord sent to him a prophet with the pertinent rebuke: "Why hast thou sought after the gods of the people who could not deliver their own people out of thine hand?"——Instead of confessing his folly and sin, the king put himself upon his dignity, suggesting to the prophet to attend to his own business: "Art thou made of the king's counsel? Forbear; why shouldest thou be smitten?" The prophet did forbear; but not without assigning his reason for desisting from further effort to bring back such a king to reason and to God: "I know that God hath determined to destroy thee because thou hast done this, and hast not hearkened to my counsel." The king who could do two things so foolish and sinful as to bring home the powerless gods of Edom to be his own national protectors, and then scornfully repel the Lord's rebuke through his prophets, could do yet another foolish thing for his own punishment and extreme humiliation; viz., to challenge Joash, king of Israel, to battle; get first a sharp and sensible rebuke from that king, and next a shameful defeat, which ended in his being made prisoner; in having his capital seized; its city walls extensively broken down; the treasures of the temple and of his own palace taken away and hostages besides —an extreme humiliation rarely visited upon any king of Judah.——It is not said whether this made him a wiser and a better man. He had shown himself not only intellectually weak but morally rotten. In closing his record of this king the historian suggests that it was *after*, and plainly in consequence of, his turning away from following the Lord that "they made a conspiracy against him in Jerusalem; that he fled to Lachish; that they sent there for him and slew him there. A man whose moral defects had made such a wreck of his good sense and judgment, and who, through sheer wickedness, had brought such calamities on his city and kingdom, was obviously unfit to reign. There were sagacious men enough in the high places of power to see this and to combine against his life for the salvation of their country. His case is one variety under the axiom: "Whatsoever a man soweth, that shall he also reap." When his sinful passions rob a king of his common sense, it is but meet that they should rob him also of throne and life.

Uzziah.

This king whose record appears briefly in 2 Kings 14: 21, 22, and 15: 1–7, but much more fully in 2 Chron. 26, was a great improvement upon his father Amaziah, whom he succeeded at the age of sixteen, to reign fifty-two years. He was one of the most energetic kings, born to push business and to work toward success. That he built Eloth [often written "Elath"], the well known port on the gulf of Akabah near Ezion Geber, is put first in the list of his exploits, perhaps because it was first in time, or because it was so characteristic of his energy. Its rebuilding indicates a revival of the India trade by sea, after the manner of Solomon.

The testimony to the moral tone of Uzziah's reign puts him not on the highest grade, nor yet on the lowest. He did right after the manner of his father—comparing him with the better part of his father's reign. He sought God in the days of Zechariah—a prophet-teacher not elsewhere spoken of. The Hebrew words, "Who had understanding in the visions of God," I prefer to translate; Who instructed in the fear of God; made men wise as to true piety. According to the universal law of God's administration, as long as Uzziah sought the Lord, God made him prosper. All history repeats evermore this great lesson.

Uzziah made wars successfully against the Philistines; breaking down their strongest city-walls. He also subdued certain Arabians and brought them under tribute. To his other labors he added extensive repairs and enlargement of the walls of Jerusalem — sadly broken down (we may remember) in the reign of his father; the reorganization of the standing army; the provision of enginery for war and for defence; and to crown all (a rare record for a king) he labored munificently to increase the productiveness of his country in the line of husbandry—the raising and the care of cattle and the cultivation of the soil.

The darker side of his character seems to have been developed under his great success and its temptations

to pride; "His heart was lifted up to his destruction"—
the word for destruction suggesting that his being lifted
up, first depraved and then destroyed him. "He went
into the temple of the Lord to burn incense"—repeating
the sin of Korah and his associates (Num. 16). When
the High Priest withstood him, he became angry and
was smitten with leprosy—a terrible infliction which
suddenly appalled him, and adhered to him—the mark
of God's displeasure—to the day of his death.——The
prophet Isaiah wrote his history for the archives of the
nation, having commenced his prophetic functions a
short time before Uzziah's death.

Jotham.

This son and successor of Uzziah reigned sixteen
years, leaving a fair record morally, fully up to the
best side of his father's, and avoiding the great sin
which brought such gloom over the closing years of
Uzziah. He followed the steps of his father in the line
of building cities, castles, towns; and in wars against the
contiguous Ammonites, who probably provoked this by
their incursions. The comprehensive generalization of
his reign is, "So Jotham became mighty because he
prepared his ways;" better—he purposely ordered, determined his ways as before God; steadfastly aimed to
please God. A worthy record!——Only seven verses
are devoted to his history by the author of Kings (2
Kings 15: 32–38). The fuller record by the author of
Chronicles gives him one short chapter (27).

Ahaz.

Ahaz, son and successor of Jotham, in his reign of
sixteen years made himself notorious for his wickedness, surpassing in crime and downright depravity all
the kings of Judah before him. In fact it is intimated
that he walked in the ways of the most wicked kings
of Israel, surpassed in sin by few even if any of them.
——To his record the author of Kings devotes one
chapter (16), and the author of Chronicles one (28), each
containing some new matter, and also some matter common to both. Both of his historians give his history
in the philosophical order; first, his great sins, and

then their legitimate results; defeat, disaster, the destruction of his immense armies; the exhaustion of his treasury by foreign exactions—the "bringing of Judah low and making her naked because of his sore transgressions against the Lord." In the line of sins he introduced Baal-worship, never brought into Judah before, save for a short time under Jehoram and Athaliah. He was the first to desecrate the famous "valley of the son of Hinnom" (south of Jerusalem), not only burning incense there to idol gods, but burning his own children there in the fire, after the abomination of the old Canaanites—a horrid worship which seems to have been kept up vigorously in Moab and Ammon. The author of Kings used the phrase—"made his son to pass through the fire;" but the author of Chronicles said in plainest terms—"burnt his children in the fire"—showing that the former phrase means nothing less than burning children to death. It is not perhaps certain that he burned more than one, though in Chronicles we read "sons," in the plural. We may be thankful the murdered son was not Hezekiah, and that God spared him to fill the throne so righteously after the death of his godless father. Perhaps the wickedness of his father was to him revolting and wrought a deep abhorrence of such crime. Did his young eyes see his little brother burned to death to Moloch? Had he a godly mother to aid him to just views of such horrid worship of devils? If we may attach any weight to the statements bearing on his age as related to his father's, he was old enough when Ahaz began to reign to appreciate his shocking inhumanity and even his guilt before God. Being twenty-five years old when he began to reign, he was nine when his father began.

For such sins judgments from God came speedily and fell thick and fast. The Syrians smote him and carried a great multitude of captives to Damascus. Pekah, king of Israel, came also upon him and "slew in one day 120,000, all valiant men, because they had forsaken the Lord God of their fathers." He also took 200,000 captives—"women, sons, and daughters," and brought them to Samaria with immense spoil. There a prophet of the Lord, Oded by name, stepped forth boldly before the conquering army, and made this very effective speech (put on record 2 Chron. 28: 9–11):

"Behold, because the Lord God of your fathers was wroth with Judah, he hath delivered them into your hand, and ye have slain them in a rage that reacheth up to heaven. And now ye propose to keep under the children of Judah and Benjamin for bondmen and bondwomen unto you: but are there not with you, even with *you*, sins against the Lord your God? Now hear me therefore, and deliver the captives again which ye have taken captive of your brethren: for the fierce wrath of the Lord is upon you."

In the result several leading men of Ephraim stood up to sustain this appeal of Oded with such effect that the army surrendered their captives. Kind-hearted men came forward to clothe, furnish, and feed them, and take them toward their homes as far as Jericho—a grand exhibition of the principles of true humanity in war, brought about by the Lord through his prophet.

The military expedition (recorded in Kings only) in which Syria and Ephraim combine under Rezin and Pekah against Ahaz, seems to have been subsequent to the events narrated above. They came up against Jerusalem and besieged Ahaz but could not overcome him. The account given in Kings (16) should be compared with Isa. 7, where the same facts are referred to, and with them are inwoven most inspiring predictions of God's future mercies to Zion. It was under the pressure of these foreign enemies that Ahaz, weakened by the loss of the flower of his army, sent to Tiglath-pileser of Assyria for help. He came; seized Damascus on his way (it being on his route); and sent many of its people into captivity to Kir, and slew Rezin their king. These facts are certified on the Assyrian monuments, brought to light within the last half century.*—— Another fact comes through the same channel, viz., that the Assyrian conqueror gathered at Damascus a group of captive kings, including those of Judea, Edom, Ammon, Moab, Gaza, Askelon, Tyre, and Arvad; put them upon their terms of allegiance and tribute; and there imposed upon them, according to the usages of

---

* The Assyrian records of Tiglath-pileser state that from his twelfth to his fourteenth year (B. C. 734-732) he carried on a war in Southern Syria against the two kings—Pekah of Samaria and Rezin of Damascus who were confederate together; that he besieged Rezin in his capital for two years, at the end of which time he captured him and put him to death, while he punished Pekah by mulcting him of a large portion of his dominions and carrying off vast numbers of his subjects into captivity." (Historical Illustrations 134).

Assyrian conquerors, a certain fealty to the Assyrian gods. To this some critics ascribe the act of Ahaz in taking the pattern of the Assyrian altar (assuming it to have been not Syrian but Assyrian), and in having one like it built at Jerusalem. The author of Chronicles, however, assumes that these gods were those of Damascus which had (so Ahaz assumed) been powerful enough to help them, and therefore he would invoke their help for himself.

Calamities by war came upon Ahaz, not from the north only, but from the south and south-west. "The Edomites came and smote Judah and carried away captives; the Philistines also invaded the cities of the low country (the great plain on the south-west), and all the south of Judah, and took several important cities (named 2 Chron. 28: 18). There is not the first hint that Ahaz in his trouble sought help from the Lord. Repeatedly he sought help from the king of Assyria, at first with the very partial success of relief from Rezin of Syria; but the author of Chronicles speaks only of disaster from this quarter: "The king of Assyria came unto him and distressed him, but strengthened him not." To buy his help or glut his rapacity, Ahaz not only robbed the temple, his own palace, and those of his princes of their treasures, but the temple of some of its ornamental and indeed useful portions, named by the author of Kings (vs. 17, 18). Even these calamities and straits utterly failed to turn the heart or even the thought of Ahaz toward the true God. He only rushed with the more infatuation to idol gods for help —(as said in this connection)—to the gods of Damascus whom he supposed to have smitten him, and wished to propitiate so that they should help him instead. "But (says the historian) they were the ruin of him and of all Israel;" *i. e.*, of his own nation.

Taken in whole the record of Ahaz is one of unmitigated crime and folly, and of consequent ruin. Not one redeeming feature appears throughout his entire history. It seems hard to account for such depths of depravity; such infatuation of guilt and folly.

Hezekiah.

In respect to both character and reign, Hezekiah stands in marked and pleasing contrast with his father Ahaz and his son Manasseh. His reign is ever memorable for the great Jewish revival of religion with which it opened; for the earnest consecration of its monarch to the God of his fathers; for the deliverance granted him from impending destruction before the great Assyrian power; for the extraordinary prolongation of his life under the special promise of just fifteen years more; and for his association with the venerable prophet Isaiah.

To his history the author of Kings devoted three chapters (18-20), and the author of Chronicles four (29-32). The former gave almost exclusively his political history; the latter, through three chapters, his religious history—a somewhat minute account of that great reformation which so distinguished his reign. Much the greater part of this political history as in Kings appears also with no considerable variation in the prophecy of Isaiah (36-39)—viz., that part which records the invasion of Judah by the king of Assyria; the embassy of Rabshakeh and his taunting speech, and the course pursued by Hezekiah with its ultimate results. It scarcely admits of doubt that the compiler of Kings drew his history of Hezekiah from the annals of his reign, prepared by Isaiah, and that in making up his own book of prophecies, Isaiah placed in it so much of these annals as we find in his four chapters. The author of Chronicles (supposably Ezra) made up his history many years later. He, therefore, assumed that his readers had access to Kings and probably to Isaiah, and thus naturally condensed very much the account found there of the Assyrian invasion, giving his attention chiefly to the great religious reformation and its results. These were matters of living interest to himself and his brethren of the restoration.

In treating of Hezekiah, I propose to pass lightly over that portion of it which appears in Isaiah 36-39, and in 2 Kings 18: 13 to the close of chap. 20, inasmuch as those portions have been critically examined in my

Notes on Isaiah; and to give chief attention to his great religious work presented in 2 Chron. 29–31.

Of this transcendently precious revival, it scarcely need be said in the outset that it came in a time of *utmost need*. The declension under Ahaz had been fearful; the temple had never been so shamefully desecrated before; idolatry in Judah had never been so bold and defiant; never before had great men burnt their sons and daughters so openly in sacrifice to Moloch. The northern kingdom had long been going down morally and religiously by a perpetual backsliding. It was at this point on the verge of political destruction and hopeless captivity. The present was the last opportunity to pluck a remnant from the open jaws of this ruin. It was the last call of mercy to the people of the ten tribes, inviting them back to the God of their fathers.*

Next it may be noted that this great revival was wrought, instrumentally, by *means of the religious institutions of Moses*. We read of no special labors of Hebrew prophets.† It is not said that there was extra preaching or any special services of reading the law. But the Mosaic ritual services were put in full requisition, and (probably) developed their utmost legitimate force toward a spiritual reformation. In this point of view, this revival may be made a valuable study philosophically, answering the great question as to the practical religious power of that ancient ritual.

Hezekiah began this effort in reform immediately after ascending the throne. Doubtless his soul had been crying out through more than one tedious year under the awful wickedness of his father's reign, longing for the time to come when he might strike for the salvation of his country and the recall of the people from their idolatrous abominations. Had he not been weep-

---

* Psalm 80 appears to have been composed for the case of the northern tribes, desolated by their crimes and the judgments sent because of them—in whose behalf the men of prayer in Hezekiah's times gave utterance to their emotions and supplications in this Psalm.

† We know however from other sources that Hosea, Amos, Micah and Isaiah had been laboring among the people, some in Israel and some in Judah, so that no small amount of preparatory work must have been done. Such men as they could never be idle during the progress of such a work.

ing over the broken altars and the polluted sanctuary, and waiting in the agony of long pent up grief and indignation for the moment to come when he might "open the doors of the house of the Lord" and summon the godly Levites "to sanctify themselves and the glorious temple".?——So when at length he came to the throne of Judah, his heart was ready; his hand was ready—for this first great measure of his reign.

First he summoned together the priests and the Levites, for these men must be his chief agents in a revival to be worked by the instrumentalities of the Mosaic Institutions. In few but telling words he sets the case before them—how the wrath of the Lord had come down upon Judah and Jerusalem for their great sins; how their fathers had fallen by the sword and their sons and daughters and wives had gone into captivity for this. "Now," said he, "it is in my heart to make a covenant with the Lord God of Israel that his fierce wrath may turn away from us."——Thus the moral pressure toward a thorough reformation, growing out of these patent facts, was immense.——Now, therefore, my sons, God lays this responsibility largely on you. He has chosen you out of all the tribes to stand before his altar and to lead in all these holy services; therefore be ye not remiss, but meet your obligations with the utmost diligence.

Then they set themselves to cleanse the temple and to restore what the sacrilegious hand of Ahaz had taken away. This being done and reported to the king (so we read 2 Chron. 29: 20)—"Then King Hezekiah *rose early*" (as one whose heart was there before the morning light), "and gathered the rulers of the city" (his officers and cabinet must combine all their personal and official influence), "and went up to the house of the Lord." A solemn service of sacrifice followed. Burnt-offerings, sin-offerings with imposition of hands and confession of sin—"an atonement for all Israel;" and accompanying this the full service of song with all the ordained instruments of music, pouring forth their mighty chorus of thanksgiving and praise during the entire service of the burnt-offering till it was concluded, after which "the king and all that were present with him bowed themselves with him and worshiped." It is specially said that "they sang praises to the Lord with the words of David and of Asaph the seer," making use of those glorious Psalms of praise which have so often in all later ages, as in the earlier ages also, borne up the grateful offerings of praise and adoration to the great Jehovah. It need not surprise us that this return to the sublime songs of the sanctuary and to the long neglected services of sacrifice and offering should have been with great rejoicings of heart. The soul of the noble king and the souls of many of his princes and people like-minded, were deeply in it.

The next great movement was the due celebration of the Passover. Neither the priests nor the people, and scarcely the temple itself—was in readiness when the appointed day—the fourteenth of the first month—arrived. So the king took counsel, and by general consent it was concluded to defer the Passover to the fourteenth day of the second month. The Mosaic law provided for this postponement under peculiar circumstances.——This gave the king opportunity for ample preparation. He wrote letters and sent out his messengers not only over all Judah but over all Israel, from Dan to Beersheba, through Ephraim and Manasseh, affectionately and earnestly inviting them to come up to Jerusalem once more and honor the God of their fathers by a joint observance of the great Passover. "Ye children of Israel" (thus we read), "turn again to the Lord God of Abraham, Isaac and Jacob, for he will return to the remnant of you that are escaped out of the hand of the king of Assyria; and be ye not like your fathers and like your brethren who trespassed against the Lord God of their fathers, who therefore gave them up to desolation as ye see. Now be ye not stiff-necked as your fathers were, but yield yourselves unto the Lord and enter into his sanctuary and serve the Lord your God, that the fierceness of his wrath may turn away from you." It was indeed the very crisis of their destiny—such multitudes of their nearest and dearest ones already cut down by the sword or borne away into captivity before their very eyes, and nothing but repentance and returning to God could by any possibility avert the same uplifted arm from blotting out the whole northern kingdom.——This tender and fervid appeal fitly closed with reminding them of God's great compassion: "For the Lord your God is gracious and merciful, and will not turn away his face from you if ye return unto him" (v. 9). "The posts passed from city to city through Ephraim and Manasseh even unto Zebulon; but" (with sorrow let it be read), "they laughed them to scorn and mocked them." This was the general fact, true of the masses; but there were some brighter shades: "Nevertheless divers of Asher and Manasseh and of Zebulon humbled themselves and came to Jerusalem."——With a high degree of probability Ps. 84 was composed and sent out with these Jewish missionaries to be not only read but sung, to back up their warm-hearted invitations to their northern brethren to gather themselves at the holy city in those lovely tabernacles of the Lord of Hosts. The sweet associations linked to the courts of the Lord; the blessedness of those who have Jehovah as their sun and shield—how finely are they portrayed in this Psalm and how exceedingly pertinent were these words to be said and sung wherever audience could be gained.——Several other Psalms of the third Book may be read in connection with the age of Hezekiah, *e. g.*, 75, 76, 80–82, and 85–89.——Judah came in well. "In Judah the hand of God was to give them one heart to do the commandment of the king and of the princes by the word of the Lord."—— A great congregation was on hand for the Passover in the second month. The idol-altars in Jerusalem were borne away and cast into the brook Kidron. Noticeably, multitudes who came up to the holy city from the northern tribes had not cleansed themselves according to the law of Moses, yet did they eat the Passover otherwise than it was written. A fair measure of sincerity was their passport, and overruled the technicalities and ritualities of the law. In the true spirit of his divine Master, Hezekiah prayed for them—"The good Lord pardon every one that prepareth his heart to seek God, the Lord God of his fathers, though he be not cleansed according to the purification of the sanctuary. And the Lord hearkened to Hezekiah and healed the people." ——This too, as well as the first great season of sacrifice, was an occasion of great gladness. They sang praises with loud instruments; they ate throughout the feast seven days; they made confession to the God of their fathers; the king encouraged all the Levites that taught the good knowledge of the Lord. Seven days proved too short for the great work before them. The Spirit of God was so manifestly upon the great congregation they could not close with the first seven days, but took counsel and by general consent kept other seven—a "protracted meeting" of fourteen days' continuance with apparently growing interest and power to the end. The record testifies in precious detail that "all the congregation of Judah with the priests and Levites; also all the congregation that came out of Israel with the strangers both from Israel and from Judah *rejoiced*." There was great joy in Jerusalem, for no such scenes had been known there since the great day of Solomon; *i. e.*, at the dedication of the temple. "Then the priests and the Levites arose and blessed the people, and their voice was heard, and their prayer came up to the holy dwelling place of God, even unto heaven."

If we were to analyze the influences that blended in this great religious movement, we might say—the ritual services of sacrifices, altars, temple, were present in their full strength; perhaps the stronger for having been long remitted. Coupled with those were the outpouring of song; the teaching of the good knowledge of the Lord; the social power of an immense congregation; the services protracted till the hearts of the people were profoundly impressed; and not least, the immediate historic antecedents—that fearful scourging of war and captivity which had sent death into so many households, and borne away so many loved ones into a captivity from which nothing but national repentance could move the Almighty to restore them. Nor let us forget the influence of the noble king, leading on with his whole heart; consecrating treasure without stint, and promptly foremost in every point where his hand could touch the springs of a great movement. All in all it was a scene of moral sublimity rarely equaled.

When this great Passover scene was finished, the people were in heart prepared for one more service imperatively demanded, viz., the destruction of idol-images, altars, and groves throughout all the cities and high places of both Judah and Israel. That they should go forth *en masse* throughout Judah on this mission was to be expected. Such a reformation would have been wretchedly superficial and shallow without it. But that they should have gone forth over all the kingdom of Hoshea as if there were no such king there; that they should go where they would with no apparent resistance:—this is truly a wonderful proof of the zealous enthusiasm and of the moral power of this great reformation.——Recalling to mind the fact that this great revival and this breaking down of idols in the northern kingdom preceded the invasion under Shalmanezer by only three years, and the total destruction of Samaria and the entire northern kingdom by not more than six years, we shall see reason to regard this as not only God's last call of mercy to thousands in the northern kingdom, but as his grand providential agency for sifting out his own chosen ones; gathering in all whom the most efficient agency could avail to save before the final storm should sweep the nation forever into ruin.

The historian of Chronicles devotes one chapter (31) mainly to the systematic arrangements for the religious services which very properly filled out and consummated this great revival. After that vigorous iconaclasm which swept the vestiges of idolatry from the land, Hezekiah set the Levites and priests in their respective courses, giving each his duties in due order, and carefully made the provisions required by the law of Moses for the payment of tithes and offerings to sustain the entire religious system. It testifies nobly to the genuineness of this revival that the offerings of all first-fruits and treasure were abundant, even almost superabundant. Ample store-houses became a necessity.——The historian concludes his account with joyous words bearing grateful testimony to the good King Hezekiah: "Thus did Hezekiah throughout all Judah, and wrought that which was good and right and truth before the Lord his God. And in every work that he began in the service of the house of God and in the law and in the commandments to seek his God, he did it with all his heart and prospered" (31: 20, 21).——Let us hope that as the fruit of his noble labors many souls were born to God and blessed with the fulness of his great salvation. If Ezra (as may be supposed) wrote out this history in Chronicles, we can readily imagine with what full heart and flowing pen he chronicled the words and doings of such a king, and laid them before the returned exiles of his time to help onward a similar reformation in souls made mellow under long and sore affliction, but then waking to new joy and to spiritual life under the precious services of a new sanctuary.

The political events in Hezekiah's reign are drawn out in detail in 2 Kings 18–20, and in Isaiah 36–39. Suffice it to say here that Sennacherib seems to have made two expeditions into Judea. In the first he came "up against all the fenced cities of Judah and took them" (2 Kings 18: 13, and 2 Chron. 32: 1); received Hezekiah's submission and tribute, but did not march upon Jerusalem. In the second "he sent Rabshakeh with a great host against Jerusalem" (2 Kings 18: 17, and 2 Chron. 32: 9), himself, meantime, laying siege to Lachish. The speech of Rabshakeh is given in detail; also its reception by the king, his bearing the case before God, and the gracious answer God gave him, followed in due time by the fearful destruction of the Assyrian army to the number of 185,000 men in one night. This effectually broke his power; relieved the holy city, and saved the throne and people of Hezekiah from being further annoyed by the Assyrian armies. This deliverance was the great event of Hezekiah's reign, and indeed, of those ages. It had been repeatedly predicted by Isaiah (*e. g.*, 10: 24–34, and 14: 24–27, and 17: 12–14, and 33: 17–24). Consequently, its historical fulfillment should find place in his book (chaps. 36 and 37).——The great moral lessons of this event are embalmed in song in Psalm 76: "In Judah is God known: his name is great in Israel. There brake he the arrows of the bow, the shield, and the sword, and the battle. The stout-hearted are spoiled; they have slept their sleep. At thy rebuke, O God of Jacob, both the chariot and the horse are cast into a dead sleep."——What a "sleep" was that! when God arose to judgment to save the meek ones of the land. Let it teach us that verily the wrath of man is made to praise God, and that it behooves his people, having vowed to God in their distress, to pay their vows with grateful thank-offerings when such deliverance comes. ——This manifestation of God's high hand against proud Assyria was a fit sequel to the glorious reformation in the first year of Hezekiah's reign. The way was opened legitimately for such prayer as God could hear, and with honor to himself could answer in overwhelming judgments on his foes.

The *date*, within Hezekiah's reign, of these Assyrian invasions has been gravely questioned by Geo. Rawlinson, as has been stated at some length in my Notes on Isa. 37. The Scripture statements are in a good degree definite and self-consistent, assigning the first invasion to Hezekiah's fourteenth year (2 Kings 18: 13, and Isa. 36: 1), and implying that the second followed the first at no long interval. The author of Chronicles is indefinite, yet seems to imply that it fell within the early and not the latter part of his reign, after the great reformation and the thorough reorganization of religious worship—his words being:—"After these things and the establishment thereof" (2 Chron. 32: 1). In harmony with these dates his sickness and miraculous recovery fell in close connection, perhaps between the first invasion and the second, since his entire reign filled twenty-nine years, of which fifteen followed this sickness and fourteen preceded.——Mr. Rawlinson, however, insists that the Assyrian inscriptions require a place for Sargon between Shalmanezer and Sennacherib, since Sargon finished the subjugation of Samaria in his first year (the sixth of Hezekiah) and reigned not less than fifteen years, and probably nineteen. Sennacherib (his son and successor) invaded Judah according to Assyrian authorities in his fourth year. These data require us to place the destruction of Sennacherib's army in Hezekiah's twenty-seventh or twenty-ninth year instead of his fourteenth. In Mr. Rawlinson's view the Assyrian authorities are so definite and strong to these points that we must either deny their authority altogether, or modify the dates of Scripture to conform to them.*

But this scheme of Mr. Rawlinson is not only out of harmony with the definite dates of Scripture (*e. g.*, the *fourteenth* year of Hezekiah, 2 Kings 18: 13, etc.), but with the general current of events, specially as given in 2 Chron. 32: 22–30. For here the order of great events runs: The destruction of the Assyrian army (v. 21); the saving of Hezekiah and his people from all other

---

* Rawlinson's views may be seen in Smith's Dictionary ("Sargon"); also in his "Historical Illustrations," 138–141, and in his Historical Evidences, 118–120.

enemies, and "guiding them on every side" (v. 22); a great influx of gifts and presents "so that he was magnified in the sight of all nations from thenceforth" (v. 23); next "*in those days* fell his great sickness" (v. 24) from which he was restored and lived after it *fifteen years*—a fact which, located here, is utterly repugnant to Mr. R.'s theory. Still after this came a period of remarkable prosperity, great riches and honor (vs. 27–29), coupled with more exploits than can be rationally supposed to have fallen within the last two years of his life. I do not see therefore how we can believe that the sacred writers put the destruction of the Assyrians within the last two years of Hezekiah's reign.

Of the later events of his reign Isaiah (in chapter 39) has given most fully the account of the embassadors from the king of Babylon: the author of Chronicles only has referred to the divine purpose in this moral trial of Hezekiah, viz., that "God left him" (*i. e.*, without special direction or without restraining grace or special admonition) "to try him that he might know all that was in his heart."

Viewed in whole his character is not unblemished, yet is in the main that of a man of prayer and of both favor and power with God, whose reign bore a glorious testimony to Jehovah's presence with his people, and to the might of his arm for their salvation. The impulses of those memorable scenes live and are borne down through all time in the sublime faith and the glorious visions of Isaiah the prophet. His eye saw them; his soul felt their utmost thrilling power. The spirit of prophecy availed itself of those present manifestations of God to exalt his conceptions of the glorious future of the real Zion—the city and kingdom of the Great God.

Manasseh.

To Manasseh, son and successor of Hezekiah, and to his son Amon, each of our historians devotes one chapter (2 Kings 21, and 2 Chron. 33). Alike these historians testify to Manasseh's great wickedness—how he set himself to undo all the noble reformatory work his father had done; how he built up the high places his father had thrown down, desecrated the temple his father had cleansed; burnt his son in the fire; practiced divination and witchcraft; built altars for all the host of heaven in the two courts of the house of the Lord; filled Jerusalem with innocent blood—supposably of sons and daughters burned to death in the orgies of devil-worship. The author of Kings attributes the destruction of Jerusalem and the captivity of Judah specially to these great sins of Manasseh, both in this chapter (vs. 10–16), and also in chap. 23: 26, 27, and 24: 3, 4.——The author of Chronicles, omitting these points, gives new and not unimportant matter, particularly that the Lord brought upon Manasseh the great Assyrian army who "took him among the thorns,* bound him with fetters and carried him to Babylon," that there in his affliction he besought the Lord his God and humbled himself before the God of his fathers and prayed to him; and the Lord was entreated of him—and restored him again to Jerusalem. Then Manasseh knew that the Lord was truly God. After this repentance he removed his idol-gods and altars from the temple; repaired the Lord's altar; offered sacrifice thereon; and commanded Judah to serve the Lord God of Israel. He also refers to the words of the seers who spake to him in the name of the Lord, and also to his prayer and confession as being on record in the national archives, "written among the sayings of the seers."

Why the author of Kings omitted the captivity, repentance, and reformation of Manasseh does not appear. Probably it occurred late in his long reign (55 years), and being followed soon by the intensely wicked reign of his son Amon, scarcely lessened the strong drift of the nation into the worst abominations of idolatry. The general influence of Manasseh on the nation was fearfully bad.

As Christian philosophers, cherishing moreover a living faith in the great promise of God to Abraham and through him to the whole church:—"I will be a God to thee and to thy seed after thee," we can by no means pass unnoticed the grave question; *How could so good a man as Hezekiah have a son so wicked as Manasseh?*

---

* The best critics reject the sense "thorns" and give to the Hebrew word the sense of *rings*—the same which were put through the jaws of a fish when placed back in the water, that by means of a cord attached they might bring him up again.

―――Every Christian parent has reason to ponder the question with personal, not to say painful, interest.――― The following considerations may serve at least to abate our surprise at the fact.―――(a) Manasseh was but twelve years old at his father's death. He was yet unborn when the great reformation in Hezekiah's first year occurred; he was not yet born when his father was sick unto death and when his life was prolonged fifteen years. According to dates and implications of the Scripture narrative, he was not living to see the great deliverance from the Assyrian power. The history of Hezekiah's last twelve years speaks chiefly of his general prosperity; of his great riches and honor; and probably includes that visit from the embassadors of the king of Babylon—in general the darker side of Hezekiah's religious life. Hence the bearing of public events upon the mind and heart of a lad under twelve may not have been specially favorable.―――(b) We know nothing of his mother save her name, and can make no account of the defects or of the possible mischiefs of her moral training of her son.―――(c) Philosophically we are entitled to make some (perhaps large) account of the law of reaction. Hezekiah's reformation left multitudes still (in heart) in their sins. Restrained while he lived from open idolatry, yet in heart real idolaters, they were ready at his death for a bold rush into those abominations. There is no reason to suppose that Manasseh moved off alone at the age of twelve in his wild career of depravity. There must have been strong surrounding influences pressing him on in that direction. It would be simply human nature if those influences were largely reactionary against the restraints upon sin in Hezekiah's reign. To this we may add that probably this reactionary law worked strongly upon Manasseh himself. The godliness of Hezekiah's family and of his personal character quite failed to change the heart of this son; it may have only chafed and fretted him by the restraints it brought upon his impulses toward sinful pleasure. When the death of his father suddenly removed these restraints and brought around him men of leading influence like-minded in their propensities toward the extreme abominations of heathenism, there is no occasion for surprise at the result.―――The moral lesson for every Christian parent in this history is primarily this: Be intensely earnest and thorough in securing radical conversion *in the very earliest years of life.* To die, leaving a godless son of twelve years to run such a career as Manasseh ran, should appall every heart with dread and intensify every endeavor to forestall it.

Returning to the course of this history, we note that Amon, son and successor of Manasseh, came to the throne at the age of twenty-two; reigned but two years, simply and only in wickedness; and seems to have outraged his people by his crimes. His servants conspired against him and slew him in his own house. A reign of vastly more interest and importance followed.

Josiah.

The history of this last *good* king of Judah fills two chapters in Kings (22 and 23), and two in Chronicles (34 and 35). "The people of the land" (says the author of Chronicles) "made him king in the stead of his wicked father," though at the very early age of eight years. It would seem that in this case also, as in that of Manasseh, a somewhat large allowance must be made for reactionary influence—here from revolting, outrageous wickedness toward a better life. Of the first eight years of his reign we have no historic notice; but in his sixteenth year of life—the eighth of his reign, while he was yet young, he began to seek after the God of David his father; and four years later began to purge Judah and Jerusalem from the images and groves of idolatry. This work was thoroughly done.——The next important measure of reform, assigned to the eighteenth year of his reign, was to repair and purify the temple. At this point the history shows that Josiah had good and strong men in high positions to aid him in this great reform, *e. g.*, Shaphan; Masseiah, governor of the city; Hilkiah the High Priest—some of whom appear in Jeremiah's book of prophecies (Jer. 26: 24, and 32: 7, 12). This last reformation in Judah was pressed forward with noble zeal by Josiah, the points specially expanded in the narrative being, the cleansing and repairs of the temple; the destruction of all idol-images and of all the appurtenances of idol-worship, not only in Jerusalem and in Judah, but extensively throughout the ancient territory of other tribes—the cities of Manasseh, Eph-

JOSIAH. 359

raim, Simeon, even to Naphtali being mentioned (2 Chron. 34: 6). Noticeably, he not only destroyed but defiled and sought to make repulsive and unendurable all localities desecrated by the abominations of idol-worship, filling those places with dead men's bones and all uncleanness. Bethel, made infamous by Jeroboam, and Tophet already foul with the blood of human sacrifices to Moloch, he sought to defile so effectually as to break forever the spell of the old associations. The historian of Kings spoke of his putting away all who wrought with familiar spirits or other magic arts, and gave him the credit of surpassing all kings before him in turning to the Lord with all his heart according to the law of Moses* (23: 24, 25).——One prominent event of this reform was a very remarkable celebration of the Passover which the author of Chronicles (characteristically) narrates quite fully (35: 1–19), closing with this high praise: "There was no passover like to that, kept in Israel, from the days of Samuel the prophet, neither did all the kings of Israel keep such a passover as Josiah kept," etc. We may hope that the legitimate influences of that great festival were turned to best account to bring the people back to the true worship of the God of their fathers, and to stem the already alarming drift of popular feeling toward the worst forms of idol-abominations.

Yet one other event has made the reign of Josiah noticeable, not to say, memorable;—the discovery of what was (probably) the original copy of the book of the law. It was brought to light as the officers were

* An inside view of the spirit and times of Josiah may be obtained from the Psalms composed or at least compiled during his reign or soon after. The fourth book of the Psalter (Ps. 90–106) falls under this description. We can scarcely be mistaken in ascribing the compilation of this fourth book to Jeremiah. The sympathy due to kindred spirit and to similar surroundings attracted him to Ps. 90—to which Ps. 91 is a counterpart. Ps. 101 well expresses the noble spirit of youthful piety and holy purpose which the history clearly assumes in the young King Josiah. We seem to have the very heart and hand of Jeremiah in Ps. 102—written in view of the events of his later years; Ps. 92 and 93 are at least pertinent to the times of that great reformation; while Ps. 106 may well refer to the first great deportation of captives. It is pleasant to hope that the joyous thanksgivings of that precious revival gave tone to Ps. 95–100 and 103–105. For a more full discussion of the historic occasion and reference of these Psalms, I must refer the reader to my Notes on these Psalms.

depositing in their proper place in the temple certain moneys contributed for its repair and worship. The remarkable things in this case, as the account comes to us, were—the surprise occasioned by this discovery; the impression made upon the king when portions of this book were read to him; the resort to Huldah the prophetess for direction from the Lord; and her message from the Lord to Josiah in reply.——This event has seemed to some rather skeptical critics to justify them in the assumption that no written copy of this law had been in existence before, and that this may (or must) have been a forgery, then for the first time brought out to the world. But the narrative gives no support to these assumptions. The profound and startling impression made upon the king by the reading of this book may have been due wholly to the fact that it brought to him the very words of God through Moses—supposably those fearful denunciations of judgment for idolatry which may be seen in Lev. 26 and Deut. 28.——The narrative does seem to imply that written copies of the Pentateuch were not at that time abundant. Very probably Josiah had no copy in his possession, as the Mosaic law required the king of Israel to have.——On the other hand it may be supposed that a peculiarly solemn impression was made upon him by the circumstance that this was (or was supposed to be) the original copy, handed down from Moses; and by the further fact that the passages read to him were those above referred to which met so pertinently the case of the men of his generation, and, therefore, seemed to bring down those fearful maledictions fresh from the lips of the Almighty, thundering against the very people for whom he was in a sort responsible as their king. This copy may have been withdrawn from view during the long reign (fifty-five years) of Manasseh—perhaps lest his ungodliness should imperil its safety. More than one generation may have passed away while its hiding-place was unknown. Then coming to light so unexpectedly at a time when its fearful maledictions were apparently (and really too) on the verge of fulfillment, it need surprise no one that Josiah was startled and his soul moved to its depths.——It should be specially noticed that the message sent through the prophetess, though speaking very kindly of Josiah and promising that these judgments should not fall on his people during his life, yet expressly declared that they were near at hand: "Thus saith the Lord; Behold, I will bring evil on this place and upon the inhabitants thereof, even all the words of the book which the king of Judah hath read, because they have forsaken me and have burned incense to other gods . . . therefore, my wrath shall be kindled against this place and shall not be quenched" (2 Kings 22: 16, 17). The appalling truth was, therefore, forced upon Josiah that all hope of saving his nation was virtually extinguished; that his great effort at reformation might delay the outbursting of these judgments; might save many individual souls from perdition; but could not permanently arrest the downward proclivity of the masses; could not effectually save the nation.——It is not easy to estimate the sad, depressing, and yet quickening impulses of such a revelation from God.——Moreover, Josiah saw that it must be so. The power of idolatry throughout his kingdom was terrific; the heart of the masses was fearfully saturated with its spirit. He could send abroad his royal mandate and find a few trusty men to arm with his authority to go forth, leveling heathen groves, crashing down idol-images and altars, burning dead men's bones on all desecrated localities; but it must have been a mountain of lead on his heart to think that the roots of this awful sin would yet remain, and that not many years would elapse before the vials of God's wrath would be poured out for sins and abominations that defied all remedy.

The great Passover and the discovery of this copy of the law are both assigned to the eighteenth year of Josiah's reign. Jeremiah had then been in his prophetic work five years. Thirteen more remained before Josiah's death. So far as can be inferred from the history he continued to reign in the fear of the Lord to his death. The manner of this death brings a slight shade over his name—the historian of Chronicles intimating that his collision with Pharaoh Necho in arms was against the will of God; " he hearkened not to the words of Necho *from the mouth of God.*" Necho had said to Josiah—then marching upon him for battle: "What have I to do with thee, thou king of Judah? I come not against thee this day, but against the house wherewith I have war" (the Chaldean), "for God commanded me to make haste : forbear then from meddling with God who is with me that he destroy thee not" (2 Chron. 35: 21, 22). This movement was on Josiah's part a mistake. How clearly he saw it to be against God's will (if at all) we can not decide with confidence. He might have asked God's will and have received a perfect answer. The result was sad; it brought deep sorrow upon all his good people. Jeremiah bewailed his noble sovereign and bosom friend with tenderest lamentation—and not without reason. There were graceless sons to succeed their godly father on his throne—not one worthy man among them all. Days of bitter trial and of stinging grief were coming upon Jeremiah, and perhaps, to no small extent, upon those other good men who had wrought in this great reformation. They must breast the fury of this storm—and with no sustaining hope of arresting the near impending doom of their country.

In explanation and partial vindication of Josiah's policy in going out to fight Necho, it may be said that he probably regarded this movement by Necho as one for conquest, and as ultimately dangerous to his own kingdom. He may have acted in concert with other powers, Syrian or Chaldean, in this effort to repel a foreign intruder and invader.——But on the other hand, we may ask—Had he sought counsel of the Lord in the case? Was he acting as the ally of Babylon or of Damascus; and if so, had he not forgotten the Mighty God of Jacob—always able to protect his own? Political alliances, offensive and defensive, were always a snare and a curse to God's people.

The Sons of Josiah.

After Josiah's death the people placed on the throne, not his eldest son Jehoiakim, but a younger son Jehoahaz, probably as giving better promise. His age was twenty-three; Jehoiakim's, twenty-five. He had reigned but three months when Pharaoh Necho "put him in bands at Riblah that he might not reign in Jerusalem" (2 Kings 23: 33); took him a prisoner to Egypt where he died; put Jehoiakim on the throne and the kingdom under tribute. He reigned eleven

THE SONS OF JOSIAH. 363

years, supremely wicked. The author of Kings, besides saying that "he did evil in the sight of the Lord according to all that his fathers" [not including Josiah we must assume] "had done," states very particularly that in raising this tribute, he "taxed the land;" "put the land to a tribute," etc.; probably implying that he took care to exempt himself entirely from these burdens, and very possibly, to enrich himself from these exactions. On the point of his covetousness and selfishness, his personal extravagance and grinding oppression of his people, Jeremiah (Jer. 22: 13-19) is very explicit and very unsparing in his animadversions. While his people were thus crushed by these exactions, he was building a palace for himself by unrighteousness, shedding innocent blood in oppression, using his royal power only in ways to make his name execrable and execrated. (See my Notes on Jer. 22.) On many other points Jeremiah's book of prophecy throws light on the character and reign of Jehoiakim, showing him to have been not only a merciless tyrant, but a heartless persecutor of the Lord's prophets—so recklessly defiant of God that he could cut in pieces the roll of Jeremiah's prophecies and burn them in his parlor fire; and withal so false to his treaty obligations that he brought upon his kingdom the vengeance of the Chaldean king. Nebuchadnezzar had defeated the Egyptians in a great battle at Carchemish (Jer. 46: 2) and forced them back into Egypt. Then coming up against Jerusalem, he put Jehoiakim under tribute,—who soon rebelled and thus brought on a more vigorous subjugation, and the first heavy installment of captives was borne away to Babylon. To this event we find allusion in Dan. 1—himself and his three friends with several thousands of the leading men being taken into captivity at that time.

The events of Jehoiakim's latter years and death are referred to only in general terms. The author of Chronicles (36: 6) seems to imply that he was bound in fetters to be taken to Babylon, while Jeremiah (22: 18, 19) assumes that he died unwept and uncared for in Jerusalem. Nebuchadnezzar placed his son Jehoiachin on the throne. He held it three months only and then was taken captive to Babylon, to lie there in bonds at least thirty-seven years—to the death of Nebuchadnezzar. A considerable number of the most capable men of Jerusalem and Judah were taken to Babylon at the same time (2 Kings 24: 12–16), including most of the royal family, the princes and all the mighty men of valor; the craftsmen and smiths—the efficient men, capable of doing something in the arts of war or peace; leaving in the country as of no particular account "the poorest sort of the people of the land."

The king of Babylon then placed on the throne yet another son of Josiah, viz., Zedekiah, who did only evil before God; proved himself treacherous to his sovereign, and after seven years provoked a final invasion of Judah and siege of Jerusalem. In his ninth year this ended in its capture and total destruction. City and temple went down together into the abyss of complete destruction—violence and fire leveling the walls of both city and temple, and leaving the whole a blackened pile of ruins. The king was arrested in his flight, his sons put to death before his eyes; then his eyes put out and himself taken in chains to Babylon and kept there in prison till his death (Jer. 52: 8–11). Only a miserable remnant were left in the land, whose history Jeremiah only has given (Jer. 40–44). For some reason he preferred to cast in his lot with them instead of going with the better class of surviving Jews to Babylon. He seems to have followed this last wretched group of inefficient men and women — infatuated idolaters — into Egypt, where he disappeared from history.

The Captivity.

Such in brief terms is a general view of the events which culminated in the deportation of the better part of the surviving Jews to Babylon; in the capture of their great city and the destruction of both city and temple.——The points most worthy of special notice are:

(1) The successive deportations of Jews, at four distinct periods; the first in the fourth year of Jehoiakim, when Daniel and his three friends were taken to Babylon. The number taken at this time was probably small, but the quality, superior. (See Dan. 1: 3–7.) Next when Jehoiachin was taken to Babylon. The author of Kings gives the round numbers and the general character of the captives taken at this time (2 Kings

THE CAPTIVITY.

24: 12–16). Jeremiah (Jer. 52: 28) locates this deportation in the seventh year of Nebuchadnezzar, which would be the eleventh of Jehoiakim, or first of his son Jehoiachin.——Next at the fall of the city in Zedekiah's eleventh and last year; the eighteenth of Nebuchadnezzar. Jeremiah puts the number of captives at this time at 832. After this the last gleanings were gathered up by Nebuzaradan, in Nebuchadnezzar's twenty-third year, to the number of 745. Thus a period of twenty-three years intervened between the first deportation and the last. The total number taken away is put by Jeremiah at 4600.* In 2 Kings 24: 14, 16, in round numbers (perhaps) 10,000. This may be the number in gross—of which some specifications appear in v. 16; 7,000 of one class; 1,000 of another, leaving about 2,000 of the high classes, princes and leading men in society.

(2) The numbers carried to Babylon were small, relatively to the immense numbers which appear from time to time, *e. g.*, in the reigns of Asa and Jehoshaphat. The crimes of Ahaz and the judgments sent for his sins cut off immense numbers. The wicked reigns of Manasseh and Amon reduced them still further. Under the wicked sons and grandson of Josiah the same process went on with accelerated rapidity. This last siege of the city was probably at a fearful cost of human life through the combined agencies of sword, famine, and pestilence.

On the moral side of this series of events let us note:

(1) That it came in fulfillment of prediction and threatened judgment, long since first made and often repeated. Through Moses (Lev. 26 and Deut. 28) these judgments were spread out in various language, with impressive minuteness, and in figures most appalling. After this, from age to age, God sent his prophets to reiterate these terrible threatenings and press them in utmost earnestness upon the heart and conscience of the people. What could the Lord have done more? How patiently and long had he been sending to them his servants the prophets, "rising up early and sending;"—but alas! they would not hear!

---

* Probably by some textual error too small.

Nothing now remained but the execution of this long threatened doom. To have postponed it longer would have imperiled the moral force of God's government over guilty men. To have ignored his threatenings and passed over this awful sin without due retribution would have broken down the divine veracity and utterly misrepresented the Holy God before both earth and heaven. It was one of those stern and awful moments in the moral history of a moral world when it is simply imperative upon the Almighty that his arm should be uplifted high in judgment and his indignation against sin should blaze forth—in the language of this inspired history—that his "wrath should arise against his" (nominal) "people, and there be no remedy" (2 Chron. 36: 16).

(2) Idolatry was the head sin. For ages the national depravity had gravitated perpetually and with fearful force toward this gigantic wickedness. Ever since Aaron made the golden calf and the people danced and shouted around it in wild revelry, this sin had been springing to the surface; giving a sad tone and dark shading to the history of the Judges; crowded back more effectually than at any other time during the reign of David; working up with strange fascination in the latter years of Solomon; darkening the whole northern kingdom during its entire continuance; and, finally, pressing in upon the southern kingdom till its spirit pervaded the mass of the people, past all moral remedies.——It is not easy in this age to conceive adequately the fascinating power of a system which had so intrenched itself in the superstitions of all nations; which drew to its support the attractions of art, taste, culture; which fostered and fed lasciviousness and lust; and yet which strangely seized upon the religious elements of man's nature and sought by the basest perversions to adjust itself to all their demands. A religion made subservient to the lowest and the utmost impulses of human depravity—who can adequately measure its capabilities to curse mankind! This was the form of sin against which the divine law thundered; against which prophets protested, and God's providential judgments and retributions were leveled and poured out age after age, culminating at last in this most terrific scourge—the blotting out (for the

THE CAPTIVITY. 367

time) of the whole Jewish nation; the fall of their holy city, and of their ever memorable sacred temple.

(3) Another evil, too great to be adequately estimated, was their reliance upon the ritualities and externals of their religion to shield them from God's retribution for their sins. Were they not the Lord's own people, and was not that gorgeous building his own glorious temple, and did not the sacred presence of the Holy One abide there? How could it be possible that God would let this temple fall before his enemies and his own holy city be laid desolate? Did not the ark of his covenant part asunder the Jordan waters and cast down the walls of Jericho; and was not the Almighty able to protect ark, temple, and holy city, from uncircumcised hands?——Thus this vain confidence took the moral force mostly out of those terrible threatenings, and in a sense made it necessary that God should let city and temple go down under an avalanche of desolation ere he could dislodge this delusion from their souls.

(4) Consequently the two great moral results sought by means of this destruction of city and temple and of this seventy years' captivity, were—(a) To cure the nation of idolatry;—(b) To break down this false reliance on the mere externals of their religious system.

The whole book of Ezekiel should be read with these points in mind. Every chapter, almost every verse, shines in the light of these truths and bears to their illustration. Of his forty-eight chapters, the first twenty-four protest with unwearied breath against the national sin of idolatry; set forth with perpetual reiteration the foulness of the sin, its terrible grasp on the national heart, its incessant and resistless demand for the most appalling retribution: while all along the prophet labors to make the captive exiles believe that their ritualities and sacred things could by no means avert from them the judgments of the Almighty. Noticeably, it was not till the tidings came to them in their captivity that the city had actually fallen and that the holy temple did certainly lie in ruins, that this vain confidence broke down!——From this point the entire tone of the prophet changes; the despondent, broken-hearted people needed the consolations of hope, and the prophet hastens to supply them. A great moral crisis had been reached in the discipline and culture of the Jewish people. Wonderfully, admirably, did the prophet Ezekiel adjust his messages accordingly.*

(5.) Bearing in mind that it was never the thought of God to forsake his people utterly and forget forevermore his promises to Abraham and the mercies made sure to David, but was rather his purpose to replant the land of promise, we may note with admiration the wisdom of his sifting processes: first, in taking away the better elements into Babylon, leaving behind in Judea the men who had sunk physically and morally so low as to be of no particular account as elements of society. The king of Babylon was not looking out for religious men; but he had need of men who had some force in them—some capability for labor and service. This, therefore, was one of the principles on which he sifted the conquered people of Judea. The other was equally simple. The men of vigor and valor were the men whom it would be dangerous for him to leave behind. They might head another revolt. Therefore it was wise to take them away.—— Thus (unwittingly as to God's plans) he took away not merely such men as he wanted and dared not leave behind, but such men as God wanted wherewith to replant his Canaan in his due time.——When seventy years had transpired and the Lord put it into the heart of Cyrus to invite the Jews to return, the sifting process was again put in requisition—this time by making it a *call for volunteers.* Such a call would of course bring out the men of vigor and stamina enough to bear the strain of the fatigues of a four months' journey, to be followed by the labors and hardships of a new settlement; and also men of heart and soul aflame with zeal and with love for the Zion of their fathers—men, moreover, whose faith took hold of God's everlasting covenant. The willing, the earnest and true-hearted—not the easy-going and indifferent—would respond to this call; the men of moral heroism who could welcome sacrifice and hardship for the love they bore to the land of their fathers' sepulchers and for their faith in the yet unfulfilled promises of his covenant.

Some one has said that in looking for seed to plant

---
* I must be allowed to refer the reader for a more full development of these points to my Notes on Ezekiel.

New England, two and a half centuries ago, the Lord sifted two kingdoms (England and Holland) for the best they had. With equal truth it may be said that the Lord of providence, on the same wise principle, sifted the Jewish people twice over to get out the best seed for replanting the land of promise.

The history of the Jews during this captivity is to be gleaned chiefly from the books of the prophets, Jeremiah, Ezekiel, and Daniel — mostly from Ezekiel, because his prophetic life and labors lay among the exiles.

Confirmations of Sacred History from Profane Records and Monuments.

On this point the period from Hezekiah to the captivity should pass under review.

Of Hezekiah's relations to Sennacherib, notice, perhaps sufficiently full, has been taken in my Notes on Isa. 36–39. His history brings to view two other foreign monarchs; Tirhakah, king of Ethiopia (Egypt also) 2 Kings 19: 9; and Merodach Baladan, king of Babylon (2 Kings 20: 12, 13, and 2 Chron. 32: 31). The former is supposed by Rawlinson to be the "Tehrah" of the Egyptian monuments, who reigned over Egypt B. C. 690–667; the third king of Manetho's 25th dynasty. The ancient, never-failing antipathy between Egypt and Assyria would naturally bring him to the help of Hezekiah against Sennacherib if his affairs at home would permit such an expedition abroad.——Merodach of Babylon was in hostile relations toward Assyria, and therefore naturally in sympathy with Hezekiah.*

The king of Assyria who took Manasseh to Babylon should be by his date Esarhaddon, who succeeded Sennacherib on the throne of Assyria.——But why should he take Manasseh to Babylon rather than to Nineveh, the proper capital of Assyria?——In answer, Rawlinson brings out two points:—(1) That on the Assyrian inscriptions Manasseh appears in the list of Esarhaddon's tributaries;—(2) That, according to their inscriptions, Esarhaddon not only took the title of "king of Babylon," but built himself a palace there, in which it must be presumed he occasionally resided. In these

* See Rawlinson's Historical Illustrations, pages 147, 148.

years the relations of Babylon to Nineveh were fluctuating—Babylon rising relatively in strength and importance; sometimes subject to Assyria, but fast attaining the power with which not long after, aided by the Medes, she subdued Nineveh and quite eclipsed her ancient glory.*

Josiah is said (2 Chron. 35: 20-24) to have gone out to war against Pharaoh Necho, then passing through Northern Palestine on his way to the Euphrates. Profane history sustains this point in the sacred record. Herodotus states that "Necho made war by land upon the Syrians and defeated them in a pitched battle at Magdolus."——In this passage "the Syrians" naturally include the Jews as seen by a Greek historian. Magdolus answers to the Hebrew "Megiddo."——Jeremiah states (46: 2) that Nebuchadnezzar (four years later) defeated Pharaoh Necho in a great battle at Carchemish on the Euphrates, and followed up this victory by smiting the land of Egypt (46: 13). With this corresponds the statement of the Scriptures that Necho "came no more out of his land" (2 Kings 24: 7) "for the king of Babylon had taken from the river of Egypt unto the river Euphrates all that pertained to the king of Egypt." Berosus bears his testimony to the same point in a fragment that comes down in Josephus (against Apion 1: 19).

In the next section of Scripture history, Jehoiakim, Jehoiachin, and Zedekiah are brought in contact with Nebuchadnezzar king of Babylon. Does profane history sustain these coincidences?

Profane history locates Nebuchadnezzar precisely here, coming to the throne of Babylon in the fourth year of Jehoiakim—the very year of the first great deportation of captives, and reigning forty-three years. Berosus records that, "having conquered the Jews, he burnt the temple at Jerusalem, and removing the entire people from their homes, transported them to Babylon."——More details on the Chaldean side would probably have come down to our age if the monuments of Babylon had been as enduring as those of Nineveh. For our knowledge of ancient Chaldean history it is unfortunate that the materials of art and architecture in Babylon were signally perishable.

* Rawlinson's Illustrations, page 150.

THE RESTORATION; ITS ANTECEDENTS. 371

Pharaoh Hophra whose name appears (Jer. 44: 30) is recognized in Egyptian authorities under the name *Apries* or *Haifra-het,* ruling over Egypt B. C. 588–586.*

CHAPTER XII.

The Age of the Restoration.

One of the great events of Hebrew history is the restoration of the captive Jews from Babylon to their own land—great as restoring the chosen people again to the land of promise; great as providing for the consummation of God's great plans for the future kingdom of his Messiah; great as the accomplishment of many precious promises and as the pledge for the fulfillment of yet other and greater; great also for its moral results upon the character of the exiled people.

The *duration* of this captivity is commonly put in both prophecy and history at seventy years. Strictly considered, the captivity can not be dated wholly from any one epoch. As we have seen, there were several successive deportations of captives, the earliest having been in the fourth year of Jehoiakim; the latest of

* Geo. Rawlinson in "Historical Illustrations" (p. 154) sums up in these words the coincidences between the sacred record and the profane during the period from the revolt to the captivity.——"They include notices of almost every foreign monarch mentioned in the course of the [sacred] narrative—of Shishak, Zerah, Ben-hadad, Hazael, Mesha, Rezin, Pul, Tiglath-pileser, Shalmanezer, So, Sargon, Sennacherib, Tirhakah, Merodach Baladan, Esarhaddon, Necho, Nebuchadnezzar, Evil-merodach, and Apries;—and of the Jewish or Israelite kings, Omri, Ahab, Jehu, Ahaziah, Menahem, Pekah, Ahaz, Hoshea, Hezekiah, and Manasseh. All these monarchs occur in profane history in the order and at or near the time which the sacred narrative assigns to them. The synchronisms which that narrative supplies are borne out wherever there is any further evidence on the subject. The general condition of the powers which came into contact with the Jews is rightly described; and the fluctuations which they experience, their alternations of glory and depression, are correctly given. No discrepancy occurs between the sacred and the profane throughout the entire period, excepting here and there a chronological one. And these chronological discrepancies are in no case serious."

much note at the point of the capture and destruction of the city, in Zedekiah's eleventh year, eighteen years later than the first. The edict of Cyrus for the restoration was seventy years after the first deportation of captives—the restoration bearing date B. C. 536; the first deportation B. C. 606.

The *antecedents of this restoration* fall naturally into two classes: (a.) The moral and religious; (b.) The political.

(a.) On the moral and religious side, we learn especially from the prophetical books of Jeremiah, Ezekiel, and Daniel, that the Jews in their captivity had humbled themselves greatly before God, were confessing their sins and seeking his face with all their heart. In point as illustrating their moral and spiritual state, see Jer. 29: 10–14, and 30, and 31; Ezek. 36: 24–38, and 37; and Dan. 9, and also Ps. 102: 13–24.

Inasmuch as the captivity occurred at all only for moral reasons, the Lord having caused his people to go into this captivity only for their great sins, so there could be no restoration until their moral state was effectually changed; till their hearts were turned from idols, broken in penitence and confession of sins, and lifted to God in prayer for mercy. On these conditions God had all along promised his pardon and favor. These conditions being in a good degree fulfilled, he returned to his people in mercy, their captive chains were broken, and they were free to return to their land.

(b.) On the political side, God made Cyrus, king of the Medo-Persian Empire, his great instrument—first, to conquer Babylon and annex it to his empire; then to issue his decree inviting all Jews who would to return to their own land; particularly encouraging them to rebuild their temple and aiding them in this enterprise. The terms of this decree are memorable:

2. Thus saith Cyrus king of Persia, The LORD God of heaven hath given me all the kingdoms of the earth; and he hath charged me to build him a house at Jerusalem, which *is* in Judah.

3. Who *is there* among you of all his people? his God be with him, and let him go up to Jerusalem, which *is* in Judah, and build the house of the LORD God of Israel, (he *is* the God,) which *is* in Jerusalem.

4. And whosoever remaineth in any place where he sojourneth, let the men of his place help him with silver, and with gold, and with

THE RESTORATION; ITS ANTECEDENTS. 373

goods, and with beasts, besides the freewill offering for the house of God that *is* in Jerusalem.

Jewish tradition holds that Daniel, occupying a high position in the court of Cyrus, brought to his attention the prophecies of Isaiah which even name Cyrus as God's servant (Isa. 44: 26–28, and 45: 1–4).

26. That confirmeth the word of his servant, and performeth the counsel of his messengers; that saith to Jerusalem, Thou shalt be inhabited; and to the cities of Judah, Ye shall be built, and I will raise up the decayed places thereof:
27. That saith to the deep, Be dry, and I will dry up thy rivers:
28. That saith of Cyrus, *He is* my shepherd, and shall perform all my pleasure: even saying to Jerusalem, Thou shalt be built; and to the temple, Thy foundation shall be laid.
1. Thus saith the LORD to his anointed, to Cyrus, whose right hand I have holden, to subdue nations before him; and I will loose the loins of kings, to open before him the two-leaved gates; and the gates shall not be shut:
2. I will go before thee and make the crooked places straight: I will break in pieces the gates of brass, and cut in sunder the bars of iron:
3. And I will give thee the treasures of darkness, and hidden riches of secret places, that thou mayest know that I, the LORD, which call *thee* by thy name, *am* the God of Israel.
4. For Jacob my servant's sake, and Israel mine elect, I have even called thee by thy name: I have surnamed thee, though thou hast not known me.

There is no good reason to question this Jewish tradition. We know that Daniel stood high at the court of Cyrus; had ready access to his ear; was familiar with Hebrew prophecy; was aware that God's time for the restoration had come and was laboring and praying for this result. In fact Daniel was raised up of God for this emergency as truly as Cyrus. The men whom God makes for a great emergency always come to time and do their duty.——The Jewish tradition adequately accounts for facts otherwise not easily if even possibly accounted for. Hence this imperial summons to all who recognized themselves as God's people—"Who is there among you of all his people? His God be with him and let him go up," etc. Wherever a Jew is found sojourning among us (Ezra 1: 4), let his neighbors aid him with silver, gold, goods, and beasts of burden, etc., and let that temple be rebuilt.

This decree paved the way for the restoration. The policy of the Chaldean kings was scarcely less hostile to the restoration than Pharaoh's to the release of the Hebrews from their bondage. It was therefore of the Lord to break down that policy by breaking down the throne that worked it and ruled under it. The Lord not only needed Cyrus but called him; not only called but *made* him. Cyrus was his servant—made all that he was, to do his Master's pleasure. He did it.

The History of the Restored People.

This is found chiefly in the books of Ezra and of Nehemiah; with some new light from the three prophets of the restoration, Haggai, Zechariah, Malachi; and the fifth book of the Psalter, viz., Ps. 107-150—all compiled and some composed, during this age.

The *book of Ezra* may on good grounds be accepted as written or compiled by himself. It has always borne his name in a way which assumes a standing tradition of his authorship. From chap. 7, onward to the close he was an important actor in the great events here recorded, and therefore probably the original author. The first six chapters are largely made up of public documents which must have been within his easy reach. The events which transpired before he arrived from Babylon may have been put on record first by other hands; *e. g.*, chap. 1 by Daniel; chap. 2 is a public document which the proper officers should prepare; chaps. 3-6 we may ascribe to Haggai or some one in like position. On this theory, Ezra's labor on these chapters (1-6) would be only that of compiler.——Moreover being by profession a "scribe of the law of God," he was of all *the man* to compile and prepare this book. We have seen good reason to assume that he wrote and compiled the books of Chronicles. Much more should we ascribe to his hand this book.

The state document in 7: 12-26 is in the Chaldaic dialect; also the passage 4: 8, to 6: 18. The rest of the book is in Hebrew, yet with a few Chaldaic words, indicating the age of the composition.

If we study with care the circumstances of the restored people and the matters—political, moral and religious— that were vital to their prosperity, we shall see that the subjects presented in this book of Ezra were of prime importance. Let us pass them rapidly under review.

DECREE OF CYRUS; GENEALOGICAL RECORD. 375

Appropriately, the great decree of Cyrus opens the book (1: 1–4). This decree must have stirred the hearts of God's true children to their depths (vs. 5, 6). All the chief fathers and those whose hearts God had touched sprang to respond to this call. Those Jews who did not join the caravan, and perhaps others than Jews, put in their aid in money, valuable goods and beasts of burden. Cyrus restored those vessels from the old temple which Nebuchadnezzar brought away—catalogued here (vs. 9–11).

Chap. 2 is the *enrollment* of the first band of returning exiles, by genealogy. It was of high importance to trace out and record the pedigree of these men. Let it be shown and known that they are indeed *Jews*—the Lord's chosen people; heirs of the promises made to the fathers. To bring out these relations will be wholesome and quickening to their hearts. Scenes of hardship and sacrifice are before them. They will endure the better if they recall their noble parentage, and remember that they go to replant the land of their fathers' sepulchers, and carry out the grand purposes under which God gave Canaan to their fathers, and all "the sure mercies of David."——A few families of doubtful or discredited genealogy are specially noted (vs. 59, 61–63). Their lack of pedigree would enhance the value of a clean record to those who had it.

The total number (v. 64) was 42,360. Besides these there were 7,337 servants; and 200 singers, making a total of 49,897—within a small fraction of 50,000. The number of their domestic animals, beasts of burden (vs. 66, 67), gives some idea of their property and of the means of conveyance for their heavy goods; for the infirm, for some of the women and children. The masses must have made the journey on foot.

Chap. 3 presents the people arrived and somewhat settled in the land—ready when the memorable seventh month opened to convene for the feast of tabernacles. Assembling on the first day of the month, they had time to prepare the great altar for burnt-offerings. Then they resumed the regular morning and evening sacrifice. Noticeably, one reason assigned for preparing this great altar was "their fear of the people of those countries" (v. 3). They needed God on their side against enemies so formidable, and therefore

must establish his worship promptly and heartily.——
Presently they commenced their preparations for rebuilding the temple, contracting for timber and materials with the men of Tyre and Zidon, as Solomon had done for the first temple (v. 7). Ezra gives carefully the *date* when the foundations were laid—in the second year and second month of their restoration. Then the foundations were laid with appropriate services of thanksgiving and praise. In this service the emotions of the great congregation rose high, expressed with ringing shouts of joy as well as songs of praise and the glorious cymbals and trumpets.——But some of the more ancient men—the venerable fathers who had seen the first temple in its glory—were sad and tearful, even to "weeping with a loud voice." Ah, it reminded them of other and better days! Even in the foundations they saw how far inferior this temple must be—not to say that the reminiscences awakened would bear their thought across the great sorrows of their captivity to the agony of those scenes of fire and blood and desolation when the city fell and the temple went down in ashes. What a tempest of emotions!——But the young were joyous to have any temple at all. It was so great an advance upon the sad privations of those dreary years of their Chaldean bondage. So there were shouts of joy and wailings of sorrow, blended in touching chorus. "The sound thereof was heard afar off."—— Was not this human and earthly? It will not be so in that other state where "God shall wipe tears away from every eye."

Chap. 4 brings to view opposition—artful, violent, formidable. It came from "the people of the land" (v. 4); *i. e.*, from the people who were there before the Jews returned—the Samaritan population. They said they were brought there by Esarhaddon (4: 2); and of various nations (vs. 9, 10). They first proposed to join the Jews in building the temple and (supposably) in the worship of God there (v. 2). This being rejected (wisely), they sought to traduce and misrepresent the Jews at the Persian court. They said that this city had been of old in rebellion against the great kingdoms on the Euphrates—not precisely against Persia, but Babylon; that when they had rebuilt their temple and made their city strong, they would withhold tribute from the

OPPOSITION FROM SAMARITANS. 377

Persian kings and detach from their sway all the countries west of the Euphrates. There had been kings (they said) who had held all the country even to the great river—referring probably to David and Solomon. By these artful representations, they obtained a rescript to arrest the building of the city. The work on the temple ceased.

When and how long was the temple-building suspended?
The answer turns upon the identity of the Persian kings named in this chapter; viz.: Darius, vs. 5, 24; Ahasuerus, v. 6; and Artaxerxes, vs. 7, 8, 11, 23.—— Various opinions have been held as to these kings, the preponderance being in favor of the theory herein advocated, viz.—that this Darius is Darius Hystaspes, fourth king of this dynasty, counting Cyrus as the first; that Ahasuerus is Cambyses, the second in order; and that this Artaxerxes is the third, better known as Smerdis the Magian. [For the convenience of the reader I place in the margin a table of this Persian dynasty, so far as to include the monarchs who appear in the books of Ezra, Nehemiah, and Esther.*]

The efforts of these adversaries seem to have been unsuccessful with Cambyses, but successful with Smerdis the Magian, whose religious notions were entirely adverse to the Jewish faith. His reign being short, the entire period of suspended work on the temple could not have been more than two years.

In Ezra 5, the prophets Haggai and Zechariah appear, calling the people to resume the rebuilding of the temple. Their books of prophecy concur with the history to this point. Under the inspiration of their prophetic messages and personal influence the work was resumed in the second year of Darius Hystaspes. Then a new opposition arose. The leaders in this instance (described vs. 3, 6) were the high officials (governors) over Syria and Palestine.——These opponents were apparently

* NAME.	REIGNED.	NO. OF YRS.
Cyrus	B. C. 536–529	7
Cambyses [Ahasuerus of Ezra 4: 6]	529–522	7½
Smerdis or Gomates, [the Artaxerxes of Ez. 4: 7, 8, 11, 23]	522–521	7 mos.
Darius Hystaspes	521–485	36
Xerxes [the Ahasuerus of Esther]	485–474 or 464	11 or 21
Artaxerxes Longimanus	474 (or 464)–424	50 or 40

less virulent and more candid than the Samaritans seen in chap. 4, and far less scornful and bitter than Sanballat and his associates, as seen in Neh. 4 and 6. It is well that the reader should keep distinct in his mind these three sets of adversaries—the first and second, withstanding the work on the temple; the third, the work on the city walls. This second class of opponents came to Jerusalem in person and demanded of the elders their authority for this rebuilding; and asked their names that they might be properly indicted before the king. This gave those elders an opportunity to refer to the decree of Cyrus under which they were acting (5: 11–15). Consequently this letter of complaint to King Darius carried with it its own antidote. It called for an investigation of the records of Cyrus' reign where Darius found the original decree and forthwith confirmed it, ordering Tatnai and his associates not only to desist from all opposition, but positively to help the work forward, making appropriations from the king's revenue for this purpose. Under these auspicious circumstances, coupled with aid and impulse from the prophets Haggai and Zechariah (referred to again 6: 14), the work moved forward rapidly to its completion in the sixth year of Darius.*

This chapter closes with the dedication of the temple —a joyful scene of glad and grateful thanksgiving to their God for his favoring hand in this work.†

Opening chapter 7, we must notice that a very considerable interval of time lies between the dedication of the temple in the sixth year of Darius, and this mission of Ezra in the seventh year of Artaxerxes. It must include—from the reign of Darius thirty years; of Xerxes (as commonly estimated) twenty-one; of Artaxerxes seven; total, fifty-eight. This was Ezra's introduction to the Jews in Judah. The history gives his genealogy

* The "Artaxerxes" of v. 14 must be, not the king of that name in chap. 4, but he who appears under this name in Ezra 7: 7, 11, 12, and often in Nehemiah—the successor of Xerxes. He is referred to here not because he bore any part in this first building of the temple, since this was completed many years before his reign began; but because he aided in rebuilding the city and was fully in sympathy with Cyrus and Darius.

† That the king of Persia should be referred to (v. 22) under the title of "king of Assyria" is due to the fact that his kingdom embraced all the provinces which originally constituted that empire.

from Aaron; also his profession as "a ready scribe of the law of Moses," "who had prepared his heart to seek the law of the Lord and to do it, and to teach in Israel statutes and judgments" (vs. 6, 10). The royal letters patent under which he was sent refer to his character in corresponding terms (v. 12). These papers are given in full, minutely defining his duties and specifying his powers, viz., to "inquire concerning Judah and Jerusalem," and under this right of inquiry, doubtless, to reform abuses and make wrong things right; to appoint magistrates and officers; also to convey to the holy city the free-will offerings of Jews yet living in their eastern homes; to draw upon the king's treasurers in the western provinces within certain specified but generous limits (vs. 21, 22), and to exempt from government tax all who ministered in the temple and its worship. The king speaks as one who has at least *some* faith in the powers of the God of Israel and who would propitiate his favor through the prayers and worship of his chosen people (v. 23). "Whatsoever is commanded by the God of heaven, let it be diligently done for the house of the God of heaven; for why should there be wrath against the realm of the king and his sons?"——For this remarkable letter, conferring powers so liberal in a spirit so kind, Ezra appropriately renders thanks to God: "Blessed be the Lord God of our fathers who hath put this in the king's heart to beautify the house of the Lord which is in Jerusalem (v. 27), and who hath extended such mercy to me before the king, his counselors and mighty princes."

Ezra (chap. 8) gave with great minuteness the genealogy of those Jews who went to Judea with him (vs. 1–14). Finding no Levites in the company, he sought and through a kind providence found some men of great worth whom he attached to his party. The journey being dangerous, he relates with touching simplicity that he was ashamed to ask the king for an armed convoy because he had previously said—"The hand of our God is upon all them for good who seek him; but his power and his wrath are against all them that forsake him." This involved the nice question whether faith in God's protecting hand should be held to supersede a guard of armed men. Ezra felt the delicacy of the question so deeply that he could not bring himself even to suggest to the king to send a guard; but turned to fasting and prayer instead. The Lord heard their prayer. Ezra joyfully testified—"The hand of our God was upon us and delivered us from the hand of the enemy, and of such as lay in wait by the way" (vs. 23–31). As they were intrusted with valuable property to convey to Jerusalem, involving no small responsibility for its safe-keeping and transmission, Ezra designated twelve priests as treasurers; consigned this property to their hand by definite count and weight; and when they arrived at Jerusalem, saw it weighed and counted over into the hands of the proper officers there—an example not to be despised. ——The time occupied in this journey—from the twelfth day of the first month (8: 31) to the first day of the fifth month (7: 9)—suggests that they took the long route—up the valley of the Euphrates to Carchemish; thence crossing the desert at its narrowest point into the valley of the Orontes and so entering Palestine from the north by "the entering in of Hamath"—which though long (900 miles) was the usual route of armies and of large caravans. Moreover, some time may have been lost in detours to avoid dangerous localities, or known enemies.

Intermarriages with Idolaters. (Ezra 9 and 10.)

The first greetings were scarcely passed and their fiducial trusts disposed of, when Ezra found painful work before him. Evils of most perilous sort had been admitted into the colony. The Jews and even their priests and Levites had been intermarrying with idol-worshiping families of Canaanite and other adjacent tribes. He learned this first from some of the princes. They stated "that the hand of the princes and rulers had been chief in this trespass" (10: 2).——Such intermarriages led toward idolatry with a social power practically resistless. The only safety lay therefore in arresting this thing instantly; divorcing all heathen wives at any cost of feeling or of family ties, and in taking a stand that should put an end forever to this violation of the law of Moses and of God. Ezra himself was the writer of this narrative and expressed in his own words his grief and horror when he heard these things (9: 3, 4): "I rent my garment and my mantle and plucked off the hair of my head and of my beard, and sat down astonished. There gathered about me all who trembled at the words of the God of Israel because of this transgression. Before them I sat astonished till the evening sacrifice"—late in the afternoon—the usual hour of prayer. In a case so sad, so critical, so perilous to the dearest interests of Zion, what could such a man do but pray! At the hour of prayer he fell upon his knees, spread out his hands unto the Lord his God, and then poured forth his heart in prayer. Here are his words, expressing shame as well as grief in view of these sins; confessing them most unqualifiedly, reciting appropriately the history of God's great mercies to his people, every remembrance of which served to intensify his sense of the great sin of his people, referring also to the admonitions God had sent through his prophets—standing appalled before this great sin in fear of God's righteous judgments—appalled, yet imploring divine mercy.——Manifestly this scene of prayer—so sincere, evincing such grief and horror toward this sin—moved the people greatly and melted many hearts. It opened their eyes to see great sin where they had seen nothing very wrong before. They saw that they had incurred the wrath of God, and their souls quivered with fear. Best of all, they saw that something must be done, and resolved it should be—to wipe out this iniquity. It is always easier to get into sin than to get out of it. In a sin of this sort, the steps backward to undo the wrong must be specially difficult. But the hearts of the people were touched—"the people wept very sore." Leading men cried aloud, "We have transgressed against our God and have taken strange wives of the people of the land; yet now there is hope in Israel concerning this thing" (10: 2). Wisely they suggest that this reform be entered upon in concert; that all the people be pledged on the spot, while their hearts were tenderly and solemnly affected, to go through with this reform as rapidly as possible. It must take time, for it was vital, (1) To bring in all the actual cases; (2) To investigate each several case thoroughly; (3) To make out the proper writing of divorcement, and settlement of estate. But let the whole matter be determined past all recall, and measures be taken to carry it through with the utmost expedition. Accordingly by proclamation, all the people were summoned to Jerusalem within three days on pain of confiscation of all their property and of exclusion from the congregation (vs. 7, 8). All the people of Judah and Benjamin were convened within the time. It was the twentieth day of the ninth month (December)—the depth of their rainy season. "All the people sat in the street [court] of the temple, trembling because of this matter, and for the great rain."——This pouring rain in the chill of bleak December put the outside face of nature in sympathy with their sad and weeping hearts. But no discomforts might postpone action in a case so critical and momentous. Ezra stood up before them and said—"Ye have transgressed and taken strange wives to increase the trespass of Israel. Now, therefore, make confession to the Lord God of your fathers and do his pleasure; let confession be followed by swift reform; separate yourselves from the people of the land and from your strange wives." Then all the congregation with one voice responded—"As thou hast said, so must we do."——Thus they committed themselves to this trying but imperative duty. They said moreover—This will require time: we can not stand in this rain to see it all done; let a commission be appointed to investigate and act on each case; let the proper authorities in every city take up the matter —prepare and bring forward each several case, and so let the work be carried through "until the fierce wrath of our God be turned from us" (vs. 12-14).

In the result Ezra and certain chiefs of the fathers, were constituted a commission or high court for the transaction of this business. After two months' labor they reported the business brought to an end.——The narrative closes with a list of the parties who, having been implicated in this sin, had put away their strange wives—some of them having become fathers of strange children.——In v. 15 our translators (probably) missed the sense of the Hebrew word "stood" (putting it "were employed"). With the preposition which follows it, the meaning is—*stood against*, opposed. Only these two men opposed; two others helped them; but, as the next verse states, the children of the captivity as a body did as they had pledged themselves to do.

The immense majority were steadfast and carried it through.

Such are the salient points of this reform, seen in their external aspects. The moral aspects deserve a few moments' thought.——Throughout these scenes Ezra's character stands forth radiant in goodness, solid in the best elements of firmness and strength. But just arrived from his far eastern home, charged with grave responsibilities, and we may presume happy in sanguine anticipations, he had not dreamed of the presence of such sin among the people of God. How was he astounded and horrified to see that the people were lapsing back so soon and so fearfully into that ruinous idolatry from which he had hoped and supposed a seventy years' captivity had cleansed them! Alas, that so soon hopes and promises so fair should be darkly clouded! He has told us how he was ashamed, alarmed, horrified; and how his heart turned away from all else to God in imploring supplication and confession, with strong crying and tears. Ps. 119—with very high probability from his own heart and hand—witnesses to his heart experiences: "Horror hath taken hold upon me because of the wicked who forsake thy law" (v. 53); "Rivers of waters run down mine eyes because men keep not thy law" (v. 136). So deeply is his heart in sympathy with God; so entirely has he adjusted his whole moral nature to the revelations of God which come to him in his pure and holy law! This sound and solid piety—utterly unlike mere sentimentalism, high above the best humanitarianism—accepts God's law as reflecting down from heaven to us his real character, and therefore knows no higher—indeed, no other standard for human duty than this.

Note also with how firm a tread he marches straight through this fearfully perplexing, trying scene. Think how many families must be rent asunder, how many ties cemented in the connubial relation must be severed. Think of children borne away from affectionate fathers, to be of their homes and households no more! Yet nothing less than this could save the colony from the ruin of idolatry; nothing less could redeem them back to the favor and protection of the God of their fathers' covenant. Therefore it must be done. Many heart-strings must quiver; many tenderest cords of earthly love be snapped in sunder. It costs fearfully to retrace the steps of a sinning life; yet there is no alternative but duty or death! Ezra believes in the wisdom of duty. Such an example of manhood coupled with piety deserves its place in this inspired history. Let us be thankful to find it here.

It is, moreover, refreshing to notice that such men have power. The hearts of the nation were swayed and melted by the manifest goodness, tenderness, holy zeal, intrepid firmness, of this one man. A great national sin which imperiled the very life of the restored community was arrested, and the nation once more saved. A seventy years' captivity had fearfully scourged the nation for the sin of idolatry and seemed to have wrought a wholesome horror of that sin; but here and now the same sin was stealthily insinuating itself under a new guise and alluring them to ruin. It may be presumed they did not think of these intermarriages as involving idolatry. All the greater therefore was their danger. It was of the Lord's wisdom as well as love that this evil was arrested so soon. Sad to say, we shall see in the story of Nehemiah that it broke forth yet once more.

Nehemiah.

The book of Nehemiah is a natural sequel to the book of Ezra, continuing the history of the restored people yet a few years further.——On the point of authorship there seems to be no ground for a question. The author says he is Nehemiah: "The words of Nehemiah, the son of Hachaliah." The book is written in the first person as if it were his private diary or journal; indeed so private that it records not only public events but private personal experiences. The only question of criticism as to author and intent would seem to be whether it were not originally written for a private diary rather than for publication. The extreme simplicity and the exquisite touches of personal experience are so very prominent as to give (may we not say?) some plausibility to this opinion. Yet if accepted, the book would be none the less valuable—none the less truthful and worthy of confidence.

The *date* of these events is fortunately beyond question. This Artaxerxes is the Persian king distinguished by his specialty—"Longimanus" (the long-handed), son and successor of Xerxes, sometimes called "the great." In his seventh year Ezra went from his court to Jerusalem. In his twentieth year Nehemiah followed; to remain twelve years and then go back to his eastern home, and subsequently return to Judea again.

Nehemiah's Story.

This is—that he was the king's cup-bearer—in an oriental court a position of very considerable responsibilities. It brought him into near and confidential relations to the king; gave him free access to his person, at least on frequent occasions, and seems to have carried with it more or less of official trusts.

Being visited at his home in the palace at Shushan by certain brethren of his from Judea, he inquired of them concerning the Jews of the restoration and concerning Jerusalem. To his great sorrow, he learned that the remnant there were in deep affliction and reproach; that the city walls were broken down and the gates burned. It affected him deeply. He wrote: "I sat down and wept and mourned certain days, and fasted and prayed before the God of heaven." His prayer is here on record (1: 5–11), in every point pertinent, earnest, humble, free in confession; fervent in supplication —closing with the request for "mercy in the sight of this man," *i. e.*, the king. He had some foreshadowings of help through the king's favor. Soon called before the king with wine, his heart still heavy with this fresh sorrow, his countenance would betray it. Simply as a child he tells his story: "I had never been sad in the king's presence before." The king said, "Why is thy countenance sad, since thou art not sick? This must be sorrow of heart." It was a critical moment. Nehemiah was "sore afraid." A king's favor is sometimes capricious. He had some hope of help from the king, but all might fail, and the issues were so great and critical that his heart trembled. But his answer was frank and full—" How can I be otherwise than sad when the city, the place of my fathers' sepulchers, lieth waste?" What would you have? said the king. Oh, what a moment! Quick as thought, his soul goes forth to God for help: "So I prayed to the God of heaven." He does not mean that leaving the question in suspense he withdrew to his closet for prayer; but this, that his mental eye was lifted to God in that spontaneous outgoing of prayer and trust which every Christian finds so natural and so precious. It proved that this "king's heart was in the hand of the Lord to turn it as he would"—and he gave Nehemiah all he could ask; leave of absence; most liberal aid; letters to his subordinate officers west of the Euphrates; authority to draw for timber and materials for the city walls and gates. The king provided also an armed escort.——Before he reached Jerusalem he met with adversaries bitterly hostile to the restored Jews, and grieved that one should appear clothed with royal authority to seek their welfare. This third set of adversaries, named here—Sanballat the Horonite (a Moabite of Horonaim), Tobiah the Ammonite, and Geshem the Arabian—represented (apparently) the old antipathy of those nations. They come to view often in the sequel of this story.

Arrived at Jerusalem, Nehemiah gave three days to rest and to a general introduction to his national brethren; then went out alone by night to examine for himself the state of the city walls. After this exploration he was prepared to say to the assembled priests and nobles: Ye see the distress we are in; how Jerusalem lieth waste; its gates burned down: "come, let us build up the walls of Jerusalem that we be no more a reproach."

As to the need and value of city walls and gates, the reader will be too intelligent to estimate it by comparison with our own times and country. That weak Jewish colony was surrounded with enemies, armed, warlike, addicted to robbery, plunder, murder. The fact that these walls were broken down and these gates burned was itself a testimony that the people were unsafe save in a fortified city. The very existence of the community was imperiled. All the precious interests garnered in that little colony of restored Jews demanded the protection of rebuilt walls and restored gates and bars.——Backing up his exhortation to the city fathers to arise and build, Nehemiah told them of the good hand of his God upon him and of the king's encouraging words. They responded, "Let us arise and build." "And they strengthened their hands for this good work."——At this point their adversaries appear again. Having heard of the scheme for rebuilding, "they laughed us to scorn, and despised us and said "What is this thing that ye do?" As if to carry the whole question by assuming this rebuilding to be treasonable, they added, "Will ye rebel against the king?" They probably knew better than they wished to know that the king sent Nehemiah for the very purpose of rebuilding these walls. But artful and false assumptions are the science of wicked men. Conscious of being powerless at the royal court, their chief reliance is upon scorn and lies and violence by arms if they get the opportunity.

Chap. 3 details minutely the distinct work done by each considerable group of citizens: by the priests; the nobles and head men—a grand personal record, of special value in those days when names signified known men, though in this respect valueless to us to whom the parties are chiefly unknown. We may profitably notice that mostly the people of the city built each over against their own house—an arrangement at once convenient as being economical of their time, and inspiring as giving them a sense of working every man for his own as well as for the public interest. ——The careful reader would notice the not quite honorable record of certain Tekoites (v. 5); that though the people wrought, yet "their nobles put not their necks to the work of their Lord." Did Nehemiah purposely make the word "*their*" emphatic when he said, not the Lord but "*their*" Lord? as if to suggest that they little deserved to be accounted noble men when they so dishonored *their* Lord. Such aristocracy, so exhibited, Nehemiah held in no great esteem.——Another party of laborers deserve from us a more honorable notice—(they of v. 12) "Shallum, the ruler of the half part of Jerusalem; *he and his daughters*." He was not too high in dignity to put his hand and neck even to the Lord's work. But what of "his daughters"? Of almost royal blood, and of true royal soul, they gave the work at least their hearty sympathy. Did they help to clear away the rubbish, or to cut the stone or to carry mortar? Enough, we must assume, to show that heart as well as hand was in the work.——After reading such a chapter it should not suprise us that in a wonderfully short time the city walls were up, the gates hung, and the holy city once more in her strength and glory.

In chap. 4 Nehemiah resumes the story of this rebuilding and gives some facts that occurred during the progress of the work, setting forth especially the opposition which sought, chiefly by scorn and plots for violence, to frustrate the enterprise.——Sanballat, their leader, hearing that the city walls were going up, was hotly indignant. He "mocked the Jews." "He spake before his brethren and the army of Samaria," obviously to excite them to join him in assault by force of arms. Tobiah the Ammonite was bitterly scornful. He thought a fox's tread would break down their stone wall!——Under these insults and dangers, which way does Nehemiah turn? First of all, to the Christian's first and only refuge—*to God* in *prayer.* "Hear, O God, for we are despised; and turn their reproach upon their own head." Having prayed, they kept on building the wall. Soon all the wall was joined together (all the breaches closed) "unto the half thereof"—*i. e.*, raised to half the contemplated height (v. 6), "for the people had a mind to work." They put their souls into it. There is a will-power which pushes the hardest work along and bears the heaviest enterprises rapidly through.

Next, their enemies (specified v. 7) conspired in force to make an armed assault upon the city and its rebuilders. Nehemiah plans the defense; first, to seek help from God; next, to set a watch day and night. Three special difficulties are noticed: (a.) "Judah"—the Jews of the country outside the city—are quite discouraged. "The strength of the workmen is failing; there is much rubbish in the way; we are not able to build the wall."*——(b.) The adversaries are planning a surprise.——(c.) The Jews dwelling by them (*e. g.*, in the vicinity of Samaria) come to us many times, solic-

* The feeble heart of the outlying Jewish population explains the purpose of the scorn manifested by Sanballat and Tobiah. They were purposely acting on these feeble souls to dissuade them from the great enterprise. They did not expect their scorn and insults would disturb Nehemiah directly; they did hope to draw off feeble-hearted Jews.

iting our laborers from the country to leave the work and go home.*

Then Nehemiah arranged his men by their families, all armed (v. 13); he sought to inspire their faith in God (v. 14); he divided his laborers into two grand divisions, half to bear arms and half to build wall; of the builders each held a weapon of war in one hand and wrought with the other—every workman with sword girded on his thigh; the trumpeter standing by Nehemiah as commander-in-chief, and all the nobles being under orders to hasten to whatever point the trumpet-blast should call. Yet further, he took the precaution to have every man with his servant lodge by night within the city, to be ready to repel a night assault if made.——Thus this godly warrior and his servants wrought and stood guard, no man laying off his clothes by night, and no man going after water save with war-weapons in his hand.† Such precautions and such unceasing vigilance seem to have forestalled the threatened assault. Thus with labor, watchfulness, and prayer, the great work was ere long completed.

A Chapter on the Poor and the Rich.

Neh. 5 has a theme peculiarly its own, unlike that of any other chapter in the Bible—*The mutual relations of rich and poor*, in a season of general scarcity. "The poor ye have always with you" (said the Great Teacher). The inequalities, property-wise, which will exist everywhere, constitute a part of the moral trial of all men.

This Jewish colony was fortunate, not to say blest, in that it was rather a brotherhood than a mere aggregation of families; for they lived and were there for a common object; enduring common privations; opposed by common enemies—in this respect illustrating not badly all Christian churches in their fraternal and life-work relations.——Here in Judea were dearth, suffering for bread, and complaints of the poor against their

---

* This is plainly the meaning of v. 12, translated badly in our English version. The margin has it better: From whatever place ye come, return to us: go home and abandon this hard and hopeless enterprise. The Septuagint has it well: "Return from all places unto us."

† This I take to be the sense of the last clause of v. 23, the marginal reading being with the Hebrew.

richer brethren. The poor came to Nehemiah; "there was a great cry of the people and of their wives against their Jewish brethren." Some with large families could not fill so many mouths; some had mortgaged every thing for bread; some had borrowed to pay state taxes; some had been obliged to sell sons and daughters into slavery, and had no means to redeem them because their lands too were gone for debt. And they could not tell this sad tale without suggesting that their children were of their own flesh and blood—as dear to them as sons and daughters were to their richer brethren who had been buying and selling their neighbor's children.—— Nehemiah, good man that he was, heard this with sorrow and indignation. He "was very angry when he heard their cry in these words." He thought the case over (perhaps he supposed it were his own); he rebuked those rich men for their oppressive usury; he brought face to face before them the many who were suffering so cruelly under their oppressions. He thought proper to speak of his own case: We have done all we could to redeem our Jewish brethren from personal slavery to foreign slave-holders; but ye are enslaving your own brethren. They could say nothing in reply. He said —Ye bring on us the reproach of our enemies; this is a disgrace to our religion and to the God we worship. I pray you, restore to your brethren those lands, those enslaved children, and that exorbitant interest—"the hundredth part"—one per cent. (payable monthly, we must presume—equal to twelve per cent. per annum), which ye have charged, not for money loaned merely, but for corn—the necessaries of life.

We may rejoice to see that they responded promptly— "We will restore; and will require nothing of them; so will we do as thou sayest." But lest second thought should bring on the grip of covetousness again, Nehemiah called in the priests to administer the sacred oath that they should fulfill this promise. Also to add the force of his own noble heart, he shook his lap and said; "So God shake out every man from his house and from his labor" (all the fruits of it) "who performs not this promise." There was some public feeling there, for all the congregation cried "Amen; and praised the Lord."

In the sequel, Nehemiah thought proper to speak of

his own personal management and finances since he had been among them—twelve years. He had taken no salary as governor, because the taxes on the people were very heavy. He and all his servants had labored on the city walls without pay. He had boarded an average of one hundred and fifty constantly at his table, besides transient visitors. Of course he must have drawn heavily on previous accumulations in his Persian home. Noble man! He expected no reward from his Jewish brethren or from any fellow-men. He only looked upward: "Think upon me, O my God, for good, according to all that I have done for this people." No doubt this prayer was answered.——Let us hope that this chapter will not be valueless to mankind. Whom does it rebuke; and whom does it bless?

In chap. 6 Nehemiah resumes the story (unfinished in chap. 4) of the opposition to their work on the city walls. First, when Sanballat and his friends heard that the work was too far advanced for their success by an armed assault, and the city too vigilantly guarded to admit of a night surprise, they sent Nehemiah an invitation (or challenge) to meet them in the plain of Ono*— they did not say for what purpose. Nehemiah was not caught in this trap. He remarks here: "They thought to do me mischief." Probably they were plotting his assassination. Yet he replied with no lack of civility: "I am doing a great work, so that I can not come down; why should the work cease while I leave it and come down to you?" This was reason enough; was manly, reasonable, and withal, safe. The principle on which it rests, applied in a thousand relationships with the world, would save Christian laborers from many a sore temptation and many a grievous fall. Let us attend diligently to our own great work, and not listen to invitations to "the plain of Ono."——Yet they sent four times—only to get the same answer every time.——The fifth messenger brought an open letter from Sanballat (copied out in this narrative) charging Nehemiah with designs wholly treasonable and ambitious—to rebel against the king of Persia and to make himself king in Judah. Withal he threatened to report this charge

*Ono appears (1 Chron. 8: 12) in the list of towns on the northern border of Benjamin, some twenty-five or thirty miles distant from Jerusalem.

to the king. On the basis of this charge, trumped up for his own purposes, he again requests an interview "to take counsel together!" The stupid fellow!—did he think to pass himself off upon Nehemiah as his personal friend, anxious to aid him with some kind advice?——Nehemiah's reply is put squarely — Not a word of truth in what you say; no such things are done as thou sayest; these charges are born of thine own brain.——Their purpose, Nehemiah said, was to alarm the builders, weaken their hands; stop their work. Therefore, as one whose habit is to look to God in every emergency, he cries: "Now, therefore, O God, strengthen my hands. What time my enemies and thine would weaken, do thou give strength!"

Other trials were sprung upon him as he came into the house of one Shemaiah. This man had been so frightened by the threats of Sanballat that he shut himself within his house as in a castle. He presses Nehemiah to do the same. "Let us gather into the temple," said he, and make that our castle, "for they will come by night and slay thee." His answer gives us those memorable heroic words: "*Should such a man as I flee?* And who is there, that being as I am would go into the temple to save his life? I will not go in." Not so much because he would not believe there was danger; but rather because, if there was danger, it behooved him to face it as a man and a hero! To have fled himself would have been the signal for all timid souls to flee likewise; and what could come of such fleeing but ruin to their enterprise?——He adds—"I perceived that God had not sent him to me with these words; but Sanballat and Tobiah had hired him." Indeed! they were arch fellows, and omitted no device to ensnare him to his ruin.——One more prayer: "O my God; think thou upon Tobiah and Sanballat according to these their works; and on the prophetess Noadiah and the rest of the prophets who would have put me in fear." The satanic arts of the false prophets had not yet ceased in Israel.

The long list of special trials closes at last with the fact of *secret correspondence* carried on between some of the nobles of Judah and those arch enemies, favored by the intermarriage of their respective families.——Tobiah the Ammonite led in this correspondence.

The work on the city walls was at length finished joyfully, having occupied fifty-two days—pushed with untiring diligence, and the energy of a noble enthusiasm. We shall meet a somewhat extended account of the joyous dedication of these walls below (chap. 12: 27–43).

Nehemiah states (chap. 7) that he put his brother Hanani and Hananiah, ruler of the palace, in charge jointly of Jerusalem, adding his testimony as to Hanani that he was a "faithful man and feared God above many"—the right man for grave responsibilities. Their instructions in regard to opening and closing the gates show that the danger of violence from enemies had not entirely ceased. Safety still demanded vigilance.

This genealogical table of the first company of returning Jews (substantially the same as in Ezra 2) may be brought out here in connection with measures for filling up the city—its population being entirely too sparse for the best interest of the entire colony. We shall see more on this subject in chap. 11 and 12.

In Neh. 8 we see an immense assembly convened on the first day of the seventh month; their public services commencing with the reading of the Scriptures by Ezra the scribe. As he read he gave such exposition as the change of dialect from Hebrew to Chaldee—then the spoken language of the people—required. It is said— "He read in the book of the law distinctly and *gave the sense*, and caused them to understand the reading" (v. 8). It was a memorable day. This reading continued (so said) "from morning till mid-day, and the ears of all the people were attentive unto the book of the law."——The accompanying devotional exercises are described thus: "And Ezra blessed the Lord, the Great God. And all the people answered, Amen, amen, with lifting up their hands; and they bowed their heads and worshiped the Lord with their faces to the ground"—a scene of no little animation; less dull and more deeply animated (let us hope) than some worshiping assemblies of our modern times. Is there not something here to be learned as to modes of public worship?

Not Ezra only but many others (v. 7) officiated in the reading and exposition of the Scriptures. The assembly was too large to be reached audibly by one human voice. Probably half the people of the colony were here; say over 20,000. We may suppose them grouped about several speakers. Was not the scene inspiring?—— Yet apparently, there was no such exhilaration as precludes serious thought and personal conviction of sin: "all the people wept when they heard the words of the law." It is rare that a religious assembly becomes too tearful and tender or even too sad of heart so as to require the treatment indicated here. Manifestly the leaders, Ezra, Nehemiah and the teaching Levites, sought to promote a more cheerful tone of feeling: "This day is holy unto the Lord your God; mourn not nor weep. Go your way; eat the fat and drink the sweet; and send portions to the destitute, for this day is holy to the Lord; be ye not sad, for the joy of the Lord is your strength." The word here for "strength" signifies *fortress*, implying that rejoicing in God is a strong power to the soul, like the walled city they knew so well how to appreciate.——We need not press this case so as to make it condemn men for sorrow and penitence in view of their sins, but should rather construe it to imply that when profoundly solemn, penitent, impressed with the words of God's law and withal sincerely docile in spirit, joy in God is appropriate and wholesome and should be cultivated. Our sadness and tears should not ignore God's great love. Since he *is* a tender Father, if we are consciously his dutiful children let us be joyful in his favor.

Convened again on the second day to continue their public reading of the law, they came upon the statute respecting the feast of tabernacles on the fourteenth of this very month. Probably this observance had been omitted for a season. The people were quite in mood at this time for such a festival, and therefore made preparation for it with enthusiasm. They gathered their boughs; constructed their booths ("tabernacles"), and ere the day arrived had all things ready. According to Moses, the book of the law was to be read publicly every day of this festival. Nothing could be more congenial with the public feeling; so from the first day to the last, the law was read.

Neh. 9, continues the record of this great convocation. If the scenes of the first day of this seventh month were memorable and the celebration of this seventh month festival, scarcely less so, the closing service, the twenty-fourth day and onward, reached the climax of religious solemnity and power. Their leaders manifestly had their hearts on turning this great national movement of religious thought, knowledge and feeling, to the best practical account. Let us note what they did and with what results.

On the twenty-fourth the eight days of the feast of tabernacles would be past. But there was no dispersion to their homes yet. "The children of Israel were assembled with fasting and with sackcloth and with earth upon them." First, they separated themselves from all strangers, severing all unhallowed alliances by intermarriage and otherwise. They stood up and read in the book of the law (and heard the reading) one fourth part of the day; another fourth part, they confessed their sins and worshiped. That we and all Bible readers in the ages onward from that hour might have a more just and full view of the spirit of this scene and of the moral value of that prayer, it was put on record and still stands in this ninth chapter. Several Levites seem to have led the devotions of the vast multitude simultaneously (possibly at different points) in this great concert of prayer. [The tone of the narrative favors the supposition of an actual concert—a unison of voices.] What they said is the more vital point, and is before us here.——"Stand up and bless the Lord your God forever and ever, and blessed be thy glorious name which is exalted above all blessing and praise." The prayer follows, reciting in most interesting detail the great historic facts of God's dealings with their fathers; acknowledging their nation's sin and their own personally; referring quite fully to their own weak, dependent colony, as needing specially such help as none but their Almighty Protector could give.—— This full recital of their nation's history—the ways of the people, sinning or obedient, toward God; and God's ways in judgment or in mercy toward them—was admirably adapted to the desired religious impression. When all these grand truths, so practical to themselves, so pungent therefore and effective, were brought fully before them, they were prepared for the solemn reconsecration which ensued. "Because of all this" (they say) "we make a sure covenant and seal it." They seem to have put hand and seal to it, not in a figure of speech only, but in fact; for here is a list, filling twenty-seven verses of individual names that were appended, and this list is followed with the statement that the rest of the people—the priests, Levites, porters, singers, Nethinims, and all they who had separated from the people of the lands unto the law of God, with their wives, sons, daughters—all who had reached years of moral understanding, *clave unto their* brethren, uniting most heartily with their leading men to bind themselves by solemn oath and covenant.

Let us take special note of the points of this solemn covenant; viz., To walk in the law of Moses; not to intermarry with strangers—the godless, idol-worshiping heathen; not to trade on the Sabbath or otherwise desecrate the holy day; to assess themselves one-third of a shekel each for the expenses of the sanctuary; to cast lots for supplying wood for the sacrifices; to bring in according to law their first-fruits and first-born, the required tithes also, and last (not least) "we will not forsake the house of our God."——This, it will be noticed, includes the great points of their religious institutions as given by the Lord through Moses. It was a *Jewish* religious covenant, looking specially toward the ritual worship under which God was training them to a holy life.

This great "protracted meeting," almost a full month—the mind and heart of many thousands held intently upon the book of the law—may suggest to some readers that this is the very atmosphere of Ps. 119: "Open thou mine eyes that I may behold wondrous things out of thy law" (v. 18). "O how love I thy law; it is my meditation all the day" (v. 97). The date and author of this Psalm are not given in the Psalter. We are left to fix its date and find its author by studying its adaptations to known history. Pursuing this inquiry we need go no further than Ezra. The entire tone of this Psalm and all its allusions to surrounding circumstances conspire to sustain his date and authorship. It is refreshing and profitable to study this Psalm in connection with his spirit and times, especially as seen in the history of this great Bible reading occasion.

The last book of the Psalter (Ps. 107–150) should be studied in connection with the times of the restoration, beyond doubt the date of its compilation. Some of these

Psalms have at their head the name of David. Why these (if really his) were not included in the first or second books of the Psalter it will probably be impossible to determine with certainty. They are here because found to be, or modified to become, appropriate to these times. The others are chiefly without name of author, perhaps because their authors were also compilers and chose to suppress their own names. There may have been inspired Psalm-writers in that age whose names as such are not on record at all. Some may have been written or compiled by Haggai or Zechariah. The spirit of Zech. 4:—" Not by might, nor by power, but by my Spirit "—is in striking harmony with Ps. 127;—" Except the Lord build the house, they labor in vain that build it." If this were originally written by Solomon of the first temple, it was yet more applicable to the second, and so would meet the sentiments of Zechariah and come into the Psalter under his hand as compiler.—— Those wonderful Hallelujah-Psalms (146–150) may have been an outgrowth of the joyful, inspiring scenes of the great meeting here before us. May we suppose them to have been written during its progress and for its occasion?

Nehemiah proceeds (chaps. 11 and 12) to speak of measures for bringing more of the people to reside within the city, protection against their enemies being the special reason. The people, subsisting so largely by agriculture, were attracted to the country. Hence a draft was made upon the country population of every tenth family by lot, to remove into the city; and a special blessing was implored upon all who volunteered to change their residence from the fields to the city.

The dedication of the city-walls (12: 27–43) testified to the general joy and thanksgivings of the occasion, the record closing with these emphatic words (v. 43): " Also that day they offered great sacrifices and rejoiced; for God had made them rejoice with great joy; the wives also and the children rejoiced (who could realize the blessings of strong city-walls better than they?) so that the joy of Jerusalem was heard even afar off." (How did it sound in the ears of Sanballat and Tobiah?)

Neh. 13. The reading of the law brought to the notice of the people the passage (Deut. 23: 3, 4) which forbade the Moabite and the Ammonite to enter into the congregation of the Lord. Consequently they proceeded to separate from Israel "all the mixed multitude," *i. e.*, those who were intermixed in blood with Moab or Ammon.——Previously to this, Eliashib the priest (supposed to have been *High* Priest, v. 28) had been allied by marriage with Tobiah (doubtless the same Tobiah the Ammonite who has appeared often in this history, for he and his son had married Jewish women, Neh. 6: 18). This Eliashib, being in official charge of the temple, had assigned to Tobiah spacious chambers which had previously been used as storechambers for the temple offerings. It was an outrage. Nehemiah felt it to be so, and at once cast forth all Tobiah's stuff from the chamber and ordered it cleansed and put to its proper use. He remarks that when this outrage was perpetrated, he was not in Jerusalem, having returned to his king in his thirty-second year, and been absent therefore from the holy city for a season. The events of this last chapter belong to the period after his return to Jerusalem. How long he was absent at the court of his king is not stated very definitely. The Hebrew phrase translated "at the end of days" commonly signifies one year. But the events that fell within this period strongly favor (not to say demand) a period longer than this.

He found another evil. The portions of the Levites had been withheld, and they consequently were driven from the temple service by the failure of supplies. He contended sharply with the rulers for this neglect, and effected a reform.——The next abuse was the violation of the Sabbath, occasioned by the tradesmen of Tyre (vs. 15-27). His expostulation with the rulers on this point appeals to judgments sent on the city for similar violations of the Sabbath in the days of their fathers (v. 18).——Lastly, he encountered yet another abuse in the line of the besetting national sin—intermarriages with idol-worshiping "strangers." Jews had married wives of Ashdod, Moab, and Ammon. Their children spake a mixed dialect, compounded of the Jewish and Ashdod tongues—a fact which shows that these tongues though related were yet dialectically different. Nehemiah's statement shows that he treated these offenders sternly, not to say roughly, manifestly regarding the offense as flagrant and determined to make his mind understood beyond mistake and his power so felt that there should be no escape. Worst of all, this outrageous iniquity had reached even the high places of the priesthood, invading the sanctity of the temple and its holiest offices. One of the sons of Joiada, the son of Eliashib the High Priest, had married a daughter of Sanballat the Horonite—that old, arch, scornful enemy of Zion. "Therefore," says Nehemiah, "I chased him from me." No wonder he did. It is astounding that the same Sanballat and the same Tobiah who appear in the earlier stages of this history as the most subtle, pronounced and bitter enemies of Jerusalem should be here related by intermarriage with even the High Priest's family. It gives a strong impression of the perils incident to this Jewish community and of the abuses which these reformers had to encounter and to eradicate.——With the prayer that God would "remember those defilers of the priesthood" for mercy and himself "for good," this striking personal autobiography of the good Nehemiah comes to its close.

This second period of Nehemiah's residence in Judea (narrated in Neh. 13) is supposed to coincide chronologically with the age of the latest known prophet, Malachi. The abuses and evils to which the book of Malachi refers are essentially the same which appear in Neh. 13. The same deplorably low moral tone in the priesthood which Malachi assumes to exist (Mal. 2), Nehemiah's story fully accounts for. Such dereliction in the High Priest would naturally deprave the whole fraternity.

Reviewing briefly the religious history of this restored people as in the books of Ezra and Nehemiah, we shall notice two very prominent facts:

1. The high and noble character of these two men, Ezra and Nehemiah.

2. Their remarkable efficiency and moral power in their work.

1. Ezra and Nehemiah are brought before the reader somewhat fully. Their personal characters stand out in the strong light of words spoken, deeds done, sympathies manifested. It is rare that we meet with nobler men, of purer motive, more earnest spirit and of more unselfish natures. How eminently prayerful! How pure and sweet is the simplicity of their devotion to the

cause of God! It is refreshing to come into contact with such men, to feel the power of such examples, and the inspiration of such spirits. They may have had blemishes of character, or sins of life; but if so, the record passes them unnoticed. Let us be thankful for such recorded lives.

2. Their labors seem to have been signally effective. In reading the account given of the reforms wrought by Jehoshaphat, Hezekiah and Josiah, we see indications of earnest endeavor and of true devotion to their work, but no decisive proof of any profound impressions made—no evidence that the popular mind was deeply moved. But here, under the labors of Ezra and Nehemiah, the record on these points is thoroughly emphatic. When Ezra first grappled with the terrible evil of ungodly intermarriages—his soul borne down with heavy grief and his spirit poured forth in mighty prayer,—"there assembled unto him a very great congregation of men and women and children; for the people wept very sore." The whole community seem to have been thoroughly aroused and deeply moved. "Men trembled at the commandment of God." The reform from its nature must needs rend asunder the tenderest ties of earthly affection; but the demands of religious purity and the authority of God were felt to be paramount to every thing else;—and the work was done.

So under Nehemiah. With what enthusiasm, and despite of what perils, and labors, and watchings did those city-walls go up! When he came to the money question and took the rich men in hand for their oppression of the poor—a reform which is wont to test and to task the sturdiest arm—the exactors said, "We will restore, and will require nothing of them." One broad, deep tide of enthusiasm swept the whole community along.——Next the record of those many days (Neh. 8 and 9)—that whole month of public Bible reading and of the magnificent celebration of the feast of tabernacles, followed by a universal reconsecration of the people to God, marks a most wonderful movement of the popular mind and heart. Where in all history do we find a record of religious services more protracted; more assiduously and heartily sustained; with more earnest attention to the revealed will of God, and more impressive devotional services—closing with such a consecration

ORIGIN OF THE SAMARITAN COMMUNITY. 401

as seemed to lift the whole people to a vastly higher plane of religious life? There must have been in the people a remarkable susceptibility to moral and religious impressions, and in their religious leaders a union of wisdom, zeal, piety, and prayer, to a degree rarely equaled, perhaps never surpassed. No doubt the good hand of God was there, carrying out his earnest purpose to redeem and to save this restored people and to give stability and strength to his earthly kingdom.

In the line of coincidences, harmonious and confirmatory, between sacred history and profane, there seems little occasion for remark in regard to the era of the restoration. The salient points of Persian history from Cyrus to Artaxerxes inclusive have been long known to the civilized world, chiefly through the ancient Greek historians. There can therefore be scarcely the least occasion to say that Cyrus appears in profane history at the right time and place and of the right character to be the restorer of the captive Jews. The same is true of Darius Hystaspes under whom the temple was finished: also of Artaxerxes Longimanus under whose long reign Ezra and Nehemiah wrought their work for the restored people. More perfect coincidences it were captious and unreasonable to ask.

In our notice of the captivity of the ten tribes (p. 316) and the resettlement of their country, allusion was made to the religious character of the Samaritan community as known to history during the entire Christian era with reference to the question—Whence came their religion, and whence their celebrated Samaritan Pentateuch and their ritual worship? Do these facts of their religious system date from Shalmanezer, or from Nehemiah, or from some other historic era and events?

The best and best-sustained opinion dates the religious elements of the Samaritan people, not from the Assyrian era but from the Persian—in the age of Nehemiah; and mainly on the following grounds:

(a.) The religion brought in at the Assyrian date must have been of the Jeroboam type—in nowise better than the worship of the calves of Bethel and Dan; would have been by no means likely to have introduced the Samaritan Pentateuch: still less likely to have provided for its preservation twenty-five hundred years—not to say that such a religious system had too little vitality to have lived till this day.

(b.) On the other hand, in the age of Nehemiah the Samaritan community absorbed into itself a renegade high priest (Neh. 13: 28) who married a daughter of Sanballat the Horonite. It may be assumed that he had the Pentateuch in his possession. His high social position would both give him the power and inspire the ambition to inaugurate a new religion and engraft it into the Samaritan community.

(c.) The intense antipathy between Jew and Samaritan in which this Samaritan religion was born accounts philosophically for the great facts of all their subsequent history—this antipathy sustained as a national characteristic, manifesting itself all through the centuries to the Christian era, and indeed to the present day.

ADDENDA *on Ezra as Scribe, Author and Compiler.*

The reader will have noticed that I have spoken of Ezra as probably the compiler of the books of Chronicles; the author substantially of the book that bears his name as well as of some Psalms. Also, that in compiling Chronicles, regard was had to the moral wants of the age of the restoration.——Here the question will arise—Was not Ezra's active life too late to admit the supposition of his agency so early as the building of the second temple?

To this I answer.

(1.) The age of Ezra when he went to Judea (seventh year of Artaxerxes) is not known. Probably he was then far advanced in life. He certainly had a national reputation as a learned and ready scribe in the law of God before he went. It seems morally certain that he must have died before Nehemiah's return to Persia; for the social evils and national sins that developed themselves then (Neh. 13) quite forbid the supposition that he was living there at that time. It is entirely reasonable to suppose that much of his literary labor upon the Scriptures was done before he went personally into Judea; possibly (perhaps not probably) some of it as early as the dedication of the second temple.

(2.) But we need not assume that Ezra labored in his

great work upon the Scriptures alone. Jewish tradition makes him the head man in "the Great Synagogue"—a group or society of learned scribes who wrought in the same field, some *with him* in time; some *before* him, and some *after*. This seems to be the true explanation of this chronological question. Such men as Haggai, Zechariah, and Zerubbabel may have commenced this great work; Ezra took it up and carried it forward; other good men, following, gave it the finishing hand.

Esther; and the Book which bears her Name.

The points properly *introductory* to this book are—the *date* and *locality* of its events; the *author* of the book and his *purpose*.

The question of *date* involves the prior question: Who was *this Ahasuerus?* I slightly emphasize the word *this*, for another Ahasuerus appears in Ezra 4:6. By almost universal consent of modern critics this one was Xerxes the Great—famous for his invasion of Greece—whose reign, commonly reckoned at twenty-one years, fell between Darius Hystaspes and Artaxerxes Longimanus. His Hebrew name was written by the Greek Xerxes; his character and acts as here correspond with remarkable precision to the character and life of Xerxes in Grecian history. I am not aware of any objection of real weight against this identification, and shall therefore assume it.

The reader will notice that, taking Ahasuerus to be Xerxes, the events of this book fall after the dedication of the second temple (second year of Darius), and *before* the labors of Ezra and Nehemiah (from the seventh to the thirty-second or some later year of Artaxerxes Longimanus).

As to locality, the reader will see that these events transpire, not in Judah, and not where they would directly affect the colony there save through sympathy; but in Shushan, the capital of the Medo-Persian Empire. The book shows that Jews in considerable numbers were scattered over that empire, many in Shushan itself. Of their fortunes under a special exigency during the reign of Xerxes this book gives an account.

The name of the author of this book can not be

ascertained with any certainty. He gives details so minutely that he must have lived on the spot. His allusions to Persian life and manners, luxury, customs and history, harmonize so entirely with what comes to us through the Greek historians as to compel the same conclusion. The writer knew too much of the Persians to have lived elsewhere than there and then.——Some think the book was written by Mordecai. It is probably safe to say—By him, or at least under his eye.

As to purpose and aim, the author recognizes the feast of Purim; indeed makes great account of it as an established institution; probably was active in making it such; and consequently prepared this history of the events that culminated in that commemorative festival. Those events were worthy of this commemoration. God's hand in them from first to last was so signally manifest, the lessons they taught could not fail to be at once impressive and instructive.——But though God's hand was in these events, too plainly manifest to be mistaken or unnoticed, yet his name is not here, not being even once written in this book. We are left in no doubt that Mordecai believed in God's covenant with his people and in his promises of salvation in their behalf (4: 14), and that both he and Esther believed in prayer, though they do not name prayer, but only fasting, when it seems plain enough that prayer is in their thought as truly as fasting. *Why* this reticence as to the name of God and as to prayer to him, is a mystery unexplained. It is natural to assume that there was some reason in their relation to Persian or to Magian ideas (philosophical, superstitious, or otherwise) which induced this suppression of names ever dear to pious souls; but what the reason was must probably remain unknown.——The contrast between this book and Nehemiah and Ezra in these respects is striking.

The story is told with great simplicity and clearness. In the third year of the reign of this Ahasuerus he convened an immense council of his subordinate officers, heads of the provinces (127) of his vast empire which continued its sittings and convivialities 180 days. It is assumed with high probability that the object of this council was to take action upon the invasion of Greece—that great but most disastrous enterprise of Xerxes, in which he took 5,000,000 of men

THE STORY OF ESTHER. 405

across the Hellespont (soldiers, servants, sutlers, etc., all counted), yet scarcely brought back 5,000. The gorgeous splendor of this great festival (1: 5–8) is quite in harmony with the historic accounts of Persian luxury and magnificence. His great army gotten up in the same style was enervated, and, against Grecian discipline and vigor, powerless.——When the king and his lords became merry and rude with wine, he gave orders "to bring his Queen Vashti before him with the crown royal to show the people and the princes her beauty; for she was fair to look on." We think the better of her that she had so much sense of womanly dignity as to refuse to make herself the gazing stock of a hundred or more half-drunken men though they were the dignitaries of the empire. The king felt his dignity hurt by her refusal, and brought the offense, as one of grave importance, before his seven high counselors. They too felt the gravity of this momentous question, taking what they seem to have regarded as very broad and statesman-like views of its bearings upon the proper subordination of all wives throughout the realm to their husbands. They advise that she be promptly deposed (shall we say divorced?) and her place filled by the most beautiful damsel to be found in the realm. It was of the Lord that this flurry in the royal harem should bring in Esther the Jewess, cousin and ward of Mordecai, to become queen of King Ahasuerus. Mordecai, it seems, held some subordinate place in the palace. Esther's nationality was not at this time known.

Another incident is on record (2: 21–23) which subsequently turned to account toward the elevation of Mordecai. A conspiracy by two offended chamberlains to take the life of the king came to his knowledge. Promptly exposing it he saved the king from assassination. Public record was made of his agency in their exposure and punishment; but no further notice was taken of it at the time.

Haman comes to light here, apparently an artful flatterer, working his way skillfully into the good graces of his king, and rising rapidly to the highest honors. All the king's servants bowed before Haman with oriental reverence—all save this Jew Mordecai, who, from conscientious scruples or contempt for the man, declined persistently. The supposition of conscientious scruples is the more probable because in this connection it came out that Mordecai was a Jew.——Haman was stung by this assumed disrespect. Disdaining the insignificant revenge of taking one human life for so grave an insult, he plotted the destruction of all the Jews in the empire. Such a measure commended itself to him (probably) as magnificent—worthy of the head prince of the great realm of Persia! To compass his object he represented to the king that the Jews were a "diverse" set of people scattered over his realm, subject to laws of their own, and, as he would imply, to no other laws—not, therefore, a profitable class of subjects for his empire. He proposed to the king to exterminate them altogether. He will pay the king ten thousand talents of silver for the desired edict for their extermination.——Under a strong love of money and a shamefully weak sense of justice, the king yielded. It does not appear that he even hesitated at all over this bloody proposition.* Apparently to relieve somewhat Haman's financial burdens, the king said to him: "The silver is given to thee" (probably in the sense of permission to confiscate all the property of the murdered Jews, to reimburse himself for the ten thousand talents); "and the people also;" do what you like with them. Haman had previously cast lots to find the auspicious day for this holocaust of human life; and the Lord had put it off to the last month of the year, so that eleven months intervened before the day of slaughter. The order having been obtained, sealed, and made irrevocable by the Persian constitution, it was promulgated throughout the empire, that on the thirteenth day of Adar, the last month of the year, all Jews were to be massacred and their property confiscated. This being done, "the king and Haman sat down to drink"—little dreaming of the retributions of the Almighty; "but the city Shushan was perplexed"— not the Jews only, but the people at large trembled before such shocking inhumanity and such a barbarous

* Such massacres of a whole race of people were by no means unknown in Oriental history. The immediate predecessor of Darius (Xerxes' father) was a Magian. On the accession of Darius, all Magians were doomed to slaughter. It is said that fifty thousand were slain.

exercise of power. How could they know how soon a similar edict might call for their own heads?

Mordecai mourned in bitter grief; and "many of his people lay in sackcloth and ashes." Ultimately he sent to Esther a copy of the king's bloody decree and "charged her to go in to the king and make request before him for her people."——This is the hour of her responsibility. She feels the critical delicacy of her position. By the law of the Persian harem she can not go before the king uncalled, except with some peril of her life. If the king takes such intrusion kindly, he extends the golden scepter: if otherwise, the intruder must die. She replied to Mordecai that she had not been called in to the king for thirty days, and could not know when she might be called again. Mordecai replied: Remember you belong to the doomed race. Think not that you will escape when all the Jews of the realm are massacred. He added—"Enlargement and deliverance will come to the Jews from some quarter." Manifestly he had faith in the God of their covenant—the God of the ancient promises. He concluded with yet another allusion to the unseen, disposing Hand:—"Who knoweth whether thou art come to the kingdom for such a time as this?" The providences that brought you there are wonderful. Perhaps God's hand shaped them that you might be the savior of your people in this terrible emergency.

What is her reply? "Go," said she, "gather all the Jews of Shushan and fast for me three days." (Why does not she say what she doubtless means—*fast and pray?*) I and my maidens will fast likewise; and so—after this —I will go in to the king, though it be not according to law; "and if I perish, I perish."——She went in, and the king extended his golden scepter, and invited her to make her request known.——The moment is so critical, the interests are so vast, the perils of the future so great, she can not bring herself to name her main request yet, but said—"Come, thou and Haman, to-morrow to my banquet." Agreed; but still her mind labored with anxious care. She dared not present her main petition yet (the Lord's arrangements were not ripe)—she therefore invited them to a second banquet the next day. Then she would bring before the king her great request.

This delay provided for certain new developments as to Haman. He is elated with the honors shown him— by all save that man Mordecai, sitting contemptuously and giving him no recognition of homage as he passed along. "All this honor," said he, "avails me nothing so long as I see Mordecai the Jew sitting at the king's gate," paying me no deference. It weighed upon his heart so badly that he talked the case over with his wife and friends. They advised him to fit up a gallows for Mordecai fifty cubits high, and ask the king's order to hang Mordecai thereon. They assumed that the king would grant this. Mordecai was nothing but a Jew, and only *one* at that—not a whole nation; and at the utmost, this would only anticipate by a few months what the king had already decreed.——Here the hand of God came in again. For some reason unknown to himself the king on the ensuing night was sleepless. To pass away the heavy time, he ordered the records of the realm to be read before him; when lo, there came up the forgotten case of the conspiracy against his life, discovered and disclosed by Mordecai the Jew. "Has any thing been done to reward Mordecai for this?" "Nothing." Something must be done without delay. [It is very much for the interest of all kings—despots as well as better men—to encourage the revelation of bloody conspiracies]. At the dinner table where Haman has it on his mind to ask the king's permission to impale Mordecai on his lofty gallows, the king has this other thing on his mind. "Haman," said he, "what shall be done to the man whom the king delighteth to honor?" That, said Haman to himself, means me; now is my time to mount to the highest honors of the realm—next below the king. So he shapes the answer to his own taste:— "Put on him the king's apparel; give him the king's horse to ride—his crown to wear; and a herald to go before him, proclaiming, "Thus is it done to the man whom the king delighteth to honor." "Go thou," said the king, "and do all this to Mordecai the Jew."—— Alas! was ever mortal man worse confounded? The king's word is law. Having obeyed it, he hastened to his house, with heavy heart—head covered. He could not conceal from his wife and friends what had happened. They see in it the augury of a sure and fatal fall.——The second banquet hastened on; the time had fully come for Esther to present her great request to the king. She does it modestly, yet with thrilling effect: "If it please the king, let my life be given me at my petition and my people at my request; for we are sold, I and my people to be destroyed, to be slain, to perish. If we had only been sold for slaves, I would have remained silent—although the enemy could not make good the damage to the king."—— "Who is the man," said the king; "where is the man that durst presume in his heart to do so?" Esther replied—"The adversary and enemy is this wicked Haman."——Alas, poor Haman! "He was afraid" [these words are weak]—"afraid before the king and the queen." The king rose suddenly from his table in great agitation, to walk in his palace garden. Haman seizes the moment to fall at Esther's feet and beg for his life. The king returning saw him there and said— "Will he even force the queen before me in the house?" At that word, the attendants forecast Haman's doom and cover his face. One said—There is the gallows, fifty cubits high, which Haman built for Mordecai. The king said, "Hang Haman there." Done; and the king's wrath was pacified.

At this stage (if not before) Esther informs the king of her relation to Mordecai. He was introduced before the king and at once promoted to high honor and responsibility. The house and estate of Haman were made over to him.——The way was at length prepared for Esther to make her final request of the king—that he reverse that horrible decree which authorized the slaughter of all the Jews of his realm. He avowed his readiness to do any thing for her and her people that he could; but a decree of the Medes and Persians, once made and sealed, no power could reverse. This however he could do, and did: Raise Mordecai to the highest honor as his prime minister; show his personal sympathy for his Jewish subjects unmistakably, and give them full authority to defend themselves everywhere; destroy their assailants; and confiscate their property.

In the event the popular sympathy proved to be intensely *with* the Jews and against their enemies. "Many of the people of the land became Jews, for the fear of the Jews fell upon them" (8: 17).——On the great day of their decreed slaughter, "all the rulers and

officers of the king *helped the Jews* because the fear of
Mordecai fell upon them" (9: 3). The story does not
indicate that any Jews fell in these two days of terror
and blood. Of their enemies there fell 500 in Shushan;
in all the provinces 75,000. The second day assigned
for slaughter and the day following were for all Jews
days of intensest exultation and joy. The day "was
turned as to them from sorrow to joy; and from mourning into a good day." That day in which they had
expected only assault, pillage, blood, death, over all the
Persian empire, proved through God's reversing providences to be a day of bloodless victory over their enemies; a day of gladness, congratulations, feasting, and
all possible demonstrations of joy.——To celebrate these
days the feast of Purim was ordained for the fourteenth
and fifteenth of the month Adar—to be celebrated
through all their generations. It has been kept to this
day. In this festival, all Jews refresh their memory
with the events of this book of Esther and their hearts
with the indications of God's kind remembrance of
their low estate, gratefully welcoming such proofs as
these that their own God knoweth how to give songs in
place of wailings; life and peace instead of the horrors
of bloody extermination.

CHAPTER XIII.

Divine Revelation progressive throughout Hebrew History.

Our study of Hebrew history will be yet incomplete
till we have given due attention to the progress made
in God's revelations of himself to men in the course of
this Hebrew history.

In the outset I must caution the reader not to confound progress in building up and purifying the church
with progress in the revelations of God. It is charming
to be able to observe progress in the tone of piety; progress in the manifestations of the religious life; and
sad to see—instead of this—a real decline, a positive
retrogression. Yet let it be distinctly said: God may
be making as real and as rapid progress in the revela-

tion of himself in periods of declension as in periods of reviving and enlargement to Zion. There are aspects of his character which shine more brightly in times of Zion's adversity.

Aiming to arrange with some method the points of noticeable progress in this portion of •Hebrew history, I remark,

1. If it was progress to give to mankind a large body of Christian experience in the inspired utterances of Psalmist and Prophet, it was but filling out more completely the exhibition of this progress to give in history the circumstances and events under which those experiences occurred. By this aid those experiences become to our apprehension more life-like, vivid, real, impressive. Indeed it were simply impossible to understand and appreciate those experiences without this historic aid. Hence I have aimed to refer from this history to the Psalms composed under the full impression of the circumstances which this history sets before us. On the same principle many passages in the prophets will be seen in their true light and felt in their fuller power if read in connection with the history to which they refer. The experiences of both Psalmist and Prophet, history serves not only to interpret, but to illustrate and even to illuminate with the radiance of their full glory.

2. It was progress to reveal the purity and justice of God both in chastising and in punishing his people when they apostatized into idolatry and lapsed into flagrant immorality. Of this we have seen countless examples throughout the history of the Judges and of the wicked kings of both Israel and Judah. It was the solemn purpose of the Lord to make his covenant people understand that such sin could not be tolerated; that such professed service could in nowise be taken for service at all. "Of purer eye than to behold iniquity" was written by the divine finger on every uplifted rod of chastisement; on every visitation of retributive judgment. While the chastisement was corrective and the judgment was illustrative of his eternal justice, both alike bore their testimony that God hated sin intensely, and must either eradicate the sin or exterminate the sinner.

3. It was progress to roll up a mass of overwhelming testimonies to *God's present retribution upon guilty nations.*

It can not be said too clearly or emphatically that nations as such have a character and life of their own; therefore must bear moral responsibilities toward the Infinite God each for itself; and—what is specially vital to consider—must have their retribution not only begun but finished in this world—*in time*—for the simple reason that *as nations* they have no future world. Hence they afford in all ages finished examples of God's retributive justice.

It should be remembered as bearing not on this one point only, but upon all the points made in this closing chapter:—It is valuable to us above all price that in this historic Bible, *the Historian is virtually God himself.* "Holy men of old spake as they moved by the Holy Ghost." Of uninspired historians some are too blind to see God's hand in history; some too perverse to honor what of it they do see. God knows his own doings and the meaning thereof. When therefore he becomes his own historian, how should we honor the history he writes, and how should we ponder solemnly, profoundly, the words which reveal the great principles upon which, as he himself testifies, he governs the nations of the earth!

4. It was progress to give so many manifestations of *God's righteous judgments upon individuals*—in a dispensation which filled out its results upon individual men so far—not perfectly indeed, yet far enough to become strikingly manifest. It has been sometimes said (upon very superficial consideration) that all the ills sent of God upon sinners in this world are discipline; none of them retribution. Our reading of this Hebrew history should have taught us better. For, what shall we say of God's "rendering their iniquities upon Abimelech and the men of Shechem" (Judg. 9: 56, 57) or upon the two sons of Eli, or upon King Saul, or upon Absalom, or Jezebel, or Jehoiakim? If there be any such thing as retribution from God upon sin, the judgments that fell from his hand upon these notorious sinners were of this sort; not indeed finished, perfected retribution, yet retribution in nature and in fact none the less. The fullness and variety of these illustrative cases make up a chapter from God's recording prophets whose testimony it were folly to ignore and fool-hardiness to disregard.

5. It was progress to give illustrations of this divine retribution in sufficient number, variety and clearness, to *disclose in a fair measure its real nature.*——The idea finds no little favor in our age that retribution for sin is neither more nor less than *sin punishing itself.* Sin (some men love to say) is its own punishment; a bad heart its own avenger—and beyond that—nothing. In their view there is no need of God in the case; and God *is not* in it. Whatever moral government there is in this world or in the world to come *runs itself.* The sinner's own nature, and this only, is judge, jury, executioner. If God even stoops to look on, it is a fact of no particular account. The process is all the same whether he do or do not.——This volume can not afford space to discuss this notion exhaustively. But it is in place here to say emphatically that these views of retribution for sin never came from the Bible. Everywhere in the inspired history of retribution on sinners, it is God's own scales of justice that measure the sinner's ill-desert, and his own hand which hurls the thunders of heaven upon the guilty. Who judged and punished the wicked sons of Eli? Were they left to the sole retribution of a guilty and accusing conscience? Was Jezebel's a case of self-torment and of self-inflicted punishment? Is there a solitary case in the long catalogue of Bible sinners suffering retribution for their sins on earth, in which you can say with the least show of reason that sin punished itself and that the government which visited them with retribution was self-acting, self-asserting, and self-vindicating? We shall need entirely another Bible for this new doctrine of retribution.

6. It is in a sort the resultant of points already made above, to say that Bible history shows God to be a Moral Governor—evermore holding men responsible to himself, and actually punishing sin by the infliction of suffering. This doctrine does not assert that God makes his administration of this moral government perfect here in time; does not deny that in large part it holds over to another world—beginning here; taught, illustrated and enforced upon the human heart and conscience by the part developed here; yet carried over for its completed result, into that enduring state of existence where there shall be no lack of either time or means or agencies to make its awards absolutely perfect. The

great fact—God the Moral Governor of all his moral subjects—stands out on every page of Bible history. It could not well have been made more plain if God had created the Hebrew race and given them a history for the sole end of teaching and illustrating this stupendous truth.

7. It was progress to show by frequent, indeed perpetual, illustrations that probation in time is purposely shaped *to afford space for repentance.* What is the history of God's ways with sinners (nations or individual men) but warning and waiting; waiting and warning—with rod uplifted but slow to fall—all as if the ever-present thought and purpose of the Great Ruler were to persuade the guilty to repent; to spare them long in patient hope; and to let fall the fearful blow only when the last hope had perished? We have read this history but poorly if we have not seen this great purpose of God radiant everywhere in the light of his patience and of his love.

8. It was progress to show that while God's judgments against sin were fearfully manifest, yet they were "his *strange work,* and *mercy his delight.*" Everywhere the record shows that he loves to forgive and does not love to afflict; that he gives pardons when he can with full heart and overflowing hand; but lets fall consuming judgments with heart-pangs of grief, and only when he must—swift to hear the cry of penitent souls for mercy; slow to wrath even against the most defiant and most guilty. A history which abounds in such illustrations ought to leave no mind in darkness as to the character and ways of the Holy One.

9. Let the remark take the broadest compass:—It is progress to show that man needs a Savior, and moreover *needs a moral law* to reveal to him this need of such a Savior as Jesus. It was consummate wisdom in God to allow some time in this world's history before the Messiah should appear. There was preparatory work to be done. In nothing was this need more imperative than in regard to just views of God as Lawgiver and Moral Governor; a just sense of sin and of the hopelessness of the sinner's case without a divine Redeemer. All along the ages of Hebrew history light was breaking forth on these cardinal points. The chosen people were often falling into great sin, and as often were

compelled to study and learn the conditions of God's forgiving mercy. Sacrifice, confession, penitence, prayer—so they found mercy, and so they marked the way to mercy for the guidance of sinning men all along the ages that were to follow. The sacrificial system gave the idea of atonement—pardon through another's blood. Confession admitted that in justice the sinner and not the innocent lamb deserved to die. So light was shed on the way of salvation through a Savior yet to come, witnessing that "without the shedding of blood, there could be no remission of sin."

10. A ritual system with indefinite ceremonial cleansings being useful to lift men's thought to the idea of spiritual purity, it was progress to guard the system against abuse by showing that the washing of the flesh merely *illustrated* but could never supersede the washing of the heart, and was by no means the same thing.—— So also, it being helpful toward just conceptions of a present God to give some *symbols* of his presence (*e. g.*, the ark; the visible glory above it; the sacred temple) it became vital to guard these ritual helps against abuse by showing that the presence of these symbols could never save men *in their sins*. Historic illustrations on such points as these became a necessity, and are among the points of real progress in the revelations of God to men.

11. It was progress to furnish prophetic foreshadowings of God's great thoughts of mercy touching a *Savior to come* and *the work he should really achieve in our world.*——We can scarcely enter upon this great subject here. Yet let it be said briefly that while the *nature* of his atoning sacrifice is largely left for its illustration to the Mosaic sacrificial system, it fell chiefly to the prophets to give pre-intimations *as to the results of the Messiah's coming* and the *extent of his blessings upon our race*. The details on these points are to be found (of course) in the prophetic books, and can not be presented here.——But it is in place to say here that these pages of Hebrew history stand in a very peculiar relation to Hebrew prophecy as furnishing to a great extent *the basis for prophetic illustration.*——Let us study this fact as seen in special examples.

(a.) In prophecy the Messiah is a king; is to rule a kingdom; is to achieve results legitimate to a well

ordered kingdom, viz., righteousness, prosperity, peace.
——Where is the model of this kingdom? Whence came the conception, the figure, which so largely underlies three-fourths of all the prophecies respecting the Messiah?——The one comprehensive answer is—*From the kingdom of David.* As David's reign made Israel great and triumphant over enemies on every side, and religious also, and peaceful and prosperous beyond any thing known in the whole range of Hebrew history, so it came to be the best type of the nation's Messiah in all the great respects here contemplated. The history well studied interprets those grand old prophecies whose imagery is built upon it.

(b.) There occurred more than once in the course of this history some signal deliverance wrought of God in behalf of his people, of a sort to set forth both the power and the love of their own Jehovah. These were seized by the prophets for the illustration of the great and benign results to be achieved by the nation's Messiah. When the Assyrian hosts were laid low so suddenly, so signally, so utterly, in one eventful night, Isaiah saw it with his own eyes, and his soul was enkindled. He saw in it not only what God *had* wrought there, but what he *would achieve* when the little rootshoot from the stem of Jesse (Isa. 10: 24–34, and 11: 1–16) should rule in righteousness, and his moral sway on human souls be far more glorious than this fall of the proud Assyrian's host. Who can say how much the lofty sublimity of Isaiah's conceptions of the Messiah may be due to the inspirations of this stupendous scene? The peace and joy felt by the daughters of Jerusalem after the Assyrian's fall passed over into his thought of the blessedness of the spiritual Zion under the glorious reign of her own Messiah.——So the restoration from captivity in Babylon served to lift the soul of many a Hebrew prophet to loftier conceptions of what God would achieve when his Son should become the world's Great Redeemer; should break every yoke; lift his people from bondage, otherwise hopeless, and prove himself able to save to the uttermost. Those glowing prophecies of Isaiah (chaps. 40–66) seem to have been built in large part on the foreseen redemption of Israel from her captivity in Babylon. Jointly, therefore, upon what Isaiah saw (the Assyrian fall) and

what he foresaw (the restoration from Babylon) his sublime predictions of the future Zion rest, and from those scenes derive their wonderful illustrations.——
These cases, the reader will remember, are not exhaustive, but are only samples to illustrate the modes of prophetic conception and the uses which the prophetic spirit made of Hebrew history.

(c.) Yet another class of prophecies find their historic illustration in another group of historic facts. There were periods (*e. g.*, in the reign of Ahaz, also of Jehoiakim, and in the age of Malachi) when Judah was brought low for her transgressions. There seemed to be no spiritual vitality left upon which to rally toward new life. Measured by human resources, all was lost.——But God still lived and his arm was still strong to save. The very emergency made a place for the more glorious revealing of his power and of his love. It was when the whole aspect of affairs looked so death-like under Ahaz that the Lord sent through Isaiah that bright prophecy of the Virgin and her son Immanuel (Isa. 7: 10–16). Drawn out in more ample detail the same principle may be seen unfolded in Isa. 59 and 60;—first a state of unparalleled moral prostration; wickedness rampant; "justice standing afar off;" "truth fallen." Then the Lord saw there was no help in man, and therefore he rose to the crying emergency; girded himself for the onset and wrought glorious victory for Zion; for here Isaiah introduces one of the grandest predictions of Messiah's reign (Isa. 60) which prophet's eye has ever seen or pen recorded. The background of this wonderful picture is the desolation that came over Zion in the wicked reign of Ahaz, or in the not less wicked reigns of Judah's last three kings, foreseen prophetically, which brought on the great captivity.——A similar moral ruin in the age of Malachi kindled the zeal of the Holy One of Israel to declare—"I will not accept your" [heartless] "offering." "*For* from the rising of the sun to the going down of the same, my name shall be great among the Gentiles; and in every place incense shall be offered to my name and a pure offering; for my name shall be great among the heathen, saith the Lord of Hosts." (Mal. 1: 11.)——
Hebrew history gives these background positions for the setting of such brilliant portrayals of Zion's transcendent glories. It was one of the elements of a pro-

gressive revelation to give these darkest historic scenes, and then put them behind the prophetic pictures for their background. Else we had failed of the full conception of the glories of our Messiah's reign.——Such emergencies, moreover, give historic occasion for the enkindling of zeal and the expression of determined purpose on the part of the Almighty—of a sort which give the richest demonstrations of his will to make the gospel under Messiah's reign a sublime and glorious success, to the full extent of "giving the nations to him for his inheritance and the ends of the earth for his possession."

APPENDIX. 419

CHRONOLOGICAL TABLES.

I. KINGS OF JUDAH.

	Began to reign B. C.	Reigned years.
Rehoboam	975	17
Abijam	958	3
Asa	955	41
Jehoshaphat	914	25
Jehoram	891	7
Ahaziah	884	½
Athaliah	884	7
Joash	877	39
Amaziah	838	27
Uzziah	811	52
Jotham	759	16
Ahaz	743	15
Hezekiah	728	29
Manasseh	699	55
Amon	644	2
Josiah	642	31
Jehoahaz	611	¼
Jehoiakim	611	11
Jehoiachin	600	—
Zedekiah	600	12
End of the kingdom	588	

II. KINGS OF ISRAEL.

	Began to reign B. C.	Reigned years.
Jeroboam I	975	22
Nadab	954	2
Baasha	952	22
Elah	930	1
Omri	929	11
Ahab	918	21
Ahaziah	897	1
Jehoram	896	12
Jehu	884	28
Jehoahaz	856	16
Joash	840	15
Jeroboam II	825	41
Interregnum	784	11
Zachariah	773	½
Shallum	773	1-12
Menahem	773	12
Pekahiah	761	2
Pekah	759	19
Interregnum	740	9
Hoshea	731	9
End of the kingdom	722	

III. HEBREW PROPHETS.

	B. C.
Joel (supposed)	830–825
Jonah	823
Amos	825–759
Hosea	between 825 and 699
Isaiah	759–699
Micah	758–699
Nahum	700
Jeremiah	629–580
Zephaniah	624
Habakkuk	610–588
Daniel	603–533
Ezekiel	595–573
Obadiah	588–580
Haggai	520
Zechariah	520
Ezra	457–432
Nehemiah in Judah	444-432 and 408–400
Malachi (supposed)	408–400

N. B.—In a few of these cases no certain data exist. The figures should be regarded as only the nearest approximation to truth possible under the circumstances.

IV. KINGS OF ASSYRIA

Which appear in the sacred history.

[On the authority of Geo. Rawlinson.]

	B. C.
Pul	800–750
Tiglath Pileser	747–730
Shalmanezer	730–721
Sargon	721–702
Sennacherib	702–680
Esarhaddon	680–660

www.ingramcontent.com/pod-product-compliance
Lightning Source LLC
Chambersburg PA
CBHW071436300426
44114CB00013B/1452